The Union of Their Dreams

The Union of Their Dreams

Power, Hope, and Struggle in
Cesar Chavez's Farm Worker Movement

MIRIAM PAWEL

BLOOMSBURY PRESS
NEW YORK · BERLIN · LONDON

Published by Bloomsbury Press, New York

All papers used by Bloomsbury Press are natural, recyclable products made from wood grown in well-managed forests. The manufacturing processes conform to the environmental regulations of the country of origin.

LIBRARY OF CONGRESS CATALOGING-IN-PUBLICATION DATA
Pawel, Miriam, 1958–
The union of their dreams: power, hope, and struggle in Cesar Chavez's farm worker movement/Miriam Pawel.
p.   cm.
Includes bibliographical references and index.
ISBN 978-1-59691-460-5 (alk. paper)
1. United Farm Workers—History. 2. Chavez, Cesar, 1927–1993.
3. Labor leaders—United States—History. 4. Migrant agricultural laborers—Labor unions—United States—History. 5. Mexican American migrant agricultural laborers—History. I. Title.

HD6515. A292U546 2009
331.88'130973—dc22
2009012310

First U.S. edition 2009

1 3 5 7 9 10 8 6 4 2

Typeset by Westchester Book Group
Printed in the United States of America by Quebecor World Fairfield

For those who believe they can change the world.
¡Que vivan!

Contents

OREGON

IDAHO

Goose
Lake

Eureka

COAST RANGES

Redding

Sacramento River

Point
Arena

Lake
Tahoe

NEVADA

SIERRA

Sacramento

Napa

Point Reyes

Berkeley

CALIFORNIA

San Francisco

Mono
Lake

San Francisco Bay

DIABLO
RANGE

Merced River

NEVADA

Gilroy

Monterey
Bay

Salinas

San Joaquin R.

San Joaquin Valley

Fresno

PANAMINT
RANGE

Monterey

Point Sur

COAST RANGES

Salinas River

Salinas Valley

SANTA LUCIA RANGE

Delano

Kern River

Bakersfield

La Paz

Tehachapi

TEHACHAPI
MOUNTAINS

MOJAVE
DESERT

Oxnard

San Gabriel
Mts.

Channel Islands

Los Angeles

San
Bernardino
Mts.

Hemet

Indio

Coachella

Coachella
Valley

Colorado River

ARIZONA

Borrego
Springs

Salton
Sea

Imperial
Valley

PACIFIC OCEAN

San Diego

El Centro

Calexico

Mexicali

MEXICO

0   50   100 Miles

0   50   100 Kilometers

Albers Equal-area Projection

Preface

The history of the United Farm Workers union begins and ends with Cesar Chavez, who had the audacity to single-handedly challenge California's most powerful industry, and the will to keep fighting for three decades. By the time he died in 1993, he stood alone again.

In the intervening years, thousands embraced Chavez's vision and joined the charismatic leader on his improbable journey. Together, they transformed the union into a vibrant community that became an intrepid experiment in organizing and a force for change.

This is the story of eight people who joined Cesar Chavez's crusade. They came into the movement from the fields, the classrooms, and the churches; they left as organizers and activists, their lives irrevocably altered by the first successful attempt to unionize farmworkers. These eight are but one cast of characters, not necessarily the most important or the most central. Each has a compelling personal story, and each also represents an archetype of the worlds that came together in a unique collaboration.

When they left the UFW, each lost something. Their lives had changed in ways they had never imagined. But they failed to pass that experience on to future generations of farmworkers, as they had hoped and planned to do. They carry that loss with them decades later, sometimes near the surface, sometimes deep down, each coping in a different way. I wrote this book to tell their story and, through them, to paint the broader, complex, grand, often messy, but supremely human story of Cesar Chavez and the farm worker movement.

In writing the book, I melded two disciplines—history and journalism. The narrative is based largely on primary source materials from libraries, garages, and attics across the country. All quotations come from letters, memoranda, notes, court files, newspaper stories, and diaries written at the time. In addition, I listened to more than six hundred hours of tapes of meetings, rallies, and interviews recorded between 1969 and 1980. The interactions captured on those tapes were a rich resource that shaped the overall narrative, as well as a source of direct quotations. To help bring the historical documents to life, I conducted dozens of additional interviews with people who lived through these events. Each of the main characters spoke with me at great length, many times, over several years. All accounts of their feelings and thoughts at the time derive from those interviews. Where not otherwise indicated in the text or footnotes, descriptions of events and conversations also are based on interviews. Where written documentation was not available, I have spoken to more than one person to verify accounts whenever possible.

Almost all previous writings about Cesar Chavez have hewed close to his version of history. This book offers a reevaluation of his legacy. His ultimate shortcomings as a labor leader do not diminish his accomplishments or his influence. The real story may be less neat than the hagiography but no less impressive.

Many books could and should be written about the history of the United Farm Workers. Many significant events and players beyond the scope of this book merit deep examination. This is the story of a different set of winners, a significant chapter of American history that deserves to be told in all its complicated glory.

Prologue

The squat four-year-old stares into the camera, pigtail hanging over her left shoulder, right foot perched on the blade of a shovel, arm wrapped around the handle that stretches far above her head. Maria de Jesus Govea, 1951, poised to pick cotton in the California fields.

One year later she entered kindergarten, where school officials decided Maria de Jesus was too difficult to pronounce. So they changed her name. Two years after that, Jessica Govea met Cesar Chavez.

Chavez was still more than a decade away from international fame when he mapped out strategy in the Goveas' backyard, sitting in a circle of chairs on dry, hot summer nights in Bakersfield, California. Jessica listened to the grown-ups make plans to register voters, organize English classes, and file police brutality suits. The details went over her head, but the purpose and the passion were clear: empower Mexican Americans to fight a racist system. "I grew up seeing poor people take charge of their destiny," Jessica wrote many years later.

As a child, she scratched chalk marks in front of the homes of potential voters, a "bird dog" pointing the way for adults who followed with registration forms. As a teenager, she starred on the debate team, where her favorite speech, "The Man with the Hoe," scored points for delivery but demerits for its radical message about desperation in the fields. At nineteen, she jettisoned her father's dream of law school and dropped out of college to spend a year working for Cesar Chavez's fledgling union. One year turned into sixteen. She went abroad, fell in love, ran union elections, organized a health clinic across the Mexican border. She rose to become a member of the executive board of the United Farm Workers of America. Then she was drummed out of the organization that had become her life.

At fifty-eight, after a decade-long battle with cancer she believed came from pesticides in the fields where she had worked as a child, Jessica Govea Thorbourne died.

Like many funerals, Jessica's memorial was a celebration of what was and a mourning for what might have been.

From across the country, the old UFW team assembled once more in Salinas, the salad bowl of the world, the hub of their union at its moment of greatest strength. They gathered on April 9, 2005, at the National Steinbeck Center, the museum dedicated to the writer whose portrait of misery in the fields still rang true seventy years later. Many of the mourners had not seen one another for decades, though they once were virtually inseparable. The picture of the pigtailed girl with the shovel greeted guests as they arrived.

They returned to Salinas to remember Jessica's beautiful voice, her fighting spirit, her intricate quilts, her straightforward compassion, and her preference for mixing cinnamon in her coffee. And they came to Salinas for the cause, for a time long ago and a movement long gone that transformed them forever. Today they are union leaders, community activists, labor lawyers, teachers, judges, environmentalists. The time they shared remains for many, as it was for Jessica, the most important in their lives. In Cesar Chavez's union they met husbands, wives, and best friends. They found work that had meaning, and discovered hope, betrayal, and disillusionment.

Jessica had asked that Jerry Cohen officiate at her service. The sixty-four-year-old lawyer looked as rumpled as ever, shirttail hanging out. He spoke of the day almost forty years earlier when the legal department of the farm workers union was in the kitchen of a cramped house and he was a rookie who didn't know which writ to file. Jessica, his twenty-year-old assistant, suggested he flip a coin. Good case, wrong writ, the judge said. "We were at our most dangerous when we were laughing loudest," Jerry recalled.

Eliseo Medina, a teenage farmworker when he met Jessica, noted how she had brought people together in death, just as she did in life. "What brought us into this union? What were those common beliefs and values that we shared?" he asked softly, standing at the lectern in the trademark purple shirt of the Service Employees International Union that he helped lead.

The colors of the UFW were on display at the far side of the room, where the union's current leaders mingled awkwardly with a handful of supporters dutifully holding red and black flags.

On the walls hung some of Jessica's quilts, including the baby blanket she had made for Gretchen Laue's first son. Gretchen had grabbed the quilt at the last minute as she left her home in El Centro, the border town where she first befriended Jessica during a strike that shut down the California lettuce fields. Gretchen had not known Spanish then; now, she spoke nothing else on the eight-hour drive to Salinas with Mario Bustamante, who once cut lettuce faster than anyone, and Rosario Pelayo, who used to pack broccoli during the day and work for the union at night.

"Jessica fought with her heart, hands, and mind," Pelayo told the mourners. Then she paid tribute to all of them. "I know there are so many people here who left half their lives, fighting for this cause."

Like many in the room, Chris Hartmire had thought he would fight for *la causa* forever, but forever turned out to be twenty-seven years. The Presbyterian minister had apologized since then for many things he had done in the name of helping farmworkers. He remembered the time Jessica was scared by ugly rifts within the movement. She had reached out to Chris, worried about her boyfriend's safety. Chris had cavalierly dismissed her fears. He was glad he had told Jessica he was sorry, long before she fell ill.

The memorial ended with a recording of Jessica singing "La Paloma" at a funeral for Fred Ross, the organizer who had recruited and trained Cesar Chavez. *Cu curu curu, cu curu curu,* Jessica sang, echoing the plaintive cry of the dove. The first time Ellen Eggers heard Jessica sing that song was a summer night in 1972 at the union headquarters, a place that Ellen thought the most exciting spot in the world. She was a wide-eyed twenty-year-old from Indiana, and Jessica seemed so confident and accomplished, though only five years older.

Ellen was one of thousands drawn to the cause. They were young and fearless and often naïve, buoyed by moral outrage that bordered on arrogance, bound together by the conviction that their cause was not only righteous but more important than any other, and intoxicated by the discovery of their own power. At the height of the boycott, seventeen million Americans stopped eating grapes so that farmworkers in California could win better wages and working conditions.

At the end of his eulogy, Eliseo talked about being a scared twenty-one-year-old farmworker thousands of miles from home, pursuing a mission that would have seemed impossible if he had stopped long enough to think. Within a few years he and an army of volunteers in a ragtag operation would force the most powerful industry in California to sign union contracts.

"We won," Eliseo recalled in his eulogy. "We won. And when we did that, we captured the imagination and the hearts of millions and millions and millions of people throughout this world. But we also raised the hopes of millions of workers around this country, who saw what farmworkers had done and said, 'Maybe I, too, can do the same thing, and if I fight, I can help change my life and create a better life for myself and my children.' "

Sabino Lopez was an irrigator with a grade school education when he went on strike in 1970. Now he was the first farmworker on the board of the Steinbeck Center. He looked around the room with pride, and sadness. Sabino thought about Jessica, how she had left her soul in Salinas, decades before she died. He thought about the lost force that had once toppled giants and transformed thousands of lives. Lost, he thought, because of some human failings. He looked at his teachers and mentors and heroes and comrades, together again, but fighting no more. They were the ones in the fields with him, fighting for the workers, day after day. Cesar Chavez was the symbol, Sabino thought. He was not the union. The story of the farm worker movement was not just his story, but also theirs.

PART I

The Grape Strike

September 1965–July 1970

CHAPTER 1

Huelga

September 1965

Eliseo

Eliseo Medina was stuck at home, watching reruns of *I Love Lucy*. You can't pick grapes with a broken leg, and there was not much else to do in Delano, California.

Life in the small San Joaquin Valley town was as monotonous as the flat landscape and as predictable as the streets that ran from west to east in alphabetical order. One-story bungalows and pastel-colored ranch houses barely broke the horizon, tapering off into miles of fields. There was only one clear boundary in Delano—the railroad tracks that split the town in two.

The serious teenager with the disarming smile lived two blocks west of the tracks, where the sidewalks stopped and the run-down housing started, and immigration agents knocked on doors in the middle of the night. Eliseo lived with his mother, two sisters, brother-in-law, niece and nephew at 418 Fremont Street, three generations in a two-bedroom frame house with a bathroom and shower out back. Behind the house ran the alley they used as a shortcut to the candy store and People's Bar, where Eliseo learned to play pool. A mile the other direction was Fremont Elementary School, where Eliseo had landed in fourth grade, speaking only Spanish after two years on the streets of Tijuana. His intelligence and curiosity propelled him to success even in a school that saw little value in educating Mexicans. He graduated from eighth grade with honors, then left school after guidance counselors explained that the Mexican students about to enter high school should all take shop classes.

The career options in Delano for a Mexican kid were simple: You could be a farmworker, or a foreman.

At age nineteen, Eliseo had been working in the fields full time for four years, summers and weekends for five years before that. He was skilled at trimming clusters of grapes, though so clumsy at spotting tomatoes when they were ready to pick (still green with just a hint of red) that people often thought him color-blind. He enjoyed the oranges best. He could find a shady, secluded perch inside a tree, where he could pick and eat at his own pace. He hated digging out potatoes, the way the rocks and roots and parched earth raked your fingertips. On those days he would wake up hoping for rain.

In the summer of 1965 rumblings of unrest broke the monotony of another season in the Delano fields. In the Coachella Valley vineyards almost three hundred miles to the southeast, Filipino farmworkers went on strike. Eliseo's mother, Guadalupe, followed the strike with keen interest. She had been orphaned young, her parents killed in the Mexican Revolution, and she grew up with a passion for social justice. The Medinas talked about how the Filipinos were better organized than the Mexicans, and they wondered if the strike would succeed.

Table grapes ripen first in the Coachella desert, kicking off the California harvest. Those early spring grapes were a prized commodity, shipped across the country to consumers who paid top dollar for the first Thompson seedless of the year. The Coachella growers had a short season and couldn't risk a lengthy strike. So they met the demands from the small Filipino workers' union and upped wages to $1.40 an hour from $1.25. By August the Filipino workers had migrated north with the harvest, expecting the same wages for the same work in the San Joaquin Valley. But the Delano grape growers weren't paying.

Rumors of an impending strike spread, expectation crackling in the dry, hot valley air. Though they toiled side by side in the vineyards, the Mexican and Filipino workers did not mix. Mexicans picked the grapes and Filipinos packed them, a job growers thought too difficult for Mexicans. On the morning of September 8, the Mexicans found out when they showed up for work that the Filipinos had refused to leave their camps. Guadalupe Medina and her daughters burst in the house that afternoon with the announcement that jolted Eliseo away from *I Love Lucy*, his favorite television show: The strike had arrived in Delano.

Eliseo hopped out on crutches the next day to look at a picket line thrown up by the Filipino union. A few days later he watched a couple hundred Mexicans and white supporters march down Eleventh Avenue, waving red flags with a stylized black eagle and inviting workers to a Thursday night meeting. They urged bystanders to join their group, the National Farm Workers Association, which they did not even call a union yet for fear of scaring workers.

Eliseo was intrigued. He had always loved to read; as a child he had read cereal boxes when there was nothing else around. Lately he had become a faithful reader of *El Malcriado*, the ten-cent newspaper the Farm Workers Association published in Spanish and English. The name meant "the unruly child," and the paper championed farmworkers, shamed labor contractors, and lampooned growers with biting cartoons and spirited satire. Eliseo followed with particular satisfaction the saga of Jimmy Hronis, a notorious labor contractor caught cheating sugar beet workers after *El Malcriado* revealed he had paid them only fifty cents an hour. The newspaper stories triggered a state investigation, a rare case of a powerful Anglo contractor forced to answer for mistreatment.

That power impressed Eliseo, his curiosity tempered by trepidation. He believed in taking important risks, but not unnecessary ones. (Though his caution sometimes backfired: He had broken his leg when a friend who was driving drunk refused to relinquish the wheel. Eliseo insisted on getting out to walk. His friend drove off, then looped back to give Eliseo a ride but accidently sent him flying over the hood.)

That Thursday night, Eliseo went alone to the meeting in Our Lady of Guadalupe Church. He squeezed into the back of the large hall next door to the sanctuary—even the second-story balcony in back was overflowing. The workers came because they had been cheated out of wages more times than they could count. They had worked in fields with no drinking water or bathrooms. They had been injured on the job, sprayed with pesticides, fired for being too slow, too old, or too outspoken. They were excluded from unemployment insurance and overtime, denied holidays, vacations, and health insurance. They endured the most backbreaking labor—with none of the basic protections and rights afforded almost all other workers in America.

A short, unimposing man rose to address the crowd. Eliseo had only read about Cesar Chavez. The teenager was disappointed by the leader's unimpressive appearance. Then the soft-spoken thirty-eight-year-old began to speak. He talked about the harshness of the fields. His own family had been driven off their Arizona farm during the Depression. He spent his childhood in and out of dozens of schools and fields, sleeping in tents, cars, and hovels. He spoke with anger about how Mexicans were treated. He told the workers things could be different if they fought together.

Chavez had started his union in Delano because he had family there. He also chose Delano because grapevines, unlike vegetables, stay in the ground all year, a permanent backdrop for strikes and protests.[1] Chavez was just as calculating in his choice of dates for this historic meeting, September 16, Mexican Independence Day. He used the holiday to drive home his revolutionary message. Think of the parallels to Mexican Independence, he told the workers in the church. They too struggled to overthrow oppressive rulers. The Mexican workers must decide, he said, whether to join the strike started by the Filipinos.

"*Huelga, huelga, huelga,*" the crowd chanted, the Spanish word for strike, soon to be emblazoned on picket signs and seared in the collective memory of Delano. The meeting ended with traditional Mexican tributes to fire up the crowd. The leader called out a *viva*—"long live"—and the crowd chanted the slogan back. *Viva la huelga. Viva Mexico.* And *viva Cesar Chavez.*[2]

Eliseo went home caught up in the fervor, enticed by the hope. He had spent too many Sundays camped outside the office of a labor contractor, wasting his one day off to collect his wages. He had seen his mother and sisters work without a single bathroom in the fields, forced to seek a shred of privacy by shielding one another. He had watched his father be fired because he could no longer keep up with the younger men in the fields.

The shy teenager from Zacatecas with a shock of dark hair tended to deliberate carefully before acting. Once he made a decision, Eliseo embraced the path with focused enthusiasm and a big, contagious grin. He went home after the meeting at the church and cracked open his piggy bank. He didn't know what a contract was, but he counted out ten dollars and fifty cents. The next day, he drove to the headquarters at 102 Albany Street, handed three months dues to Helen Chavez, and joined her husband's union.

Chris

The same day, Cesar Chavez placed a call to a young Presbyterian minister in Los Angeles. On the eve of a strike he was unprepared to wage,

Chavez could count on only a few people for help. Chris Hartmire topped the list.

From a fifth-floor office on Olympic Boulevard, Chris ran the California Migrant Ministry, a largely ignored stepchild of the Council of Churches. For decades, the small Protestant ministry had offered spiritual counseling to farmworkers and toys to their children, visiting bleak migrant camps in a fleet of station wagons named "the Harvesters." Quietly, Chris had been engineering a radical shift in the ministry's approach. The catalyst for that change was the man now calling from Delano for help.

Cesar Chavez had been one of the first people Chris sought out in 1961, when the young pastor moved reluctantly to California. Chris had loved his job in New York, running a youth ministry in East Harlem. But when his wife was mugged in the elevator of their apartment building, their two-year-old in her arms, he knew they had to move. The offer to run the California Migrant Ministry seemed serendipitous, yet unappealing. Chris dreaded the tedium of an administrative job.

He made lists, in his neat script. "California: Assets." "California: Liabilities." Even after he accepted the job, his doubts persisted. "Never before have I felt so helpless and so small," he wrote church officials, explaining apologetically that he could not promise to stay more than two years. To himself he wrote: "Perhaps God arranged the pressure of events knowing that I was too timid to say yes under other circumstances. Perhaps this *is* His will for me at this time in history."[3]

He drove cross-country with his wife, Jane, his best friend since seventh grade, better known by her nickname, Pudge. The Hartmires settled in the Los Angeles County suburb of Culver City. They came to appreciate a backyard for the kids and even, over time, to root for the Dodgers. The day Cesar Chavez outlined his vision of community organizing over lunch in an East Los Angeles café, Chris began to think his destiny was in California after all. He was captivated by the idea of a ministry that helped poor people organize themselves.

Chavez sketched out the work he did as director of the Community Service Organization (CSO), a grassroots group that organized citizenship classes, voter registration drives, and lobbying campaigns in poor Mexican neighborhoods across California. Chris met Fred Ross, the lanky founder of CSO, who had discovered Chavez and taught him how to organize. Then Chavez and Ross installed Chris in a dilapidated rooming-house in Stockton for a month, so the young minister could see for himself how CSO taught Mexican Americans to take on the powerful institutions that denied them education, justice, and civil rights.

Even as Chris embraced the CSO model, Chavez was growing frustrated by its limitations. The CSO board refused to organize farmworkers. The CSO members, once empowered, increasingly voiced middle-class aspirations, more concerned with their own advancement than with helping the poor. Their attitude infuriated Chavez. Poor people were what he cared about, and farmworkers were the poor whom Chavez knew best. Chris was in the audience at the CSO convention in March 1962 when Chavez rose to announce his resignation. Chris couldn't understand why people didn't beg the leader to stay.

Chavez struck off on his own and founded the National Farm Workers Association. The Migrant Ministry loaned him a mimeograph machine. Chris's aides drove Chavez to key appointments and handed him their credit cards when his money ran out. The Migrant Ministry hosted the Chavez family at the group's bimonthly retreats. Gradually, Chris began to assign his staff to work as organizers. He rejected the ministry's historic milk-and-cookies approach as "dishonest attempts to salve conscience while hanging onto an unjust social system which benefits 'our kind of people' at the expense of the poor."[4]

From his mother, Wayne C. Hartmire Jr. had learned to embrace the underdog. From his father, he had learned to love baseball. Chris grew up in a working-class family in a Philadelphia suburb, the middle child of an insecure mother and an emotionally absent father. Chris was short, as undistinguished at sports as he was outstanding at academics. He won a scholarship to Princeton and graduated Phi Beta Kappa in engineering, but decided science offered little opportunity to help others. After three years as a navy engineer, he entered the seminary. When he began to work with Chavez, Chris felt he had finally found his calling.

Chris found Chavez an irresistible force, a presence that belied his slight stature. Chavez was dark-complexioned with faintly Mexican Indian features, his dark hair parted on the left, slicked back or occasionally falling over his penetrating, perpetually tired eyes. He used those eyes when he wanted something, looking right at you, but otherwise he glanced down a lot. Sometimes a brief smile flashed across his face, or a mischievous grin. He dressed in work clothes, donning a shirt with a Nehru collar or embroidery for special occasions, never a tie. His speech, like his appearance, was unremarkable; his profound thoughts delivered in a flat voice, with run-on sentences often punctuated by "you know." He was at his best in small groups, a good listener who left his audience convinced that their words mattered—even as he listened intently to make sure his points had gotten through.

Chris had an earnest, boyish innocence that made the minister seem much younger than his thirty-three years. Chavez needed that youthful sincerity. The Migrant Ministry had resources. And Chavez knew Chris would never say no. He was fast becoming a disciple, ready to risk it all for a cause he believed in. So the day after the crowd roared its approval in Our Lady of Guadalupe Church, Chavez summoned Chris to Delano to help turn the shouts of "huelga" into action.

That Friday, Chris drove 140 miles north from Los Angeles, over the Tejon Pass and down to the lush floor of the San Joaquin Valley, nothing but farmland on all sides. In Delano he mediated a meeting on Sunday between the Mexicans and the Filipinos at the Stardust Motel. The Farm Workers Association agreed to join the strike on Monday morning.

Chavez had been building his union slowly for three years. He had less than one hundred dollars in the treasury, a small credit union managed by his wife, and a death benefit program for the handful of members who paid $3.50 a month in dues. He didn't believe his tiny union was ready for a strike. He had always said a union should strike only after organizing workers. But like many decisions that would follow, this one was made for him.

Chris helped Chavez and the Filipino union forge a tentative alliance and pledged support from the ministry: cash for gas and phones, food and rent money for strikers, and clergy to walk picket lines. Chris knew his early support earned him a position of trust. So with no sense of the consequences, no agonizing or making lists, almost overnight Chris turned the Protestant ministry into an adjunct of Cesar Chavez's union.

Eliseo

"Este hogar es católico, no aceptamos propaganda protestante ni de otras sectas" read the sign on Eliseo's front door, a common warning on Delano's west side. This is a Catholic home, we don't accept propaganda from Protestants or other sects. Eliseo was not sure what to expect from Protestants and uncertain he had ever actually met one. Certainly not a Communist or a Jew. Wide-eyed, he watched in the fall of 1965 as they flocked to Delano—college dropouts, families, nuns, Communists, Protestants, Jews, long-haired guys, and Berkeley girls.

Help poured in as soon as the strike began, transforming the anonymous farming town of twelve thousand people into the new cause célèbre. White civil rights activists casting about for another cause after the Mississippi Summer were drawn to the farmworkers' struggle. Delano was only 250 miles from the University of California at Berkeley, where Jerry Rubin organized teach-ins against the Vietnam War and students burned their draft cards. Each Friday after the strike began, Delano's population swelled with weekend volunteers from the Bay Area and food caravans that delivered provisions to the communal strike kitchen.

The only white people Eliseo had known before the strike were growers and teachers. Now the west side of Delano filled with more white people than he had ever seen. They lived among the Mexicans on the wrong side of the tracks and at night they drank beer and played pool at People's Bar, around the corner from Eliseo's home.

As alien as the out-of-towners were to Eliseo, the civil protests that drew them to Delano were even more foreign. And equally alluring. A few weeks into the strike, the teenager heard the union was paying people to picket. He went to inquire with his friend. The two walked uncertainly into Filipino Hall, a community center that served as strike headquarters. Follow me, an old man said, grabbing some of the big, round strike signs that looked like giant lollipops. They jumped into his car, and he deftly navigated through the acres of vines, taking them to the field of a company where workers were breaking the strike. Police cars followed close behind. Eliseo was sure he would be arrested, maybe even deported. His mother had waited almost two years in Tijuana until she could bring her children across the border legally. The memory of swearing to uphold the laws when he entered the country was still vivid.

The old man got out and stood beside a field, shouting at the workers in the vineyard and urging them to honor the strike. Some heeded the message and walked off the job. The police just observed. Eliseo's fear dissolved into relief, then awe. In his world, there was only one way to protest working conditions: quit. The seductive power of this public challenge quickly overcame his fright. After that, Eliseo went out on the picket lines every day, even though the rumored payments never materialized.

Within weeks he became a picket captain. In the disorganized and understaffed union, eagerness quickly translated into greater responsibility. Each morning, Eliseo assembled his crew and received his assignment. The union called strikes at more than two dozen ranches spread over several hundred square miles. To select strategic locations to picket, volunteers with two-way radios drove around the fields each morning before dawn. They tailed crews to figure out where strikebreakers were working and radioed the information back to headquarters so coordinators could dispatch picket crews. Police followed the picketers, took pictures, and opened files. Just a few weeks into the strike the FBI opened a probe into "Communist Infiltration of the National Farm Workers Association."[5]

Eliseo led his crew each morning in a caravan of cars to the designated field. They stood in the road at the edge of a vineyard, about twenty strong, and exhorted workers to join the strike. Sometimes they used megaphones; usually they just shouted from the road or the tops of cars. Often the supervisor moved a crew out of earshot. That was a partial victory—vines that needed picking were left untended, and ripe grapes quickly rot. Sometimes workers dropped their tools and walked out of the fields. They were welcomed with cheers.

As hard as Eliseo was fighting to coax workers out of the vineyards, Martin Zaninovich was fighting to keep them in. Zaninovich had grown up on the vineyard he now ran. He belonged to the second generation of one of the many interlocking Slav families that had settled in Delano in the 1930s. Grape growers from the island of Hvar off the coast of Croatia, they had picked Delano because the soil and climate nurtured the same grapes they had farmed back home. The Slavs owned the bulk of the seventy vineyards around Delano, all but two family-owned. Martin Zaninovich's Jasmine Vineyards was a few hundred feet down the road from another Slav ranch, Dan Tudor and Sons, where Eliseo had picked grapes before he broke his leg. The Monday when the Mexicans joined the strike was the first time Zaninovich saw the red flag with the black eagle, alongside the round sign that said "Huelga." He had no idea what the word meant.

Zaninovich's Delano was the peaceful "United Nations of the Valley" featured in Chamber of Commerce literature: Slav, Italian, and Armenian growers, an Asian-American school board president, a Mexican American police chief, and a stable workforce of comparatively well-paid farmworkers. Suddenly, hippies marched down Main Street. Students, religious liberals, and labor organizers lectured those who made their living off the land. Zaninovich saw them as ignorant, spoiled children of the middle class on a crusade to upend the economic and social order. They yelled threats and obscenities at workers who did not walk out on strike, workers whose lives the outsiders could not possibly comprehend.[6]

The Delano growers had to recruit additional workers from Mexico to replace the strikers. But most of the workers stayed in the fields, out of either necessity or fear. Many who had walked out soon returned to work. Forced to choose between the cause and the job, workers overwhelmingly picked the latter. After a few weeks Eliseo was one of the only farmworkers still on the picket lines. One day Eliseo even ran into his friend who had started picketing with him, working in a field. Astonished, Eliseo ran over to talk, but the police blocked the entrance to the vineyard, and his friend disappeared.

Eventually Eliseo, too, needed a paying job. He waited till the grape harvest ended and the fields were almost empty, to lessen the impact of his departure. Then he took a job at a nursery, away from the strike. The work seemed even more tedious than before. The highlight of his week was always the Friday night union meeting, timed so that weekend visitors could take part. Filipino Hall filled with the smells of fish soup and *adobo*, the warm camaraderie of shared struggle, and the spirited voices of all ages, joined in traditional songs of protest. Speakers told jokes to punctuate reports about the picket lines, food bank, garage, and health clinic. Chavez acknowledged setbacks, but always looked ahead to the next success. He understood the importance of giving people victories to hold on to. The Teatro Campesino drew laughter with improvised skits that mocked growers and *esquiroles,* scabs. Eliseo and his mother were among the contingent of faithful Delano supporters, but the audience, like the picket lines, had more students and volunteers than farm workers.

The Reverend Jim Drake often opened the meetings with a prayer and sometimes presided when Chavez was away. Drake worked for the Migrant Ministry, but his office was a desk built over a toilet in a bathroom of 102 Albany Street. A few months into the strike, a nurse from the Bay Area walked into the union headquarters for a weekend visit. Drake looked up and asked if she could type. Marion Moses nodded. He handed her a form letter to type and address to twenty-five supporters. Moses soon returned to Delano to volunteer for a week. She paid the fifty dollars' rent on her San Francisco apartment for two more months but never went back. The first in her family to go past high school, Moses put her plan for premed studies on hold. She worked in a makeshift health clinic in a bedroom and slept on the floor of a nearby house for months before a bed opened up.

Doug Adair, a liberal Republican graduate student, had ended up in Delano because of a political argument with Moses on the Berkeley campus when she was recruiting volunteers. She had challenged him to see how farmworkers lived. The twenty-two-year-old Adair ended up picking plums and moving to Delano when the strike began. "Doug" pronounced in a Spanish accent became "Duck." Soon everyone just called him Pato, the Spanish word for duck. The son of a prominent American historian, Pato worked for *El Malcriado*, first delivering the paper and then writing and editing stories.

To Martin Zaninovich, the young people looking for a cause were proof the strike was not a labor dispute but a civil rights action, fueled by outside agitators.

To Eliseo, who began to befriend the outsiders on picket lines and at Friday night meetings, they were an exotic community, an eclectic mix united in their single-minded focus to help Cesar Chavez and to fight for the cause they always called "the Union," as if there were no other.

Chris

Chavez was counting on Chris to deliver something largely absent from the passionate army of volunteers: credibility.

Chris first aimed his earnest entreaties at religious supporters. He appealed for Christmas presents to offer children of strikers and public commitments to bolster morale. He cloaked the cause in an unambiguous appeal to Christian conscience. "There is no relevant middle ground on a moral issue that is as clear as the farm workers' fight for opportunity and self-respect," he wrote. "Silence and neutrality inevitably become the allies of the established, unjust way of doing things."[7] You are with us, or you are against us.

Chris compared the farmworkers' strike to the Watts riots that had taken place in Los Angeles just one month earlier, in August 1965. He invoked the church's role in the South, speaking of Selma, Alabama, and Martin Luther King Jr., as he proselytized for the new civil rights movement of the West. Chris decried the radical imbalance of power, glorified the justness of the workers' cause, and reminded Christians about their duty to help the weak and poor. He quoted the Gospel in one breath and government statistics in the next: Farmworkers earned about $2,500 a year, one third the median family income in California.[8]

Chavez also needed Chris to help win over a very different audience—farmworkers who were scared, skeptical, or both. The movement lacked support from the Catholic Church; the Protestant clergy would have to suffice as symbols of the workers' religious allies.

Chavez's sense of staging made the most of his small band of religious supporters. When a farmworker began to read Jack London's "Definition of a Strikebreaker" out loud on a picket line, a deputy sheriff warned that voicing such seditious sentiments would lead to arrest. The Reverend David Havens of the Migrant Ministry took up the challenge. Havens was arrested minutes after he recited the withering passage that begins: "After God had finished the rattlesnake, the toad and the vampire, he had some awful substance left with which he made a Strikebreaker."

Two days later Chris rounded up nine ministers to join a Demonstration of Christian Concern as they defied the latest police edict: shouting "huelga" was disturbing the peace. At 10:53 A.M. the sheriff's deputy turned on his tape recorder, and forty-four protesters chanted *huelga* with all their might. "These workers, we believe, have the right to organize a union just as other Americans," Chris declared. Each time the sheriffs used their radios to communicate, the demonstrators shouted louder to drown out the police. While television cameras whirred, all forty-four were charged with unlawful assembly and hauled off to jail.[9] Chavez timed the protest to coincide with a speech he delivered at Berkeley. He announced the arrests, and students handed over thousands of dollars in lunch money to help.

Even a legal system stacked in favor of the growers was vindicating the farmworkers. "The court finds that there was no 'clear and present danger' involved in the present situation. No persons were about to riot nor was any form of civil disorder incipient," wrote the judge who dismissed charges against the Reverend Havens. "While the court does not think that the passage read from Jack London was in good taste under the circumstances, nonetheless the court must hold that no violation . . . has occurred."[10] The ensuing national attention spurred more donations, sympathetic coverage, and weekly visits from clergy. ("With collars," Chris stressed.) They walked the picket lines "as a reminder," Chris wrote, "to police, grower security guards, and growers that the rest of the world was watching."[11]

The more credibility Chris lent the movement, the more he became a target. Growers formed the bulwark of the local churches, and the backlash against Chris was swift and fierce. The Delano Ministerial Association denounced the Migrant Ministry's tactics as unethical. Protestant churches in the valley and the Episcopal diocese passed resolutions condemning the Migrant Ministry. Churches canceled contributions and urged the California Council of Churches to suspend funding for its errant offspring. The Council of California Growers devoted its October 4,

1965, newsletter to an attack on the Migrant Ministry for encouraging "class conflict and ferment." Outraged growers pointed out that the meddling clergy were not even Catholic.[12]

Hundreds turned out to castigate Chris at church meetings. When he and Chavez arrived at the Visalia Methodist Church to debate the head of the Farm Bureau, the church had already installed loudspeakers on the lawn to accommodate an overflow crowd—growers, their families, their friends, and the business people who depended on them. They're more angry at you than me, Chavez told Chris as they waded through the hostile audience.[13]

Chris scrambled to justify his own actions. "Christians should be willing to say by word and deed: 'The workers are important people who should be dealt with as equals.' That is what the Migrant Ministry and other churchmen are trying to say by their presence in Delano," Chris wrote. "So long as growers refuse to recognize independently organized workers then Christians must continue to help the workers be strong and press their employers to bargain."[14]

Martin Zaninovich was emerging as a leader of the Delano growers, though his vineyard was far from the largest. Growing up, he had one lesson drummed into him: the most important thing, no matter what, was to keep your workers in the field. Tend the vines and harvest the crop. Now he took pride in his ability to keep the vineyard operating despite the unrest. He and the other growers in the valley were harvesting the largest crop in history. Most of his regular workers had stayed. He had worried whether Mexicans would be able to replace the Filipinos as packers, but that turned out not to be a problem.

"There is no strike in Delano," Zaninovich kept telling people. But even if he was winning what he always referred to as "the so-called strike," he was losing the public relations war. Zaninovich turned his wrath on Chris, infuriated as the minister become the public face of religious leadership. "Religious hierarchies have elected to abdicate their positions as representatives of all churches by entering into the field as union organizers," Zaninovich fumed.[15]

In the spring of 1966, the strike passed the half-year mark as a new season began in the Delano vineyards. More strikers returned to work, and national attention faded. Then came the march to Sacramento. A devout Catholic, lacking support from his own church, Chavez set off during Lent on a religious march of penance, a twenty-five-day pilgrimage from Delano north to the state capital. "The farm workers feel that this is a

Chris Hartmire and Cesar Chavez during the march to Sacramento, March 1966. (Ken Thompson)

religious pilgrimage borne out of their cultural tradition, their suffering and their need to express their God-given worth," Chris wrote, urging supporters to join the march on Good Friday and Easter Sunday. "It is of crucial importance that the churches join them in this effort."[16]

Steeped in Mexican traditions, the *peregrinación* resonated with workers in the dozens of small farming communities along the spine of the San Joaquin Valley. They lined the roads to watch, they offered the marchers food and drink, they cheered as Chavez and a small group slowly, sometimes painfully, walked the three-hundred-mile route. Some days the march stretched out for a mile, workers who had never dreamed of such militant action silhouetted against the fields in the relentless sun, their flags casting shadows as they walked in ones and twos along Highway 99. They sang "Nosotros Venceremos" and shouted "*Viva la huelga.*" Always at the front of the procession was the banner of the Virgin of Guadalupe, the most sacred cultural symbol for Mexicans. Catholic churches along the route had no choice but to open their doors to the penitents.

Chris was on the march the day a lawyer best known for his mobster clients tracked down Chavez. Sidney Korshak said he was authorized to negotiate a contract on behalf of Schenley, a large liquor company whose wine grape vineyard had been the union's most recent target. The fields were one small piece of Schenley's empire; the company would rather negotiate than risk bad publicity that could hurt its sales. Chris and Chavez broke off from the march and drove to Los Angeles to meet Korshak at his Beverly Hills mansion. Over cocktails and hors d'oeuvres, they discussed the terms of the recognition agreement. Jubilant, Chris drove Chavez back to northern California to join the end of the march.

Thousands rallied outside the capitol on Easter and cheered the Schenley victory. Chris rose to address the crowd. He thanked Chavez and those around him: "They have taught us new things about courage and honesty and hope. Most of all they have helped many of us see the world as it really is, in place of the pleasant world we imagine for our comfort's sake." He spoke of Jesus, resurrection, and the march as a beginning of new hope. Then the Protestant minister concluded with a quote from an atheist— Nobel Prize–winning author Albert Camus: "What the world expects of Christians is that Christians should speak out, loud and clear, and that they should voice their condemnation in such a way that never a doubt, never the slightest doubt, could rise in the heart of the simplest man. That they should get away from abstraction and confront the blood-stained face history has taken on today. The grouping we need is a grouping of men resolved to speak out clearly and to pay up personally."[17]

CHAPTER 2

Showdown at DiGiorgio

June 1966

Eliseo

In the late spring of 1966, Eliseo walked into the union office looking for a job. He walked out with a calling.

Eliseo wanted to work picking wine grapes under the union's new contract at Schenley Vineyards. He persuaded two friends at the nursery to quit and figured they would pick up the fourth they needed to form a team. Then he went to see Dolores Huerta at the union headquarters. Eliseo had met her when he was a picket captain. He thought he could parlay the connection with a top union leader into a job at Schenley. Sure, she told him, but since the harvest hasn't started, help us out first for a month on the strike. So Eliseo signed on for the union's battle against the DiGiorgio Corporation, the largest grower in the Delano area. As Eliseo was leaving the union office, Chavez walked in. Huerta told him she had enlisted a new organizer, and the two men shook hands.

Eliseo joined a fight in progress on two fronts. Chavez was trying to leverage political and public pressure to force a union election among table grape workers at DiGiorgio, an agricultural conglomerate whose holdings included several large vineyards. At the same time Chavez faced a new adversary vying to represent farmworkers: the Teamsters.

The Teamsters were a corrupt, discredited union that had been thrown out of the AFL-CIO. That stigma only endeared them to the growers, who

Eliseo Medina learning to be an organizer during the DiGiorgio campaign, August 1966. (Jon Lewis/www.farmworkermovement.us)

already had Teamster contracts in packing sheds and trucking operations. To the DiGiorgios, the accommodating Teamsters presented an attractive alternative to Chavez's militant movement. An alliance with the Teamsters would offer a union label with little sacrifice. So DiGiorgio invited the Teamsters to woo the workers in the fields, confident the rival union would not challenge management.

To spearhead the two-pronged struggle against DiGiorgio and the Teamsters, Chavez recruited his own mentor. Fred Ross, the man who had trained Chavez at the Community Service Organization, returned to help his protégé in a fight both men thought would make or break the young union. Ross became Eliseo's teacher.

The union's message resonated with DiGiorgio workers, just as it had for Eliseo when he first heard Chavez speak. But the bare-bones union faced significant hurdles. Just finding DiGiorgio workers presented the first challenge. Teamsters were ushered in to speak with workers on company time; Farm Workers Association organizers were run out of the vineyards and camps. The union scattered between thirty and two hundred pickets around the 4,400-acre DiGiorgio ranch, hoping to catch workers at 206 entrances along an eleven-mile boundary. Company trucks barreled by the strike lines, nipped picketers on the ankles, and sprayed them with sulfur dust.[1]

Ross compensated for the difficulties by imposing a discipline that left nothing to chance. Eliseo learned to follow Ross's exacting methods. He created an index card for every DiGiorgio worker who was eligible to vote. Each morning, organizers collected cards for the workers they were assigned to see. They tracked down their workers and made notations on the card. Each night, Ross sorted the cards into three piles before they were locked away: yes votes, no votes, and maybes. Early morning, midday, and evening, Ross met with Eliseo and the other rookie organizers. He grilled them about every interaction, what they said, the reception, the response. He drilled lessons into them. Count with your mind, not your heart, he would say.

Eliseo learned from his own interrogation, but he also listened closely to the experiences of others. He fine-tuned the message that Ross called the rap, the speech Eliseo used to sell the union and to counter blandishments from Teamsters and threats from the company foremen. Eliseo talked about higher wages, but also about dignity and respect, about the right to speak up. But you're Mexican, he would say to a worker—how can you support the Teamsters? You must be with us. We have to stick together, that's the way we will win. He talked about his own experiences in the fields. He emphasized results, the point that had sold him on the union. Look at the Schenley contract, where wages went up from $1.40 to $1.75, and workers received medical and life insurance and paid vacation. Look at Jimmy Hronis, the corrupt labor contractor whose case had first piqued Eliseo's interest when he read *El Malcriado*. A year after the union forced an investigation, a judge had ordered Hronis to pay back wages to the beet workers he had cheated. That, Eliseo told the DiGiorgio workers, is what the union means.

Chris

Chris plunged into the intrigue of the DiGiorgio campaign, working as an organizer, masquerading as a minister.

His first mission was to crusade against the very thing the union wanted: an election. DiGiorgio unilaterally scheduled an election and decreed that only current employees could vote—excluding workers who had walked out on strike. With the contest rigged against him, Chavez obtained a court order to remove the union's name from the ballot, leaving only the Teamsters. He urged workers to boycott the election in protest. On election day Chris led a group of observers from the Migrant Ministry, who watched DiGiorgio supervisors put crews on company buses, deliver them to the polling place, and pressure them to vote. Chris joined a line of protesters outside the small railroad depot adjacent to the DiGiorgio ranch. The picketers shouted as each bus rolled by, urging workers not to vote.

Chris knew one driver very well. He yelled and shook his fist when Joe Serda drove his workers to the polls. But the minister was confident they would not vote. Serda was a submarine—a loyal foreman by day, a union spy at night. He had first learned about the union when his daughter came home with bruises on her ankles, where the DiGiorgio trucks hit her while she was on the picket line. Serda went to Chavez and offered to help; Chavez told the foreman to stay right where he was. Chris often attended the late-night meetings at the union office where Serda filed his daily reports. He relayed any intelligence he could garner. He described Teamsters pulling up in Cadillacs and offering free food. He collected garbage from wastebaskets in the company office, torn-up notes that the union team spread out on a table and pieced back together, gleaning information that helped them preempt DiGiorgio's strategic moves. When he drove his crew back from the polls, Serda watched workers embrace, tears in their eyes. They had challenged the company for the first time, by the simple act of refusing to vote.[2]

Between the submarines, the loyal Chavistas, and the threats from picketers, almost half the 732 DiGiorgio workers driven to the polls refused to vote. Within three days, Chris had turned the testimony of the clergy witnesses into a formal protest to the governor. Their report detailed the dishonest election: No neutral party monitored the vote. Non-farmworkers cast ballots. Supervisors pressured workers to vote for the Teamsters. The next day Governor Edmund G. Brown met with Chris, Chavez, and a group of farmworkers. Brown agreed to appoint an arbitrator to investigate.

The following day Chavez ratcheted up the pressure. He pulled workers out on strike at a second vineyard owned by DiGiorgio, near San Diego. He summoned Chris and told him to bring as many clergy as possible. Chris could round up only one priest on such short notice, so the three met just outside the DiGiorgio property. Chavez planned to force a confrontation by accompanying strikers in to the labor camp to retrieve their possessions. Chris did not relish the impending showdown. But he had no choice; he could not back down and maintain his self-respect—or the respect he craved from Chavez.

"When I arrived on the scene, the company had a barricade of trucks, security guards and dogs on the roadway between the camp and the entrance to the property," Chris wrote to church leaders a few days later. "Father Salandini and I offered to go with Cesar and the workers in order to help affirm their basic rights. The workers responded with enthusiasm. For most of them it was to be an entirely new and frightening experience. Our presence was in fact an important source of moral strength."[3]

The group drove in around eight at night. A quarter-mile inside the Borrego Springs ranch, DiGiorgio supervisors made a citizens' arrest. For three hours, Chris sat captive with the others in a pickup truck the company used to transport farmworkers around the fields. Then sheriffs arrived. The trespassers were strip-searched, chained together in groups of three, and placed in police cars. When the eleven men arrived at the San Diego county jail at two thirty A.M., they were strip-searched again. By four A.M. they had been booked on two charges of trespassing and placed in cells. Six hours later they posted bail and headed back to the strike.[4]

Chris spread the word about the demeaning strip searches, triggered by the most minor offense. The saga demonstrated yet again the power of the growers—in collaboration with police.

A few weeks later Chris stood trial in a local courtroom, a legal confrontation that mirrored the social upheaval. The facts of the minor trespass incident were not in dispute. Workers testified they had been scared of the armed guards and dogs and had asked the union leaders to accompany them. When Chris took the stand, the judge admonished the witness in a tone so hostile that the defense moved for a mistrial. Prosecutors painted Chris and Chavez as radical communists manipulating the workers. The union lawyer objected to the prosecutor's use of the phrase "Karl Marx tactics" (overruled) and "henchmen" (sustained). The jury took less than two hours to acquit the workers and convict Chris, Chavez, and the priest. Each was fined $276 and placed on probation for two years.[5]

Chris returned to Los Angeles and reverted to his more traditional roles. He resumed his daily appeals. He solicited food for the Delano strikers. He asked each church supporter to contribute fifteen dollars— so the children of strikers could return to school with new shoes. And Chris asked for volunteer drivers to transport workers to the polls on August 30. The governor had ordered a new election.

Eliseo

The union had won the right to a fair election; now Chavez had to win at the polls. Fred Ross stepped up his drills, and the pressure to deliver weighed heavily on Eliseo.

The election rules favored the union—as long as organizers could turn out their voters. Anyone who had been on the DiGiorgio payroll when the strike began almost a year earlier was eligible to vote, as was anyone who had worked at least fourteen days before the election. DiGiorgio had fired workers almost as fast as the union could win them over, homing in on any outspoken Chavista. So many of the union's sure votes no longer worked at the ranch.

Strikers had scattered as far away as Mexico. Organizers labored to track them down. The union sent a bus to Texas and guaranteed round-trip transportation, food, and lodging in Delano. Chris identified "drag-net areas" and asked contacts in Texas, California, and Oregon to go door to door in farmworker areas asking the following questions: did they work for DiGiorgio, if so for how long; where, at what job; what was their Social Security number, and would they come back to vote. "If they are afraid, then they should know that we will get police protection as needed."[6]

On the ground in Delano, Eliseo concentrated on making the case. He handed out the "Mosquito Zumbador," the union's bilingual flyer where the cartoon character Mosquito buzzed about, spreading the news of the day. Eliseo carried summaries of the Schenley contract to show workers how favorable the terms were compared with recent Teamster pacts. He explained to workers what the election ballot looked like.

As the vote approached, the Mexican and Filipino unions merged under the auspices of the AFL-CIO. Bill Kircher, the AFL-CIO's director of organizing, had been one of the union's staunchest allies, in and out of Delano almost since the beginning. He explained the merger to workers at meetings, took votes, and posted the tallies on a blackboard he carried around. At the Friday night meeting on August 19, 1966, Kircher proposed a name for the new union—the United Farm Workers Organizing Committee, or UFWOC (an acronym the younger workers found amusing). The members approved, 199 to 25.[7] Eliseo questioned Kircher: Who are the organizers going to be? You are, Kircher said: farmworkers.

Two days later, Eliseo and another organizer drove through the Di-Giorgio camps, a megaphone mounted on top of their car, inviting

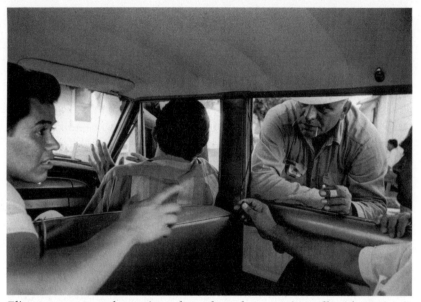

Eliseo gestures to make a point as he and another organizer talk with DiGiorgio workers. (Jon Lewis/www.farmworkermovement.us)

workers to a union barbecue a week later to celebrate the birth of UFWOC. They had broadcast announcements through the main camp and were just leaving the women's camp, Eliseo at the wheel and his partner on the microphone, when the Teamsters pulled in. They surrounded Eliseo's car. First they heckled; then they reached in and punched. His friend tried to fend them off with the microphone while Eliseo stepped on the gas. He escaped with a badly bruised face and a swollen lip that needed several stitches. The union used the attack in its campaign literature. "Violence is a 'way of life' with the Teamsters! Now it has started in Delano," read the union leaflet. "Sunday is the Lord's day. It is a day of rest and peace for most people . . . BUT NOT FOR THE TEAMSTER ORGANIZERS . . . They smashed Eliseo in the face and cut his lower lip."[8] Eliseo celebrated at the barbecue by drinking beer—out of one side of his mouth.

Two days later a brigade of cars waited before dawn to take workers to cast votes in the first secret-ballot election held for American farmworkers. Volunteers from as far away as San Francisco and Los Angeles had responded to pleas from Chris to provide the armada that Fred Ross requested. Ross insisted that volunteers pick up every pro-union voter and drive them to the polls. The lesson Eliseo learned: Don't take anything for granted, or leave anything to chance. After the polls closed, the ballots

The crowd in Filipino Hall carries Chavez around the room after he announces victory in the DiGiorgio election. (Jon Lewis/www.farmworkermovement.us)

were driven to San Francisco, where the count was to be supervised by the American Arbitration Association. Each side sent an observer to accompany the ballots; Joe Serda the submarine had surfaced and stood guard for the union. He took dexedrine to stay vigilant on the all-night trip up north.

In Delano, the organizers and workers gathered in Filipino Hall the next morning to await word. Eliseo was full of doubts. He thought about what he had done, what he hadn't done, what he might have done. A victory would be historic; a loss would mean they had let Chavez down. Eliseo looked at the union leader from afar with reverence bordering on hero worship. Eliseo was crestfallen when he saw Chavez drinking at a strategy session one night—breaking his own rules. But the transgression only momentarily tarnished the image.

On the morning of August 31, Filipino Hall was silent when the call from San Francisco finally came. Chavez stood in front of a microphone mounted on a stand almost as tall as he. A cigarette in his right hand, he read numbers off a small piece of paper in his left hand. He announced the results of the green ballots, from the small group of workers in the packing shed: Teamsters, 94; UFWOC, 43. And then the white ballots, the vote from the fields. Teamsters, 328. He paused dramatically. Eliseo's heart fell. UFWOC, 528. There was silence for a moment; then the crowd erupted. They lifted Chavez up and carried him around the room. People laughed, cried, hugged. Only twelve workers had voted for no union.

Years later, Chavez would say he had thought his union lacked sufficient credibility to survive had it lost the vote.[9] Eliseo would say he never again experienced the pure joy of that moment of victory. For both men, the DiGiorgio election was proof that the power they talked about could actually produce results.

CHAPTER 3

Out of the Fields, Into the Streets

July 1967

Eliseo

The shy farmworker stood center stage, playing emcee at a grand fiesta at the Bakersfield fairgrounds for a crowd of thousands on a summer Sunday. The farmworkers were celebrating a recently signed contract with DiGiorgio as the union geared up to take on the largest table grape grower in the valley, the Giumarra company. In between songs, Eliseo introduced one labor luminary after another who pledged support for the strike—Bill Kircher from the AFL-CIO, Jimmy Herman from the Longshoremen, Jack Conway from the United Auto Workers, even officials from the Teamsters, who had signed a no-raid pact just two days earlier. Then Eliseo introduced his hero. Chavez asked the Giumarra workers if they were ready to walk out. They shouted their approval.[1]

The enthusiasm masked reality. After almost two years of shouting "Huelga," the union had failed to stop the harvest of grapes. Even as he prepared to call the Giumarra workers out on strike, Chavez was putting in motion a new and untried strategy. The union would shift resources to the retail end and attempt to shut down the consumer market for grapes. An ad hoc boycott organized by supporters in a few cities had showed promise. Now Chavez wanted to send out farmworkers to plead their case. Impressed by Eliseo's performance at the July 23 rally, Chavez tapped the farmworker to be in the vanguard of the new campaign.[2]

Eliseo had worked full time for the union for almost a year since the DiGiorgio victory, a whirlwind that felt as if he had parachuted into an adventure movie. He lived for two months in the basement of a black church in Los Angeles, then moved to a union supporter's San Francisco home. He tasted sourdough bread for the first time and saw his first jazz concert, starring Miles Davis. He sat on the docks to make sure grapes weren't loaded on ships, cleared nonunion wines off liquor store shelves, went to jail for the first time with Dolores Huerta, and helped clean up a rogue melon strike in Texas. His picture was on the cover of *El Malcriado* as one of the young *capitanes,* the next generation of leaders.

When Chavez asked Eliseo to go to Chicago for a few weeks to organize a consumer boycott of grapes, the farmworker asked only for directions and when he was to leave. He had no sense of the distance and knew nothing about the Windy City. A few days after the Bakersfield fiesta, Eliseo took his first plane ride. He had one hundred dollars in his wallet and a bag of UFWOC buttons to sell. He landed in Chicago without winter clothes and with only one name.

John Armendariz, a postal worker active in his union, met Eliseo at the airport and took him home until he could find a place to live. Eliseo was so green that the older man wondered how the farmworker would even cope in the big city, let alone stop the sale of California grapes in the third biggest market in North America. Eliseo's first move didn't assuage the apprehension. He opened the phone book, called the A&P, explained that he was a farmworker on strike, and asked them not to buy grapes. Then, slowly, working out of a desk in the Hispanic ministry of a local Catholic church, he set out to develop contacts.

The first big break came less than two months after he arrived, at the September convention of the Illinois Federation of Labor in Peoria. Bill Kircher helped. He introduced Eliseo to local labor leaders and promised that his story would energize any labor gathering. "Veteran trade unionists find in the current union effort of farm workers an emotional common denominator that brings them back to the days of their great struggles," Kircher wrote.[3] Eliseo's new labor friends put him on the convention agenda. The twenty-one-year-old was so nervous about speaking in public that they fortified him with a couple of stiff drinks. When he addressed the delegates, he described how he felt as a farmworker, robbed of dignity and treated as a disposable tool. He talked about the Teamsters and what they did to him. "I'm smiling now," he said. "But I wasn't for quite a while after I got my mouth knocked in on a picket line." The audience gave him a standing ovation. The conference donated $1,500. Eliseo collected cards along with promises of further help. Back in the office, he typed up a list of eleven names and numbers for follow-ups, ranked by the likelihood that the contacts would pan out.[4] By hand, he wrote in Spanish to Sr. Chavez, addressing him in the formal *usted* and asking Chavez to send a personal thank-you note to Mexican American leaders who had collected $89 during the Mexican Independence Day parade.[5]

Eliseo polished his new rap at colleges, high schools, community forums, churches, temples, and labor halls, growing ever more confident in his adopted language. He distilled his basic message to two salient pleas: Don't buy grapes, and give us money. Eliseo had been the first of three workers dispatched from Delano to cities that handled the largest volume of grapes. Soon four others joined him in Chicago as the union expanded the boycott operation. They were boycotters in the union's lexicon, though their job was to persuade others to boycott. They lived in barely furnished apartments that Eliseo rented for $175 a month. They slept on army cots, relied on donations from two Mexican bakeries to stretch the five-dollars-per-person weekly food budget, and finessed invitations to as many meals as possible. Eliseo's rule was they went only where they all were welcome. They counted on supporters to donate everything—jackets, furniture, pens, a chess set. They wore thin summer jackets long after the leaves fell from the trees around Lake Michigan.

At Christmas, Eliseo went home to Delano but soon headed east again. On the first Friday of 1968 a yellow school bus christened *El Caballo* (The Horse) left Delano for New York with about fifty farmworkers aboard. The bus was named by Denver UFW supporters who raised $7,500 to purchase the vehicle, which they drove to Delano filled with Christmas presents.[6] Chavez wished the boycotters well, Jim Drake prayed over the bus, and El Caballo headed east into winter. Though the bus was new, the heat worked only in the first few rows. Each time they tromped off the bus and back on, the passengers dragged in slush and snow that slowly melted. Eliseo tried to sit up front. They warmed up inside churches and supporters' homes, where they ate and slept after a rote performance each night: they were introduced, told their stories, and sang "De Colores," a folksong that had become the unofficial union anthem.

Chavez had sent the group to New York to dampen sales of Giumarra grapes in the company's largest market, and to train under Fred Ross. The veteran organizer moved temporarily to New York and divided the boycotters into teams. Eliseo led a group that visited stores each day and

asked owners not to carry Giumarra grapes. If the store refused to honor
the boycott, Ross dispatched another team to picket. Ross replicated tactics that had been successful in California—where the union had long-
standing supporters ready to help and accustomed to picket lines.

Eliseo found the regimen in New York largely irrelevant to the job he
had begun in Chicago. Landing in a strange city and setting up a boycott
required different techniques and ingenuity. In Chicago, he didn't have a
ready-made picket line at his disposal; he had to organize one. He had to
build popular support, navigate the political scene, form alliances with
clergy and union leaders, and devise strategic approaches tailored to pres-
suring different stores.

In the fields, Eliseo drew on his own experiences to win over workers.
He was one of them. In Chicago, he had developed an entirely different
pitch. The boycott required convincing people who knew nothing about
the world of farmworkers that they needed to help. Eliseo was unim-
pressed by Ross's training in New York and eager to return to Chicago. He
wanted to see if he could use the network he had begun to assemble to
persuade supermarket chains to stop buying grapes.

Chris

The foot soldiers in the boycott were as familiar to Chris as the farmworkers in the field were to Eliseo: middle-class white people looking for
a cause that would make them feel good about themselves. Chris had a gut
instinct for identifying people who craved the sort of meaning in their
lives that he had found in the farm worker movement. His strategy for en-
listing their help was simple. He would make the cause as irresistible as
the wringer on the washing machine.

As a child, Chris could not resist playing with his mother's old-
fashioned washing machine, sticking his hand between the rollers as they
revolved and squeezed water out of the clean clothes. He summoned that
sensation in an analogy he loved to repeat. "When one's fingers are caught
in the wringer of a washing machine, the rest of the body is inevitably involved," he said. "Some parts will get dragged in physically—but all parts
will participate, whether they want to or not."[7]

He first used the image to describe how the wayward Migrant Ministry
had shamed the religious establishment into confronting the plight of
farmworkers, an issue the church preferred to avoid. Now he applied the

analogy to the way the movement was attracting converts across the country. Chris saw the progression over and over: First, attend a meeting. Then buy a button. Then wear the button. Then show up to hand out leaflets. Before they quite realized what was happening, people were drawn into the cause.

The controversy over the church's involvement, a distraction at first, now helped publicize the boycott and recruit volunteers. Some came from the religious community, like Ruth Shy, who had picketed supermarkets in her hometown of St. Louis and then helped the Sisters of Loretto boycott grapes in Denver, where she was studying to become a nun. College students joined the movement after spending a summer as interns with the Migrant Ministry. A few started even younger. Tom Dalzell first volunteered in high school. The Philadelphia teenager grew up hearing his mother's stories about working with Fred Ross in California migrant labor camps. When the boycott began, Tom signed up and learned to picket, then talked his way into a summer in Delano, though he was just sixteen.

Chris generated much of the information that boycotters across the country relied on to dispense facts and counter criticism. His office was down the street from the union's Los Angeles headquarters, across from Loyola Law School. Chris escaped the ever-present cacophony by ducking into the law school library, emerging a few hours later with a new missive written in his neat longhand. (He had never learned to type.) His "Friends of the Grape Strikers" mailing list morphed into a much lengthier "Action Mailing List," as informational updates from Delano turned into specific appeals for help. Chris wrote letters to the editor, gave interviews, spoke at churches, schools and synagogues, debated growers, and recorded messages for "dial-an-issue" hotlines. He quoted Simone Weil on power and Cesar Chavez on sacrifice.

As he spread the gospel to the middle class, Chris became an ever-more-polished propagandist. His quick pen and facile mind framed the issue as a clear-cut moral crusade. He offered point-by-point rebuttals of common criticisms, skillfully overlooking or writing around facts that conflicted with his conviction. It's not true that the strike is dominated by outsiders, he wrote. Cesar Chavez is a migrant worker himself with long family ties to Delano! It's not true that the strike is foundering—I personally watched hundreds of workers walk out of the fields! It's not true that the picket lines are dominated by nonworkers—thousands of farmworkers are on strike. "No one has ever claimed that all farm workers in Delano are on strike," Chris wrote, to counter Martin Zaninovich's insistence that the strike was a fiction. "In addition to local strikebreakers, large numbers of scabs have been brought in from the outside. The fact that many farm workers are willing to cross picket lines says nothing about the existence of a strike. Rather it highlights the poverty and insecurity of the people and underlines the importance of supporting grass roots organizations that can reach farm workers and bring unity and dignity and strength where there is fear and weakness. A movement is underway in Delano. *Your support is urgently needed.*"[8]

In "Straight Talk on the Grape Strike," Chris listed common attacks—Chavez was power hungry, the workers didn't really want the union, the boycott hurt small, innocent growers—and then dismissed each as grower propaganda. Yes, small growers were caught in the boycott, Chris acknowledged, less able to withstand the economic pressure and perhaps less culpable. But even small growers sent their kids to college. They had access to credit and a place as decision-makers in the community. For years, Chris pointed out, the church had ministered to employers—and neglected workers. Thus the church had facilitated a system that concentrated power in the hands of a small group who controlled the $4 billion-a-year agricultural industry. The time had come to even out that imbalance. Only radical change could right a corrupt system.

Chris had a clear, strong response when sympathetic people ventured concern from time to time that the Migrant Ministry might be too close to the union, sacrificing independence for access. We are supporters, Chris said. We support whatever the farm workers union decides to do because they know best. We do not make policy. He politely refused to let anyone shift the debate away from an undeniable truth: farmworkers needed help. He invited church people to come see conditions for themselves. He did not invite them to debate the proper role of the church.

His unquestioning devotion earned him the trust and praise he craved. "We have had priests with us before, during and after the strike," Chavez said in a speech in New York. "The priests of the California Migrant Ministry, Chris Hartmire and Jim Drake, have been with us from the beginning. They took losses in their church because of the Migrant Ministry and the suffering they accepted was for the migrants and for justice. It was from them that we learned the importance of the support of the church in our struggle. The church is the one group that gives help and never qualifies it or asks for favors."[9]

Jerry

As the boycott escalated and the strike waned, Chavez needed to open a third front in his crusade against the growers. He was casting around for a suitable warrior when Jerry Cohen wandered into People's Bar.

Jerry was a wisecracking navy brat who thought out loud as he talked, his mind usually several steps ahead of everyone else's. His father was a captain in the Navy Medical Corps, and Jerry had attended eight schools before college. He thrived on the frequent moves. Jerry was at once an all-American kid—varsity athlete, student council president—and an agitator on the lookout for causes to champion. He had challenged hazing in high school, campaigned against fraternities at Amherst College, and then gravitated toward more political fights as he came of age during the 1960s. He chose law school because he admired Clarence Darrow and was enamored of the movie depictions of heroic attorneys in *To Kill a Mockingbird* (Gregory Peck), *Anatomy of a Murder* (Jimmy Stewart), and *The People Against O'Hara* (Spencer Tracy). Jerry liked to debate and excelled only in classes he enjoyed, particularly constitutional law.

Jerry craved action, and by the time he passed the California bar at the end of 1966, the hot action was in the fields of the San Joaquin Valley. He took a job with California Rural Legal Assistance, a federally funded organization, expecting to help craft legal strategy in conjunction with Chavez. Jerry soon discovered that the funding conditions barred him from helping a labor union. He chafed at the work he was given, mostly domestic disputes.

Jerry began hanging out at People's Bar, mingling with the union staff. When he saw Jim Drake and a group of protesters being kicked out of a Mayfair parking lot in Bakersfield one afternoon, Jerry went over to offer legal advice. He cited the cases that protected equal rights to free speech in public places and negotiated a compromise with the store owner. That intervention led to a meeting with Chavez and Bill Kircher, organizing director for the national labor federation. In a note to his boss, AFL-CIO president George Meany, Kircher explained that Chavez badly needed a full-time attorney: "We have investigated this thoroughly and I have found a young man who, in my opinion, 'fits the bill.' He is anxious to help farmworkers. He is married. He and his wife are both under 30 years of age. She too, wants to help."[10] At the Friday night meeting on May 12, 1967, Chavez introduced Jerry to the crowd in Filipino Hall. By loud acclaim, the members approved a motion to name Jerry the first general counsel for the United Farm Workers Organizing Committee.[11] He had just turned twenty-six.

Unlike most of the union staff, Jerry received a salary. Kircher arranged for the AFL-CIO to pay Jerry $750 a month. The compensation was not much, nor was Jerry the only union staff member funded through outside sources. The Migrant Ministry paid some of Chavez's aides. Others had their college loans or mortgages paid in lieu of wages. Eliseo had arranged a monthly stipend of $115 for his mother, his share of the family income. Most volunteers, including Chavez, lived on the union's standard five dollars per week plus room and board. Chavez believed strongly in the symbolic and practical benefits of subsistence wages. But he was pragmatic, and willing to pay for talent he needed. Jerry thought sacrifice was fine and good, but he had a family to support.

Inexperienced in labor law but blessed with a keen eye for surmounting obstacles, Jerry plunged in. He had confessed he didn't know the law that well, and he loved Chavez's response: That's okay, I don't either; we'll learn together. There was no precedent for what they were trying to do. Farmworkers were excluded from almost all labor laws, which denied them protection but liberated their lawyer. Jerry felt empowered to take risks. He relished guerrilla warfare, and so did Chavez.

Jerry Cohen, recently hired as the first counsel for the farmworkers union, makes a point to Chavez as they confer. (Walter P. Reuther Library, Wayne State University)

Jerry's first major skirmish centered on a tactic central to the boycott: the right to urge consumers to shun a store that sold nonunion grapes. Boycotting stores had become one of the union's signature strategies. Such "secondary boycotts" were prohibited under the National Labor Relations Act, but since the federal act excluded farmworkers, the union was free to boycott. Then the growers figured out a loophole. Because the union's contract with DiGiorgio included a handful of members who worked in a peanut-shelling plant—performing jobs that fell under the jurisdiction of the federal labor act—the law applied to the entire union. The growers obtained an injunction banning the secondary boycott. Jerry solved that conundrum speedily. He created the United Peanut Shellers Union Local No. 1 and moved the workers out of UFWOC. The secondary boycott stayed in the union arsenal.

Next came the bullhorn fight. Just days after Chavez launched the strike at Giumarra, the company obtained a court order barring the use of bullhorns. The noise, they argued, disrupted business. For union picketers, standing at the edge of the road and shouting to reach workers in the fields, bullhorns were essential. "To take away petitioners' right to speak to the workers is to take away their only weapon," Jerry wrote in an August 28 writ.[12]

The writ was served by Jerry's young assistant, Jessica Govea. They worked in the makeshift legal office carved out of the kitchen in the Pink House, the building next door to 102 Albany Street that the union had taken over as the staff expanded. Jessica had grown up in the nearby barrio of Bakersfield, the neighborhood known as Little Okie after the first migrants who settled there. A decade earlier her father had helped Chavez form the Bakersfield chapter of the Community Service Organization. Jessica started organizing young; in high school she formed a Junior CSO and ran meetings under *Robert's Rules of Order*. After the strike started, she dropped out of college and went to work for the union. She started in the Service Center, helping workers with taxes and bureaucratic problems. Then she moved to the legal department, where it was even easier for Jerry to bum Benson & Hedges cigarettes, to feed his two-to-three-pack-a-day habit.

The bullhorn fight succeeded, after an initial setback. At Jessica's suggestion, Jerry flipped a coin to decide which writ to file. Heads was Writ of Supersedeas, tails was Writ of Prohibition. The coin came down heads. The right writ was prohibition. Jerry refiled.

Even when he lost, the union leaders made Jerry feel good. Gilbert Padilla, who had been with Chavez since the CSO days, patted Jerry on the back and told him the union had never gotten this far before and the lawyer was doing a hell of a job. Chavez found ways to turn losses into public relations victories. Nothing thrilled Jerry like a good fight. The worse the odds, the greater the fun.

CHAPTER 4

The Fast

February 1968

Eliseo

The boycotters in New York gathered each night at the Seafarers Hall in Brooklyn, where their union brethren were providing the farmworkers with food, shelter, and cars. Fred Ross was unusually somber on the mid-February night when he broke the news to the farmworkers far from home: their leader had embarked on an indefinite fast.

Chavez was frustrated with the demoralization seeping into the Delano troops, a response to little progress in the strike or boycott. Picket lines had become almost nonexistent. Falling spirits led to desperation that led to demands for more aggressive tactics. Vandalism and violence were becoming more common. Packing sheds had gone up in flames. Growers had discovered vines chopped down. Refrigerator cars carrying grapes had been sabotaged. Chavez, an avid admirer of Gandhi, decided to fast as a wake-up call, a jolt, he called it, to enforce discipline.

Only a handful of people knew that Chavez was already fasting when he called the Delano strikers and union staff to Filipino Hall on February 19. He announced he would fast until everyone in the union agreed to embrace nonviolence. Anything less, Chavez warned, would endanger the whole movement. Impassioned arguments broke out as soon as Chavez left the room. Some objected to the religious overtones. Leftists found the idea particularly distasteful. His own family urged him to abandon the protest.[1]

In New York the response was equally emotional, but more supportive. Ross told the volunteers that they had to be strong. He urged them to write letters to Chavez, expressing their commitment. Eliseo responded with sorrow and reverence; he felt sad that Chavez believed circumstances dictated such dramatic action, and awed that he would undertake such a personal sacrifice.

"He told us that he was fasting as a prayer—it was not a hunger strike and its purpose was not strategic but as an act of prayer and of love for us. He felt that he was responsible as the leader of the union for all the acts of any of us," Marion Moses wrote in a letter from Delano.

> The most important thing he said, in my opinion, was that we as a union and as a movement have aroused the hopes and aspirations of poor people . . . and we have a duty and responsibility to those people . . . we cannot by resorting to violence crush their hopes and destroy what we have done. He said that even if all of us in the room were to disappear the movement that had been started would still go on—but that did not mean that we could sacrifice the aspirations that we had aroused.[2]

After he left the meeting where he explained his fast, Chavez walked three miles from Filipino Hall to a scrubby lot on the western edge of town known as Forty Acres. The union had acquired the undesirable plot, between a dump and some radio towers, for its new headquarters. As yet only a few trailers and a half-finished gas station dotted the barren land. Chavez set himself up inside a room in the back of the gas station. A handful of close aides found a fan for ventilation, a bed for him to lie on, chairs for visitors. Moses became one of his caretakers as well as a gatekeeper, regulating access to Chavez as he lay in bed to conserve his strength.

Three thousand miles away in New York, Eliseo worried about Chavez's health. He wondered how the fast would sap his strength, what would happen to the movement if Chavez fell ill. Knowing that Chavez would risk his own health for the people on the strike and boycott, for all the farmworkers, made the twenty-two-year-old in Brooklyn determined to go out and work harder.

Jerry

The response of the farmworkers transformed Jerry from skeptic to true believer almost overnight.

Jerry was one of the inner circle who had known about the fast a few days before the announcement, shortly after Chavez stopped eating on February 14. Jerry had been so annoyed that he plotted to foil the plan. He and a few other union leaders would stop eating until Chavez started. Chavez preempted that idea when he addressed the meeting. To shun food as a negotiating tactic was a hunger strike, Chavez said, not a fast. If anyone in the room thought of not eating to pressure him to end the fast, he would not respond. He suspended picket lines and any strike-related activities for the duration of the fast, saying he intended the fast as an act of penance, not to give himself leverage.

"He sacrifices for us! And his sacrifice demands a response from each and every one of us," read the flyer inviting workers to mass at Forty Acres. "The fast of Cesar Chavez has moved farm workers throughout the state to come to talk with him this week. He turns away no one. He desires to see the people." [3]

Jerry watched workers stream into Forty Acres to pay respects, moved often to tears by the sacrifice Chavez was making on their behalf. Jerry dubbed the fast "a pilgrimage in reverse." He found the experience so powerful that he took the uncharacteristic step of starting a journal. "When the union began, non-violence was at the center," Jerry wrote, recording Chavez's comments. "Now we seemed more concerned with paid vacations and an extra dime an hour." [4]

In Jerry's typically mercurial manner, he became the fast's biggest booster. Jerry was a nonpracticing Jew, but he attended the outdoor mass at Forty Acres every night. He took on the liberals unhappy with the religious pageantry and its intimations of martyrdom and argued with those who condemned the fast as a manipulative distraction. When Chavez asked Doug Adair why he wasn't attending the masses, Pato expressed disgust at the workers worshipping outside the leader's door. Why weren't they out on picket lines instead? Pato asked. Some of Jerry's own staff wondered why the attorney wasn't spending more time in the office and less time hanging around Chavez.

When workers camped out on the grass at Forty Acres and asked how they could help, Marshall Ganz had the answer. The son of a Bakersfield rabbi, Ganz had dropped out of Harvard to join the Mississippi civil

Jerry, left, and LeRoy Chatfield support a weakened Chavez as he leaves the Kern County Courthouse on the twelfth day of his fast. (UCLA Charles E. Young Research Library Department of Special Collections, Los Angeles Times Photographic Archives, Copyright © Regents of the University of California, UCLA)

rights protests in 1964, returned to the San Joaquin Valley shortly after the grape strike began, and found a home in the farm worker movement. Now his job was to redirect the workers who came to honor Chavez. No, there's nothing you can do for him here, Ganz told them. But there's a liquor store over there that's selling scab wine. Let's go picket. On the second week of the fast, Ganz took the workers to the nearby city of Bakersfield, to measure the hallways and courtyards of the county courthouse.

Jerry was preparing for a contempt hearing, his first one. Chavez was due in court to answer Giumarra's charges that the union harassed strikebreakers and violated an injunction that limited pickets to one every hundred feet. Jerry was nervous. On the twelfth day of the fast, he arrived with Chavez at the Kern County Courthouse. Hundreds of farmworkers lined the approaches from the street all the way in to the courtroom. Ganz and the workers had figured out the maximum number of people that could fill every available space.

The courthouse had always been a place Jerry expected to lose even when the law was clearly on his side. For the first time, he felt the union had the home-court advantage. The judge declined Giumarra's request to evict the workers who quietly filled the halls and chambers, a move that would only have enhanced Chavez's stature. As the leader shuffled weakly onto the escalator, he turned to Jerry and winked.

Chris

As Chavez grew weaker, penitents arrived at Forty Acres and walked up the entrance road on their knees. Dozens, then hundreds, camped out to be near the leader. Tents covered the grounds. Makeshift memorials sprang up. Each day, workers sewed another cross onto the union flag draped around the altar where they held a nightly mass.

Chris didn't really know the extent of violence or the degree to which it troubled Chavez. Chris was aware of sheds burning and property damage. He knew about the iron stars placed on the roads to rip up tires. But that wasn't knowledge useful for Chris, so he wasn't privy to details. The minister saw the fast as much more than a statement about nonviolence. The very public sacrifice was a powerful demonstration of Chavez's faith.

Almost everyone who stuck with the union was willing to sacrifice—you had to be, to work for free, sleep on floors, eat baloney sandwiches every day on the picket lines. But in a single act, Chavez upped the stakes. The appeal resonated most with the deeply religious and the overwhelmingly Catholic workers. "Please keep Cesar and the movement in your prayers," Chris wrote to Migrant Ministry supporters. "The fast is a crucial event in the life of the farm worker's strike. It is a fast of penance directed toward the temptations and failures of the past; but more importantly it is a powerful act of leadership pointing the farm worker's union toward a militant, non-violent and united struggle in the future."[5]

As his doctor began to warn about irreversible damage, Chavez made plans to end the fast. Chris drafted a statement; then Jim Drake and Chavez refined the message. New York senator Robert F. Kennedy, a presidential contender who had become a major supporter of the union, flew in for the ceremony. Chavez chose to break his fast on a Sunday, the farmworkers' one day off. He told Chris he wanted everyone to be able to participate and charged the minister with making arrangements so the crowd could partake of the symbolic breaking of bread. Chris directed his staff to spread out among the throng with hundreds of boxes of bread. Chavez was too weak to read the statement himself, so Drake read to the thousands gathered in a Delano park on March 10:

Chris hands Chavez the bread to break his fast, as Chavez's wife, Helen, and Senator Robert F. Kennedy look on. (Walter P. Reuther Library, Wayne State University)

"The Fast has had different meanings for different people. Some of you may still wonder about its meaning and importance . . . the Fast was first for me and then for all of us in this Union. It was a Fast for non-violence and a call to sacrifice.

> Our struggle is not easy. Those who oppose our cause are rich and powerful and they have many allies in high places. We are poor. Our allies are few. But we have something the rich do not own. We have our own bodies and spirits and the justice of our cause as our weapons. When we are really honest with ourselves we must admit that our lives are all that really belong to us. So, it is how we use our lives that determines what kind of men we are. It is my deepest belief that only by giving our lives do we find life. I am convinced that the truest act of courage, the strongest act of manliness is to sacrifice ourselves for others in a totally non-

violent struggle for justice. *To be a man is to suffer for others.* God help us to be men!"[6]

Chris approached Chavez, who sat between his mother and Kennedy. With great pride, the Protestant minister handed the Catholic leader the bread to break his twenty-five-day fast.

CHAPTER 5

Please Don't Eat Grapes

July 1968

Eliseo

The midwestern radio host struggled to sound neutral as he moderated a debate between Eliseo and a lobbyist for the agricultural industry.

"Did your group pass a resolution opposing extension of unemployment insurance coverage to farmworkers," the host asked the lobbyist, "because it would, quote, 'undermine motivation and place a premium on idleness'?"

Indeed, replied William Callan, executive secretary of the Associated Farmers. "Why should the farmer in California or anywhere else be criticized for hiring these people who are not suitable for work in other industries? If the farmer's good enough to give these people a job, why should all these restrictions be put on the farmer?"

"You're taking a paternalistic attitude toward these people then, is that it, sir?" the host asked.

"In a sense, I suppose you could call it that," Callan responded.[1]

Eliseo was back in Chicago, trying to get grapes out of town. He had learned from watching Chavez to turn opponents' actions against them. Adversaries like Callan helped. "I asked him if the workers didn't want a union, and our 'illegal' boycott was causing a lot of problems, why hadn't they just agreed to elections and gotten rid of us?" Eliseo wrote to Chavez, recounting the exchange. "He really made a real ass of himself. The program went very, very well."[2]

Eliseo was finding it easy to muster public sympathy, but far harder to translate that good feeling into pressure that would affect the decisions of businessmen such as Harry Beckner. Beckner, the president of the Jewel Tea Company, was Eliseo's principal antagonist. With more than two hundred stores in metropolitan Chicago, Jewel controlled one-third of the market and set policy for the whole region. If Jewel pulled grapes, the other chains would follow. Eliseo had figured out that the boycott would not be won on picket lines, persuading one shopper at a time; to dampen sales enough to pressure the California growers, the union had to force major supermarket chains to stop stocking the fruit.

Eliseo worked hard to make himself a public pest, always looking for inventive approaches that would garner attention. He organized ministers to conduct "pray-ins," blocking the produce aisle in front of the grapes. "Lord, though sinners we pray to you on behalf of National Tea Company, that their hearts might be turned from darkness to light," began the Service for the Conversion of the second-largest chain store in Chicago. The clergy sang "We Shall Overcome" and left just ahead of the police.[3]

Again cloaked in the company of ministers and nuns, Eliseo barged into the office of the grape broker for the Giumarra company. The delegation harangued Philip Balsamo about his principal client and called the broker an immoral profiteer who made his living from the misery of farmworkers. Balsamo just gritted his teeth and listened. If he called the police, the boycotters would get even more publicity.[4]

Eliseo organized supporters to jam phone lines of a selected store on a certain day, deluged Balsamo with postcards denouncing Giumarra, and packed city council meetings to ask for resolutions of support. He led groups that stood all day in the parking lot of Jewel stores, sandwich boards strapped around their necks, signs that read "Don't Buy Here—Support Farm Workers." They stopped each car and asked shoppers to please go somewhere else until Jewel stopped carrying California grapes. The Chicago boycotters' quixotic quest attracted media attention—eight volunteers, far from home, living on five dollars a week plus room and board, asking consumers to make a small sacrifice and shop elsewhere so that farmworkers could have a better life. Beckner declined to meet with the union, and Balsamo found Eliseo less than genial, but newspaper

Eliseo teaches a workshop for Lutheran youth at the Walther League in Chicago to enlist help in the grape boycott. (R. Paul Firnhaber)

stories called the boycott leader tireless, brilliant, jaunty, astonishingly articulate, and, invariably, young.

Eliseo was competing for attention during an era with no shortage of news. He had returned to Chicago from New York just weeks before Martin Luther King Jr. was assassinated on April 4, 1968. Riots erupted and thousands of National Guard troops patrolled Chicago. A few months later massive antiwar demonstrations overshadowed the action inside the Democratic National Convention, then led to the arrest and trial of the Chicago Eight.

Eliseo focused single-mindedly on his own Chicago eight, the boycott staff. He took account of events only as they intruded on his work. "The riots have hurt our program, but hopefully not too much," he wrote Chavez a week after King's assassination. Religious and labor allies were distracted by the riots and had not gotten out mailers they promised. The retail clerks union had a crisis: "Seems when a lot of stores were burned, a lot of their members were out of a job." But Eliseo reported his team was now sending twenty-five postcards a day to Balsamo, demanding that Giumarra recognize UFWOC and negotiate a contract. A nun who had written Balsamo reported he had called her to argue that he was only a middleman, so the union deduced he was most susceptible to pressure from Catholics and upped the ante accordingly. They stockpiled postcards and mailed them out in successively larger numbers to make it appear that pressure was mounting.[5]

By the time the grape harvest peaked in the summer of 1968, Giumarra had figured out a way to evade the boycott. The grape giant borrowed labels from growers who were not boycott targets and secretly shipped the crates under different names. The union found out and sued for false advertising. Giumarra's action backfired on the other growers who had been helpful: Chavez extended the national boycott to all California grapes.

Day after day, seven days a week, Eliseo explained the rationale: Farmworkers were denied the right to organize that other workers enjoyed under the National Labor Relations Act. The growers refused to negotiate contracts or allow fair elections. The proximity of the border with Mexico and the ability to easily import labor meant the farmworkers could not win with a strike alone. So the union turned to people in the cities to help.

"This organization is involved in a life and death struggle with the large growers that seek to perpetuate what are called factories in the field," the president of the International Association of Machinists and Aerospace Workers said, as he introduced Eliseo to the machinists' convention. His speech was personal:

> When the kids go to school, they get told: "Why do you want to go to school? You are just going to grow up to be a stupid farm worker. Why do you want to waste your time?" Let me tell you that no matter how much you want an education, when you have that day after day after day, a child doesn't want to go to school. The reason is simple, because the growers own the political system, so they own the school boards. So they feel, keep the children stupid and we will always have our cheap labor supply. Keep them stupid, and we will always have them for our needs. And we are tired of that. We want to be able to determine when and if our children are going to go to school. We want to be able to determine their future.

Eliseo always wove in a few jokes—this time he complained that California governor Ronald Reagan had not been nominated as vice president. ("I'm not sure if you want him, but we don't," he said to laughter. "Somebody has to have him.") He told about the latest outrage: California officials had refused to allow Jerry to review records detailing what pesticides were used on the grapes. If you don't want to boycott grapes out of principle, Eliseo said, do it for your health. As always, he ended with a simple message. Please don't buy grapes. The delegates passed around a wastebasket and collected $2,733.11.[6]

A typical speech, on a typical day: the machinists union at lunch, the Council on Foreign Relations at dinner, a staff meeting in between. Eliseo studied the union's few contracts and took care to publicize specifics. The wine grape contracts, he pointed out, mandated one bathroom per twenty-five workers and required the company to provide protective goggles in the fields. But he also relied on his personal rap. He often talked about his father, who came from Mexico as a bracero, a temporary worker with no rights, and worked in the fields for low wages and no benefits until he was too old to keep up. He returned to Mexico, where he died in 1965. "Farm workers have no social security or any other benefits. What should be done with people who are too old, or too weak, or too sick to work for themselves?" Eliseo appealed to the members of the Chicago Typographical Union. "Should they just be thrown away like a husk?"[7]

He talked about poor schools, second-class health care, and two tiers of justice, one for the rich, one for the poor. He addressed religious and labor groups who were his chief allies but also students not much younger than he. When he spoke to the social science club at Elk Grove High School in suburban Chicago, one of ten schools where he had a regular following, students took home paper bags full of Huelga buttons to sell for Eliseo.[8]

The money they raised helped support the Chicago boycotters. Anything left over, Eliseo sent back to the union headquarters. Eliseo had reduced the rent to $70 a month, though he reported apologetically one month that unforeseen travel expenses had pushed their expenses to $744.24. Still, the daily ledgers—in which he recorded every expenditure as minute as a ten-cent parking fee—showed a surplus. They had raised $853.35 that month, and Eliseo mailed the difference to Delano.

He missed home and felt cut off. He signed letters, "on behalf of the Forgotten Workers," and appealed to Dolores Huerta: "We do have one beef—and I believe very firmly that it can be corrected. If someone will just take a minute of their precious time, even though we fully realize that you're all very busy, to please let us know what is happening in Delano, as *we* still feel we're part of the Union."[9] He requested a transfer—to Acapulco, or Huanusco, his home town in the Mexican state of Zacatecas. "We would very gladly send you to Acapulco but we have received word that there are no grapes there now and the city has been shut down," Chavez replied. "Huanusco the local padre told the congregation that it was a sin to eat grapes and we had no more problems there."[10]

When Chavez brainstormed with his staff in Delano about ratcheting up the boycott, he praised two qualities in Eliseo: his honesty and his relentlessness. Most boycott directors in other cities exaggerated their success to make themselves look good, Chavez said. "Eliseo, the last time I saw him, he looked discouraged," Chavez related. "And I said, 'Are you discouraged, brother?' He said, 'No, I'm not discouraged. I'm discouraged that I can't give you a good report. Things are bad.' I said, 'Well, the only way it's going to break is keep at it.' I said, 'I don't know what to tell you. What I'm going to do, I'm going to go back to Delano and pray for you. But keep at it.'"[11]

The prayers and hard work paid off. Sometimes with two steps forward and one step back, the Chicago campaign was dampening sales of grapes, cutting the volume sold and forcing down the price. The second September that he addressed the Illinois AFL-CIO meeting, Eliseo did not need drinks to bolster his confidence. The convention endorsed the boycott and called on Chicago mayor Richard Daley to ban grapes from city institutions. When Daley stalled and the labor federation wasn't applying enough pressure, Eliseo worked the phones and told all his labor contacts that the federation wanted them to send telegrams to City Hall. The mayor received the telegrams, and the city stopped buying grapes.

In October 1968, Harry Beckner tried a halfway measure: he put up signs in Jewel stores informing customers of the controversy. Eliseo rejected the move as an attempt to placate the union without taking action that would hurt the California growers. Eliseo declared November 16 "Get Jewel Day" and mobilized supporters to boycott Jewel stores throughout the Chicago area. In December, Jewel announced its stores would no longer carry grapes "to insure freedom from harassment to our customers, their families and Jewel people."[12] As soon as fresh grapes became available in the spring, Jewel reneged. A few months later, Jewel again pledged not to handle California grapes. One month later, grapes were back.

"The boycott seems to be holding up pretty well, though some of the chain stores are backing away from their agreements," Chavez wrote to Eliseo. "I understand that Jewel is your number one problem now, and I know it must be frustrating to see that happen. But I know you will mop them up soon . . . The battle continues, and to be honest, the solution is in the boycott. We all know that."[13]

Chris

Two milestones occurred in the summer of 1969, completely unrelated save that both would have been unfathomable less than a decade earlier: Neil Armstrong walked on the moon, and Cesar Chavez's portrait landed on the cover of *Time* magazine. "The Little Strike that Grew to La Causa" was the headline on the story that portrayed Chavez's quest as a civil rights battle for Mexican Americans as well as a farm labor strike. The grape boycott, the magazine concluded, was the only issue on which Gloria Steinem, George McGovern, and Chicago mayor Richard Daley all agreed.

Chris, the true believer for so many years, now had a lot of company. He was about to see just how much.

For more than a year Chavez had been an invalid on and off, often confined to his bed after his famous fast had exacerbated a long-standing back problem. When he felt well enough to travel, Chavez asked Chris to organize a cross-country trip to visit the major boycott cities. A supporter donated a small camper, and the crew headed out—Chavez, Chris, a driver, a scheduler, and a nurse, Marion Moses. The twenty-eight-city tour in the fall of 1969 was a coming-out party for the union leader who had become an international icon, profiled in the *New Yorker* and overseas publications as well as in *Time*. The farther Chavez traveled from the fields of California, the more his popularity soared.

Chris watched the impact Chavez had on people, the way they swarmed around the folk hero, not because of his words—which were not particularly well chosen or well spoken—but because of what he had done. Hundreds of people approached him at events, often expecting Chavez to remember them from some earlier encounter. I'm terrible with names, Chavez would say, but I remember your face. Often in pain, Chavez addressed crowd after cheering crowd. He always told the same joke: A mother and her small son were in a store. The mother had been boycotting grapes for years. They passed the grape display, and the boy tugged on his mother's sleeve and said, "Mommy, when can we buy some of those boycotts?" At one appearance Chavez was so tired he left out a key line in the middle of the joke, then wondered why no one laughed.

When they arrived in Chicago, the forty-two-year-old celebrity filled the Chicago Coliseum. Congressmen and aldermen compared him to Gandhi and Martin Luther King Jr. Confetti rained down, and the crowd chanted "Cesar, Cesar" as he took the floor.[14] The appearance raised spirits as well as $2,043.82, Eliseo reported: "Your visit to Chicago has inspired and encouraged everyone here to continue on in our struggle for La Causa. All of our Chicago supporters are fired up to keep on fighting until Chicago is clean of grapes and the boycott has won!"[15]

The two-month trip turned into three. Chris found the pace grueling, but the rewards great, as he saw how the farmworkers' struggle resonated. Similar trade-offs defined his life when he finally returned home, where Pudge juggled the demands of four children, the oldest thirteen. Chris went out on picket lines every week. He worked hard not to miss Little League games, birthdays, and school events. To see his family, he dragged his kids to hand out leaflets in supermarket parking lots or to march in the hot sun. The payoff was the spiritual high he felt when watching a poor woman turn away in the parking lot of a store in response to the boycotters' pleas, or the strength he drew seeing a scab worker summon the courage to walk out of the fields. "Sometimes it seems like everything I know (or think I know) about life and human nature were absorbed in these past five years," Chris said in a sermon.[16]

He even fasted himself. Chris and Joe Serda fasted for two weeks in the parking lot of a Los Angeles Safeway, urging consumers to boycott the supermarket until it stopped selling grapes. "For both of us, it is a simple

At the rally in the Chicago Coliseum, Chavez recognizes Eliseo, who waves to the crowd. His boycott staff—two farmworkers from California and four volunteers from Chicago—join in the applause.

desire to put all of ourselves into the struggle at a time that is very critical. We *have to* get them this year!" Chris wrote to Chavez, telling him about the fast. "I feel very close to you."[17]

Not everyone emulated Chavez's commitment to sacrifice. Some resented it deeply. The fast and Chavez's ensuing fame were exacerbating a split within the loose-knit group of union leaders who had worked together since 1965. Chavez wanted to force out those who did not share his strict work ethic and commitment to subsistence living. The union's scarce resources should be used to subsidize more boycotters, he argued, instead of supporting those who did not pull their own weight. "You make your place in the union by hard work," he declared to Chris and a few others at a staff retreat. "Because I decide. I have that one prerogative—to decide who makes it."

Chavez related to Chris and the others a recent conversation with some of the early union leaders, who felt shut out. "They said that it was a one-man union. I said, 'Yes, that's true. If I leave, I bet you that most of the volunteers who work with me would leave.' I said, 'They're here mostly because of me.'" Chavez predicted a showdown with the unhappy union leaders and warned of long-term consequences: "In a confrontation, I can beat them. I can beat them because they haven't been around organizations, they don't know how to stab each other. And I know how to do every fucking stab. But once you do that, so you do it to save the union, then every time there's opposition developing, boom, you get them. Because, well, you want to save the union . . . In other words, I got to pull a Joseph Stalin, to really get it. And I don't think I want to do that. By the time I do that, then I'll be a different man. Then I'll do it again for some other reason. More and more and more . . ."

Chris offered a different option: Keep recruiting for *la causa* so that "people with guts for the struggle" overwhelm the malcontents. "What you're saying is the weeding-out process might be fatal," Chris said to Chavez. "If the weeding-out process is fatal, then really the only alternative is to do what we can to get more people."[18]

In the following months, the internal conflicts subsided as news from the boycott improved. More grapes were sitting longer in storage, because they could not be sold. A group of growers in Coachella asked to negotiate for the first time, though the discussions went nowhere. Chavez launched several successful diversionary tactics: Jerry crusaded against pesticides, claiming the union had found grapes that tested positive for a noxious poison, and Marshall Ganz researched a theory that sounds played at certain frequencies would relax the sphincter muscles. Ganz played horrible noises but never achieved the desired effect. But he did figure out how to place a dry substance in portable toilets that turned into tear gas on contact with liquid. When John Giumarra Jr. testified to Congress that the union had gassed his workers when they used bathrooms in the fields, he was ridiculed.[19]

As the holidays approached at the end of 1969, Chris was tired but hopeful. The new crop of grapes was unusually large, which would drive down the price and assist the boycott. "Life is a little slow back here compared with the trip," Chris wrote to Eliseo in December. Chris wrote primarily to thank Eliseo for attending the National Council of Churches convention in Detroit, where Eliseo debated a Coachella grower. The church group held firm in support of the boycott.

Chris concluded his letter with a small personal request, in the midst of all the crises and weighty issues. The first time Eliseo had to order a batch of Huelga buttons to sell in Chicago, he had no idea what size to request. The salesman suggested an inch and a half. The tiny buttons were less than effective, but they proved extremely popular collectors' items. "Could you send me one of the small, red boycott buttons?" Chris wrote. "I lost my only one—after nearly a year. I will pay, pay, pay!!!"[20]

CHAPTER 6

Making History

January 1970

Jerry

The first break came when Jerry sat down with an unlikely ally: the wife of Kelvin Keene Larson, a small grape grower, hundreds of miles from the Delano fields.

Larson's influence in the Coachella Valley far outstripped his modest vineyard. Larson was a quirky grower, known for his commitment to quality and an inventive streak. He was the first to pack grapes in cooler trucks in the fields, to protect their sweetness, and the first to use a bath brush to thin delicate grapes. Jewel was Larson's largest customer, because Harry Beckner knew that Larson waited till grapes were sweet, while other Coachella growers rushed to market to cash in on the high prices. When Chavez extended the boycott from Giumarra to all California grapes, overnight the price fell a dollar on every twenty-two-pound lug.[1] Larson was outraged. He viewed himself as an innocent victim of the dispute in Delano. He did what they had taught him in the Naval Academy in Annapolis: when you have a problem, go to your chaplain.

The Reverend Lloyd Saatjian had started a Methodist church in Palm Springs, and Larson was one of his charter members. After talking to Larson, Saatjian met with Lionel Steinberg, the biggest grape grower in the Coachella Valley and the most sympathetic to the union. Then Saatjian went to Delano to hear the other side. The Methodist minister wasn't part of the Palm Springs church royalty, and he didn't feel he needed friends among the growers or the union. He saw the intense enmity between the two camps in Delano, and the paralyzing hatred reminded him of the relationship between the Turks and the Armenians, his own people. He admired Chavez, but he also understood the problems of the grape growers. Saatjian thought he might play a useful role.[2]

When Larson debated Eliseo at the National Council of Churches meeting in Detroit at the end of 1969, Saatjian encouraged the grower to call for elections among workers to resolve the question of representation and end the boycott. Eliseo gave his standard response: We welcome elections under the proper circumstances. In fact, the union wanted contracts, not elections. Contracts meant members and dues. Eliseo's comments in Detroit prompted some internal grumbling.[3] But Chavez asked Eliseo to put the Coachella grower in touch with Jerry.

On Monday, January 26, 1970, Jerry went to meet Keene Larson at Saatjian's church. Saatjian was there—with Larson's wife. Jerry was incensed that Larson had stood him up and was reluctant to negotiate with his spouse. But he accepted Saatjian's assurance that Patricia Larson, known as Corky, was more level-headed than her husband and spoke with full authority. The Larsons wanted to make peace before the season started. They had been badly hurt by the boycott the year before, unable to make the mortgage payments on their 160-acre ranch.[4]

In the two-hour meeting, Jerry reported, they discussed, "first, the general aura of mistrust, second, the specific problems in working out regulations governing an election, and third, problems relating to the boycott. On the first topic, I informed Mrs. Larson that it would take a series of many meetings to reduce tension and change distrust to trust."[5] Jerry explained that the union wanted a contract, not just recognition; he would insist on negotiating a pact before an election was held.

A month later, Corky Larson and Lloyd Saatjian traveled two hundred miles from Palm Springs to Santa Barbara, where Chavez was having a retreat at St. Anthony's Mission. The three walked around and around in circles on the seminary track, trying to reach an understanding. "On the positive side, Mrs. Larson indicated very little interest in having an election and indicated that she was interested in working out a reasonable contract," Jerry noted. Wages and a hiring hall run by the union were not obstacles. "On the negative side of the board she was worried about what she considered to be Union irresponsibility . . . Cesar assured her that she should try the union out by sitting down and talking."[6]

Jerry confronts a sheriff's deputy in the Imperial Valley during a demonstration (Cris Sanchez)

Chavez worried that signing a deal with only one or two growers would complicate the boycott. Larson said she believed others were interested. The growers in the Coachella Valley, where the Filipinos had first gone on strike five years earlier, were split. Smaller growers were hurting, and many had gone out of business. With a short, early harvest, and no ability to turn their grapes into raisins or wine, they had fewer options and more losses than the Delano growers. A hard-line group of about a dozen Coachella growers opposed dealing with the union at all. The head of Tenneco, a large ranch owned by a multinational corporation, was inclined to strike a deal but reluctant to antagonize his colleagues, who browbeat the Tenneco official whenever he appeared to waver. Larson and Steinberg were most interested in contracts.

Steinberg, a prominent Democrat whose politics made him sympathetic to the union's cause, was first to sign. During around-the-clock negotiations at a hotel near the Los Angeles airport, they reached a deal: $1.75 an hour, plus ten cents an hour for a health and welfare fund, and a bonus of two cents per box. Jerry slept at Steinberg's lawyer's house, and they finished the contract language the next day.[7] The pact was signed on April 1, 1970, the day after Chavez turned forty-three. Ten days later the Larsons held an election on their ranch, supervised by religious leaders. The workers voted for the UFWOC, 78 to 2. A contract, which had been drafted beforehand, was signed days later.

Other growers ostracized Larson and denied him space at the storage facility he normally used. When the Reverend Saatjian attended an Armenian potluck and joined the dinner line, everyone else left. The Larson and Steinberg grapes reached the market in crates that carried the union label and the distinctive black eagle. The grapes commanded a premium; jubilant union organizers called it "the bird tax." Pressure on the other growers increased.

Howard Marguleas, the head of the Tenneco ranch, was the next domino. The negotiations started in a twelfth-floor conference room overlooking LAX and finished up in a Bakersfield hotel. During a break, before the growers returned to the room, Jerry drew a picture on the blackboard of two boats. One had Marguleas in it, sinking. The other carried John Giumarra, calling out "Don't give up the ship." Jerry and Marguleas signed a contract the next day.[8]

Eliseo

Eliseo measured his success in rail-car lots. The boxes of California and Arizona table grapes unloaded in Chicago between 1966 and 1969 had fallen by 42.8 percent—a steeper decline than in any other major city, almost twice the average drop.[9]

But Eliseo still hadn't gotten Jewel. He had staged marches and sit-ins, gone to jail, and enlisted support from congressmen, mayors, rabbis, and the Catholic Church. He bought a 1250 Multilith offset printer that churned out leaflets with pictures. He proudly ran off his own letterhead with a drawing of stylized workers carrying produce crates that featured the black eagle label. He hosted conferences. Harry Beckner was still selling nonunion grapes.

In early 1970, Eliseo convened a brainstorming session in Chicago. There was nominally a national boycott coordinator in Delano, but in practice each city was on its own. So Eliseo had free rein, as long as he raised enough money to cover expenses and send a little back. He emerged from the retreat with a three-pronged plan of attack. First, Eliseo escalated the boycott by circulating tear-off cards that shoppers signed, pledging not to shop at Jewel. Half the card went to Beckner; the other half went back to the union, often with a contribution. Second, Eliseo formed the Jewel Citizens Committee. With donations, the union purchased 120 shares in Jewel at $45 each and geared up to disrupt the company's annual meeting. The third piece of the campaign was to be a massive march through Chicago, with stops for rallies in each ethnic neighborhood and an overnight tent city.[10]

The boycotters plastered posters around the city: "In a two-day march for justice the farm workers will bring the strike home to the front doors of Jewel, the biggest strikebreaker this side of California! TELL IT STRAIGHT TO JEWEL: JOIN THE MARCH!!" Eliseo lined up guest speakers. Musicians offered to play along the route. Students solicited donations. Kathy Fagan, a freshman at Northwestern University who had been boycotting supermarkets near the Evanston campus, took charge of organizing support for the overnight march. She published appeals asking supporters to loan tents, lanterns, canteens, sleeping bags, trucks, and a bus.[11]

Less than a year earlier Fagan had entered college and found the sorority environment so disturbing that she almost fled home. Then she discovered the farm worker movement. By the spring of 1970 she was working practically full time for Eliseo. When Chavez agreed to come to Chicago for the march on Jewel, Fagan was so pleased, she wrote to him in Delano: "Eliseo and all the rest of us on the march committee were really excited to hear you are coming here to lead it. Thank you so much for taking your time to be here with us. I wanted to thank you especially because it made Eliseo so happy! He is the hardest worker of any of us, yet he always has a smile and a word for us."[12]

Two weeks before the march, Jewel caved. "Until such time as the parties involved in the 'grape issue' have resolved their conflict, either through the passage of appropriate legislation or through meaningful negotiations, Jewel Food Stores will not offer table grapes for sale to our customers," the company said in a statement.[13] The news was overshadowed by the death the same day of four students on the campus of Kent State, shot by National Guardsmen during a protest against the Vietnam War.

The day the march was to have begun, Eliseo and the others were sitting around the office when the police showed up to ask where the marchers were. We won, Eliseo said. It's over. The message to the California grape growers from supermarkets around the country was clear: Solve your own labor problems. We've had enough.

A few grape growers in the San Joaquin Valley had signed contracts, and the union represented workers at about one-third of the table grape industry—but the large Delano growers were still resisting. Eliseo was on his way back from a meeting at the Catholic Service Center in Gary, Indiana, when Chavez called the Chicago boycott apartment around nine P.M. on July 16. "Tell him to call, it's very important," Chavez said.

When Eliseo called back, Chavez delivered the news, switching from English to Spanish and back: The union had received a call from Philip J. Feick saying he was authorized to begin negotiations on behalf of twenty-five Delano table grape growers. Chavez began to read the names. Eliseo tried to write them all down, but he couldn't keep up. Never mind, we'll send you the list, there isn't time, Chavez said. He was calling each boycott office, tape-recording the historic calls.

In Montreal, Jessica Govea reacted to the news with the same giddiness as Eliseo. "Are you kidding?" she exclaimed when Chavez read the list. "Oh wow. This is like heaven. That's amazing. How did that happen?"

"I don't know, I think the boycott," Chavez answered warmly, with a chuckle.

On each call, with his customary dramatic flair, Chavez withheld the names of the biggest growers, adding them almost as an afterthought. On the phone with Eliseo, Chavez saved Giumarra for last. Eliseo let out a yell. "Beautiful, beautiful," he murmured. We have our bags packed, he told Chavez. Keep up the boycott, make it stronger than ever, Chavez told him. It's not over yet. "*A toda madre*," Eliseo said, meaning, roughly, awesome.[14]

Jerry

The much-heralded negotiations ended quickly in a deadlock. After the second day the growers walked out. A key reason was one of the union's unusual demands: the Delano school board must reverse a recent decision to oust several students, including Chavez's daughter and nephew. They had not been allowed to graduate from high school because of a strike-related controversy. The growers protested that the school dispute had nothing to do with a contract for farmworkers. The growers controlled the school board, Jerry and Chavez responded. As both sides had seen five years earlier, the strike challenged the social order as well as conditions in the fields.[15]

A week after negotiations broke down, John Giumarra Jr., the Stanford-educated son of the grower known as the Grape King, called the Cohen house around nine P.M. Jerry's wife took a message. Giumarra called back an hour later and told Jerry they needed to meet right away. Jerry said Chavez was out of town, on his way home. An hour later Giumarra called back. By midnight, Jerry had reached Chavez at home; they set a meeting for two hours later.[16]

At two thirty A.M. in Room 44 of the Stardust Motel in Delano came the beginning of the end. Marion Moses was massaging Chavez's ailing back. John Giumarra Jr. and his father sat in a corner. They talked till after dawn, then agreed to meet later that afternoon in the auditorium of St. Mary's School. Thirty-four growers gathered in the school auditorium, and the two sides went through issues one by one. Martin Zaninovich knew the growers really had no leverage at all.

The last unresolved item was about the schools. "We know it fits into the strike," Jerry said, demanding a meeting with the grower on the school board. "It's a community problem that has resulted because of the strike." Someone began to interrupt, and Jerry answered sharply. "Let me finish! We want total peace. I think it's time all of us in Delano sit down together to solve our problems." When Giumarra suggested the union call the school board member directly, Chavez exploded: "We cannot accept no for an answer . . . I have kids who didn't get their diplomas, who didn't get credit for the work they did at school, and the roots come from the conflict of the strike. The day is gone when you can isolate a problem."[17]

Finally Giumarra said Louis Lucas, one of the younger growers who was related by marriage to the school board member, would call to arrange the meeting.[18]

Two days later the massive hall at Forty Acres was overflowing. Chris rode up on a bus full of boycotters from Los Angeles, whooping and screaming and crying. Kathy Fagan, who had come from Chicago to Delano as a summer volunteer, squeezed into the back of the hall. Jerry was up front, with John Giumarra Sr., the family patriarch, and his son John Jr. All the growers were present. Chavez had insisted on that as a condition of the deal.

"Today when we see so much violence in our country, in our midst, this event here truly justifies the beliefs of millions of people that through non-violent actions in this nation and across the world, that social justice can be gotten. We are proving this here every day," Chavez said. "Without the help of those millions upon millions of good people who believe as

Chavez and John Giumarra Sr. sign the historic grape contract at Forty Acres. Onlookers include (left to right) Bill Kircher, Jerry Cohen, Bishop Joseph Donnelly, Monsignor George Higgins, Gerard Sherry, editor of the Catholic Monitor, *and John Giumarra Jr. (Walter P. Reuther Library, Wayne State University)*

we do that non-violence is the way to struggle, without that help I'm sure that we wouldn't be here today."

Then he talked about the future. "We give hope to millions of millions of farm workers throughout the land who are coming to us every day, almost every day around the clock . . . begging for us to go and represent them and organize them. And we will not, we will not disappoint them."[19]

John Giumarra Jr. also looked ahead. He hailed the contracts as a mutual victory, and he challenged the union to live up to its new responsibility, as the world focused on the small farming community of Delano. "If it works well here, if this experiment in social justice as they call it, or this revolution in agriculture however you want to characterize it, if it works here it can work elsewhere. But if it doesn't work here, it won't work anywhere. And so there's a fantastic responsibility on the part of your people and on the part of my people, that we work together to make sure that this is a historic moment."

Overnight thousands of workers became members of the United Farm Workers Organizing Committee. The only election that had taken place was on the tiny Larson ranch.

PART II

Growing Pains

August 1970–April 1973

CHAPTER 7

Strike in the Salad Bowl of the World

August 1970

Sabino

The cool ocean air that the lettuce loved wafted into the Salinas Valley from the nearby Pacific coast. Tourism was the major industry along the stunning shoreline of the Monterey Peninsula. Just over the Santa Lucia Mountains thousands of workers toiled in the Salinas fields. Many never saw the ocean, less than twenty miles away. Life behind the lettuce curtain revolved around agriculture. More lettuce grew in the Salinas Valley than anywhere else on earth.

Artichokes, broccoli, celery, tomatoes, and peppers all flourished in the Mediterranean-like clime, but lettuce was the dominant crop—more than 650,000 tons tended and harvested by the *lechugeros* and the steadies.[1] Lechugeros were the firemen of the fields: tough, strong lettuce cutters accustomed to working as a team. Paid by the piece, a trio of elite lechugeros could cut and box as many as 2,400 heads of lettuce an hour. They followed the crops, from the early lettuce in the Imperial Valley into Yuma, Arizona, in the late winter, and then up north to Salinas. The steadies were irrigators and tractor drivers, who could work nearly year round at a single company. Lechugeros looked down on the steadies' routine labor, but the steadies viewed themselves as an elite with special skills that earned them a nickel more in their hourly pay.

Sabino Lopez was a steady, an irrigator like his father. Sabino had

Sabino Lopez, upper right corner, poses with co-workers during his first season working in the California fields.

made his first trip to Salinas from Mexico as a teenager, joining his father at a company where the older man had worked for years. They lived in Rancho 17, one of several labor camps on the large D'Arrigo Brothers ranch. The housing was cheap and convenient for workers without a car. The small run-down room in the barracks was up against the railroad tracks that ran along Highway 101. Sabino knew the schedule of almost every train, especially at night.

From his father, Sabino learned to cook, to wash his own dishes, and to adjust irrigation valves. The slight seventeen-year-old was a quick study, and at the end of the season the foreman suggested Sabino move in with him and work year round. The teenager was tempted, but his father grimaced at the idea of returning home to Mexico for the holidays and facing his wife without their son. Work never ends, Julio Lopez told his son in Spanish. Sabino declined the foreman's offer, repeating his father's counsel: *El trabajo nunca se acaba.*

The following spring, father and son returned to Salinas and walked from the bus station to the D'Arrigo ranch. The foreman told them there was no work for them. We'll wait, Sabino's father said, thinking they had arrived too early. There won't be any jobs for you two, the D'Arrigo foreman replied. As they stood in the road, with no money and no place to go,

Sabino's father asked what his son had told the foreman the year before in turning down the permanent job. *El trabajo nunca se acaba*, Sabino said. Then Julio Lopez explained to his son why they had been fired: Work ends when the foreman says so. To suggest otherwise was unacceptably presumptuous. The foreman could replace an irrigator as easily as a broken tractor.

The comment the teenager had made unthinkingly sent the pair of irrigators walking down Harkins Road, looking for work. They found jobs at Merrill Farms, one of the larger ranches in the Salinas Valley. There they were paid more than at D'Arrigo, fed hot meals at lunch, and given enough time to water the fields carefully. Irrigators worked in pairs—one in the fields, checking the water flow in each row; the other up at the control valves, making adjustments according to hand signals from his partner below. Sabino enjoyed the work and liked to think about the variables; the dirt varied from spot to spot and year to year in how much water it could absorb.

Sabino first heard about the union when he went for help with his taxes. The young irrigator showed the tax preparer all the pay stubs he had saved, another habit acquired from his father. The tax man clucked over Sabino's long days, all at $1.10 an hour, never any overtime. There is a man coming to help farmworkers, he told Sabino. Cesar Chavez is working in the grape vineyards now. Sabino tucked the information away and waited. Mexican unions were powerful in his home state, Jalisco. They were frequently corrupt, but Sabino had also seen their ability to shift power from employers to workers.

In the midst of the grape strike, Chavez came to Salinas. Sabino was one of hundreds of farmworkers waiting expectantly at the Towne House Motel. A short Mexican wearing a large hat brushed by Sabino and excused himself as he made his way to the front of the room. When he took the podium, Sabino realized he had just had his first encounter with Cesar Chavez. Just as in Delano, his unimposing stature stood in sharp contrast to the inspiring speech. Chavez talked about wages and working conditions, but also dignity, justice, and respect. The message resonated with Sabino, isolated in the fields with only a few years of elementary school, no English, but great pride. Quietly, Sabino burned at the way growers viewed Mexican farmworkers—industrious but never smart. The Mexicans had a saying: *Como dios a los conejos, chiquitos y orejones.* The way God looks at rabbits, short with big ears. Sabino had few complaints about his situation at Merrill. But he could not forget the way his father had been cavalierly fired after years of good work, just for an offhand remark by his clueless son.

Chavez returned to Salinas sooner than he had planned. On the summer day in 1970 when he sat down in Delano to finalize the historic grape contracts, the Teamsters signed secret agreements in Salinas.[2] The vegetable growers had invited the rival union in to preempt Chavez, confident that the Teamsters would neither interfere unduly with management rights nor empower workers. At Merrill Farms, Sabino's bosses brought Teamsters in to proselytize to the workers on company time. But the workers knew about Cesar Chavez's union. Angry that their fate had been determined in secret, the workers felt sold out.

As soon as the Teamsters appeared in the fields, Chavez set up temporary headquarters in Salinas. Sabino and his father joined the large crowds that rallied around the union leader, condemning the grower-Teamster alliance. Workers demanded a strike. Chavez announced the action on August 24, and the next morning thousands of workers shut down the Salinas lettuce fields at the height of the season. The harvest dropped to one fourth of normal.[3]

Harkins Road, the street Sabino and his father had walked down when they were turned away from D'Arrigo two years earlier, now filled with flags and Huelga signs. The farmworkers marched, sang, and waved homemade banners, each company boasting a distinctive flag. When the Teamsters waved American flags to counter the red and black UFWOC banners, the union picked up red, white, and blue flags too. Soon there was not an American flag to be bought in Salinas.

Sabino proudly walked out on strike from Merrill Farms, the cautious steady confidently leaving a coveted job despite the warning that he would never work there again.

Jerry

The vegetable fields of Salinas were foreign territory for Jerry, but his metabolism matched that of the lechugeros. The boy who had thrived on moving from school to school shifted excitedly from the grape victory to the next battle, walking away from the Delano celebration without a backward glance.

He noticed differences in Salinas immediately. The response to Chavez among the vegetable workers was more muted, respectful but not worshipful. The workers were committed, but practical. They wanted to know if the union would help support them during a strike. They listened intently and cheered Chavez with a quiet militancy but without the adulation of Delano.[4]

Vegetable workers tended to be single men, rather than the families that predominated in the vineyards. The lechugeros worked piece rate—paid by the box instead of a flat hourly wage. They negotiated rates that could fluctuate daily, depending on the field, the conditions, and the season. They were a close-knit fraternity, far more accustomed than the grape workers to challenging authority. That trait meshed with Jerry's personality. Anxious to exploit the new terrain, he watched workers stream into the union office, asking for representation, eager to picket, ready to form committees.

The union drew strength from another ally that had been conspicuously absent during most of the Delano strike—the Roman Catholic Church. The bishops had appointed a committee to deal with farm labor issues, and Monsignor George Higgins, a Washington, D.C., cleric, had emerged as the dominant voice. Higgins, known as "the labor priest," had shuttled back and forth a dozen times in six months to facilitate negotiations with the Delano grape growers. In August he made his first trip to Salinas, hoping to mediate a resolution between Chavez and the Teamsters.[5]

Negotiations culminated in an all-night session at the Towne House Motel, Higgins attempting to broker a deal between Jerry and a Teamster leader. Around dawn, Jerry and a law school classmate he had recruited took a break and walked around the hotel parking lot. Bill Carder had joined the union staff only a few months earlier, after a chance encounter with Jerry at a Chavez speech on the East Coast. At Boalt Hall School of Law in Berkeley, Carder had admired Jerry's irreverent confidence and his ability to motivate people. Swayed again by Jerry's personality, Carder moved his family across the country, landing in Delano just as the grape strike was ending. He feared he had missed the major action. Then the lettuce strike began. At dawn in the Salinas hotel parking lot, Carder gratefully inhaled the cold, fresh air. His day had started twenty-four hours earlier on a picket line at four A.M. As negotiations droned on inside the hotel room, he had been taking notes just to keep himself awake. He marveled at his friend's stamina; Jerry showed no sign of wear. Carder, Jerry said exuberantly as they paced the parking lot, we've got the world's greatest jobs.

The negotiating session ended with a brief but ultimately unsuccessful détente. Just as in the 1966 DiGiorgio fight, the union battled the growers and the Teamsters—a formidable alliance. Jerry went into the fields to talk with workers at Hansen Farms on the second morning of the lettuce strike and found himself surrounded by a semicircle of ten pickup trucks and a dozen Teamsters. While Jerry exchanged sharp words with the owner of the ranch, a Teamster known as "Tiny" began menacing the attorney. Jerry weighed about two hundred pounds, but Tiny outweighed him by half and easily lifted Jerry off the ground.[6] The last thing Jerry remembered was a black-gloved fist approaching his head. Jerry ended up in the hospital for several days with a concussion. His picture ran in the newspaper, and the union reveled in the publicity. "I didn't have a chance to test my commitment to nonviolence because I was pinned by this other guy," Jerry quipped.[7]

Though the workers' militance made picket lines far more effective than they had been in Delano, Chavez pursued essentially the same strategy: He focused on two large ranches owned by multinational companies whose products were susceptible to boycott pressure. The top target was Interharvest, a large lettuce grower owned by United Fruit, which also marketed Chiquita bananas. Eager to avoid a banana boycott, United Fruit agreed to negotiate a contract if a majority of the two thousand workers signed cards favoring the union.

Monsignor Higgins was selected to count the cards. A United Fruit official kept wandering into the office where Higgins was tallying the votes. Finally the company official beseeched Higgins: We need the union to win decisively so that we can negotiate without antagonizing other growers. United Fruit wanted cover. The labor priest kept the conversation secret. When Higgins finished the count, he announced the union had won. He declined to reveal any numbers, and the union trumpeted an overwhelming victory. "Eighty-five, ninety percent of the workers had signed cards. No question who represented the workers," Jerry boasted.[8] In fact, Higgins's careful tally showed the union had narrowly fallen short of a majority.[9]

The union signed a contract with Interharvest that provided job security, grievance procedures, $2.10-per-hour minimum wage, and a ban on the use of DDT. Two other ranches followed suit, but the overwhelming majority of companies stayed with the Teamsters, and the workers stayed on strike.

As economic pressure mounted, the growers devised more sophisticated legal strategies to break the impasse. When Jerry came out of the hospital after his concussion, Carder took his boss to a borrowed office, the floor covered with stacks of injunctions. Each grower had filed a separate suit to block the union from picketing. Carder received a continuance from an unfriendly judge when the lawyer pointed out he had to respond to twenty injunctions in three counties in the next eight days.[10] In the first month of the strike Monterey County judges granted sixty injunctions, and the union appealed almost every one.[11]

The growers argued they were innocent victims, caught in a fight between two unions; in California, strikes were illegal in jurisdictional disputes. Jerry decided to challenge that underlying legal assumption. He thought he could prove that the Teamster deals, signed with no input from the workers they purported to protect, were not legitimate contracts. Carder had an idea for another counterattack based on the same reasoning. Collective bargaining agreements were exempt from antitrust charges—as long as the contracts were legitimate. The union had amassed piles of evidence that the growers had signed contracts in secret to preempt the workers from joining the union of their choice. Late at night, Carder worked with a pencil and a yellow legal pad in the deserted Monterey County Courthouse library. (He had gotten a key after he noticed the growers' attorneys had access.) Unions had never been sued under antitrust law, but Carder thought he could argue that the growers and the Teamsters had colluded to artificially depress wages for workers.

"Often we act on what well may be mistaken assumptions," Jerry wrote in his journal. "No mistake seems fatal or even important so far. Cesar has been able to breed amazing confidence in some of us who actually believe and act on the proposition that there is no ill from which some good will not flow."[12]

Eliseo

Summoned to Salinas along with boycotters from around the country, the erstwhile picket captain from Delano saw immediately that this was not Martin Zaninovich's "so-called strike." The vegetable workers were really on strike. Eliseo was not in California long enough to see much else.

By the time he arrived in Salinas in early September, after driving from Chicago, Chavez was seeking a way to end the strike. Dozens of injunctions had crippled the protest. The union had run out of money. Gas alone cost a thousand dollars a day. "I have to call a boycott," Chavez told a group of boycotters who had rushed to California to help. "See, that's the only card that we have that we haven't played."[13]

Chavez called a rally on September 16, Mexican Independence Day, the fifth anniversary of the meeting in the Delano church that had launched the grape strike. He told the strikers to return to work. He told them to find jobs where they could, and to continue organizing around the committees they had formed during the strike. To win, Chavez stressed, the union needed to turn again to the tactic that had won contracts in the grape vineyards. He announced the lettuce boycott the next day, calling it "the most powerful weapon that can be used."[14]

Eliseo longed to stay in California, preferring action in the fields to selling the cause in a distant city. Chavez asked the farmworker to return to Chicago. Eliseo deliberated for several days. He talked to Dolores Huerta, who had recruited him in the 1966 DiGiorgio strike. He told her his heart was in helping the grape workers in his home town, now that they had contracts.[15] Finally he decided that if he worked for the union, the union's needs took precedence.

Eliseo was not the only hard sell. Chavez had to work to re-recruit the old boycotters, the vast majority of whom were not eager to return to the cities. The lettuce workers voiced even more reluctance to leave their jobs and travel across the country. Only a few agreed. "The strike will never generate the kind of power that the boycott can generate. It just can't. It's just not made that way," Chavez exhorted them, making his pitch for boycott volunteers. The union must exert pressure from the outside to

Eliseo uses a bullhorn to reach the crowd at a rally during the Salinas lettuce strike. (Walter P. Reuther Library, Wayne State University)

win, he argued. They must move the fight to the cities, away from communities where the agricultural interests held sway.[16]

When he was ready to make boycott assignments, Chavez asked Eliseo and the other boycott leaders to address the volunteers. Dorothy Johnson had first worked on the boycott as a student at the University of Washington, picketing Seattle grocery stores. She had taken her sleeping bag to Delano and camped out in Filipino Hall during spring break her senior year, then headed back to California right after graduation. She ended up on the Washington, D.C., boycott. When the Salinas strike began, she joined the caravan of boycotters who traveled west, more cars joining in at each major city along the route. She celebrated her twenty-second birthday along the way, a week before arriving in Salinas. When Chavez asked the boycotters to select three cities for their next assignment, almost everyone ranked San Francisco first. Johnson did too, though she knew she lacked the seniority to land such a coveted spot. For her second choice, she wrote down Chicago. Eliseo's reputation was well known among boycotters, and she had been impressed by his speech. He interviewed her briefly and accepted her on the Chicago boycott team. They headed east.

Back in Chicago, Eliseo tried to redirect all the goodwill and credibility he had built up during the grape boycott. But the lettuce boycott was as murky as the grape boycott had been simple. Stores *were* selling union lettuce—mostly harvested by Teamsters. Eliseo struggled to explain that the Teamsters had sweetheart contracts imposed through an unholy alliance with the growers. At the same time he tried to promote lettuce harvested under the handful of UFWOC contracts. Eating habits worked against the boycott too. Grapes were a luxury item, lettuce a staple. The per capita grape consumption was two pounds a year; for lettuce, the figure was 22.3 pounds.[17] Persuading people to eat cabbage salads was not easy.

Just before New Year's 1971, Eliseo borrowed a supporter's Winnetka home for a staff retreat. They tried to develop strategy to rebuild the boycott and treasured the rare respite. "Not only did we enjoy the pool table and the fire place, but we also genuinely appreciated all the food you left us," Eliseo wrote in his thank-you letter. "Our budget does not allow for many turkeys, and we usually find ourselves in a rut as far as the kinds of food we do buy. The variety of food, then, was also greatly appreciated."[18]

The boycott limped along. By March, disarray had set in across the country. Boycotters were confused about which produce to target. UFWOC

Dolores Huerta joins Eliseo for a march in Chicago to draw attention to the boycott and strike.

leaders in California did not have a complete list of union contracts.[19] With little direction from Delano, Eliseo took matters into his own hands. He named himself Midwest boycott coordinator. He convened a regional conference to formulate strategy. About one hundred volunteers from a dozen cities, as far away as Philadelphia and Boston, traveled to Chicago and paid three dollars to cover food for the weekend. "As you requested, I am sending you my impressions," Eliseo reported to Chavez afterward. "I think, Cesar, that at this point morale is somewhat low." In his forthright style, Eliseo offered a detailed critique of missteps by the union's central administration. He aimed to pass on useful information, in the same spirit that boycotters had pooled their knowledge at the conference. Eliseo assumed all union leaders shared his interest in thoroughly dissecting problems so that they could devise solutions.

His most withering criticism involved the union label. Volunteers had relentlessly educated consumers to look for the trademark black eagle. With grapes, the union label had commanded a premium. With lettuce, the black eagle brought the growers grief from the Teamsters. So union companies had quietly dropped the UFWOC label. The boycotters found out from supporters who were spot-checking produce. "The biggest gripe—and we aired quite a few—was the decision to leave off the eagle on some lettuce boxes," Eliseo wrote Chavez. "The entire conference was literally outraged that such a decision had been made in the first place. But there was a also a lot of discontent with the fact that we had not even been informed of the decision . . . Frankly we look like fools when our supporters come to us asking questions that we cannot answer."

He ticked off a host of other deficiencies on the part of the Delano administration: Not meeting orders for buttons and bumper stickers. Sending out stickers that did not hold up to the midwestern winters. Passing on inaccurate information. Failing to send key documents, such as existing contracts and details on pesticide usage. Issuing shifting and contradictory directives. Eliseo ended with a recent example: The Chicago team had scrapped a major six-week offensive after receiving an order to suspend the boycott because the union was in negotiations—only to be told days later that the boycott was back on. "I hope we find out soon what is going on," the twenty-five-year-old concluded. "Confusion is not conducive to effective boycotting."[20]

Weeks later, Eliseo was headed back to California, uncertain of his next assignment. "Anyone that worked with me during the past years in Chicago knows that one of my favorite sayings was 'Boy, will I be glad to get back to California.' But now that the time has come, it's a little harder than I thought it would be," he wrote in his farewell newsletter, printed on the offset press whose acquisition had made him so proud. "For a long time I have wanted to get back to the fields and work with the people who do and will make up the union. For the opportunity and challenge to finally come, I am grateful. On the other hand, our union is what it is today largely because of the sacrifices made by people in Chicago and other cities. Leaving the people who have helped to form our union is difficult, and finding words to thank them is even more difficult."[21]

Those he had worked with in Chicago thanked Eliseo in return. "From your Illinois friends, our lives here have been enriched and will never be the same because you have shared your life with us," read the inscription in a copy of Studs Terkel's *Hard Times*. From Kathy Fagan and two fellow Northwestern students who had organized the Jewel boycott in Evanston, Eliseo received a copy of Saul Alinsky's book about organizing, *Rules for Radicals*. The inscription read: "Eliseo, from three radicals you helped break the rules."

CHAPTER 8

The Union Is Not La Paz

May 1971

Chris

Four dozen religious leaders gathered at an isolated compound in the foothills of the Tehachapi Mountains, the loud whistles of passing trains the only intrusion. A few small homes, two hulking, run-down hospital buildings, and some small offices dotted the grounds of the former tuberculosis sanatorium. Cesar Chavez saw something different. He sketched for the clergy a grand vision of what the complex would become: a home for the union's leaders, an educational center, and a place to experiment with collectives. A wealthy union supporter had surreptitiously bought the hundred-acre campus about thirty miles east of Bakersfield, and Chavez was gradually moving the union's headquarters away from the vineyards of Delano to the tiny town of Keene, California. He wanted a name that combined religious imagery and peace. He christened the retreat Nuestra Señora de la Reina de la Paz.[1] Our Lady Queen of Peace. The compound quickly became known simply as La Paz.

The visiting clergy were handed a list of items urgently needed to transform the ramshackle buildings into the communal home Chavez envisioned: 240 sheets, 60 mattresses and covers, 100 blankets, 400 towels, 200 pillows, a commercial washer and dryer, a large heater, a floor buffer, a tractor, a jeep, a chain saw, a large coffee maker, and latex and enamel paint.[2] The guests were escorted to their rooms in one of the former hospital wings—decrepit, dingy dorms with shared bathrooms. Accustomed to a subsistence lifestyle, Chris had not thought twice about the accommodations. Besides, he had brought the religious leaders to La Paz for symbolic rather than practical reasons. They were charter members of the National Farm Worker Ministry, and Chris wanted to tie the new group as tightly as possible to Chavez.

Like everyone else, Chris had rushed to Salinas when the lettuce strike began. He coordinated one of four marches that converged in Salinas the first Sunday, the weekend he was supposed to be picking up his middle son from camp. He helped raise money and sent out news alerts. With a militant workforce in the vegetable fields and support from the Catholic Church, Chris was not needed the way he had been in Delano. Chavez had other plans for the minister.

The union had a foothold in the vegetable industry and more than one hundred contracts in the grape vineyards, covering a total of about 48,000 jobs.[3] Chavez turned his attention away from the mechanics of running the union. He focused on how to sustain his movement. He talked about a Poor Peoples Union and farmworker cooperatives. He spoke admiringly about the Jehovah's Witnesses, sending an aide to research how they organized conferences, won court cases, and successfully distributed their newspaper.[4] He viewed a broader effort to organize the poor as the next struggle. He had studied movements that failed and was determined to avoid their mistakes; a new battle was vital to keep people engaged. "You get a union, then you want to struggle for something else," Chavez said. "You just keep struggling like that, that's the only way."[5]

To support his crusade, Chavez suggested that Chris transform the California Migrant Ministry into a national ecumenical organization. A national ministry also would head off another potential problem. Dozens of groups had sprung up to help the rural poor, taking advantage of federal funds available from the War on Poverty. Chris and Chavez wanted to establish an organization they could control, that would consolidate power and ensure that the religious community spoke for farmworkers with a single voice.

Selling church people on a broad-based movement to help the poor was not difficult. Chris quoted Chavez in the Migrant Ministry newsletter: "Our goal is a national union of the poor dedicated to world peace and to serving the needs of all men who suffer." Religious support was crucial, Chris wrote, to build "a union that intends to serve the needs of all rural poor people and that intends to join with other organizations in fighting for peace and justice throughout the world."[6]

Chris's largest hurdle was defining the relationship between the new ministry and the union. To close the deal, Chavez traveled to Atlanta in January 1971 to attend the founding convention of the National Farm Worker Ministry. His message was not subtle, and some of the union's strongest supporters privately balked. In a confidential letter after the Atlanta meeting, Monsignor George Higgins described Chavez's presentation to the clergy:

> He made it abundantly clear that what he wants is a national organization of religious leaders who will support UFWOC 1000 per cent with staff and funds and will do so without asking any questions or offering any advice. In my judgment, he appealed very crassly to the guilt feeling which so many Protestant social actionists seem to harbor in their souls and even went so far as to threaten them with the enmity of the poor (meaning, in this case, farm workers) if the religious community fails to measure up to his expectations.[7]

Chris scornfully dismissed such criticism, particularly from Catholics. They had not even been around in the early days, when friends really mattered. Even now the Catholic Church had not endorsed the boycott, choosing instead to anoint the bishops' committee as a mediator. Chris also rejected arguments that the ministry risked losing its independence and objectivity by forming such a close alliance with Chavez. Chris was convinced the way to be most effective was from the inside.

When the National Farm Worker Ministry (NFWM) board met for the first time at La Paz, Chris easily addressed one set of complaints: He promised to use hotels the next time instead of the old hospital rooms. The fight over the new ministry's mission was trickier. Chris engineered two moves that bound the group tightly to the union and set the ministry's course for decades. He insisted other groups be allowed to join NFWM only with the approval of Chavez. Then he called a vote on the mission statement he had drafted: "NFWM is a movement within the churches to be present with and support farm workers as they organize a national union under the leadership of the UFWOC to overcome their powerlessness and achieve equality, freedom and justice." After much debate, the motion passed 14–5, with eight abstentions. Chris was unanimously elected director.[8]

Chris returned to La Paz a few months later to attend a conference of California boycotters. He spoke with his usual combination of earnest but passionate rhetoric and practical advice. They were fighting for the rights of others, he reminded the boycotters. He walked them through a typical organizing scenario: Form an interfaith committee. Visit store managers and explain the farmworkers' cause. Stress the moral responsibility to help. When the managers say they have a responsibility to their customers, tell them that's not good enough. Then tell them you'll just have to go to the customers yourself. "The boycott is a legitimate moral weapon that the farmworkers should have . . . that's got to be our position," he told the boycotters. "Keep hammering it again and again and again."

The National Farm Worker Ministry would recruit volunteers for the boycott and subsidize union staff, Chris said. But he saw his role as helping to build something greater in this new, more mature phase of the movement: "There is a sense in which the religious community keeps reminding people, even after the struggle gets real old, keeps reminding people that what this is all about is human beings who are suffering and are trying to take hold of their own lives and build something beautiful for themselves and for all the rest of us."[9]

Eliseo

Eliseo dreamed of building something too, no less ambitious than Chris's soaring vision. When Eliseo finally returned to the fields, he encountered an operation in as much disarray as the old hospital buildings at La Paz. Eliseo set out to build a local union.

He had driven home from Chicago to Delano, in a blue 1969 station wagon that members of United Auto Workers Local 600 had chipped in to buy for $2,860.[10] He was home only briefly before heading to his new assignment: field office director in the Imperial Valley. Chavez went along to help orient Eliseo to the job in Calexico, a border town at the southeastern corner of California. Chavez traveled as usual with his security guard and dogs, Boycott and Huelga. Eliseo followed, driving with Dorothy Johnson. The caravan stopped in Palm Springs because Chavez wanted bagels and lox. Dorothy had never eaten either. She had grown up in a Presbyterian home in Seattle and was accustomed to the boycott diet of baloney and white bread. In Chicago she had started working on the boycott in a suburb and then moved downtown to be closer to Eliseo. They soon became a couple. They shared a quiet reserve and complete commitment to the cause, and each offered the other a passport into a foreign culture.

They arrived in Calexico in summer, the desert heat so enervating that Dorothy spent the first few days in bed before her body could adjust. The Imperial Valley was a desolate desert transformed into a lush agricultural paradise by the country's largest man-made irrigation system. Water from the Colorado River flowed into the American Canal and then into thousands of miles of canals and ditches that cut a checkerboard pattern as they nourished acres of cotton, melons, and vegetables. In winter the Imperial Valley produced 90 percent of the country's lettuce. Many of the Salinas growers had fields in Imperial, so they could harvest and ship vegetables almost all year round.

Eliseo walked into a mess. The union's tiny storefront office in the Hotel El Rey was infested with crickets. The first staff person to arrive each morning went around with a pail and broom, sweeping up buckets full of crickets and dumping them outside. The files were in chaos; opened letters had been returned to their envelopes and dumped into drawers. Eliseo moved to more spacious quarters around the corner, put in a counter to separate the meeting area from the office in back, and organized a filing system.

As the winter lettuce season began, Eliseo faced more complex problems. A key provision of the contracts required that all jobs be filled through a hiring hall run by the union. Growers placed orders for workers; the union dispatched them on a seniority basis. The hiring hall was supposed to eliminate favoritism and the capricious power of labor contractors. In practice, the system created dislocation and chaos. Longtime workers at one ranch were dispatched to a new company. Families were split up. Workers returning from Salinas wasted time by having to apply for their jobs all over. The union, with little administrative capability, was in charge of maintaining complicated seniority lists. Accusations of favoritism were common, and side deals had been the norm—as Eliseo discovered when workers tried to curry favor and secure jobs by bringing food and candy.

Compounding the problem, union leaders had adopted rules that required members to pay dues each month—whether or not they worked. The back of the membership card had twelve squares, one for each month. Dorothy ran the Calexico hiring hall, and her orders were not to dispatch anyone unless each square had a colored sticker showing that the

$3.50-a-month dues payments were up to date. Often workers owed several months for time they had been unemployed. For large families, the amounts added up.

The problems were new to Eliseo. But the hiring hall had been inciting anger in the grape vineyards since the contracts were signed more than a year earlier. Most workers in the Delano and Coachella vineyards had evinced little active support for the union. The growers had acquiesced to contracts because of pressure from the boycott. The hiring hall and the union's rigid policies were antagonizing workers rather than winning them over. Union officials, in turn, looked with disdain at the ungrateful grape workers who had not fought for their contracts and did not appreciate the benefits—bathrooms, drinking water, reliable employment, fixed hours, and overtime.

Cesar's brother Richard saw the difficulties clearly and had been trying to get Cesar's attention for months. A carpenter by trade, Richard Chavez had been on his way to a middle-class life in 1962 when his older brother convinced him to help build a union for farmworkers. When the lettuce strike started and all the union leaders flocked to Salinas, Richard Chavez was left alone in Delano to set up a hiring hall and figure out how to administer dozens of new contracts. Practical by nature, he grasped the problems right away. After visiting all the field offices in mid-1971, he grew increasingly concerned that the union was alienating its members. His brother brushed off the warnings. Richard Chavez thought the union's punitive measures—collecting back dues and fining members who did not attend meetings—so destructive that he simply stopped enforcing them.[11]

Eliseo knew none of that. The field office directors did not compare notes. The union ethos was sink or swim; you solved problems on your own. Eliseo soon decided the Calexico hiring hall made no sense for workers returning to the same jobs year after year. He abolished the hiring hall for all but new workers. To address the back dues problem, he came up with the Comité de Cuotas (Committee on Dues). When a worker owed dues and objected to paying, Dorothy sent him to the comité, representatives from each union ranch. Workers made their case to their peers, and the comité decided whether to grant a hardship exemption. The comité served double duty: It deflected anger away from Eliseo while helping to build leadership among the rank and file.

Eliseo quickly made an adjustment of another sort. He jettisoned the rhetoric of the boycott as he absorbed the reality of the fields. For four years, he had been selling the story of militant poor people fighting for their rights. In Calexico, he found workers focused on their jobs, not on the cause. "I was beginning to believe that all the farmworkers have a little red book stuck in their hip pocket and they're all ready to go out there and start the revolution with rifles in their hands," Eliseo told a meeting of boycotters. "Then I come back and I find an entirely different story. The farmworkers aren't there, you know, running down the streets by thousands with rifles in their hand. They're people who are just trying to make a living. A decent living. These are people who are trying like hell to get themselves a strong union."[12]

The workers learned about Eliseo too. They had been accustomed to a hiring hall where the union replaced the labor contractor as patronage dispenser. Workers watched skeptically to see if Eliseo really meant what he said about enforcing strict seniority and union rules. They discovered he was a by-the-book guy. He went into the fields to make sure workers were not cutting deals with foremen to bypass the dispatch system. Farmworkers began to read the contracts and learn their rights.

Eliseo seized opportunities to show members how the union worked for them. When he won $163 in back pay and reinstatement for a fired worker, Eliseo presented the check in front of hundreds of workers. He told stories about the boycott and explained the crucial leverage it provided in negotiations. Motivated by Eliseo's enthusiasm, workers voted to help picket supermarkets in Los Angeles. They arranged a schedule and traveled north one crew at a time.[13]

With his staff of seven and monthly budget of $2,400 (including living expenses),[14] Eliseo steadily built the union's base. Attendance at weekly meetings grew, and workers carved out time to volunteer. Rosario Pelayo had seven children and worked full-time in the broccoli fields. Her first encounter with the Calexico hiring hall had left her furious—Dorothy had refused to issue a dispatch because Pelayo owed back dues. But Pelayo watched the system change. She saw Eliseo treat people with respect, and she saw the results. She and her friends became a team of committed volunteers—Becky and Guicho and Pancho the poet, who read his verses at union meetings. Eliseo became convinced that the ranch committees—the leaders elected at each company to represent their co-workers—were key to the union's success.

In La Paz, Chavez focused on a different key to success. He convened a meeting at the new headquarters to relaunch the lettuce boycott. Volunteers in San Francisco were close enough to the fields to hear criticism about the hiring halls. They had drafted a letter in preparation for the conference, questioning whether the union had sufficient staff and asking why grievances piled up. In his opening speech Chavez angrily rebutted criticism of the union's contract administration. He put forward field office directors from Fresno and Delano to refute the charges. They piled on the boycotter who had written the letter. Then Chavez called on Eliseo.

The Calexico field office director refrained from the personal attacks that the others had used. He did not address the complaints directly, other than to suggest that those who grumbled generally didn't have enough work. Instead he talked about his own experience in Calexico. He talked about the importance of having workers take ownership of the contract. "It doesn't do us any good to have a good leader and good directors or anything, unless the people themselves are really with it, unless they're organized and are really doing everything in their power to enforce those contracts," Eliseo said. "See, we don't enforce the contracts—they do." He told them about the power that came from sitting down with a committee of workers to negotiate in a grower's office. He told them the growers were coming to respect the workers and to understand they needed their cooperation. Everything Eliseo was learning in Calexico was shaping his idea of how the union should work.

"I want to make this one thing clear," Eliseo told the group. "The union is not Cesar Chavez. And the union is not La Paz. The union is out in the field offices, where the people themselves are building it."[15]

Sabino

The quiet irrigator from Jalisco was one of those people building the union. He regulated the water in the fields of one of four vegetable ranches under contract in Salinas—the same companies Eliseo worked with during the winter in Calexico. In a union organized around personality and devoid of structure, the two offices took different approaches. From the start, Salinas was the militant heart of the union.

Sabino worked at Freshpict, which was owned by Purex. The consumer products conglomerate had dumped the Teamsters and signed with the union rather than risk a boycott of Purex's well-known products, which included Sweetheart soap and Brillo pads. Sabino faithfully attended union meetings, watching and listening. He became friends with an older union leader at the ranch who mentored the irrigator. Sabino in turn helped his friend, whose rigid union dogma and rough edges often antagonized others. Sabino discovered that his own calm demeanor and willingness to listen helped him play the role of conciliator and broker compromises. He was elected union steward for his crew of steadies. For the first time, he could make a difference not only in his own life, but in the lives of others.

Sabino's new post, the lowest rung on the union ladder, offered a vantage point from which he observed the battle to establish power in the vegetable fields. The union's aggressive tactics in Salinas delighted Chavez, who was frustrated by the recalcitrant workers in the vineyards. He soon began extolling the "liberated ranches" of Salinas, triumphant islands amid the hostile "Ranch Nation" controlled by greedy growers.

The differences between Delano and Salinas began with the crops themselves and the fabric of the lives of those who tended the plants. A grape grower nurtured the same vines year after year; he was invested in the fields and tethered to his land. His workers often returned to their same jobs and worked with the same crews, for the same supervisors, in the same fields. Vegetable growers could pick up stakes and plant anywhere. They mostly rented land. They could switch fields every three months, as soon as a lettuce crop matured. The total number of acres under cultivation changed frequently, altering the supply and the price. The structure of the vegetable industry further complicated the economics: There were growers, harvesters, packers, and shippers. They made deals with one another in combinations that shifted depending on the market, the weather, and the workforce. Some vegetable growers shipped their own produce. Some shippers bought all their lettuce from growers. Some shippers hired crews to harvest crops planted by third-party growers. "Union-grown lettuce" often meant lettuce that was planted and harvested by nonunion workers but shipped by a company with a union contract. Freshpict and Interharvest were unusual in that they did everything: hired workers who grew, thinned, irrigated, harvested, packed, and sold the vegetables.

The first ranch to be "liberated" was Interharvest, which had been first to sign a contract in the summer of 1970. A year later the foremen resisted giving up the power they had traditionally wielded. Grievances accumulated, unresolved. Frustrated, the workers introduced the company to *la tortuga*—the turtle. They worked so slowly, they cut production to 20 percent of normal, reducing their own wages by 80 percent. The union staff from the field office went into the fields and theatrically yelled at the workers, chastising them for breaking the contract. Everyone enjoyed the show—except the growers. Crew leaders strictly enforced the slowdown, arguing for hours with workers who wanted to return to normal speed and make more money. Lettuce was wilting in the fields. Finally the union and the company had a summit meeting. The company met the workers' demands.

The ranch leaders at Freshpict learned from Interharvest. At Freshpict, the tension grew until there were thirty-seven grievances and no resolution in sight. The company brought in a nonunion crew to harvest some lettuce. Workers decided that one particular foreman who was harassing union members had to go. The tortuga began. The company sent telegrams every day to La Paz, complaining about illegal work stoppages. The two sides met at La Paz, and the company agreed to get rid of the crew boss who had touched off the slowdown and become the symbol of the old power of the foreman. When Freshpict put him back to work two weeks later, the tortuga returned. The company fired all three lettuce crews for violating the contract. The next day the broccoli and celery crews reduced their harvest to 20 percent of normal. Sabino and the other irrigators cut back the flow of water so the crops were getting a fraction of what they needed. The company capitulated in the face of the workers' new-found solidarity.[16]

Sabino saw the tortuga as an extraordinary measure, not to be used lightly. The turtle evened out the scales. For years, workers had suffered arbitrary treatment; now they were a force to be reckoned with. No longer could growers take workers for granted. When he went home to visit Mexico, Sabino's family and friends listened in amazement to his tales about the tortuga, the power of the union, and its fight for justice.

From the vegetable workers, Chavez frequently recounted, he had learned what had to be done in the grape vineyards. The grape workers blamed the union for anything that went wrong. They had to be trained to get angry at the company instead, Chavez said. They had to be taught to subvert the contracts. "If we don't teach them that, first of all, they don't deserve a union, and we don't deserve to be leading," Chavez said. "The places we really have a good union is where they've gone through this kind of a fight," he said, describing the Salinas vegetable workers' battles. As he and Marshall Ganz went across the country meeting with boycotters, they told the story of the tortuga. And Ganz always bragged about how the irrigators made sure that the water ran slow.[17]

Jerry

As the union slogged through its building phase, not quite at peace but for the moment not at war, Jerry's mission shifted. Instead of fighting injunctions on picket lines or confronting growers in court, he bantered with them in hotel conference rooms. Jerry found himself cast in a role he relished: negotiator.

Jerry had been drawn to the law because of his natural ability to talk rings around others. He had expected to spend most of his time as a lawyer framing arguments; he had not anticipated so much deal-making. Jerry thought fast on this feet and could argue both sides of an issue, enabling him to anticipate opponents' moves. He honed his natural instincts by observing his new teacher, a master negotiator.

Chavez was a "gentle intimidator" who used "adversity as an ally, sacrifice as a positive good," Jerry wrote. He analyzed Chavez's tactics: "Work and penance. His ability to relax. To clown, to be mean as hell—unreasonable."[18] Together Jerry and Chavez schemed and plotted pressure points they could push that would in turn exert pressure on the enemy. Just like the carom shots that Chavez was fond of executing at the pool table: You hit one ball that hits another to make the shot. The boycott had proved they could play that game.

Jerry watched Chavez use meetings as a negotiating tool, knowing exactly where he wanted to end up and patiently steering the conversation until he reached that point. Chavez held out for what he wanted even when there were costs. He wore down the opposition, sometimes with a bluff. The union contracts required that employers contribute to a jointly administered health fund. Chavez insisted the union control the fund, and for more than a year he refused to spend the money at all. Growers became increasingly irate about paying into a plan that wasn't benefiting farmworkers. Finally at a summit meeting Jerry presented a complicated legal argument that asserted the union was exempt from certain federal laws and thus had the power to act unilaterally. He was not at all certain that was true.

Chavez sat in the rocking chair he used for his bad back and rocked back and forth as Jerry made the case. "It was really a hell of a bluff," Jerry recounted gleefully. "They gave us complete control of the plan. We castrated them that day, which was exactly what they deserved. They agreed to be a rubber stamp . . . I learned a lot about negotiating that day."[19]

Jerry felt Chavez trusted him, and the union leader gave the lawyer leeway to devise his own strategies. Their styles meshed. Jerry was quick and brash, feet up on the table and a toothpick in his mouth so often that growers placed them next to his plate at lunch. He joked that he'd given up smoking and gotten Dutch elm disease instead. He was known for his quick repartee and poor dress. When a grower's attorney asked Jerry how many of the four buttons on his shirt should be open, Jerry responded: It depends on the amount of hair on your chest.[20] The more conservative Delano grape growers tended to take Jerry's insults personally and found less common ground. His banter held greater appeal for the vegetable crowd. Whether they liked him or not, adversaries admired Jerry's intellect and feared his memory for detail.

Throughout 1971 Jerry held out hope of reaching an agreement that would void the Teamsters' sweetheart contracts in the lettuce fields. He held on-and-off-again bargaining sessions with lawyers representing several blocs of vegetable growers. They met as often as twice a week, in hotel suites from Marina del Rey to San Francisco. The most progress Jerry made: "On July 23rd at 2:38 in the afternoon, they agreed to the bulletin board clause," he reported dryly, referring to the standard clause about what could be posted on the company bulletin board.[21]

By the end of the year, Jerry focused on arguments to present to a meeting with Chavez and AFL-CIO president George Meany. Meany had condemned the Teamster contracts, but the AFL-CIO did not like boycotts; its members worked as meat cutters and retail clerks at the stores the farmworkers boycotted. Meany had asked the union to suspend the boycott and engage in good-faith negotiations, and Jerry had dutifully complied. But the months of glacial progress yielded nothing more than the bulletin board clause. "I sat there for seven months listening to these schmucks," Jerry told a meeting of union volunteers. ". . . It's a lot more fun to be fighting than it is to be listening to this stuff." Now the union was going to ask the powerful labor federation to support a more aggressive approach, including a lettuce boycott. That would probably mean an independent charter for the farm workers union, so that they could undertake the boycott without compromising the AFL-CIO.

Jerry also looked beyond the lettuce battle to his next negotiating task—the grape contracts, which would begin to expire in early 1973. Complaints about the union's administration had intensified. The handful of growers who had been the earliest union supporters were now among the most vocal critics. The growers had signed the contracts to buy labor peace. Chaotic hiring halls, wildcat walkouts, and tortugas defeated the purpose. They appealed directly and through intermediaries in an effort to straighten things out before renegotiations commenced.

Several growers went to Monsignor Roger Mahony, a Fresno cleric who served as secretary to the Bishops' Committee on Farm Labor, and Mahony wrote Chavez to relay the complaints. Keene Larson was trying to make the contract work but found himself stymied by inexperienced, zealous union volunteers, such as the one who ordered him out of his own fields. Workers had so much trouble paying back dues when they returned to Coachella at the beginning of the season that Larson stood outside the hiring hall with several hundred dollars, handing money out to his employees so they could pay up.[22] Instead of breaking bonds with employers and transferring authority to the union, the new system often did the reverse. Mahony warned Chavez that farmworkers across the Fresno diocese expressed resentment and the bishop encountered "increasing animosity towards the UFWOC efforts, in particular by many Mexican-American groups."[23] Chavez sent a curt reply: "You must know things that I don't."[24]

Lionel Steinberg, the first grape grower to sign, praised Chavez's leadership but questioned his administrative ability. Steinberg urged the union to get help from experienced negotiators in the AFL-CIO—an offer Chavez had previously turned down—to avoid problems like back dues, or contracts that expired at different times. Because he had signed first, for example, Steinberg's wages went up to $1.90 per hour while a competitor was still paying $1.75. Chavez had the opportunity to become one of the great labor leaders of the country, Steinberg said, but only if he focused in that direction. "Is it a social movement or is it a trade union?" Steinberg asked.[25]

Once in a while Jerry privately shared some of those concerns. He confided to Fred Ross that finding plaintiffs for some suits in Salinas had become difficult because the union wasn't organizing aggressively enough. He urged Ross to talk with his protégé about staying focused on the farmworkers.[26] Richard Chavez intensified efforts to persuade his brother that the union was alienating workers. Cesar needed to be out with the people more, his brother told him. He was losing touch, living in La Paz, away from the fields. He was fooling himself if he thought the people loved the union. The poor staff and rigid policies were backfiring. Richard Chavez went so far as to warn that the union would lose the contracts. But no one took him seriously.[27]

With more than one hundred grape contracts and tens of thousands of dues-paying members, Chavez moved confidently to expand into a national union. The AFL-CIO granted the farmworkers an independent charter, and he began to draft a constitution. When Arizona passed an anti-union law, Chavez staged a twenty-four-day fast in Phoenix and organized a drive to recall the governor. In Florida he signed the union's first major contract outside California, covering twelve hundred workers who picked oranges for Coca-Cola's Minute Maid division. Chavez saw Florida, with thousands of farmworkers and horrendous conditions in the fields, as the logical place for the union's next major base. He pulled Eliseo out of Calexico and sent him to Florida to oversee the new contract and build a statewide operation.

Chavez had finished shifting the union headquarters to La Paz, and he wanted Jerry to move there too. Jerry was resisting. He much preferred Delano. With People's Bar and two movie theaters on Main Street, Delano was a major metropolis compared to Keene, a crossroads with nothing more than a post office, a general store, and the former tuberculosis sanatorium. Nearby Tehachapi, less than half the size of Delano with five thousand residents, held little appeal. The isolated environment at La Paz made Jerry claustrophobic. He did not like meetings, and there seemed to always be an endless meeting underway. It was harder to escape meetings, and harder to escape, period.

Most of all, Jerry shared Richard Chavez's concerns about being out of touch. Jerry felt removed from the action when he visited La Paz, far from the communities of workers, growers, and attorneys with whom he interacted. Only the railroad tracks of the Southern Pacific, constructed through Keene to bypass the Tehachapi Mountains, connected the rural retreat to the fields of the Central Valley. The tracks built to transport produce from the fields to the cities of southern California ran smack through La Paz, and freight trains regularly rumbled by, their deafening whistles bringing conversation to a halt.

Chavez badly wanted Jerry at La Paz. As an incentive, Chavez offered Jerry any accommodation on the grounds. In the summer of 1972 the Cohens moved into a double-wide trailer at the end of a dirt road, as far as possible from the hospital buildings and offices at the compound that Jerry dubbed "Magic Mountain."

CHAPTER 9

Back to the Boycott

June 1972

Ellen

Cat Stevens was singing "Morning Has Broken" on the car radio as Ellen Eggers drove from Nevada into California, just a few weeks after graduating from Ball State University. She had come west from Indiana largely by chance. A friend had given her a church brochure listing dozens of summer programs, and Ellen had picked the National Farm Worker Ministry. The ministry was advertising for help on the Los Angeles boycott, and Ellen was looking for a meaningful experience before heading to graduate school in social work. She knew nothing about the lettuce boycott and wasn't too sure of the difference between Cesar Chavez and Che Guevara. But the internship sounded in line with her career goals, and she was eager to see California.

On June 15 a dozen summer volunteers gathered for orientation at a Los Angeles church on Sepulveda Boulevard, and Ellen met Chris. He showed films about the history of the union. Then he explained the boycott, which Chavez had officially relaunched a few weeks earlier. Within minutes Chris won over the enthusiastic twenty-year-old from Muncie. He conveyed the justness of the cause and the urgency, and Ellen could see how much he cared. Chris sketched out for the new recruits the moral imperative. He stressed that farmworkers were counting on them. Just days before, Ellen had gorged on lettuce to get her fill for the summer. Swayed by Chris's passion, she moved quickly from ignorance to outrage.

Chris divided up the summer interns among the coordinators and assigned Ellen to a group led by Sister Ruth Shy. Shy had grown up in St. Louis, where she had helped host Chavez on his 1969 national tour with Chris. She moved to Denver and joined the Sisters of Loretto, one of the most progressive orders of the Catholic Church. The sisters had invited the Denver boycott director to a meeting. After listening to the story of the farmworker from Delano, the nuns endorsed the boycott. They picketed Safeway supermarkets, went to jail, published stories about the boycott in their newsletter, and sewed black and red Huelga flags for a Salinas protest march. By the time she took charge of Ellen's boycott group in the summer of 1972, Shy had been working full time for the union in California for more than a year. She helped set up the new union headquarters at La Paz, then moved to the coast and organized farmworkers on weekend bus trips to picket Los Angeles supermarkets. When he geared up the lettuce boycott, Chavez sent Shy to Los Angeles to help. She was a rail-thin, no-nonsense, chain-smoking workaholic, always at her desk when Ellen arrived, and still there in the early hours of the morning, double-checking plans for the next day. Shy was as committed and single-minded as Chris, and Ellen liked them both right away.

Ellen's group was assigned to the San Fernando Valley, the large suburban swath of Los Angeles to the north of the Hollywood Hills. First they had to find a house that would also serve as an office, and a landlord willing to rent to a group of unrelated activists. The best prospect turned out to be a house owned by the internationally famous transsexual Christine Jorgensen. She wanted to meet the people who would live in her home. Ellen and the others looked at the woman they had read about and tried not to stare at her hands as Shy explained their work. They moved in, and Ellen told friends back home that she was definitely in southern California.

Shy taught the volunteers how to conduct a house meeting campaign to educate consumers about the need to shun nonunion lettuce. Fred Ross had pioneered the house meeting, a Tupperware-style mode of organizing: Ask a supporter to invite a few friends over for a small meeting. Then enlist the friends to invite over their friends, until you reach a critical mass. Shy had the new recruits map the area, drive around, and note friendly churches, likely supermarket targets, and sympathetic community organizations. Then Shy gave them lists of contacts and sent them out to make more.

Ellen was inspired by and a little in awe of the older woman, who had worked directly with Chavez and always had ready answers for the intern's questions. Shy drummed the history of *la causa* into the young people who had not lived through it, so that they could pass on the lore. Ellen spent days knocking on doors, persuading people to sign cards pledging not to eat nonunion lettuce. She learned her first Spanish: *Esta es una promesa ni comer ni comprar lechuga.* (This is a pledge not to eat or buy lettuce.) One of the farmworkers in the house patiently helped Ellen memorize the words to "De Colores" so she could join the singing at union meetings. The kid from Indiana who had never seen a tortilla learned that burritos were named after donkey ears, while Malcriados were not food but newspapers that she was expected to sell.

Ellen told the union's story over and over. She had never seen Cesar Chavez, but she was proficient at reciting the details of his life. Finally, the first weekend in August, her boycott house was summoned to La Paz. Volunteers from around California gathered in the North Unit, one of the old hospital buildings, to hear Chavez outline their next crusade: Defeat Proposition 22. The growers had gathered enough signatures to place an initiative on the California ballot that would ban secondary boycotts and mandate elections in a way that would effectively disenfranchise all seasonal farmworkers. "The only time we come together is when we're in trouble," Chavez welcomed them ruefully. "We have two days of hard work to determine the best and most efficient course we can take to overcome this threat against our union on Election Day."

His speech was rambling, his manner alternately funny, informative, and stern. Star-struck, Ellen took pictures. Chavez lectured the volunteers on his twin pet peeves: excessive phone bills and poor care of union cars. He shared news of recent victories: a grape grower had finally agreed to negotiate. He outlined a campaign to register one million new voters to help defeat Prop 22. Humbly, Chavez credited the hard work of the people in the room for the union's success. "It is always a source of amazement to me how our union can withstand attacks and stay a viable force and continue to make progress," he said, picking up a bullhorn to be heard over the passing Southern Pacific trains.

Then he shifted from proud father to stern patriarch. At La Paz, people worked harder than anywhere else, he said. He demanded it. If you were not willing to work around the clock, he warned, better leave now. "We are servants of people in need," he told the group. "We don't get paid. None of us . . . If you see someone not doing his work, you tell them so and work it out. We don't have time to deal with people who are confused. We work day and night, and don't need the extra burden of having other problems."[1]

Ellen was so mesmerized by the charismatic leader that she scarcely paid attention to the substance of his talk. Besides, she was going home in a few weeks; she would not be around long enough to fight Prop 22. But she loved being at La Paz. At night she listened to Jessica Govea, her beautiful voice singing union songs and traditional Mexican ballads. Ellen soaked up the atmosphere of people drawn together by a common purpose.

The next week, boycott director LeRoy Chatfield summoned the Los Angeles boycott staff from around the county to a meeting downtown. The union was in a life-or-death struggle, he told the volunteers. All of them would be expected to work seven days a week, instead of six, until Election Day. The summer volunteers would please stay on. You're staying, Shy said to Ellen as they headed back to the San Fernando Valley. It was a statement, not a question. Ellen demurred. She reminded Shy of the reasons for going home: a new nephew she'd never seen, a new boyfriend waiting, and the wedding of her college roommate. In the car, Ellen thought about what she had been telling people all summer, about the sacrifices she had been asking them to make. By the end of the half-hour ride, she had changed her mind.

Ellen called her mother and sobbed as she explained the importance of the union's struggle and why she had to stay. Ten years from now, she reasoned, she would not remember whether she went back to see her nephew and her boyfriend. But she would always remember if she left when the movement needed her to stay.

Chris

The theologian Chris admired most, Dietrich Bonhoeffer, believed in a suffering God on earth. During World War II the German pastor had condemned his own church for valuing its survival above the cause of saving Jews. He was executed for helping Jews escape the Nazi regime. In the union, Chris saw opportunities to practice the sort of servanthood that Bonhoeffer preached.

Chavez described sacrifice as a powerful weapon that made others want to help, to be near those willing to give up so much. Chris was exhibit number one. He often said Chavez had a genius for reaching in and pulling out the best in those around him. Ellen's decision to stay was a good example. "We'll organize workers in this movement as long as we're willing to sacrifice," Chavez told a group of church leaders. "The moment we stop sacrificing, we stop organizing. I guarantee that." He already saw danger signs. Three times during his short speech, he mentioned rumblings of dissatisfaction with the union's five-dollar-a-week allowance for its staff. Voicing particular impatience with farmworkers, Chavez said those interested in making money should go back to the fields, where wages had increased substantially under union contracts. "So we tell the workers, 'If you want to make that kind of money, go back. That's where the money's going to be. Not here.'"[2] Chris thought the speech so significant that he typed up a transcript for supporters, left copies in the office as handouts, and often quoted the text in his own tracts.

Chris knew he could not match the standard that Chavez set. Chris would be home at night watching TV with Pudge, while Chavez was reading labor history and Gandhi. "I need first of all people who can work as much as I'll work," Chavez told a group of volunteers. "I don't like them to take vacations. I don't like them to run around in expensive cars. I don't like them to wear ties. I'm a son of a bitch to work with . . . I work every day of the year. I just sleep and eat and work. I do nothing else."[3] Chris pushed himself relentlessly to do more, and where he fell short in hours, he compensated with efficiency and loyalty. Chavez said he could name only five people he could count on to get something done, with no excuses. Chris was one: "They just look at me and blink their eyes and do it. I may be wrong, they still do it. But it's also a reciprocal thing, they have more influence with me than most anybody else."[4]

So when Proposition 22 qualified for the November ballot, Chavez again relied on Chris. Voters in California could legislate by initiative; anyone who gathered a sufficient number of signatures could place a measure on the ballot. The agricultural industry was hoping to defeat Cesar Chavez at the polls.

In the late spring of 1972, reports trickled in to the union suggesting that supporters of Prop 22 had used fraud to obtain the hundreds of thousands of signatures necessary to place the initiative on the ballot. Chris loaned LeRoy Chatfield a couple of tenacious diggers who worked in the farm worker ministry. They produced enough evidence for the union to launch a full-scale campaign to document the extent of fraud.

Ellen joined the small army who worked off barely legible lists of names and addresses to track down people who had signed the petitions.

Many lived in the poorest neighborhoods of the city. They readily acknowledged they did not realize what they had signed. Most voters said
they had believed the proposition would help farmworkers. At the end of
each conversation, Ellen asked the hoodwinked voter to sign an affidavit.
Within weeks union volunteers across Los Angeles had amassed hundreds of sworn statements from people who had been told that Prop 22
would lower food prices, help farmworkers, and support Chavez.

Then the union volunteers located people who had circulated the petitions. The paid petition-gatherers testified they had been told to cover up
the attorney general's neutral, accurate description with a bright pink or
yellow card. They called them "dodger cards," because they dodged the
real intent, saying instead that Prop 22 promised to "give agricultural
workers their true choice of union representation." As one signature-
gatherer told Ellen, he was paid thirty-five cents per signature and used
the subterfuge because "many people would not sign the petition if they
found out that it was against Cesar Chavez and the Farm Workers
Union."[5]

Once the union had collected hundreds of declarations, Chris and
Chatfield took a small group to meet with Secretary of State Jerry Brown.
They asked him to pull the proposition off the ballot. Brown declined, but
said he would help. He denounced the fraudulent tactics, opened an in-
quiry, issued subpoenas, and requested district attorneys initiate criminal
investigations. The publicity raised Brown's political profile, established
an alliance with Chavez, and gave the union a new line of attack as Election Day approached.

Chatfield oversaw the campaign, and Chris was in charge of the final
push in Los Angeles: a massive human billboard campaign. "No on 22" and
"Prop 22 is a Fraud" read the giant black and white signs. Chris culled
through city data to calculate how many cars passed through major intersec-
tions at different hours. He figured out where to station billboards for maximum impact during morning and evening commutes. From all over the
state, farmworkers poured into Los Angeles to help, camping out in tents in
an East Los Angeles park. Volunteers came from around the country. Ellen's
mother flew in from Indiana, to see for herself the cause that had been too
important for her daughter to come home.

Each morning around five, the volunteers gathered in Lincoln Park.
Over coffee and *pan dulce* donated by Mexican bakeries, they listened to a
pep talk from Chris. Then he dispatched them for the morning rush hour.
Each team piled into a van that had been stocked the night before with

Ellen Eggers, right, works to defeat Proposition 22 alongside her mother, who flew to Los Angeles from Indiana to help in the campaign. (Ken Doyle)

the giant signs, on foldable poles so that they would fit into the vehicles. Once at their posts, the volunteers spaced themselves out, six or eight to an intersection, and waved the signs at motorists. The novelty alone attracted attention—so much so that Chris quickly jettisoned his plan to position demonstrators on highway overpasses. During the first day they caused several car accidents when motorists looked up to wave.

At lunchtime the volunteers regrouped in the park, and Chris called out statistics on how many cars had driven past their billboards during the morning rush. He went over the theme of the day. Sometimes the billboards stressed endorsements: "Catholic Bishops say No on 22," or "LA Times says No on 22." Then he sent the troops out again from two P.M. to six P.M. for the evening commute. Ellen's arms ached at the end of the day.

Single-minded, the union workers paid scant attention to the presidential campaign that was also going on. Merrill Farms, Sabino's old employer, printed endorsements of Richard Nixon on its lettuce crates. At the Democratic convention in Miami, the union made "boycott lettuce" such a pervasive phrase in speeches and signs that Senator Edward Kennedy began his address with "Greetings, fellow lettuce boycotters."

On Election Day, Nixon, who had proudly eaten grapes during the boycott, won California in a landslide. But Proposition 22 lost overwhelmingly. The union defeated the measure by a margin even greater than Nixon's win over George McGovern. More than 58 percent voted no on Prop 22, and only 24 percent in favor. Ellen had been so nervous during the day that she smoked a joint, defying the union's strict policy against drug use. At the victory party she danced with Chavez. Still groggy, she very much regretted breaking the rule.

Chris celebrated in a more sober fashion but with no less joy. The union had risen to the challenge once again, everyone pulling together, united in the face of the enemy, and proving that a righteous cause and hard work could triumph over the most powerful industry in the state.

Sandy

Sandy Nathan left his Pennsylvania home for Columbia Law School in 1966 with the nebulous idea of ending up some cross between a small-town lawyer and a social crusader, a character like Atticus Finch. Higher education also seemed a pragmatic approach to avoiding the draft. Though he had a medical classification that took into account a mild hearing impairment, by the time Sandy graduated from college the Vietnam War was conscripting even those whose status had seemed relatively safe. Sandy marched in antiwar demonstrations, campaigned for Eugene McCarthy, and joined students occupying buildings at Columbia during protests in 1968.

He graduated from law school and headed west, still far from enamored of his chosen line of work. He gravitated to political activists in Los Angeles. When Sandy passed the California bar, he and three friends arrived at the formal swearing-in dressed in jeans and work shirts—in solidarity with the workers. They leafleted the well-dressed crowd at the Dorothy Chandler Pavilion before the ceremony began. Then they were sworn in as lawyers, and the four young men thrust their right fists in the air.

Sandy worked for a poverty law project at UCLA, then joined a lawyers' collective in Venice, then traveled in Europe. By the beginning of 1973, he needed a job and heard the farmworkers were looking for a lawyer in Los Angeles. He interviewed with Jerry and LeRoy Chatfield at the end of January. They asked Sandy to work for next to nothing. He accepted on the spot.

After defeating Prop 22, the union had decided to focus on a secondary boycott against Safeway supermarkets. They urged shoppers to shun the stores until the dominant chain in southern California stopped carrying nonunion lettuce. Sandy's job was to sue Safeway, both as a nuisance and to generate fodder for boycotters around the country. Chris had organized the Interfaith Committee to Aid Farm Workers, which served as the plaintiff for the lawsuits Sandy drafted. As their first collaboration, they held a press conference to display organic cookies purchased at Safeway, carefully preserved in the freezer—and full of bugs.

Next, the Interfaith Committee sued Safeway for selling inferior grades of meat at higher prices. Rosemary Cooperrider, a longtime supporter in northern California, consulted animal diagrams in her cookbook to gather examples of how Safeway mislabeled meat. At a San Francisco press conference announcing the suit, Chris brought along a cooler containing evidence—samples of neck bones labeled as spareribs.[6]

By the end of his first three months with the union, Sandy had filed eleven nuisance suits. Then federal inspectors detected a residue of the pesticide Monitor 4 on some California lettuce, and the union decided to sue every supermarket chain in California that could be selling the contaminated produce. Sandy knew the approach was so broad that a judge would almost certainly dismiss the suit, but the charge made good headlines. The union served notice on hundreds of supermarkets, and incredulous lawyers flooded the union office with calls. Chris sent Ellen and a group of boycotters to camp out in a legislator's office until he agreed to hold hearings on the poisoned lettuce.

Ellen had been on the Safeway campaign for several months, assigned to picket the Safeway at Third and Fairfax and then the store at Third and Vermont. The union was turning away as many as three thousand people on weekends from eighteen Safeway stores across the city; the chain claimed it was losing more than $5,000 a day at each store.[7] Ellen lived in one of two "boycott houses" in Los Angeles, a two-story Victorian on Hobart Street, home to as many as two dozen volunteers. At night the boycotters went "Dumpster diving" at Safeway stores to try to find useful information—or food. Ellen had a sweet tooth and always looked for the day-old sweet rolls. On Sundays, her one day off, she often headed to Venice Beach, where Sandy lived. She borrowed his bicycle and rode along the boardwalk by the ocean, her only escape.

Sandy was expecting to move to Salinas in the spring. Just before he was hired, the union had won a significant victory in the California Supreme Court: The judges ruled that the Teamsters had signed sweetheart deals with the Salinas vegetable growers, without any input from workers, who appeared in fact to favor Chavez's union. The court refused to void the contracts. But the judges ruled that the strike was not a jurisdictional dispute, since the Teamsters had no legitimate claim to represent the workers. That opened the door to strikes and picketing. The union planned another run at the big vegetable growers. Jerry had told Sandy he would help out on the strike when the lettuce season got going in late spring. The union had received its charter and was now the United Farm Workers of America (UFW).

The three-year grape contracts expired in spring too. Unhappiness with the hiring hall and the administration of the contracts had not abated, but Chavez dismissed the problems as grower propaganda emanating from "unliberated ranches."

Sandy had been working in Los Angeles for less than four months when he was sent to Coachella in April for a few days. He drove his beat-up MG convertible east from Los Angeles, past the Palm Springs oasis for which the Coachella desert was famous, to the hot, dusty, poor farming areas, acres of grapes and citrus and dates. The grape contracts signed in 1970 were expiring, and the Teamsters were taking them away. The Coachella grape growers had seen how well the sweetheart contracts with the Teamsters worked for the vegetable growers. They wanted the same deal.

When Sandy arrived in Coachella, he called Jerry. Jerry told Sandy he was staying there indefinitely. The union was going on strike.

Sandy was stuck in a hole-in-the wall hovel in the sweltering desert, some days writing out briefs by hand when he couldn't borrow a typewriter. For the first time in his life, he felt good about being a lawyer. He was making a difference in people's lives. And having a blast. He told his parents he was proud of the work he did, and that meant the world to him.

PART III

War, Again

April 1973–June 1975

CHAPTER 10

Holy Week

April 1973

Jerry

The contracts expired on Palm Sunday. The strike began Monday.

Jerry arrived in the Coachella Valley on the eve of the action, summoned by Chavez to help with last-minute negotiations. Jerry had ignored the urgency in the message, confident that deliberations could wait. Determined not to miss a Lakers playoff game, he stopped at a bar en route and watched his team lose to the Bulls in game six of the Western Conference semifinals. Jerry was driving south from La Paz with Tom Dalzell, the Philadelphia kid who had first arrived at the Delano bus station in the summer of 1968, a high school senior in seersucker jacket and penny loafers. Dalzell had gone back and finished high school, then college. Now he dressed in jeans and T-shirts. The lanky twenty-one-year-old wanted to be a lawyer, and he looked up to Jerry the way others did to Chavez. As they approached the Coachella Valley, a tourist hub with lush golf courses and first-rate resorts, Jerry explained why the strike would be fun. Dalzell took notes: "You can climb up on the canal banks and overlook the whole fields and action, (2) the valley is small enough so that you can get from one field to another easily enough, (3) the cops are political (4) the judges are assholes, (5) it's not too hot yet, and (6) the movies in Palm Springs are good."

Jerry and Dalzell walked into the Reverend Lloyd Saatjian's Methodist church around ten P.M. Jerry feigned surprise when Bill Kircher passed him a note with the final score of the basketball game: Lakers 93, Bulls 101. As Jerry had surmised, he arrived in plenty of time. Chavez was finalizing a deal with the only two growers still talking to the union, Lionel Steinberg and Keene Larson. Jerry joined the negotiations; Dalzell talked music with Steinberg's son. Billy Steinberg had recently graduated from Bard College and formed a band called Billy Thermal, named after his hometown. He wrote poetry and dreamed of being a rock star, but he was learning the family business, just in case. Early Saturday morning Dalzell fell asleep on the floor of the nursery in the Palm Springs church. He awoke to the sound of Jerry yelling. Soon, Steinberg and Larson signed a deal—the only contracts the union kept in the Coachella Valley.[1]

"It is hard to believe that it is happening," Chris wrote to supporters as the union called workers out on strike at twenty-eight ranches.

> The farm workers struggle and sacrifice for five years to make some progress and then the growers and the Teamsters steal the contracts away with a stroke of the pen! This is a painful and worrisome time for Cesar and the Union. But you can't stop a movement that won't stop . . . It is Holy Week: the farm workers are going to jail in Coachella and the struggle for justice is as difficult as ever. Please remember Cesar and the farm workers in all that you do. And join us on the picket line.[2]

In the vineyards of the Coachella Valley, Teamster leaders saw an opportunity to replicate their lucrative collaboration with the Salinas vegetable growers. Grape growers saw the Teamsters as a painless way to keep a union label without sacrificing management prerogatives. Workers were caught in the middle, given no say, their allegiance claimed by all sides.

An avalanche of assaults soon eclipsed the question of which union the workers preferred. The growers were willing to pay to keep their workers in the fields: $67.50 a day for each of the Teamsters' "security personnel." Dozens of large beefy men, covered with tattoos and armed with baseball bats, knives, chains, and clubs, descended on the Coachella fields. They arrived each morning on a flatbed truck the sheriff's deputies called the "Animal Wagon," or A-Wagon for short.[3] They taunted the UFW pickets, screamed epithets, beat up strikers, smashed car windows, and burned trailers.

The violence was not all one-sided. UFW supporters chopped down vines, torched packing sheds, threw rocks and clods of dirt, and occasionally crossed an unwritten line: Attacks on property were unofficially condoned, violence against people was not. Cognizant of Chavez's commitment to nonviolence, UFW allies engaged in covert acts, often at night. But the Teamsters reveled in committing brazen attacks. One morning a Teamster leader broke the nose of a priest as he ate breakfast in a diner with a *Wall Street Journal* reporter.[4]

While the self-proclaimed "Coachella Gorillas" patrolled the fields, the growers opened a second front—in court. Superior Court Judge Fred Metheny didn't bother holding a hearing. He declared the strike a jurisdictional dispute between two unions and ruled that the UFW picket lines were illegal. Infuriated, Jerry prepared to fight back.

On Maundy Thursday, Jerry picked up a bullhorn and addressed hundreds of workers and union supporters massed in the small Coachella park that had become strike headquarters. "Those injunctions are unconstitutional. They're meaningless! They're just useless pieces of paper. They say we don't have the right to strike, but we do have the right to strike. They didn't give us notice before they went into court, and that's unconstitutional." Jerry paused while his remarks were translated into Spanish. "You have to make the decision what you want to do in terms of where you want to picket and how you want to conduct the strike. But as a lawyer, and as a lawyer representing the union, I'm just advising you that those injunctions are worthless!"

"Huelga, huelga, huelga," the crowd shouted.

Jerry passed the bullhorn to Chris. The minister led the crowd in prayer, as earnest as Jerry was enraged. "Today is the very day Jesus was betrayed . . . But Jesus is alive with Cesar, and with you, and with all people everywhere in this world who have decided to give their lives to help other people to be free."[5]

They were ready to violate the injunction. The crowd piled into dozens of cars, then proceeded in a long caravan to the Tenneco vineyard. They defiantly waved flags, then knelt by the side of the fields while deputy sheriffs carried the limp protesters into vans. Chris prayed until he too was arrested, one of 147 that day and 458 the first week of the strike. Dalzell stayed to collect the flags they left behind and rescue a van that was stuck in the sand.[6]

On Good Friday, Judge Metheny realized that Jerry was right. Metheny had erred in issuing the injunction without giving the union notice. He tried to rectify the mistake by letting the prisoners go. The judge went from one holding tank in the jail to the next, asking protesters to sign papers so they could be released. Jerry followed him, shouting "I object!" every time Metheny opened his mouth. To sign anything, Jerry argued, would be to acknowledge an illegal order. The prisoners chanted and cheered from behind bars, and Jerry played to the crowd.

Captain Cois Byrd heard Jerry before he met him, the lawyer's indignant bellows echoing from one end of the jail to the other. Byrd was the Riverside County deputy sheriff charged with keeping the peace in the Coachella Valley. He was a square-jawed, thirty-four-year-old ex-Marine devoted to law enforcement. But the Riverside native also understood something about the fields and about what it meant to be poor. As a child, he had accompanied his mother when she sneaked out of the house to make ends meet by picking grapes. Now Byrd juggled work with studies, finishing up a master's degree in public administration at the University of Southern California. He had just been promoted to captain and had barely settled in as commander of the Indio substation when the strike began.

Overnight, he found himself running an operation on a scale no one in his department had ever handled: mass arrests, national media, busloads of protesters, an armed war between Teamster goons and UFW zealots. Even the logistics of feeding more than one hundred deputies out in the fields all day, six days a week, became a challenge. Byrd requested Abba-Zaba bars, his favorite candy because the caramel and peanut butter confection didn't melt in the triple-degree heat. Sometimes focusing on the mundane kept Byrd's mind off his real worry: whether he could get through the summer without a major disaster. The day he first met Jerry, screaming in the jail, Byrd realized he would be spending a lot of time in court. He needed to understand the laws he was supposed to enforce.

Jerry emerged from the courthouse that afternoon victorious. "Even Clarence Darrow couldn't get three hundred and twelve dismissals in one day," he quipped. Then he turned serious. "The farmworkers won a terrific victory today because all of the workers who were arrested for violating the court order were freed and the charges against them were dismissed. That's because the order was unconstitutional."[7]

The judge had even taken aim at the Teamsters with what Jerry dubbed the goon clause: "No person shall threaten either workers or pickets with guns, knives, lead pipes, baseball bats, billy clubs, grape stakes or other dangerous instruments."[8]

As Jerry explained the victory, he shouted to be heard over the back-

A UFW picket gestures as he talks to Teamsters, who stand guard outside a Coachella vineyard to block the union from talking to workers in the field. (UCLA Charles E. Young Research Library Department of Special Collections, Los Angeles Times Photographic Archives, Copyright © Regents of the University of California, UCLA)

drop of rival chants. A line of Teamsters was sandwiched between the workers in the field and the flag-waving *huelgistas* in the road. Each side tried to drown out the other. "Chavez sí, Teamsters no." "Teamsters sí, Chavez no." The union pickets gained the upper hand when they began to sing one of their anthems, "Solidaridad Pa' Siempre," some singing the Spanish verses the union wrote, others singing in English:

> Solidarity forever,
> Solidarity forever,
> Solidarity forever,
> For the union makes us strong

Eliseo

Eliseo stood on top of a car, five foot nine but a commanding presence. On the road in front of him, triumphant picketers mingled with dozens of workers who had just dropped their tools and walked out of the Karahadian vineyard. In the field, two dozen workers still trimmed vines. Eliseo rallied the crowd with clear instructions: Persuade the holdouts with words, not threats or violence. He directed each picket to zoom in on one specific worker and make the case for the strike. Then he climbed down and led the charge, the picketers clustering in small groups around each worker. The guerrilla tactic overwhelmed the supervisors. By the time the sheriffs arrived, the field was shut down.[9]

Week One, and already the battle of Coachella was taking its place in union lore. Boycotters, union leaders, and volunteers from around the country converged in the desert valley. A few busloads of workers came from Salinas, calling themselves the Division del Norte after Pancho Villa's revolutionary army. The fight was starkly defined in black and white, the unity as uplifting as the loss of the contracts was catastrophic. Eliseo soaked up the solidarity—on the picket lines, at the evening rallies, and during a brief stay in jail. But just as during the Salinas strike, he was back in the California fields only long enough to be told that the most important job was in the cities. Chavez reactivated the boycott and assigned Eliseo to Cleveland.

So less than two weeks into the strike, Eliseo flew home to Florida and prepared to move yet again. Over the past year he had expanded the union's presence in Florida beyond the Coca-Cola contract. He organized striking sugar cane workers, publicized slave labor conditions and a typhoid epidemic, then masterminded an improbable victory in the state capital. The agricultural industry had introduced a law that would cripple the union's ability to organize. Florida labor leaders advised Eliseo to lobby for a weaker measure. He opted instead to try to kill the bill. He barraged legislative leaders with letters and staged gripping testimony in a House committee meeting from an orange picker who had been imprisoned in a slave gang. The bill died. Eliseo gained his first taste of navigating in the political world. When he returned from the Coachella strike, Eliseo packed up and took his staff with him to Ohio, shuttering the union's expansion into Florida.

In Cleveland, Eliseo took familiar steps. He made a list of "key friends in labor" and wrote each one asking for support. He contacted religious leaders, researched local supermarkets, and recruited volunteers. The Watergate hearings were on TV, but almost no one in the UFW office watched. Within a month, Eliseo had opened four boycott offices around Ohio, held a statewide conference to educate volunteers, and worked with local bishops to set up interfaith committees. He divided Cleveland into five sectors. "We haven't moved as fast as I would have liked to," he reported in a letter to La Paz. "To a large degree we have had to start from scratch as far as getting pickets out to help us. Lots of sympathy, but few people willing to walk the lines with us. And we don't need all that sympathy if we don't have the pickets."[10]

By the end of June, as the Coachella harvest was winding down, Eliseo organized his first big fund-raiser. He worried nobody would show up. With relief, he saw a full house in the St. John's College auditorium when he peeked from backstage. "There's a very serious situation developing in the Coachella Valley in California," Eliseo somberly told the audience of almost eight hundred. "To a large degree, what happens here is going to decide the future for farm workers throughout this country." The issue was not a simple dispute between two unions, he said. He spoke his appeal slowly, pausing as if to choose his words with great care, though he had delivered virtually the same speech many times. "To me, what's at stake here is whether farm workers are ever going to get the right to live and work as free men and women. The issue here, is one again, of social justice."

Then his demeanor changed entirely. He scolded the audience gently for not cheering loudly enough. He told them they didn't know how to clap, and that they'd better get organized or he'd lose his job. And where could he find a job that paid five dollars a week plus room and board? He taught them to shout back *"¡Viva Chavez!"* the way he had first shouted on Mexican Independence Day in 1965 in the Delano church. Then he taught them the rhythmic farmworker clap: starting slow and quiet and building, faster and faster. Like waves that begin small far from shore and crash on the beach, he said. An unstoppable force. It was one of his standard lines. "You have to be organized to be able to face the kind of opposition that we're facing. And so the farm workers are organized even when they clap."

Eliseo introduced Cindy and Chuck, the Huelga Troubadours, and the two boycotters sang "Which Side Are You On?" Finally Eliseo brought on stage the featured guest, Cesar Chavez. The union leader reported that two days ago the temperature had reached 121 on the picket line in Coachella. The goons had moved into the San Joaquin Valley, where they beat UFW pickets the day before with pipes and baseball bats, injuring fourteen and sending four to the hospital. Juan Hernandez, sixty-seven, was hit in the head with a lead pipe; a seventeen-year-old boy had two ribs broken by a baseball bat.

The strike had an upside, though, Chavez said. In 1970 the growers had signed contracts because of the boycott, not the strike. "We've learned that there's a great difference between a member who has never been on the picket line and had a contract handed to him and a member that had to fight for his contract," Chavez said. ". . . The attitudes are very different. Many of the people who are striking today never had the opportunity to win a strike for themselves because we haven't had a way to have them survive while they were striking." This time would be different. With a strike fund, he said, he would win. "I have never seen love develop among human beings as I do on the picket line."[11]

Chris

Chris knew that if he could just get church leaders to Coachella to see that love, the Teamsters would take care of the rest. With the help of his friend John Moyer, Chris pulled off a coup that would be talked about for decades.

Two time zones away from the picket lines, two thousand delegates and visitors gathered in St. Louis for the Ninth General Synod of the United Church of Christ. The farmworker strike was a last-minute starter on the Assembly's agenda of urgent crises, joining the Watergate scandal and the bombing of Cambodia. Chris expected support from the denomination and particularly from Moyer, a minister in the church and staunch ally. But Chris was taken aback when Moyer called from St. Louis: The religious delegates were debating not whether to help but how. One suggested they charter a 747 to take the whole Assembly. Others preferred to donate the $25,000 that a trip would cost, arguing Chavez needed money more than visitors. Chris didn't bother checking with Chavez. Send the people, he told Moyer.

A chartered DC-9 left St. Louis late on Sunday, June 24, with ninety-five religious leaders aboard. They landed at the Ontario airport, east of Los Angeles, in the middle of the night, took three buses to the desert, and arrived at the Coachella park around four A.M. Dozens of farmworkers swarmed around the guests, hugging the religious delegates and ushering them to the small platform on the bandshell. The sleepless clergy heard about the clash the day before between UFW supporters and Teamsters with iron pipes, clubs, tire irons, and machetes. Chris watched with satisfaction as those who had been sent from St. Louis to make "objective reports" lost any pretense of objectivity before they even left the park. Chris split the visitors into small groups and sent them to the picket lines along with about 750 union supporters. Captain Cois Byrd had received intelligence that Teamsters intended to escalate attacks, so sheriff's deputies traveled along with each group.

One caravan was headed south on Highway 111 around five A.M. when another group of cars merged in. The strikers assumed the cars carried more UFW supporters. Suddenly one car turned to block the road. Teamsters emerged, surrounded a tan Chevy truck owned by Salvador Ochoa, pulled two strikers out and bashed their heads with baseball bats. A Teamster kicked one of the men as he lay on the ground semiconscious. As sheriff's deputies reached Ochoa's truck, they saw Gundar Hansen smashing the back window with a baseball bat, while two women huddled on the backseat.

Hansen, six foot five and 350 pounds, relished a physical fight the way Jerry savored verbal battle. Hansen had been running the local on the Long Beach docks before the Western Conference of Teamsters sent him to Coachella. He had gone out to the desert with a few hundred of the biggest guys he could find. Hansen was an adventurer who rode away from his Philadelphia home on a 1946 Indian Chief motorcycle when he turned eighteen, sailed ships around the world, and ended up working for the Teamsters. He believed in the Teamsters, and he believed that decent wages and pensions were all that really mattered to the average farmworker. His mission was clear: Scare off the college kids and hippies who harassed and threatened the people they called scabs, workers who just wanted to make a living. Hansen was proud of his work, unrepentant, and unperturbed when deputies arrested him for assaulting the UFW caravan.[12]

Shaken, the clergy regrouped in the Coachella park after witnessing the confrontation. Chris drove home his message. "Some of you were involved in some very, very heavy stuff," he said, describing the attack on Highway 111. "Some of you saw that. And some of us met them as they were on their way to the hospital." Chris urged them to share their experiences on the trip back to St. Louis.

Chavez asked Chris for a prayer, and the Reverend W. Sterling Cary obliged. "Oh God, we confess that there are experiences in our world which deny and contradict the intent of thy creation," prayed the president of the National Council of Churches. "May the day quickly come when even the Safeway chain corporation shall say no to the Teamsters and yes to the farm workers union. Bless their leader, Cesar Chavez. May he not grow weary in well doing."[13]

Chavez thanked the large group for making the long journey. He echoed Chris's plea that they spread the word about the battle of Coachella and the conspiracy between the Teamsters and the growers to steal the contracts away. He talked about the silver lining; a new cadre of strikers, bewildered by the confrontation but growing strong in the process. "A month and a half ago, a month ago, a week ago, people on the picket line hadn't been in a strike before," he said. "And they're now striking and they're being asked to change their lives radically and to make this very difficult commitment to nonviolence. So your presence here is important and very helpful."

"We are here trying to say to the farmworkers who are on strike that you are not alone, you are not forgotten, that your battle, your struggle is our struggle," the Reverend Cary responded. "It is the struggle of America itself, as America tries to find ways to be on the side of those who are locked out of the system."[14]

Chris was so consumed with logistics that the magnitude of the visit did not sink in until much later. Moyer's group returned to St. Louis less than forty-eight hours after they left. Tired, dirty, and sweaty, they burst triumphantly into the synod on its final day and reported on what they had witnessed. When they returned home, the "Coachella 95" formed a network of UFW support groups across the country.

The Teamsters made it so easy for Chris. He never had to explain why so many workers stayed in the fields, or why many of those arrested on the picket line came from out of town. He didn't have to address problems with the old contracts, unhappiness with the hiring hall, and the concerns that Richard Chavez had flagged two years earlier. Chris didn't have to make the case that farmworkers really wanted the UFW and the union was a victim. Gundar Hansen and the Teamster goons did that for him.

Chris went out on the Coachella picket lines with Moyer on one other occasion. They arrived just in time to see UFW supporters throw clods of dirt and rocks at cars taking workers to the fields, an operation orchestrated by Marshall Ganz. Chris was stunned, not so naïve as to be unaware such things happened but surprised by Ganz's arrogance in conducting the maneuver in front of religious supporters. Chris castigated Ganz for stupidity: Don't you realize these church supporters actually believe that you believe in nonviolence? Moyer was dismayed, but not dissuaded. The incident was one of the rare times Chris allowed himself to recognize that the strike was more complicated than the story he told.

Sandy

Sandy harbored fewer illusions than most about the purity of the union. For Sandy, the farmworker movement was not a romantic summer adventure or an instant community, not a substitute family or a place to practice servanthood. The union was a vehicle that enabled the child of the '60s to meld his legal skills with his inchoate political desires. For Sandy, the union was a place to make change.

His early efforts to document dead bugs in Safeway cookies and pesticide on lettuce paled next to the urgent quest to overturn injunctions and document violence on the picket lines. In Coachella, Sandy plunged into an emotional ground war, surrounded for the first time by farmworkers. At the Friday night rallies he gamely used pidgin Spanish for walk-on parts in skits that poked fun at the powerful enemies, to lessen workers' fear. His six-foot-one frame got him cast as a Teamster goon, though he was long-haired, lean, and lacked tattoos. *Yo soy un Timster*, Sandy said his first time on stage in the little bandshell in the Coachella park. After the skit he reverted back to *el abogado* and presented a report every week, even when there was not much new, just to show workers they had lawyers on their side. Each time Sandy forced Judge Metheny to back down or sprang picketers from jail, workers saw the power of the union.

On Memorial Day weekend the union planned a dance and rally in Indio, the date capital of the country. Indio was adjacent to Coachella and twice the size, home to the sprawling Riverside County Fairgrounds. When Sandy applied to hold the dance in the Arab-motif buildings on the fairgrounds, county officials denied the permit. Writing by hand because he couldn't find a typewriter late Friday afternoon, Sandy drafted an appeal and scrambled to find a judge who would hear the case before the holiday weekend. Sandy ended up before a municipal judge who gave him a hearing but denied the appeal. Chavez was delighted. He said he would take the first dance with his wife and get arrested. Don't bail me out, he told Sandy. As the party began, Cesar and Helen Chavez took to the floor and danced a slow dance, and the police wisely decided not to interfere.

At twenty-eight, Sandy was one of the older union staff. He didn't quite share the Chavez worship that was so prevalent. Sandy had seen Chavez inspire crowds but had not yet had much personal contact. Sandy's first close encounter with Chavez made a lasting impression.

Sandy and a few of the sisters who had become full-time volunteers sat talking in the Coachella strike office at the end of the day, weary from the relentless pace and frightened by the Teamsters' violence. Chavez walked into the small storefront in the strip mall. He launched into a tirade about their phone bills, cursing profusely in front of the nuns. Here he was, groveling with labor leaders in Washington to raise donations for a strike fund, while the union staff wasted money on phone calls.

Sandy found the outburst so incongruous he almost laughed. Any romanticized notions of Chavez evaporated. He was a leader, a symbol, a useful tool, and in the end, as the phone-bill tirade demonstrated, very human. The world of the UFW cleaved into those drawn by the man and those attracted to the cause. With the union at war, that distinction blurred almost entirely. The diatribe over phone bills in the midst of so many real crises reminded Sandy that the man and the movement sometimes diverged. For Sandy, the cause always transcended its leader.

Sandy's life settled into routines amid the chaos. He ditched his MG convertible, its floor full of used tissues because his allergies were so bad, and bought a more practical Dodge caravan. He lived in the van for a while. Then he moved into a run-down apartment infested with ants and cockroaches—and invariably crowded with volunteers crashing on the floor. He grew to rely on his sidekick, Tom Dalzell, whom Sandy nicknamed the Dazzler. The Dazzler woke before four each morning to mariachi music on the radio, headed to the park where the strikers met, then joined a caravan to a picket line. He took declarations to document Teamster violence, wrote affidavits, typed interrogatories, and kept track of clerical details for Sandy. More important, the Dazzler became Sandy's guide to the organization he had joined less than six months earlier. The Dazzler was only twenty-one, but his romance with the union had begun when he was a teen. He had vacuumed up information for five years; now his knowledge and political acumen helped Sandy navigate.

Each week ended with a Friday night rally, where Sandy often appealed to the workers for help. "It looks like the things that the Teamsters are doing best right now are breaking a lot of windows," he told the crowd in the park in late June. "Every time that it happens to anybody, I want you to contact the law student that's on your picket line or come into the office so we can write it down and keep track of it." He asked them to look for crates of grapes illegally shipped out with the union label. And he asked them to report workers illegally crossing from Mexico and working as scabs. "We need your help if we're going to stop it," Sandy said, as Chavez translated the message into Spanish. "If you know something about a smuggler, or about some illegals, let us know. Let the picket captain know or let the law student know or let me know, and we'll try to get the border patrol out there."[15]

Chavez consistently blamed "illegals" for the union's failure to win

Sandy Nathan speaks at a Friday night rally in Coachella, while the tape recorder runs and Chavez talks in the background with Marshall Ganz.

strikes. But many times he also expressed confidence that with a strike fund, he could win. In May the AFL-CIO had provided one: $1.6 million. The union offered seventy dollars a week in strike benefits, then upped it to ninety dollars. Still, they had to bus in workers from Salinas and the San Joaquin Valley and students from Los Angeles and the Bay Area to supplement the picket lines. The UFW strikers were fervent but only a small percentage of the workforce. The strike created confusion and violence and cost the growers money. Poor weather caused a significantly delayed harvest with inferior-quality grapes. But the total harvest was only slightly below normal, and the strike did not come close to shutting down the fields.

By mid-July the short season in Coachella was all but over and the strike was moving north. Sandy shaved his beard and did his Mick Jagger imitation at the going-away party he and the Dazzler hosted for the summer law students. In a last hurrah, Sandy filed a class-action lawsuit against the Teamsters and twenty-seven Coachella grape growers, seeking $45 million in damages for union members and volunteers injured during the strike. He also filed thirteen personal-injury suits, asking for another $3 million. The suits alleged that the Teamsters' campaign of terror, orchestrated with the encouragement of the growers, was "designed to ultimately destroy the collective economic and consequent political strength of the UFWU and thereby force them into a life of poverty, deprivation, humiliation and powerlessness."[16]

Captain Cois Byrd watched the caravan of cars leave the Coachella Valley, surprised at his own mixed emotions. He felt enormous relief that life could go back to normal. The department had spent half a million dollars, more than half in overtime alone—the largest law enforcement job in the history of the Coachella Valley.[17] From that first encounter with Jerry and Judge Metheny in the jail, Byrd had been in court for every hearing. The judge came to rely on the captain; by the time Byrd returned to his office, Metheny was usually on the phone for a private consultation. Byrd clandestinely took the judge out to see the picket lines for himself.

Byrd had observed Chavez only from a distance—the UFW president would never attend meetings with the sheriff—and noted his quiet charisma. He walks on air, Byrd's deputy said, as they watched him at a rally. When Chavez was around, the UFW supporters never gave the sheriff any trouble. Even in his absence their restraint was admirable, and their misdeeds paled against the Teamsters' reckless acts. The captain had come to respect and even like Jerry and Sandy, the one loud and dramatic, the other quiet and serious, both so clearly invested in their work. Byrd and the union attorneys argued on the picket lines during the day, but at night everyone ended up drinking together at the Date Tree Motel in Indio. Byrd had learned in the Marines that you could do more than you thought, but he emerged from the summer with a different kind of confidence. He had survived car bombs, arsons, and armed confrontations and earned sometimes-grudging praise from all sides for keeping the peace. No one could ever throw anything at Byrd that would faze him after that. Chavez instilled in his people a liberating sense of fearlessness, the conviction they could take on anything. In an odd twist, the farmworkers' battle in the summer of 1973 delivered the same gift to Cois Byrd.

CHAPTER 11

Fill the Jails

July 1973

Jerry

Unlike most people in the union, Jerry always carved out a life. He made time to play with his kids, follow sports, and read novels. He quit smoking on June 29, after watching one of the Teamster leaders chain-smoke through a deposition. The asshole is killing himself, Jerry thought, then realized he was doing the same thing. Now he was trying to lose weight. The six-foot-one lawyer was down to 220 pounds by July 8, he noted in his *Playboy* datebook. He took his son to his first hockey game, taught his daughter to play chess, and followed Hank Aaron's pursuit of Babe Ruth's home run record. In between work, while the strike raged, Jerry tackled James Joyce's *Finnegans Wake* and Jane Austen's *Emma*. On the second weekend of the Coachella strike, Jerry left Chavez a note saying he was off to get supplies. Jerry drove with the Dazzler to a movie theater eighty miles away to watch *McCabe and Mrs. Miller*. For the fifth time. Warren Beatty's portrayal of the dashing negotiator who ultimately overplays his hand was Jerry's favorite film.[1]

In July the strike moved north, away from Cois Byrd's even-handed justice and into the hostile San Joaquin Valley, where the power of the agricultural establishment permeated the cops and courts. Law enforcement officials were openly sympathetic to the growers. Judges granted multiple injunctions against picket lines. Police beat protesters. "All summer long the police have used excessive force," Jerry declared angrily. ". . . Because the police here are racist, and if you have someone they're dealing with who has a different color skin from them, they beat the hell out of them. That's the kind of justice they mete out here in Kern County."[2]

Jerry responded with a novel legal gambit. A few years earlier California's highest court had heard the case of Colin Scott Berry, a college student who demonstrated in support of striking county workers. He was arrested for violating an antipicketing order. The court overturned his conviction, ruling that the injunction Berry broke was an unconstitutional infringement of his right to free speech.[3] Jerry grasped the implications of *In re Berry* immediately: You could prove an injunction unconstitutional by deliberately violating the order. The strategy required a keen legal mind, because a loss put you in contempt of court. But a victory would overturn bad rulings with dramatic flair, far faster than pursuing lengthy appeals. A lawyer who appeared frequently before a local judge might think twice before accusing that judge of acting unconstitutionally. UFW attorneys had no such compunctions. Union leaders began orchestrating demonstrations to violate injunctions that limited pickets in the San Joaquin Valley.

Jerry still hoped that the union could keep the bulk of its grape contracts by reaching agreement with the Delano growers. The contracts did not expire until the end of July. Negotiating a deal in the vineyards where the union had started became Jerry's priority, a goal he assumed that Chavez shared. Jerry's talks with the Delano growers had convinced him that they wanted to avert a strike or boycott.

Martin Zaninovich did not want to endure the economic pressure of the boycott or the emotional turmoil of another strike. Hostilities from the last one still scarred the small city of Delano. His son Jon, born just weeks before the 1965 strike began, was finishing third grade. But Jon no longer attended St. Mary's Catholic School. The diocese had recently adopted a new catechism that included passages on Cesar Chavez. Jon's mother was ousted as president of the school board after she refused to use the new text. The growers began their own catechism class in Slav Hall, and Jon enrolled in public school. Zaninovich was eager to avoid another open conflict in the fields. But like the other Delano growers, he could no longer live with the UFW hiring hall. The lost time and money added up. Chavez had said everything was on the table, and Zaninovich hoped for an accommodation.

Jerry met with the Delano growers as often as four times a week. He felt he was making progress. At Chavez's request, John Giumarra Jr. had brought almost the entire industry together to attempt a master contract. Giumarra urged quick negotiations, warning that the Teamsters were "a spreading cancer." The growers wanted more control over who worked in their fields; the Teamsters' Coachella contracts complicated that exigency. The UFW wanted to deny jobs in the Delano vineyards to those who had worked under Teamster contracts in Coachella—scabs, in the union's view.[4]

The hiring hall and the union's right to determine who were members in good standing—thus eligible to work—emerged as key stumbling blocks. But after a July 19 meeting alone with Giumarra, Jerry thought he was close to an agreement.[5] He had ten days left. On July 24 hundreds of workers at a Delano rally voted by acclamation to authorize a strike if the contracts were not renewed. "We're far apart on some issues, but the point is, I think, we're meeting and there's an outside chance," Jerry told the crowd. He exhorted the workers to demonstrate visible support for the union. "I think really whether we get a contract or not depends on how strong we are as union members and how much strength we can show the growers."[6]

Jerry and Chavez often played a good-cop–bad-cop routine during negotiations. Jerry was the Anglo lawyer who joked about baseball and talked their language. Chavez could turn without warning from humble, soft-spoken organizer to rabid Chicano activist. He aimed tirades at his strongest supporters, like Lionel Steinberg, playing off their liberal guilt. After a Chavez outburst, Jerry would come back as the reasonable guy with whom the growers thought they could deal. Jerry and Chavez laughed about how it worked every time.

But during negotiations the night before the Delano contracts expired, Chavez left his own lawyer as mystified as the opposition. Jerry and the growers were prepared to work all night to close a deal. Jerry was so confident that he called the Dazzler and told him to bring typewriters to the Bakersfield Ramada Inn; they would need to type up contract language. During the meeting Jerry worked through the contract clause by clause. Shortly after midnight he came to the housing section, and Chavez interrupted. He began to berate the growers for allowing whores, gambling, and cockfights in the camps where workers lived. "We have a responsibility to the membership to change the quality of life," Chavez said. "There's a hell of a lot of gambling that results in fights and deaths. The foremen make money from controlling gambling, chicken fights, prostitutes . . . You must destroy the camps be-cause they are used to break strikes. When people have their minds on gam-bling, they don't think about the union."[7]

Jerry was so frustrated by the whores-in-the-camp tirade that he sat there making lists of all-star baseball teams where the players' names all started with the same letter. M was best. Mantle, Mays, Musial, Marichal.

The negotiations collapsed. The union lost all its remaining contracts in the table grapes. They were back on strike, eight years after the historic Delano grape strike, in the same vineyards.

Jerry was shaken. He had thought keeping the contracts was of para-mount importance, and he was sure he could have closed a deal. But Chavez had a different agenda. Sandy was there later when Jerry turned his acerbic wit on his boss. Jerry told Chavez that if he wanted to commit suicide, he should stand on the capitol steps, pour the pesticide parathion on his head, and twitch to death. At least he would be making a point.

Chris

Chris paced expectantly in the early morning darkness of a small San Joaquin Valley park, less than twenty-four hours after the Delano con-tracts had expired. For years he had nurtured a network of supporters who found meaning in their own lives by helping farmworkers through the boycott. Now he called on them to do even more. He called on them to bear witness.

He spotted a few familiar faces arriving in the park. Rosemary Cooper-rider, whose Palo Alto home had become a haven for boycotters in search of a home-cooked meal, a free phone, or a bed. But the large group Chris awaited was a bus full of strangers: eighty-five priests, nuns, and seminar-ians from around the country who were attending an Ignatian spirituality conference in San Francisco. A Bay Area priest and union stalwart had called to ask how the Jesuits might help. Come to the fields, Chris said. Tomorrow, at five thirty A.M.

Now he stood before them as the sun rose and briefed the group. There would be two picket lines: One would protest in accordance with the in-junctions and go home that night. The other would deliberately violate the restrictions and end up in jail. The goal was to fill the jails and help Jerry overturn the antipicketing injunctions by proving them unconstitu-tional. Chris estimated Fresno County might take three days at most to process and release the prisoners.

The church people had come to California expecting to reflect on Jesuit principles in the quiet of a San Francisco university. Instead they found themselves confronting the battle between good and evil at dawn in a Selma park. The caravans were leaving within minutes. Chris told the delegation each person had to make a choice. More than half volunteered to go to jail, most for the first time in their lives.

Chris's longtime supporters did not think twice about which picket line to choose. Cooperrider came to the park prepared. When Chris had asked her to bring a carload to Selma, she called three friends, then made her list: sleeping bag, camera, hat, toilet articles, postcards, stamps, reading material, change of clothes, Huelga buttons, knitting, and a flag that had been gathering dust in her church's belfry. Cooperrider was a preacher's daughter with a visceral feeling for farmworkers rooted in more than her Christian principles. During the Depression her father had left his Washington parsonage and gone to work cutting celery and spinach in the San Joaquin Valley to support his family. Three decades later, Rosemary Cooperrider met Chris.

On Tuesday, July 31, she was in the park by five thirty A.M. and on the picket line outside a nectarine orchard at six thirty. Three hours later she had been booked, fingerprinted, and strip-searched, along with the religious delegation. By the end of the day, more than two hundred farmworkers, priests, nuns, and supporters filled dank cells in the Fresno County jail, the surplus spilling over to the honor farm. The nuns strung blankets around the toilet. They all scrawled "Huelga" across their green jail uniforms.[8]

On Wednesday, Chavez visited the jail after lunch, climbed on a chair, and thanked the prisoners for their sacrifice. The judge was refusing to release them on the grounds that many lived out of town and might not return to court. Chavez vowed to bilk county taxpayers for as long as possible.[9]

On Thursday, Chris began nervously making long-distance phone calls to worried relatives. He had promised the priests and nuns they would be out in three days. He felt reassured by the camaraderie developing inside the jail. The religious folk were absorbed in conversations with farmworkers. The more they learned, the greater their outrage. Soon they began a solidarity fast. Excitement increased when the newest wave of prisoners included Dorothy Day, who had flown from New York to Fresno just to get arrested. All the women signed the gown of the founder of the Catholic Worker Movement.

On Friday, Chris drafted a letter to the chairman of Safeway, blaming the company for the strike. He signed the names of sixty religious leaders currently residing in the Fresno County jail. "Those with power and influence in our society have failed to exercise their corporate moral responsibility to assist the most oppressed people of our society, the farmworkers, achieve their just rights," the letter read. "For this reason, we the undersigned religious people have chosen to join our struggling farm worker brothers and sisters in their challenge of an injunction which is clearly a grave infringement of their constitutional rights of free speech and free assembly."[10]

As the week wore on, the jailers made an exception and allowed men and women to worship together. Priests provided daily updates during mass about the recently exposed bombing in Cambodia, which Congress had ordered President Nixon to halt. Daniel Ellsberg visited, and Joan Baez sang in the prison yard.

A week after the arrests Chris was out in the Selma park again at five A.M., dispatching a new group to violate injunctions. Then he headed to the Fresno jail and began a vigil while the union lawyers went to court. Once again, the judge refused to release the protesters. Jerry argued that the court's action constituted arbitrary punishment without proof of guilt. He finally prevailed on appeal. Two weeks after they had entered jail, the priests and nuns walked out to chants of "Huelga" and "Chavez sí, Teamsters no," and celebrated a victory mass on the lawn outside the jail.

More than thirty-five hundred arrests across the San Joaquin Valley during the summer of 1973 did nothing to directly help win the strike. But the civil disobedience boosted union morale, publicized the boycott, and raised money. The union collected $300,000 in donations in July, a record for a single month.[11]

"Hundreds of people began to care in a personal way about the suffering of farm workers because they care about you and learned that you were willing to go to jail with striking farm workers," Chris wrote the delegates from the Jesuit spirituality conference.[12] He apologized profusely for having misled them into thinking they would be out in a few days. But no one complained. They told Chris the two weeks ranked among the most moving times of their lives. The gripes came from those who had opted for the picket line that obeyed the injunctions. They had been forced to make the decision too fast, they grumbled to Chris.

Police in Kern County subdue, club, and arrest UFW pickets, including teenager Marta Rodriguez, who walked out of the Giumarra vineyard during the protest. (© 1978 Bob Fitch/Take Stock)

Chris saw the saga as a modern parable, and he loved to tell the story: The people who played it safe, unwilling to risk arrest, ended up feeling cheated and angry. Those willing to sacrifice emerged from the ordeal enriched, certain that the experience had changed their lives.

CHAPTER 12

The New Union

September 1973

Eliseo

The call came from the leader of the lechugeros at Interharvest: The nominating committee had tapped Eliseo to run for a spot on the first executive board of the United Farm Workers of America. Eliseo was honored to be on the official slate, though not entirely clear what the commitment entailed.

Eliseo arrived at the union's Constitutional Convention as the Cleveland boycott delegate, one of 352 representatives of ranches, boycott cities, and union offices who gathered in the cavernous Fresno hall. Jessica Govea came back from the Montreal boycott, bringing a contingent of Canadian supporters. Ruth Shy was a delegate from Philadelphia, where she had taken charge of the boycott. Ellen drove from Los Angeles with a group of boycotters. Sandy came from La Paz, exhausted from six months of fighting, lonely with everyone out on the boycott. The Dazzler arrived at three A.M., just a few hours before the convention opened, with five hundred copies of the constitution that he had helped collate on deadline at La Paz.

The UFW's new charter from the AFL-CIO marked a significant shift in status, elevating the farmworkers from a committee that operated without formal rules or structure, under the umbrella of the national federation. The delegates needed to adopt a constitution and elect a board to complete the transition to full-fledged union. The mood was ebullient,

despite the union's somewhat perilous state. The new union had only ten
contracts and a handful of dues-paying members. They depended on donations and a generous subsidy from the United Auto Workers, which had
been contributing $10,000 a week since the Coachella strike began.[1]
Chavez had exhausted the $1.6 million strike fund from the AFL-CIO and
then burned through another $1.1 million; the union was no closer to win-
ning back contracts lost to the Teamsters.[2] Two workers had been killed in
strike-related violence just weeks before the convention, one shot on a
picket line. Chavez used the deaths to call off the strike.

Now the union president stood at the podium, dwarfed by a twenty-
four-by-sixty-foot mural commissioned for the event.[3] In the style of the
great Mexican artists, the painting depicted the Teamsters' brutal assault on
a UFW picket line. "The forces of evil threw caution out the window and
determined that our union should not exist," Chavez declared in his opening address to the historic assembly. He denounced the Nixon administration, the Teamsters, and the growers for conspiring to take away the union's
contracts.[4] In English and in Spanish, Chavez quoted the carefully crafted
preamble to the new constitution:

> We, the Farm Workers of America, have tilled the soil, sown the
> seeds and harvested the crops. We have provided food in abun-
> dance for the people in the cities, the nation and the world but
> have not had sufficient food for our children . . . We devoutly be-
> lieve in the dignity of tilling the soil and tending the crops and re-
> ject the notion that farm labor is but a way station to a job in the
> factory and life in the city. And just as work on the land is ardu-
> ous, so is the task of building a Union. We pledge to struggle as
> long as it takes to reach our goals.

Chavez had carefully balanced his selections for the first UFW board:
"All colors, all shapes, all sizes, Mexicanos, Filipinos, a Black brother, a
Jew, woman—all," he proclaimed.[5] Two had never been farmworkers; five
others had worked at jobs outside the fields before joining the union staff.
The mix did not sit well with a group of Mexican farmworkers who had
manned picket lines and boycott cities since the strike began. They felt
workers were getting short shrift on the Chavez slate and decided to
nominate competing candidates—Mexicans who had come directly out
of the fields. The organizers of the opposition had known Eliseo since the
start of the Delano strike; they, too, asked him to join their slate. Eliseo

believed, as Chavez often said, that the union should be run by farm-workers. Eliseo perceived no conflict in being on both slates and readily agreed to join his friends.

The farmworker slate targeted Marshall Ganz, who had been asked by Chavez to run for the board. Suddenly Eliseo found himself dropped from Chavez's team. The Dazzler typed the new list: In Eliseo's place was Esther Uranday, an early Chavista.[6] Finally Chavez's cousin Manuel, who often functioned as a deal broker, took Ganz and Eliseo out into the hall to nego-tiate. You can be on one slate or the other, he told Eliseo. That choice was easy. Eliseo had stumbled due to political naïveté, never viewing himself as anything but utterly loyal. He withdrew from the challengers' slate and went back on the Chavez team.

All the opposition candidates except one withdrew, but the delegates engaged in a robust nominating process. "Eliseo Medina was one of the first strikers with Cesar Chavez, and when Cesar Chavez would go around to the boycott, he would tell us that Eliseo Medina was the champion of the boycotters in Chicago," said Epifanio Camacho, one of the original Delano strikers. "And it is for that reason that we know exactly who Eliseo Medina is. We know him through Cesar and we know his merits." The delegate from White River Farms seconded Eliseo's nomination: "He is 100 percent farm worker who came out of the fields of Delano."

The older board members included those who had been with the union from the beginning—Chavez, his brother Richard, Dolores Huerta, Gilbert Padilla, and two of the Filipino leaders, Philip Vera Cruz and Pete Velasco. Eliseo, Ganz, and Mack Lyons, a black union staff member who had been a tractor driver at DiGiorgio, were the younger group.

It was late at night by the time Chris administered the oath of office, asking God to help the new officers: "May they be blessed with strength and wisdom and courage. And may we, dear God, keep learning from each other that the best thing that we could do with our lives is to give them for our brothers and sisters in the struggle for justice." The hall rang with shouts and applause.

Eliseo took his copy of the oath of office and asked each new board member to autograph the piece of paper. He wrote the date and time, one A.M., September 23, and asked another worker to witness the signatures. Then he tucked the document carefully away with his other memorabilia—newspaper clips, the stock certificate from Jewel, and all his UFW member-ship cards, from the very first one issued on that September day in 1965 when he broke open his piggy bank.

In the Salinas fields, where Sabino Lopez worked as an irrigator under the only union contract, the delegates returned from Fresno full of stories about the weekend. His friend told Sabino how the delegates had debated point by point. And he told him about the young farmworker, born in Mexico, who had been elected to the board. He is a future leader, Sabino's friend said. He is one of us.

Chris

The convention felt as momentous to Chris as it did to Eliseo. Like each of the speakers, Chris entered the hall escorted by an honor guard of farm-workers, almost two dozen marching in a double line, waving UFW flags as the audience rhythmically stomped its feet and clapped. The entrance matched Chris's sense of the historic occasion.

Chavez introduced Chris as a member of the family. "I have asked him at least a million times, if not more, to help me on the problems that we have—on the day-to-day problems. He has *never* said no. But such is the respect for the Farm Workers Movement that he has that he doesn't even question it."

Honored to speak but uncertain what to say, Chris asked the boycotters to stand and be recognized. "Every day in every part of the country some of the best people God ever made stand in parking lots talking to shoppers about the farm workers' struggle," Chris said. He recapped the triumphs of the Safeway boycott, the bugs in the cookies, the mislabeled meat, and the poisoned lettuce. He told them people loved Cesar Chavez because of the example he set. "As long as we reach for people, and as long as we do not stop, there is no force on earth that can stop this struggle. The farm work-ers will overcome."

The more dire the union's plight, the more Chris felt needed. Chavez made clear that he considered the boycott key to the union's very survival. "The only weapon left for us is the boycott," Chavez told the convention.

Chris had invited church people, and Chavez made sure to recognize them. He pointed out Rosemary Cooperrider, attending on behalf of the Santa Clara Council of Churches, and reminded the crowd that she "spent two weeks in jail with us." He singled out the priest who had been ar-rested, chained, and strip-searched along with Chavez and Chris after the trio trespassed on the DiGiorgio ranch. John Moyer had come to repre-sent the United Church of Christ, and Monsignor George Higgins on behalf of the Catholic bishops. In more than thirty years of attending hundreds of labor conventions, Higgins said, he had never seen such a hard-working group. You will win, the labor priest said, to cheers. "You will long be remembered in the annals of the American labor movement as the founding fathers of one of the greatest organizations in the history of the movement."

The delegates met for fifty hours over three days, the last session a twenty-three-hour marathon that finished at seven on Monday morning. They debated each article of the constitution, elected the new board, and then acted on twenty-seven resolutions. They set dues at 2 percent of members' salaries. They condemned the dictatorship of Philippine president Ferdinand Marcos. The workers set the tone the first day, when Chavez referred to *Robert's Rules of Order* and one of the delegates questioned the bureaucratic procedures. "What are these Roberts rules of order, who established them?" the delegate asked. ". . . I've been to other conventions and I've never heard of Roberts."[7]

The religious supporters marveled to Chris at the democratic feel and the empowerment of farmworkers. Opposition was free to come forward—though they were then crushed by the well-organized Chavez team. Whenever the debate became too spirited, someone moved to close the discussion and vote. Chris termed the convention an exercise in "controlled democracy."

Chavez used a slightly different term. In a private conversation on the eve of the election of the new board, Chavez rued what he called this "so-called democracy." Late Saturday night, he both embraced and denounced the "so-called democracy" in which, he said, the leader must inevitably get rid of his strongest people because otherwise they will get rid of him. They will all be going back out on the boycott now, his biographer noted. That doesn't matter, Chavez replied. It is inevitable. The convention has sown the seeds.[8]

CHAPTER 13

Dark Days

November 1973

Sandy

On November 8, 1973, the last day of the twenty-ninth year of Sandy's life, he and the Dazzler paid a dollar each to see the new movie *Paper Moon*. The next morning, Judge Metheny rejected the union's motions against the Teamsters and sent Sandy stalking out of the Indio courtroom, in no mood to celebrate. But at their Palm Desert house, the Dazzler had simmered vegetable soup all day, barbecued chicken over coals, and baked carrot cake. They took a walk after dinner, the Dazzler wrote in his journal, and "Sandy, as per our agreement of earlier, begins to tell the story of his life, growing up in small-town Western Pennsylvania and then Penn State and the world, how a boy gets from [a] small town in Western Pennsylvania to here being the way he is." The story ended on the porch, the Dazzler playing guitar to accompany the birthday tale.[1]

Sandy and the Dazzler were back in Coachella, calling themselves the Advance Desert Strike Task Force as they waited for action and reinforcements when the grape harvest began in spring.

"The growers are scared of the boycott, very disturbed about a strike, and poorer for their legal hassles with us," Sandy wrote optimistically to Chavez weeks later, at the start of 1974. "They will be ready for talking—or, at least a lot more ready than a year ago." But he added a word of caution:

"If we don't really hurt them on the boycott, they may be very difficult to negotiate with."[2]

Sandy was glad to be in Coachella. He had lived at La Paz during the end of the strike and took a visceral dislike to the isolated campus, the dingy former hospital rooms that lacked reliable heat. During the height of the civil disobedience he had driven hundreds of miles a day visiting courtrooms and jails in farmworker towns across the vast San Joaquin Valley. Then the drives from jail to jail segued into months of slogging through paperwork to clear up the 3,589 arrests from the summer protests. Sandy and the Dazzler shared a small Bakersfield apartment, their barely furnished living room lit by a single bulb. For months they met almost every day with twenty-five-year-old Phil McNutt, the greenest lawyer in the district attorney's office, who had drawn the tedious task of sorting through the arrests. The depressing sprawl of Bakersfield offered little respite. Sandy listened over and over to a Kris Kristofferson hit: *I've come from just the other side of nowhere, to this bigtime lonesome town . . . Just the other side of nowhere, goin' home.*

The Coachella desert offered a welcome change. Sandy enjoyed learning about farmworkers, each crop with its different culture. The *palmeros* who picked dates were loners who enjoyed the high-wire harvesting, climbing up to the dangerous heights of the date palms. The lemon pickers were tough, scaling thorny trees in hardhats with buckets in hand and earning money by the piece, not the hour. The Filipinos who dominated many of the grape vineyards were quiet, industrious, and suspicious of the Mexican union. But at Lionel Steinberg's vineyard Sandy found strong support among Filipino workers. Sandy was preparing for contract negotiations with Steinberg and Keene Larson, whose one-year pacts would expire in mid-April. Sandy had never negotiated a contract before. In the union you had to do things you weren't sure you could pull off. Sandy liked that ethos.

Keene Larson's wife, Corky, began urging Chavez at the beginning of 1974 to meet quickly and agree to a one-year extension with a new wage scale. Chavez brushed off her repeated requests, as well as Larson's warning that the Teamsters were hovering. "The UFW must bear responsibility for the complications which will surely arise if you delay," she wrote after Chavez canceled a meeting. Larson also complained about the new nineteen-year-old director of the Coachella office. He was "capricious and dictatorial and doing devastating harm to the image of the UFW in the Coachella Valley," she wrote.[3]

The Larsons had stuck with the union when almost all the other growers had fled to the Teamsters. But now Keene Larson's passion for quality and control had run smack into the union's young, untrained staff. The small vineyard employed fewer than one hundred workers during harvest, about 40 percent of them related to a forewoman who had worked there for thirteen years. The union viewed her as a labor contractor who interfered with the hiring hall and gave preference to her friends; the Larsons valued her as essential to their operation. In mid-January the new UFW director kicked her out of the union. That meant she would lose her job.

Chavez watched the drama unfold and chose not to interfere. He knew the forewoman had been improperly ousted from the union and would win her appeal on technicalities. He believed the Larsons would break the union contract, if necessary, to keep the forewoman. That prospect did not trouble him: It would make the grape boycott cleaner. "I don't think they want to deal with us," he said about Larson and Steinberg. He planned to negotiate "but get into a dispute with them, get into a strike. And boycott everything."[4]

Sandy did not know Chavez's strategy when the two sat down three days later in the Reverend Lloyd Saatjian's Palm Springs church to open negotiations with Corky Larson and Lionel Steinberg. The second morning Larson walked in and dropped a bombshell: The Larsons had held an election only hours earlier, and the workers rejected the UFW. She claimed farmworkers had petitioned for the vote; the UFW claimed the workers had been coerced into signing and that the Larsons had been secretly planning an election while bargaining in bad faith.

Sandy knew about problems with the hiring hall, allegations of favoritism, and anger over the firing of the Larsons' forewoman. But he believed the UFW represented the workers in a fundamental way that the Teamsters did not. The union was about giving workers a voice in their own lives. The Teamsters were about money, not empowerment. As the leader of the Western Conference of Teamsters explained in an interview that the union disseminated, he saw no point in having membership meetings for farmworkers: "I'm not sure how effective a union can be when it is composed of Mexican-Americans and Mexican nationals with temporary visas . . . As jobs become more attractive to whites, then we can build a union that can have structure and that can negotiate from strength and have membership participation."[5]

When Corky Larson staged a secret election, Sandy was sure the vote

Chavez and Sandy talk with Lionel Steinberg as they open contract negotiations in March 1974.

was a ploy to bring in the Teamsters. "All the procedures we are entitled to were violated," he fumed. "It wasn't an election, it was an absurdity."[6]

Like the Larsons, Lionel Steinberg had suffered for his allegiance to the union. The hiring hall posed major problems and cost him time and money. Vandals had torched his packing shed, a $300,000 loss that had sent him scrambling for a place to store grapes at the height of the season. But Steinberg's politics kept him with the UFW. A few weeks after the Larsons defected, Sandy and Steinberg reached agreement on everything except wages. Steinberg offered $2.50 an hour, a 10-cent raise. Chavez had ordered Sandy to get $2.51—one penny more than the Teamster contracts. Steinberg wouldn't budge, and the workers were happy with $2.50.

They embraced the UFW because they believed in Chavez, and they believed the union was committed to represent their interests.

Sandy called La Paz and said in his flat Pennsylvania drawl that the Steinberg workers wanted to accept the deal. Screw the workers, Chavez responded. Get the extra penny. Sandy objected, though he understood the principle and did not expect his objection to hold sway. Sandy never knew exactly who Chavez called on to exert political pressure, but Steinberg finally went up the extra cent. The new contract was signed April 16, the one-year anniversary of the Coachella strike.

The same day, Corky Larson announced they would negotiate with the Teamsters. "From beginning to end," Sandy responded angrily, "this Larson matter smacked of a sweetheart deal."[7]

The next day Larson trumped Chavez at his own game. She signed a contract with the Teamsters that paid $2.52 an hour.

Eliseo

The spring grapes ripened in Coachella, and the backup for the Advance Desert Strike Task Force never arrived. Just as Sandy had surmised, the boycott again became the union's principal weapon. Cleveland was a far cry from Chicago, which had a sizable Mexican-American community and a long, storied past of supporting labor. But Eliseo was light-years removed from the twenty-year-old who had opened the Chicago phone book, called A&P, and asked them not to sell grapes.

In Cleveland, Eliseo wrote a primer for Fred Ross to use in training boycott volunteers, a five-page, Roman-numeral-labeled outline that covered everything from how to approach local unions to how to structure a four-part speech to supporters, sample humor included. "I always tell them we all make $5.00 a week so that their money goes to support the strikers, not for fancy salaries," he wrote. "And that if they have any old, moldy money that they have been meaning to throw away, now is their chance. That we'll take from 25 cents to 30 million dollars. This usually cracks them up and makes their giving something they want to do and something they feel part of, instead of something they have been pressured into doing."

He spelled out the research necessary to decide which stores to target:

1. Who owns it?
2. What percentage of the market do they have? If they crack will others follow?

3. Where are the stores located? (white reactionary areas or liberal, Black, Chicano neighborhoods)
4. Any alternative stores for shoppers?
5. Are the stores located in big shopping centers or are they single stores?
6. Union or scab?
7. How strong are you?
8. Will the fight be won quickly or will it be a long one?[8]

Eliseo targeted Fisher-Fazio, the Cleveland area's largest chain and, like Jewel, the one that other stores in the area would follow. He began with the standard moves: picket lines and publicity urging consumers not to shop at Fisher-Fazio until the chain stopped buying nonunion grapes and lettuce. He sued them for advertising sale items that weren't in stock. He filed complaints about the use of the union eagle on non-UFW produce. When Chavez came through Ohio on a national tour, Eliseo set up events in eleven cities across the state, reaching audiences of more than twelve thousand.[9]

But Eliseo made only incremental progress. The union was trying to boycott three different items—grapes, lettuce, and Gallo wine. The boycott was no longer fresh. And labor was fractured. Two strong unions in the AFL-CIO, the Meat Cutters and the Retail Clerks, actively opposed the boycott. Their members worked at stores the union was boycotting, and the meat cutters had close ties to the Teamsters. The two unions chose Ohio to make a stand and took out three-quarter-page ads in Cleveland newspapers denouncing the boycott as "ineffective and offensive." Their campaign undermined labor support and confused even ardent boycott supporters, like church groups. Chavez called Eliseo to a summit meeting with AFL-CIO President Meany in Washington, D.C., and the national labor leader brokered a deal. Meany announced that the federation would throw its full support behind the grape and lettuce boycott. In exchange, the UFW agreed to drop the secondary boycott; they would urge consumers to boycott grapes and lettuce but not to shun entire stores.

The agreement freed Eliseo to campaign all out at the Ohio AFL-CIO convention. He prepared packets for each delegate and draped two thirty-six-foot banners from the balcony in the convention hall: "Help Farm Workers—Don't Buy Grapes." He collected $6,300 and an endorsement from the convention. In return, Eliseo invited delegates to sample union wine in the farmworkers' hospitality suite at the Cleveland Plaza Hotel.

(The garment workers, electrical workers and steelworkers unions each picked up one day of the $29.03-a-day room tab.) Eliseo directed the four Ohio boycott offices to bring two cases of wine—"beg, borrow, steal, hustle or buy"—and assigned each city a specific brand to avoid duplication. "We did most of our organizing there," Eliseo reported to Chavez. "The delegates went home with the farm workers in their minds, hearts, and hangovers."[10]

Eliseo set a fund-raising goal for each city—$10,000 a month—and chastised them when they fell short. And he wrote letters, and letters, and more letters. Any donation of time or money, no matter how small, merited a personal note of thanks. Dorothy typed dozens a week, on onionskin paper in duplicate, one copy for the files. Eliseo thanked the Newspaper Guild official who donated paper for the union newsletter, the garment worker who handed a boycotter five dollars for bus fare, the priest who invited farmworkers to live temporarily at the Catholic Youth Organization center. And Eliseo thanked his own staff. In the middle of his first executive board meeting, he wrote home: "Greetings from beautiful downtown La Paz. We have just completed the third day of our board meeting and I'm awfully glad I came. It has been a very educational 3 days. I have learned so many things that I did not know or was only superficially aware of. The meetings start at 8 A.M. every day and we finish by about 11:30 or 12 midnight. While Cesar works us long hours, it's the kind of work that you enjoy." Then he got to the point, congratulating them on the successful Christmas fiesta held the day before he left for California. "I was just floored when I walked into the hall and saw the whole place jammed. Even better, when Dorothy told me that we raised about $2,300, I was walking ten feet tall . . . All of you deserve, and are getting, the credit."[11]

Fund-raising helped the union, but contributions would not force Fisher-Fazio to capitulate. After the AFL-CIO agreement boycott leaders in most cities abandoned the effort to lobby grocery chains and set out instead to win over consumers one by one. Eliseo rejected that as a losing approach. He sought alternative ways to generate pressure that would force stores to stop selling grapes and lettuce. On a chilly fall night, Eliseo ate refried beans and tortillas, then began a fast outside a Fazio store. "We could not reach Mr. Carl Fazio with our words; perhaps we can reach him with our actions," Eliseo said. "I will fast in the hope that Mr. Fazio will search his heart and recognize that he has a moral responsibility to the farm workers. Going without food will be difficult but it is worse going without dignity."[12]

Eliseo camped out in a beat-up red Ford van in the Severance Center shopping plaza. Supporters held vigils and sent mailgrams. Local officials and Ohio senator Howard Metzenbaum came to visit. After fourteen days Eliseo broke the fast at his doctor's urging. Others took up the "Fast for Justice," taking turns going without food in the parking lot. One was Kathy Fagan, who had helped boycott Jewel as a college freshman in Chicago four years earlier. Her volunteer stints with the farmworkers had inspired her to become a doctor, and she enrolled as a medical student at Case Western Reserve.

"The boycott teaches. He who learns the boycott can organize anything," Eliseo told *El Malcriado*. Eliseo had discovered during his one-year stint in Calexico that the organizing skills he had learned in the city could be put to use in the fields. He was eager for that opportunity. "The boycott is giving rise to a new wave of young, but experienced farm worker leaders. After the boycott is over, they will have much to contribute in the administration of the new contracts."[13]

Chris

The outside world was losing faith. But not Chris. Eliseo's difficulty breaking through in Ohio was echoed around the country. By 1974, *la causa* was growing stale. The '60s generation had moved on. AFL-CIO President Meany disparaged the Coachella strike as "almost a disaster" because so few workers took part.[14] The *New York Times Magazine* pronounced the union on life support. Chris redoubled his efforts to prop up religious allies and dispel a growing perception that the UFW was in trouble.

Union leaders defiantly dismissed the critics, confident of prevailing in the long run and winning on their own terms. "If as the obituary in the *New York Times* indicates, we are dead, then why have there been so many injunctions filed against us in the last three months?" Jerry wrote. ". . . Perhaps what crawled into the orifice of the *New York Times* and died there was not us but something called 'liberalism.' "[15]

Chavez acknowledged difficulty in Coachella. "The strike in Coachella did not materialize as we hoped it would," he reported to the board. He blamed a lack of leadership, because the union's best people were out on the boycott. He blamed growers' ability to import workers from Mexico. And he blamed federal authorities for not enforcing immigration laws.[16]

So in the spring of 1974, as Chris struggled to bolster spirits, Chavez launched a crusade that made the minister's job tougher: the Campaign Against Illegals. He deemed the effort more important than the strike, second only to the boycott. "If we can get the illegals out of California and Arizona we can win the strike overnight," Chavez told the executive board.[17] He instructed all union offices to find illegal workers in the fields and write them up. The union circulated examples, urged the government to step up deportations, and publicized enforcement failures. The government was complicit with the growers, Chavez charged, providing a ready supply of workers to break the strike.

Chris knew church people would not embrace the illegals campaign. The union's traditional allies had higher expectations now that the UFW had a history, a track record, and an internationally famous leader. Friends found it hard to excuse unpopular positions like the call to deport immigrants. Labor leaders made jokes about Saint Cesar and his fasts.[18] Seafarers Union president Paul Hall, one of the union's die-hard allies, urged Chavez to consolidate his gains rather than always fight. The boycott is like a gun, Hall said. The less you use it, the more effective. The best place for a gun is in its holster. The more you point it at someone's head, the more tired your arm. "We'll buy you fucking kneepads if you want to fight a holy war," Hall told Chavez at a meeting to meditate an accord with the Teamsters. You can't build a union while you fight. "Let's not make it a cause, let's make it a fucking union." Chavez was resolute: He would not compromise. He remained confident that the public pressure generated through the boycott would eventually force the Teamsters out of the fields.[19]

Chris carried the message of unrelenting struggle to the wavering supporters. He moved his office across Olympic Boulevard into a warehouse partitioned in half so that he could share space with the UFW's Los Angeles headquarters. Proximity to the action was important. No one had time to brief him, and Chris needed to be up to date at all times, so he could interpret the changing events to middle-class church people who didn't automatically assume that workers were right.

Chris stressed two messages as he tried to keep boycotters and religious supporters in the fold: The farmworkers' struggle was an unremitting fight that allowed no time off, and those who quit hurt those left behind. Chris rejected the possibility of tiring. Two kinds of organizations seek change, he said. One depended on an all-consuming work ethic. Time off might happen occasionally, but you couldn't plan on it. The other kind of organization featured normal hours and vacations. One makes change and the other doesn't, he repeatedly preached. The growers are working twenty-four hours a day; it's their life, their livelihood. We have to outwork them to win.

By the end of 1974 prospects looked gloomy even from the inside. The union had spent a million dollars in the summer and fall on scattered, largely ineffective strikes. In December the union was so broke that checks bounced.[20] Chris vowed to work harder. When volunteers approached about working for the ministry, he resolved to raise money to pay their subsistence salaries. When the boycott lagged, he proposed a National Farm Worker Week. He set goals: How many churches in each city would post boycott signs on their front lawns? He stressed the positive: Chavez had an audience with the pope. The bishops had finally endorsed the boycott. Gallo's vocal response to the boycott showed the union was hurting sales.

Chris summoned all his zealous devotion when he addressed his staff at a ministry retreat. "Cesar and other key UFW leaders have set the pace of the struggle. They are in a hurry to change things for farm workers everywhere in our country. There may be a different way to do the struggle but that is irrelevant unless we plan to give our lives to proving that. Cesar and UFW represent the *only* way that is known about. We have to relate to their way or get out or make our own revolution."

He castigated those who even thought of quitting. "People who leave are really betraying the commitment of the UFW cause. By leaving they say it is not really that important. Cesar and the leaders of UFW can't help but be hurt by that choice to leave . . . people who leave because of personal injuries have escalated their own importance above the needs of farm workers who are being *brutalized* by agribusiness power."[21]

Eliseo

Eliseo never thought about doing anything else. When his spirits flagged in Cleveland, he looked forward to recharging in California. Every three months, he attended marathon meetings of the union's executive board. They helped Eliseo feel connected, even if the board accomplished little more than ratifying Chavez's decisions. The novelty far outweighed Eliseo's frustration with the meetings' length and plodding pace.

Eliseo approached his new responsibilities as seriously as he did all other tasks. He was conscious of his status as the youngest board member, the only one born in Mexico, and certainly not part of the inner circle. He instinctively called the union president "*César*," though everyone else—including Chavez himself—used the American pronunciation. Eliseo listened appreciatively to war stories told by Jerry and the close-knit group who had been the brain trust for years. He came to meetings well prepared. He took copious notes and checked off each item on his agenda. He was the board member most likely to invoke rules, to spot mistakes, to remind the board about its own policies, and to ask speakers to slow down and spell names so he could keep up as he took notes. He contributed confidently to policy debates when he had expertise and stayed quiet when he did not. He questioned decisions and raised ideas with a single-minded focus on work and a straightforward innocence that verged on naïveté.

When the executive board discussed why the boycott in Michigan was in trouble, board members told Chavez the problem was his new son-in-law, Artie Rodriguez. Disappointed he had not been appointed to run the Detroit boycott, Rodriguez had been undermining the new director. Eliseo was moving to Chicago to rebuild the boycott in that key city. He named a couple of volunteers he would be willing to take from Michigan. "Oh they'd like to go there!" Chavez said. "And Artie too?"

"No," Eliseo said after only a split-second pause. "I'd much rather not deal with your relatives."

Chavez assured the board his relatives could be treated like anyone else. Rodriguez stayed in Detroit.[22]

Chavez was adjusting to a freewheeling board, loyal and subservient but certainly not shy. He still dictated decisions, but now he had to maneuver them through the outspoken board. "Watch!" he often said, prefacing an explanation of what the board should do. Chavez's style and the lack of trained administrators or financial experts guaranteed that board meetings ran for days. (Eliseo suggested time limits for speeches and submitted a cartoon on one report cover that showed two board members crawling out of a meeting, exhausted.) Chavez struggled to impose order not only on the meetings, but on the whole union. He railed about inefficiency in the volunteer organization, with its often-shifting roster of staff working in seventeen field offices and thirty-seven boycott cities. He told stories about finding stacks of checks that had never been cashed. He began to rise at three thirty each morning to open every piece of mail himself.[23]

Board members told Chavez he needed help. The administrative chaos was attracting widespread notice. Letters and phone calls to La Paz went unanswered. Promised follow-ups never occurred. Car insurance for volunteers never materialized. Even the union's best friends wondered how they would survive—once they had contracts and members. "People you wouldn't think they'd tell you this, people you have to listen to," Richard Chavez told his brother. "That we're screwed up administratively. We're fucked up. See, everybody knows it. We can't cover it anymore."

Chavez flatly rejected the suggestion that he needed help. All he needed was to stop traveling. "Just give me some time to be in La Paz," he told the board. "I can do my job. I don't need any help."

"No, no, I don't think you can," Eliseo responded. He had never seen an organization that functioned well with only one person in charge of everything, he told Chavez. "I think that for instance you need, number one, some good, strong department heads. You need a chief of staff to coordinate everybody else's work, to make sure it gets done . . . an Al Haig type of person."

"Somebody's got to be here to do the job, and I got to do the job. Nobody can do it for me," Chavez replied.[24]

He insisted on making decisions on minute matters such as car repairs and telephone calls. If a spark plug needed changing, he wanted to know about it, Richard Chavez complained: "If you don't trust me, and I'm your brother and you know that I would go to hell for you . . . you are not ready to give, to hand out that responsibility and I'm sure nobody is going to work against you if that's what you're afraid of."[25] In Ohio, Eliseo raised more than twice what the operation cost—in 1974 the six offices spent $50,619 and sent another $61,111 to Delano.[26] Yet Chavez called Eliseo to question why he had overspent $234.82 on gas and $190.67 on car repairs one month before the union president agreed to approve $60 to fix the front end of Eliseo's car.[27]

By the fall of 1974 even Fred Ross openly questioned his star student's management style. The boycott was in trouble, Ross said. The lack of structure was insane. Someone had to be in charge. He nominated Eliseo. Ross touted Eliseo as the longest-tenured and arguably strongest boycott leader, someone who could play the "circuit rider" role that Ross and Chavez had played years ago when they built CSO chapters around the state. Chavez said he agreed with the need for a director, then torpedoed the idea. Alternately amicable, angry, and defensive, Chavez offered one justification after another for maintaining the disorganized status quo.

Eliseo also reacted negatively to Ross's suggestion. "I would not like that job," Eliseo said without hesitation, describing the boycott director as a troubleshooter who jumped from place to place putting out fires. "I for one like to be somewhere where I can build something." But he remembered his angst as a young boycotter in Salinas in 1970, when Chavez had asked Eliseo to return to Chicago. He had badly wanted to stay in the fields. "But it also dawned on me later that if I was going to work for the union, it would have to be where I was needed the most," he told the board. "So I went to Chicago." He told them he felt the same way now about being boycott director. "What I'm saying is, I wouldn't want that job, but I'd take it I guess if it's the only ballgame in town."[28] Chavez assured him there was no need.

Eliseo focused on a different, longer-term issue: how to involve farmworkers in running the union. Chavez had explained at the 1973 convention that he had run out of time to write a key section of the constitution—rules to govern ranch committees, the workers elected at each company with a union contract. More than a year later the executive board finally began the discussion. Eliseo urged the board to think about how the union would compensate workers who took time off to investigate grievances, handle medical claims, negotiate contracts, or lobby in Sacramento. "You're talking about several thousand people actively enforcing and building and doing things to make a union possible," Eliseo said, looking forward to when the union had dozens of contracts. Traditionally, workers had taken up collections to cover the salaries of their co-workers who took days off for union work. The new UFW constitution forbade that practice, because of Chavez's conviction that pots of money handled by local committees would lead to trouble.

Eliseo's comments triggered vociferous debate among the usually collegial group. Board members denounced the idea of compensation as a sure-fire way to destroy the movement. Money corrupts, they said. We'll end up like all the other labor unions in the country that sold out thirty years ago, they warned. Eliseo became exasperated, sure that he understood the workers' mentality better because of his own experience in the fields. "You're not ever going to get them to give up two, three weeks to go running around and processing grievances without any pay," Eliseo said. "Be realistic."

"They don't have to run around," Dolores Huerta argued.

"Oh come on, Dolores, they will have to run around. If they're putting time in to process grievances, investigate grievances, putting time in to help organize . . ."

"You have to be careful, Eliseo."

"I *know* that, Dolores. All I'm saying is, it's a real problem that's going to have to be dealt with and we should look at it."

"The day we start doing it for one person," Huerta said, "you're not going to get anybody else to do it unless you pay everybody. And we are screwed."

"I think we're even more screwed if we think they're going to do it for free forever," Eliseo retorted.

Only Richard Chavez backed up Eliseo. To effectively administer a union of one hundred thousand workers required thinking differently, he said. "You've got to drop that Goddamn mentality of a movement, you know, if you want to build a union. If you don't want to build a union, then you keep that same mentality and you'll wind up in the same goddamn place we're at."

Eliseo tried to draw a picture for those less familiar with the fields: "If you've got a guy that's got seven kids and you ask him to take the presidency of the ranch committee, and that's going to entail, to really do a good job, a lot of time and a lot of effort, you watch to see how many times that guy's going to be able to take off three days out of the week, and two days out of the week before the seven kids and the wife start yelling and the car and all that other shit . . . Sure, the guy's got all his heart right here in *la causa*—So what's he going to do, leave his wife and his kids so he doesn't have to worry about them? Come on. I just don't think you guys are realistic."

Chavez missed the heated exchange. He returned toward the end and amicably set aside the debate as moot until the union won back contracts. "That discussion is the one that's going to give us the biggest problems," he said. "I've been dealing with it all these years, my way, you know. But now it's your decision . . . That decision affects the union, more than any other . . . We have enough sense. We'll know what to do when the time comes. We always do."[29]

CHAPTER 14

The Best Labor Law in the Country

August 1974

Jerry

Jerry was viewed in the state capital as an irreverent hustler with a brilliant legal mind. His power derived not from the usual sources—money and connections—but from the union's ability to mobilize people and make demands. As an outsider in the clubby world of state politics, Jerry didn't worry about offending the Sacramento establishment. He could berate the Assembly speaker as the kind of liberal that made Jerry puke, then share a drink with the legislator the next day.

The freedom to take an outrageous stance strengthened Jerry's hand as he began to negotiate a law to govern union activity in the fields. He didn't particularly care what others thought about his tactics or positions. He played to win, as absolutist in negotiating the law as Chris had been in soliciting religious support. Besides, neither Jerry nor Chavez was all that anxious to succeed. Chavez was loath to forfeit what he fondly called the nonviolent Vietcong approach.

But the union had no choice. In exchange for the $1.6 million strike fund from the AFL-CIO during the battle of Coachella, Chavez had agreed to support legislation that would establish a procedure for elections. National labor leaders viewed a law governing union activity in the fields as the only long-term solution. Jerry had stalled as long as he could, sharing Chavez's concern that a law would force the union to give up the boycott in exchange for elections. Chavez viewed the boycott as a crucial weapon to exert public pressure. Jerry reassured him: "One way of doing it is to introduce a bill that can't be passed ... see what reasonable-sounding things we can put in there that are impossible."[1] So Jerry prepared a bill so favorable to the union that the chance of passage seemed remote. The bill included the union's four key points: secret-ballot elections in peak season when most workers were present, a bargaining unit that included all agricultural employees, expedited elections first with challenges heard afterward, and the right to boycott.

Ronald Reagan was governor, sure to oppose the measure. But Reagan was in his waning days in 1974, and Jerry was building a relationship with the Democratic candidate for governor, Jerry Brown. Two years earlier, as secretary of state, Brown had helped the union when he investigated fraudulent petitions during the successful campaign to defeat Prop 22. Now Brown the gubernatorial candidate sat down with Jerry for an hour and a half, agreed to support the boycott, and promised to help pass a strong law.[2]

Jerry took up residence in Sacramento ahead of Brown. The attorney became the union's point person, camped out in the capitol office of a friendly legislator. Jerry sifted through reports from the union's assorted lobbyists, boycotters, and friends. When he needed to get people in line, Jerry picked up the phone and sweet-talked, bullied, cajoled, threatened, or yelled, whatever suited the situation. When the bill Jerry had helped draft came up for hearings, the union packed the room with farmworkers.

In mid-August, a week after Richard Nixon resigned as president, a bill to promote union elections in the fields moved out of committee. Democrats were threatening to water down the measure on the Assembly floor. Jerry tried unsuccessfully to reach Brown, the titular head of the Democratic Party and the best person to pressure his fellow Democrats. Jerry wanted Brown to publicly endorse the bill and to keep the leadership from diluting the measure. A floor vote was expected within forty-eight hours. By evening, Jerry had still not heard from Brown. So Jerry dispatched Sandy to San Francisco.

Sandy drove the eighty miles from Sacramento, arriving after midnight at the local boycott house. By seven o'clock the next morning, he had two dozen boycotters and farmworkers on the second-floor mezzanine of the Fox Plaza office building, in front of the still-locked doors of the Brown for Governor headquarters. They read Brown's newspapers while they waited. When Brown's chief of staff arrived, Sandy explained that his orders were simple: not to leave until Brown personally assured him that he supported the farmworkers' election bill and would make sure the measure passed the Assembly. After several hours Brown called. On Friday morning he held a press conference and expressed support for AB 3370. On Monday the bill passed the Assembly, with no amendments.[3]

When Jerry called Chavez to tell him about the victory, Chavez reacted with resignation, not joy. He knew a law would fundamentally change the rules of the game. Jerry reassured Chavez that the Teamsters would kill the measure in the Senate. Jerry was just thinking about the end of session. Chavez was thinking further ahead.

Opponents employed technicalities to keep the bill from coming to the Senate floor, but Jerry had established the key parameters. Chavez explained his strategy to the executive board: In 1975 the union would put forward a Farm Worker Bill of Rights so loaded with favorable provisions for workers that the legislation could not pass. Then the union would collect signatures and place the measure on the ballot in 1976. A presidential election year would draw a large Democratic turnout. Jerry believed they could turn an initiative into a constitutional amendment—far preferable to a law that could be eroded by future legislatures. "We go to the voters, and I think the voters will give it to us," Chavez said confidently.[4] He did not foresee that the next governor of California would stake his first year in office on delivering for farmworkers the right to free elections.

Ellen

Ellen intended to work for the union forever, but the once-starry-eyed Indiana grad had begun to tire of standing in Safeway parking lots. Drawn to Jerry's quirky but charismatic style of leadership, she began to think about the law. "He's the 'famous' UFW attorney," Ellen wrote her mother, describing Jerry. "Young, handsome, very fast-moving, energetic—lots of nervous energy and is really a riot!"

So one afternoon Ellen sneaked away from a Los Angeles picket line, leaving her post outside the Safeway on 3rd and Fairfax to drive to the UCLA campus and take the LSATs. She was unprepared for the first question: Which two law schools did she want to receive her scores? She listed the only two that came to mind: the University of California at Davis, because a union volunteer had told her it was a good school, and Valparaiso in Indiana, her father's alma mater.

By 1974 Ellen had become a boycott coordinator, as Ruth Shy and Jessica Govea had been two years earlier, when Ellen first arrived. Jim Drake ran the Los Angeles boycott, and he sent Ellen out to Long Beach to organize from nothing. First she had to find a place to live. Drake gave her the name of a Communist bookstore owner; Ellen slept under the dining room table, since the house lacked a spare room. She set up a house meeting campaign and trained volunteers to do what she had learned her first summer. The volunteers sent out to Long Beach were inexperienced, but she made the best of it. She had stayed close to Chris; whenever she had qualms or thoughts of leaving, he crushed them with his customary optimism.

The goal of Ellen's house meeting campaign was to build toward a big community meeting in October that would launch a full-scale boycott of grapes, lettuce, and Gallo wine. Ellen's father planned a big family trip to Hawaii in late August and bought tickets for his three daughters. Ellen felt guilty leaving even for a week, but she went. She felt like she was not doing justice either to the union or to her family. She was accepted at Valparaiso but decided to defer law school a year to stay for the big October meeting. Soon afterward, she felt so wiped out that she headed home to Indiana.

Chris called just after the Christmas holidays, and Ellen already was pining for the union. He asked her to return to help organize the premiere of a movie that had been filmed during the violent summer of 1973. *Fighting for Our Lives* had taken almost two years to assemble and was scheduled to debut around the country on April 16, the second anniversary of the Coachella strike. Chavez had designed a fund-raising campaign around the movie.

Ellen flew back to Los Angeles, moved into an apartment on Sunset Boulevard, and went to work selling hundred-dollar tickets for the film premiere and sponsorships in the program booklet. The ACLU shared its donor list, and Ellen's team divided up the solicitations. Her primary responsibility was church people, while others focused on labor leaders and Hollywood celebrities. Ellen also got her share of celebrity calls, including Michael Douglas, Cloris Leachman, and Joanne Woodward.

Ellen's father flew out from Indiana for the premiere. Steve Allen emceed the gala event at the Sportsmen's Lodge in the San Fernando Valley. A roster of celebrities joined union leaders in the benefit, which netted $60,000. The showing was punctuated by frequent cheers as the audience applauded their friends: The Dazzler righteously telling a deputy sheriff that if the protesters

Ellen leads a boycott protest in Los Angeles in 1974.

had to be sixty feet away from each side of the road, that put them somewhere up in the air. Strikers being carted off from the Karahadian vineyard,
after Eliseo stood on the car and exhorted them into the fields. Thousands
mourning the worker shot on the picket line.

The union coordinated showings around the country. Eliseo raised

$26,000, with an advance VIP hundred-dollars-per-person showing at the Pick Congress Hotel in downtown Chicago and then a three-dollars-a-ticket performance at the Palacio Theater, emceed by Studs Terkel. More than fifteen hundred people in the sold-out crowd stood up and cheered when they watched Rosario Pelayo shout, "Viva la huelga" as she and her sisters were carted off to jail. Dorothy Johnson wrote the filmmaker a note to tell him about the emotional response.[5]

After the premiere Ellen went to La Paz to write thank-you notes to all the sponsors, using a programmable typewriter that spit out the text and left room for her to fill in the name, using the standard union salutation. That format yielded her favorite note, the one addressed to Tommy Smothers: *Dear Brother Smothers.*

Then once more Ellen was persuaded to stay after she had planned to go home to Indiana. Jerry asked her to help for three months on the antitrust suit, the case that contended that the Salinas vegetable growers and the Teamsters had conspired to artificially depress wages for farmworkers. The UFW had drawn a sympathetic judge and received favorable rulings. Jerry saw the class-action suit as leverage in negotiations with the growers and Teamsters. The longer and more complicated the case, the more money the opposition was shelling out for high-priced lawyers. And last but not least, as Jerry explained to the board, the discovery process forced growers to give the union "complete, total access to every goddamn record that the growers have, relating to their relationships to the union, their relationships to each other, their relationships to the Teamsters."[6] The paperwork had grown so voluminous that the union rented bank vaults.

Ellen's job was to research answers to one subpart of a subpart of an interrogatory, the legal term for questions each side asks the other during the discovery phase of the case. Ellen enjoyed her tiny piece of the giant fishing expedition, an open-ended query about the nature of the lettuce boycott. She tracked down and interviewed boycotters who had worked for the union in the early 1970s, posing dozens of questions about the lettuce boycott: what they did, who they talked to, what kind of leaflets they produced.

She was back in Los Angeles for a few days when her father suffered a stroke. Ellen flew home the next day to Indiana; he died a week later, on Father's Day. She stayed with her family until she entered Valparaiso Law School, promising to come back and work for the union as soon as she finished.

Jerry

Jerry thought he saw an endgame in Sacramento. Local law enforcement officials were weary from processing thousands of arrests; grape growers had become disenchanted with the Teamsters; Gallo wine owners were nervous about the boycott; supermarket executives were eager to avoid picket lines; and labor leaders were ready to end the costly strikes and turmoil. Most significantly, at the center of the capitol offices known as "the Horseshoe" sat Governor Jerry Brown, a former Jesuit seminarian. In a fifteen-paragraph inaugural address that set records for brevity, Brown had devoted two paragraphs to farmworkers. It was time, he said, to provide unemployment insurance to those who worked in the fields, and also "to extend the rule of law to the agriculture sector and establish the right of secret ballot elections for farm workers."[7]

Jerry had used the legislative battle in Sacramento as an excuse to leave La Paz. "It is almost impossible to function in an offensive manner from here," he wrote Chavez, referring to Keene. Jerry offered to resign as chief counsel.[8] Chavez wanted Jerry to stay. So with the union president's permission, if not his blessing, Jerry moved the legal department to Salinas, in the midst of one of the largest concentrations of farmworkers, and nearer the courts and the capitol. Sandy and some of the other legal staff moved into the "White House," a sprawling Victorian a few blocks from their new office. The Dazzler, studying to become a lawyer through the unusual route of apprenticeship rather than law school, shuttled between Salinas and Sacramento, helping Jerry with negotiations.

When Jerry arrived at La Paz for the executive board meeting in the spring of 1975, he found spirits very low. "There was a real sense of almost desperation out there," he noted shortly after the March meeting. "I had always been sort of buoyed up by the attitude of some of the people because they were so cocksure. But I found myself in the role of trying to buoy them up."[9] Jerry had reason to be upbeat. Just ten days before the board meeting, he and Chavez had held their first long meeting with Brown at the governor's house in Los Angeles. Chavez made his priorities clear: His first choice was to use the threat of legislation to negotiate the Teamsters out of the fields; second, to avoid any bad laws; his third, to get a really good bill. Jerry hadn't thought there was any way to get a law that would take effect before 1976, but Brown was more optimistic. "About three o'clock, he invited me for a walk," Chavez recounted to the executive board. "We walked out, and that's where we made some deals."[10]

The basic strategy was simple. Publicly, the union would take an extreme position. Privately, Chavez trusted Brown, who knew the union's bottom line. Jerry sat down with Chavez, drew up twelve key points, and sent them on to the governor's office. He didn't hear anything back till the night before Brown introduced his bill. Then the dance began, with the union publicly denouncing the bill while privately negotiating with Brown. Sometimes Jerry thought the stratagem was working. Other days he had blow-ups with Brown's staff and decided the union's public stance really reflected the truth—they were not allies after all. Brown, a smart, quirky politician, could be hard to read. He preferred late-night meetings and uttered profound statements that left Jerry in bemused confusion. When Brown proclaimed "a moment of polar lucidity" in the negotiations, the line became a standing joke between Jerry and Sandy. But Brown personally negotiated the bill to an extraordinary degree, calling in chits, leaning on labor allies, and putting his prestige on the line to achieve a fragile peace among interest groups that loathed one another.[11]

Jerry used Sandy and the Dazzler as sounding boards and as foils. The Dazzler tracked movement on the bill and relayed messages back and forth. When a United Auto Workers lobbyist criticized the union's negotiating stance, the Dazzler delivered the message to Chavez and then went back to the lobbyist with Chavez's response: "If he doesn't trust brown people to make their own decisions and make their own strategy he can go fuck himself."[12]

For weeks alliances shifted; friends were enemies, then friends again, Jerry playing one against the other as he walked through the halls of the capitol whistling the theme from *The Sting.* He felt like he was jumping from crest to crest in high seas—the trick was to ride the wave and jump off just before it crashed. His nimbleness in navigating charmed most of his sparring mates, who preferred to see Sandy as the angry and unreasonable opponent. Rose Bird, the governor's agriculture secretary, got so mad at Sandy that she wouldn't speak to him.

Jerry became impatient with the lack of progress and leery that the governor was not sufficiently supportive. On April 30 Jerry and Sandy waited in San Francisco for an expected meeting with Brown. In agony, Jerry watched Rick Barry blow a shot, costing the Golden State Warriors game two of the Western Conference finals of the National Basketball Association. Still no word from the governor's office. Jerry called Chavez three times at a funeral in San Jose to warn him about problems. The next night they finally convened in Brown's sparsely furnished apartment. The meeting was contentious, the two Jerrys arguing over who wanted the bill more. Jerry and Sandy left depressed.

But Brown spent the next day working on the problems and called them back. They all worked on the bill together on Saturday. Then Jerry took Sandy and the Dazzler to see *Young Frankenstein* to make sure they were not reachable until late at night. They started negotiating after the movie ended at eleven thirty P.M. Jerry filibustered and talked about "four levels of boycotts." With one crucial legal point about the union's right to boycott still in doubt, Jerry played fast and loose with a precedent-setting court case. The *Tree Fruits* decision had established the constitutional right to leaflet outside stores. Jerry stretched the meaning of the decision, using a combination of theatrics, bluffing, and artful legal parsing, to get language in the bill that preserved the union's right to secondary boycott.

By May 5, they had a deal. Jerry went to see *Godfather II*. The next evening Brown did round-robin diplomacy in the Horseshoe—the growers in one room, the Teamsters in another, the UFW in a third. Finally they staged a phone call to Chavez, putting the union leader on speaker phone as everyone assembled in Brown's office. The governor outlined the final terms, and with great dramatic flair and a show of reluctance, Chavez agreed. At three A.M. Jerry called the White House in Salinas, where Sandy and the other lawyers had gathered to await the news. The governor enforced one more unusual, and key, demand: The bill must pass the legislature without a single change. Otherwise the deal would unravel.

On June 5, Governor Jerry Brown signed the Agricultural Labor Relations Act, the first law in the country to promote union activity in the fields, to give workers a route to organize and hold secret-ballot elections, and to penalize employers who interfered or retaliated against union supporters. Jerry's claim to having midwifed the best labor law in the country was not an idle boast. He had negotiated in so many favorable clauses that the growers and Teamsters had overlooked some when they agreed to the deal. *The Packer*, an industry newsletter, had to run a correction after reporting that the bill outlawed boycotts. No other union in the country had unilateral power to determine the good standing of its members—in effect, controlling their right to work. The union prevailed on almost all key points, from saving the boycott to having elections first, challenges after. Existing contracts would be in effect only until an election was held; the Teamsters would have to fight to defend all their contracts. Because the bill had passed in emergency session, the law would take effect within months, in time for the fall growing season.

After the bill was signed, Jerry focused on the next round: drafting rules that would be enshrined as regulations. He wanted to negotiate access to the fields for union organizers, and make sure the ballots had symbols as well as words. Chavez was thinking about something else: how to preserve his movement in a world about to turn upside down.

"The whole fight's going to change," he predicted. Until now, his movement had been rooted in the quest for recognition, "which is the one that appeals to the human mind and the heart more than anything else."[13] From now on the fight would center on issues Chavez considered more mundane—contracts, wages, benefits, and grievances. The battleground would be Delano, not D.C. The passionate urban supporters would fade in importance, and farmworkers with middle-class aspirations would make more demands. To preserve the spirit of the movement, Chavez told the board, it was time to evolve into the Poor Peoples Union. First, they should reach out to senior citizens and welfare recipients, people on fixed incomes who could pay for services but needed support. Let them use the UFW's credit union, the service centers, and the health clinics. "Show them some love," Chavez urged, become their extended family, and win their allegiance in return. "The potential to make real ardent followers and supporters, the potential to make a *causa* out of this is fantastic," he said. "It's there. Besides, we don't have a choice." If they did not expand to embrace poor people in the cities, Chavez warned, the movement would wither.

He looked ahead portentously to the start of elections in the fields and the end of the boycott. "The more we win, the weaker we're going to get," Chavez said. "The moment we pull our troops from the cities, back to our own, we lose power. We're going to lose a hell of a lot of power. The power right now is out there: It's borrowed."[14]

PART IV

The New World

June 1975–March 1977

CHAPTER 15

Elections in the Fields

June 1975

Eliseo

After all those long midwestern winters organizing picket lines, fasts, and protests, Eliseo was about to see the payoff: farmworkers across California voting for the union of their choice. He arrived at La Paz for the summer board meeting, eager to digest details of the new law and to ascertain his role in the historic elections. One week and twenty-four pages of notes later, Eliseo left with a clear mandate: Beat the Teamsters. But just as when he first went to Chicago to stop the sale of grapes, Eliseo headed for his new assignment with little idea of strategy or tactics. He didn't even have a car.

The last time the union had engaged in an all-out campaign to win workers' votes, Eliseo had been a twenty-year-old neophyte, beaten up during the election at the DiGiorgio ranch. Nine years later the UFW was gearing up to compete against the Teamsters and the growers at the polls again—in dozens of elections, often several the same day, in fields across the vast state of California, from artichoke ranches to apple orchards. The union organizers had less than three months to prepare, and hardly a clue what to expect.

Chavez invited a large group to La Paz and asked Jerry to present a tutorial on the law. The lawyer began with the basics. To trigger an election, the union needed to present signed cards from more than half the workers asking for union representation. The petition must be filed during peak season, when more than half the employees at a ranch were working. The election would take place within seven days after the petition was filed. Jerry enumerated illegal practices that could overturn an election. An employer could not threaten to go out of business, promise benefits for a no-union vote, intimidate, demote, or fire union supporters. "If it's a threat or a promise, we can get them," Jerry said. But the growers could and would fight back, he warned. Some were already giving workers two paychecks—one for the two percent of their salary they would pay in union dues if they joined the UFW. "If it's free speech," Jerry said, "we can't get them."[1]

Eliseo took notes as Jerry reviewed details such as which jobs were covered, how to challenge company ringers, and which strikers were eligible to vote. Finally, on the fourth day of the meeting, the union leaders began to discuss strategy. They made little progress beyond agreement on their pitch: The UFW was the union of the workers. That was what made them different from the Teamsters. *"Ahora es Cuando,"* Eliseo wrote. That was the new election slogan: Now is the Time.

Eliseo suggested splitting the ranches into two groups—those with Teamster contracts and those without. The union should focus on the second group, he argued. Growers with no union would have little incentive to help the Teamsters. "We know they cannot organize unless the growers help them, right?" Eliseo said. The Teamsters would have to focus their limited resources to defend the contracts they had; the rest of the companies would be wide open. Chavez endorsed the opposite approach, relishing a fight. He numbered the areas of the state according to the severity of the Teamster threat. Then he assigned Eliseo to Oxnard, telling the board that the coastal area an hour north of Los Angeles was the region where the Teamsters were strongest.[2] "Oxnard, we've got that son of a bitch there," Chavez said, naming the most accomplished Teamster organizer. "Oxnard is going to be a big battle with the Teamsters . . . You've got a real fight on your hands."

Eliseo accepted the assignment without a word. Chavez assured him he would like the terrain. "Ever been in Oxnard? It's the biggest Chicano concentration of people living together outside of Los Angeles . . . Just like little Mexico."[3]

Chavez listed all available organizers, then assigned them around the state. "All I got is two?" Eliseo asked plaintively at the end. He inquired about a car to get to Oxnard; Chavez wasn't sure any were free. The union relied on a fleet of ancient white Plymouth Valiants and donated cars that broke down more often than they worked. To start Eliseo's car in Chicago required two people: One held a screw driver on a connection under the hood while the other turned the key.

Eliseo had ten weeks to figure out how to win elections, during an interregnum when the law was not yet in effect and nobody knew whether its provisions would apply retroactively. In addition, he inherited an ongoing strike at the world's largest egg ranch, home to three million chickens and hundreds of unhappy Teamster members. Eliseo called Dorothy Johnson and told her to pack up and drive to California—hoping the car would last. He headed west to Oxnard, a place he had never seen.

Chavez also left the board meeting without a clear plan. He traveled to a rally in Calexico and watched *Fighting for Our Lives* with a group of workers. "I was sitting in the movie thinking, you know, 'Well, everybody is assigned now, what am I going to do?' " he explained. "I couldn't see myself at La Paz, you know, behind a desk, even though, you know, it would have been helpful in some ways." So he decided to tap into powerful Mexican traditions and march from the San Diego border north to Sacramento. "The sacrifice, they understand," he said, in the midst of what he called the thousand-mile march. "Mostly women will come, some men, and they will embrace me, and they cry . . . and they say, 'Stop walking, it's too much sacrifice. It's too much.' "[4]

He believed his own sacrifice drew workers to make a spiritual commitment to the union. He did not need to talk much about elections. "It's like a common language, especially with the Mexican worker . . . I know that if you walk, something happens to people. If they walk, something beautiful happens."[5] The march, Chavez said, engaged workers the same way the images in *Fighting for Our Lives* conveyed Teamster brutality more powerfully than words. Every night, for weeks, he sat with workers and watched the movie that chronicled the battles of 1973, now eclipsed by the new law.

Eliseo was settled in Oxnard by the time the marchers approached. Dorothy had survived the trip from Chicago; she traveled with another boycotter to start the car and slept outside in her sleeping bag at rest areas along the way. Chavez held his first large farmworker rally of the march in a park a few blocks from the union's Oxnard office. Eliseo bought an hour of time on Spanish radio to broadcast the rally live. He introduced Chavez, who spoke only briefly. Eliseo improvised, corralling mariachis to play and fill out the radio time.

Dorothy Johnson, second from left, links arms with UFW volunteers as they sing the traditional song "De Colores." (Cris Sanchez)

The next day Eliseo walked about ten miles with Chavez through the barrios and lush fields of the Oxnard plain. The march seemed removed from the frantic preparation for elections. But Eliseo saw the warm response and admiration that the quiet leader elicited. Tired after walking only half a day, Eliseo was impressed again with Chavez's powerful appeal and his commitment to sacrifice, for the workers.

Sandy

Sandy was in the crowd at the Oxnard rally, by necessity not choice. He was scrambling to get ready for dozens of elections, and the march was a baffling distraction. Every day he was frustrated by a new grower or Teamster outrage and confronted with a dozen decisions on uncharted legal matters. He was acutely aware that his responses could determine whether the union won or lost.

Sandy and Jerry often needed answers in a hurry, and Chavez was off walking. The lawyers had to drive hundreds of miles and talk with the union president as he walked. Sandy couldn't understand why Chavez deliberately removed himself from organizing for elections—not even routing the march primarily through areas that would be targeted in the first round of votes in September. The way the growing seasons fell, the fields along the central coast, stretching from south of Oxnard to north of Salinas, would be the prime area during the late summer harvest.

July and August became a free-for-all in the fields, everyone operating in a no-man's-land until the law went into effect. UFW organizers tried to invoke provisions of the new law that promised them equal access to workers and protected union supporters from retribution. Teamsters and growers locked the union out and denied the law had any impact until the end of August. Sandy directed volunteers to document incidents that could be appealed later—workers who had been threatened, fired, or denied access to fields. When Salinas police and immigration agents raided labor camps a week before elections began and tried to deport thirty-two workers, Sandy went to find them in the lockup and protest. He ended up under arrest, chained to two union organizers. But a judge ruled the workers could stay. "Workers have a right to vote in the upcoming elections," Sandy said triumphantly.[6]

Sandy ends up handcuffed to Marshall Ganz in the Salinas Border Patrol facility after telling workers about to be deported that they had the right to stay and vote in upcoming elections.

Finally, on August 28, the California Agricultural Labor Relations Board came to life. In English it quickly became known as the ALRB. In Spanish the agency was simply called *La Ley Laboral*. The labor law.

By coincidence, the eve of the opening of the new state office fell on Labor Day. In the parking lot of a U-shaped Salinas strip mall on Laurel Street, several hundred farmworkers held a late-afternoon rally. A priest said mass from a flatbed truck parked in front of the standard government-issue office. The workers celebrated with food and song. Then they lined up to play their small role in history. They settled in for an all-night vigil to make sure they would be first to file election petitions on Tuesday morning. Seven days later, there would be elections. Many workers would cast votes for the first time in their lives.

Shortly before the office opened at eight A.M., Sandy joined the expectant crowd, fourteen election petitions in hand from Salinas and five from Oxnard. The festive atmosphere dissolved as soon as the doors opened. The ALRB director tried to sneak Teamster officials in ahead of the line. Sandy and the workers stormed the office, determined to file first, for the historic symbolism.

They prevailed, but the confrontation presaged weeks of stormy exchanges. Most of the three dozen board agents hastily hired to supervise elections lacked any experience with farmworkers. Those who had conducted union elections under federal labor law were accustomed to employees voting in offices, not exuberant crowds in fields and parking lots. They could not fathom the need to hold elections at three A.M., before work began, or to refrain from voting on Mondays because many workers commuted on weekends to Mexicali. Many agents didn't speak Spanish. They were unfamiliar with Mexican names, so the tradition of using both paternal and maternal last names caused endless confusion. The agents invariably believed the polite employers, as opposed to the scruffy union attorneys and Mexican farmworkers. "Our objections are met with distaste, as if a child were throwing a tantrum and the parent decided that the best way to deal with it is to ignore it," Eliseo reported.[7]

Sandy's normally taciturn demeanor gave way to his own public temper tantrums. Day and night he was in that little office in the Salinas strip mall, leaning over the counter screaming at board agents and reading them the law. He demanded they give him the companies' lists of employees, challenged the inflated numbers on growers' lists, and made them review cards they had discarded because they couldn't read the handwriting.

Once the state accepted petitions, Sandy's fights centered on the pre-election conferences, chaired by state agents to work out rules, time, and place for each election. Sandy arrived with workers; state officials tried to kick them out. Materials were not translated into Spanish. "There's a board agent at this place that really believes, and she's stated this, that these elections are held for the state's benefit, not the workers," Sandy fumed. "It's so frustrating to go there . . . They don't know what's been going on for ten years. They're totally ignorant of it, and they just have no conception. They think: well if we lose an election, so what?"[8] Imbued with the union's life-and-death ethos, Sandy fought for every vote. With his long hair and cowboy hat, he denounced the racist, classist mentality that assumed the growers' attorneys were right. When workers begged to have elections off company property, he sought to make state officials understand how intimidated the workers felt.

The next problem was figuring out who won. Elections began on September 5, and dozens were held the first week alone. But growers persuaded the state agency to impound the ballots in many cases until various legal issues were resolved. That fueled the enormous distrust of the electoral process that the union had been working hard to dispel. Corrupt elections were the norm in Mexico; to many workers, an honest vote count was an oxymoron. Sandy made sure board agents held the ballot boxes upside down before each election and shook them in front of the crowd. Workers stood guard as election observers. When the polls closed, the boxes were sealed with reams of tape. The election observers and board agents signed their names on the tape, to serve as proof, when the boxes were opened, that there had been no tampering.

Sandy felt discouraged, then apprehensive, unsure the law would work. The physical demands were exhausting. The union staff was going all day, not eating till close to midnight, dinners at Rosita's Armory Café, catty-corner from the Salinas legal office. All this energy going into elections, and Sandy felt like he had accomplished little. Then he went to the pre-election conference for Interharvest, the only company that had had a UFW contract since 1970. The conference was going as badly as all the others. The board agent overruled the union on point after point. When the hearing resumed after lunch, the agent physically ejected a law student working with the union, because she had not been at the morning session. Then the agent allowed in a company vice president, even though he had not been present earlier. When workers questioned the disparity, the agent explained that the vice president was the *dueño*—the owner of the company.[9] The workers walked out in protest. Sandy considered calling off the election. The lechugero who was head of the ranch committee turned to the lawyer and calmly offered reassurance. We're not afraid, the lechugero said. His simple confidence caught Sandy short. If the workers weren't afraid, why was he panicking?

That strength and dignity spread in the weeks that followed. More workers volunteered to serve as election observers, unafraid to proclaim their allegiance to the union. They embraced a process that gave them standing for the first time in a world where they had had none. When the votes were finally counted two weeks later, the Union de Campesinos won overwhelmingly at Interharvest: UFW, 1167; Teamsters, 28; No union, 18. The first weeks of tallies showed the UFW racking up more votes, while the Teamsters won slightly more elections and many remained undecided.

As Sandy worked with the Interharvest committee, he grew increasingly impressed with the confidence of the lechugeros and steadies who had been working for years under a UFW contract. Their self-assurance was a tangible reminder of why he was there, and how the union changed lives.

"To me, it was really clear what it meant to have a union, forgetting wages and benefits and everything else," Sandy said after the Interharvest election. "Just seeing the difference in the people."[10]

Eliseo

Less than one month after elections began, the UFW was the largest union for farmworkers in Oxnard. Once again, Eliseo was making it up as he went along: Diagnose a problem, devise a solution.

When the Egg City strikers were picketing the farm and fighting with the scabs, Eliseo enlisted their help in Plan Escoba—Operation Broom. He divided Oxnard into grids and sent teams out to sweep up as many cards as possible from any workers they could find. Before the board even opened, Eliseo had seven thousand cards he could use to petition for elections. The strikers kept busy and stopped antagonizing the Egg City workers, so Eliseo could send organizers inside the ranch to campaign. He needed both the strikers' and the workers' votes to win.[11]

When immigration agents began raiding ranches just before elections, Eliseo devised a diversionary tactic. He instructed all the workers with legal papers to swarm around the border agents, ask questions, and create a stir. The federal agents were taken aback. The workers were delighted by their power to sidetrack *la migra,* the agents who had come to deport union supporters.

When Eliseo saw how growers intimidated workers during the days just before an election, he figured out how to file his petitions at the last moment, right before workers were laid off for the season. The petition qualified because the company was still at more than half its peak workforce when Eliseo filed. But by the time of the vote, most of the workers were home—instead of in the fields facing pressure from their bosses.

And when Eliseo found himself with a skeleton staff, he looked for help among the longtime Chavistas in the area. At Interharvest, he found Jose Manuel Rodriguez, a thirty-year-old who had been enthusiastically volunteering to help the union since 1970. During the day he picked and planted celery, broccoli, and lettuce; in the evenings and on weekends, he picketed Safeway supermarkets all over southern California and demonstrated outside liquor stores that carried Gallo wine. During the Prop 22 campaign he had gone to Los Angeles and slept in Lincoln Park for two weeks to help on the human billboard campaign. He had lobbied for the labor law in Sacramento, and now he was eager to see the results. He and Eliseo came from the same Mexican state, Zacatecas. They made a good team. Rodriguez knew the local fields, and he knew everyone in Oxnard. Eliseo knew the union, and he knew how to organize.

Rodriguez was a natural schmoozer, at ease chatting with anyone. But the first time he had to run a meeting, he froze. He knew how to fire people up to support the union, but he had never had to keep track of cards or votes, count crews, or conduct a house meeting. He learned. Rodriguez resisted Eliseo's entreaties to give up the job at Interharvest and become a full-time union organizer. Eliseo persisted. Finally Rodriguez signed on, taking the five-dollar-a-week salary and the hundred-dollar stipend for rent, gas, and food. He had been an outspoken leader even when he first came to the country as a bracero, a guest worker. He believed in the union, and his sincerity was infectious. Rodriguez had landed at Interharvest after being fired from a company called Donlon Produce because he refused to take a supervisory position. When Eliseo posted a list of the companies he wanted to target and asked for volunteers, Rodriguez's hand shot up. He took Donlon. The first time he went to meet with workers, the company called the police and threw him out. The police dropped him off a few miles away, and he walked back, cheerfully asserting his access rights under the new law.

Jose Manuel Rodriguez, holding a short-handled hoe, works with his wife, Maria, in an Oxnard celery field. They both worked under the Interharvest contract until Jose Manuel went to work full-time for the UFW. (UCLA Charles E. Young Research Library Department of Special Collections, Los Angeles Times Photographic Archives, Copyright © Regents of the University of California, UCLA)

After a quick reconnaissance of the 275 companies in Oxnard, Eliseo had focused on twenty-two growers for the fall elections. Half had contracts with the Teamsters, which would be void if the UFW won. Eliseo researched each target. He recruited a staff of twenty-nine, half of them full-time organizers. He divided the ranches among them. Then he dispatched each organizer to work the companies crew by crew and identify workers who could be union representatives. At meetings from early morning till late at night, Eliseo grilled his organizers, sometimes together, sometimes individually. He made lists on the back of flyers, envelopes, receipts, or whatever he had at hand. He broke each company down by job—irrigators, tractor drivers, celery, cucumbers, lettuce. Then he split each of those categories into three columns: total number of workers, cards signed, sure yes votes.[12]

Cards, the 3¼-by-5¼ pieces of paper certifying that a worker wanted to be represented by the UFW, became critical currency. The organizers were obsessed with cards—getting them, logging them, sorting them, locking them up safely. But the cards, Eliseo stressed, had to be more than just a signature. Anyone could be talked into signing, just to get the organizer to go away. Cards had to be a real commitment to the union, an indication of support. Eliseo wanted cards signed by 75 percent of the workers at a company before he filed for an election. He passed on lessons he had learned from Fred Ross almost a decade earlier: Count with your head, not with your heart.

Eliseo worked out of the union office in the *colonia*, the neighborhood where most workers lived. He mounted loudspeakers outside the office to broadcast music and entertain workers who began to congregate outside at four each morning, waiting for jobs. The Teamster organizers hammered on problems with the UFW hiring hall, forced participation in the boycott, and the 2 percent dues. "In some cases it has had an effect that we have had to really work to overcome," Eliseo noted. He coached his organizers on how to respond. But the union's biggest advantage was its staff. Unlike the Teamsters' professional organizers, Eliseo and Jose Manuel Rodriguez came from the fields.

Between staff meetings, Eliseo visited the vegetable fields and labor camps. To participate you don't need to speak English or be a lawyer or even a citizen, he told workers. The only thing you need is courage. This will be hard work. Growers will threaten you. But the fight is for our children. How many of you are willing to struggle? he always asked as he wound up his speech. How many are willing to work? How many are for the UFW?[13]

Eliseo piled up victories at smaller ranches, then took on the Teamsters' most important local contract. West Foods, a large mushroom grower, operated year round, providing an important base of union dues. Eliseo left nothing to chance. When he heard that several workers lived in the dry creekbed that ran behind the mushroom ranch, he took Rodriguez and went exploring. They found a small path leading into the tall bamboo rushes and overgrown brush. They followed first the worn path, then the faint sound of music. The mushroom pickers welcomed the organizers into their abode beneath a tarp and offered food and drink. Then they signed union cards.

Two days after Eliseo filed for an election at West Foods, the border patrol staged predawn raids and arrested more than thirty workers at the mushroom grower, including several of the UFW's strongest supporters. The Teamsters and the grower had collaborated and were using the border patrol as "an instrument of fear," Eliseo charged at a press conference.[14]

Despite the immigration raids, the union triumphed at West Foods, 136–39, a resounding win at a Teamster ranch. The UFW took another contract away from the Teamsters at Donlon, where Rodriguez celebrated victory over the employer that had fired him. They beat the Teamsters eight times and took away almost six hundred members from the rival union, with one big election at Egg City still undecided. Eliseo marked each victory in his pocket calendar, scrawling <u>WON</u> over the notation about the time and place of the election. In four weeks he lost only one election unexpectedly, a small vegetable farm where the owner had doggedly made his case to workers day after day, one on one. At the end of September the score in Oxnard was UFW 11, Teamsters 3, Company, 1.

Everything about Oxnard brought out Eliseo's competitive spirit. Beating the Teamsters. Competing with other organizers for the most wins. Oxnard also offered a chance to get even with the same Teamster leader who had led the fight at DiGiorgio—where Eliseo had been beaten up. When one of the union's attorneys was scheduled to depose the local Teamster boss, Eliseo suggested holding the interrogation at the union office. Word spread, and the workers poured into the room. With farmworkers circling around him, the Teamster leader sat in the midst of the UFW stronghold, forced to answer questions. Eliseo used the deposition to demonstrate the union's strength and to puncture the aura of invincibility that had surrounded the growers and the Teamsters.

The fertile soil and temperate seaside climate of Ventura's Oxnard plain meant crops grew all year—tomatoes in September, celery and lettuce in November, lemons in January, and strawberries in March. Eliseo started plotting longer-term strategy. He commissioned a study of tomato acreage to devise a plan to get the bulk of the industry under union contract. He had lost staff to other areas of the state and was down by almost a third. He badly needed more organizers and legal aides. "There is a lot of work all year round, so the organizing has to be an ongoing campaign," Eliseo reported to Chavez in late September. "If we can get more help we are going to be in great shape."[15]

Such long-range building was not to be. Two weeks later Eliseo was transferred to Coachella.

CHAPTER 16

Transitions

September 1975

Chris

Like Chavez, Chris sensed as soon as the Agricultural Labor Relations Act passed that his world would become radically different. The boycott, which he had nurtured and championed and shaped into something that meant so much to so many people, was no longer the life-and-death struggle. What mattered was winning elections.

Chris perceived that his role would be less vital, removed from the action and the front lines. For the first time in more than a dozen years, he wondered if he should seek a new mission. "I am bored with NFWM," Chris wrote to himself when the law was signed.[1] In public he remained far more circumspect. "Our relationship to Cesar and the UFW is solid but not as intimate because of the growing size of the union and its entities," he told his board. He tried to generate excitement by looking ahead to a time when church people would again play a greater role: "The UFW is planning an organizing effort among the poor (particularly senior citizens and welfare recipients) . . . When it comes it will be an opportunity for churches to relate to the militant poor in their own communities."[2]

But first the UFW had to be stabilized. Pressure from the boycott and religious supporters would be necessary to ensure the law worked and companies negotiated contracts in good faith. An election victory only won the union the right to represent the workers. "Celebrate . . . But don't relax!" Chris wrote supporters. "No law can guarantee strong contracts."[3] He strove to guard against complacency, a sense that the fight was over, time to move on to some other cause. Bishop Roger Mahony chaired the new ALRB; Catholics assumed all was well. Supermarkets happily resumed the sale of grapes, pointing out the union had gotten what it wanted—elections. Confused boycotters called Chris for advice. Then Chavez elevated confusion into crisis.

Three weeks after elections began, Chavez summoned Chris to La Paz for an emergency meeting with union leaders. In full battle mode, Chavez ticked off problems they had all experienced with the new state agency. He painted the situation in dire terms: "I haven't sensed, in the whole history of the union, a period of so much frustration as we have had these past two weeks." He railed about the state agents' failure to protect workers' rights. He denounced the growers for conspiring with the Teamsters. Chavez focused on the defeats, not the victories, and warned that unless the state board changed dramatically, the whole union could be destroyed. Outside Oxnard, Salinas, and San Diego, the union organizers had struggled; Chavez blamed their losses on others and even hinted at hanky-panky with vote counts and ballot boxes with fake bottoms.

He dismissed Eliseo's wins in Oxnard and Marshall Ganz's successes in Salinas. "We're not going to win any more elections," Chavez told them. "You're kidding yourselves."

"What the hell are we going to do?" he asked. "Boycott the elections? Cry? Continue to cry about what they're doing to us?"

He quickly received the answer he sought. "Go after Brown," Jerry said with gusto, referring to the governor. "Fuck Brown." Jerry was itching for a fight. He had filed more than one hundred unfair labor charges the first day the state agency opened, complaints that were supposed to receive priority attention. "They didn't do a damn thing."

"Brown! Brown! Brown!" Chris chanted. "Get him!" Brown claimed credit for the landmark law; he should take blame for its failures. "It's a big feather in his cap. Let's put mud on it!"

Chavez played devil's advocate, one of his favorite techniques. "So we don't like what he's doing, what can we do? . . . He's the most popular governor in the history of California."

"He responds to pressure," Jerry countered. "You know he does. The slightest bit of pressure, he jumps like a baby."

"He's ambitious," Chris added, referring to Brown's presidential aspirations and suggesting the union bring one of his Democratic rivals to California to campaign.

Chavez's mood lightened as he schemed out loud. The union would demand that the governor fire the ALRB's chief counsel. First, they would organize supporters to send a hundred thousand letters of protest. Next, put farmworkers on buses and send them to the capitol. Occupy the governor's office if need be. Bishop Mahony called, and Chavez interrupted the meeting to take the call. "I told him we're going on a public campaign," Chavez reported when he got off the phone. "I told him, 'We're working full time. We don't want to win elections anymore. We want to prove to you and everybody else that the whole thing stinks.'"

"We're better at that anyway," Jim Drake said ruefully, and everyone laughed.

Chavez had already contacted sympathetic reporters and presented allegations of election fraud, forged signatures, and bribes. He planned to attack the state officials on television and radio. But the first step was to summon "independent" outside observers. "We have to bring in some credible people to California, have an investigation, have a press conference, say the whole goddamn thing stinks," Chavez said. Once again, he turned to Chris.[4]

Out of duty rather than passion, the minister went to work. He crisscrossed the country delivering pep talks to religious leaders and boycott committees. He spent hours explaining how the law should work—then enumerating its failures. He detailed case after case where employers had illegally retaliated against Chavistas and the union had filed charges—but the backlogged state agency let the complaints languish. In late fall Chris brought seventy-two religious leaders from seventeen states to California. They toured Delano, Oxnard, and Salinas and then reported their findings to a state committee. They met forty farmworkers who had been fired after the UFW won an election at an Oxnard vegetable grower. They talked to workers who had lived for years in a labor camp—suddenly facing eviction because they demonstrated support for the union.[5]

Chavez's strategy succeeded. Brown, invested in making the law work, appointed a commission to straighten out the problems. Seeing the injustices re-energized Chris. When he brought the NFWM board to Oxnard for its semiannual meeting in November, he overcame his own weariness and warned forcefully against the attitude he sensed in conversations around the country. "There is an awful lot of whatever it is out there, an awful lot of desire to back away from this issue to do other things; to assume that the law is solving the problem; to want to not boycott anymore because it is complicated now," he told his board. Now comes the real test of commitment, he preached, recovering his old fervor. You must push back hard, hammer at the message, expect people to call you crazy and irrational, "just keep fighting and fighting and fighting and fighting for what we know that the farm worker needs and that is just simple things: their own union."[6]

To the outside world, Chris's strong and determined front betrayed little of his waning enthusiasm. But in a "Personal and Confidential" letter to Chavez that he wrote and then rewrote, Chris confessed to having felt restless since spring. He posed several options, all of which would bring him to La Paz to work more closely with Chavez. One idea was to move the NFWM to La Paz. Another was for Chris to work directly for Chavez, on a temporary or permanent basis. Chris recognized that scenario created the problem of finding a new leader for the farm worker ministry. "I have thought about this a long time," Chris wrote. "I realize that the churches trust the NFWM, partly because of the leadership. I think we are going to have a real problem if I leave. But maybe it is time for the NFWM to be something different. It will go downhill anyway if I do not have the spirit for the work."[7]

Sabino

As the UFW scored election victories in the vegetable fields, the union no longer struggled for legitimacy. Now the fight revolved around contracts. The union office on South Wood Street in Salinas bustled with excitement, and Sabino liked to stop by after work. The union staff began to call more often on the irrigator, a dependable and persuasive salesman for the cause. Sabino began to learn more about the world of the union beyond the Salinas Valley.

He attended his first UFW convention in the summer of 1975, proud to be elected to represent his crew of steadies. He felt even prouder when he picked up his delegate badge—a stylized metal eagle with a slot in the middle, a slip of paper inserted with his name and company neatly typed: "Sabino Lopez—Interharvest." He mingled with delegates from ranches around California and boycott cities around the country who came together in Fresno for the second UFW convention. Jessica Govea brought a busload of supporters from Toronto, stocking up before she left on peanut butter, crackers, jam, cookies, nuts, and dried fruit for the long trip.[8] Chavez welcomed the contingent warmly and called upon Jessica to sing. "You will have to excuse me," she told the delegates. "We came in a bus from Canada, which is three thousand miles away. We were singing for three days on the road and I lost my voice. We will do our best."[9]

Sabino marveled at people who chose to live on subsistence wages in order to help farmworkers. But what thrilled him most was when Chavez talked about his vision of a union run by farmworkers: "We have not come to the point yet, but it is our intention: the workers on the ranch governing their union . . . It must be this way because the only way to achieve a democratic union is to base it on the workers." The ranch committees on which many delegates served were the key, Chavez said. "The only way that there can be democracy in the Union now and tomorrow and thereafter is to have those ranches, those ranch committees, retain as much power to run their affairs as possible."

The imagery matched Chavez's words. Rising Chicano artist Carlos Almaraz and his Los Angeles collective, Los Four, had created a 24-by-44-foot mural for the convention hall entitled *Why We Struggle*, a depiction of workers building their own union and triumphing over a greedy grower (skeleton), biased police (a piglet), and corrupt Teamsters (a rat).[10] Building a democratic union is hard work, Chavez explained, as he fielded questions from delegates about the ranch committee system. "Nothing comes easily. Headaches. Brothers and sisters who have just joined the union and don't know how things work make mistakes. But the important thing is that they are always working." The effort would pay off, he promised, as together they built a union unlike any other, rooted in its members, who would learn to run it themselves. "No one in a movement is born knowing that he/she has to deal with the Constitution, the contract, the law and all the rules and orders and all the requests and problems," Chavez said. "No one can comprehend it all at once; it takes time to understand these things. But little by little, little by little."[11]

Sabino took that counsel to heart. He had been working at Interharvest since his old company, Freshpict, shut down a few years earlier. Sabino regulated water at the Shrine Ranch, a thousand-acre parcel south of Salinas, sandwiched between Highway 101 and the foothills of the Santa Lucia Mountains. Interharvest had bought the smaller ranch, and the workers now fell under the union contract. The UFW field office director had dispatched Sabino to teach workers about the union, a task that required patience and a thick skin.

The crew was one very large extended family from Chupicuaro, a village in the Mexican state of Guanajuato. They had never taken part in the strikes—in fact, they had been insulted by the strikers, cursed for being scabs. They had heard horror stories about the union. Now they paid 2 percent of their salaries to the UFW, since the contract forced them to join the union. They viewed Sabino with suspicion. He told the UFW field office director he needed help. Soon his father, brother, and a few other union partisans were dispatched to the Shrine ranch.

Little by little, Sabino won over the family from Chupicuaro. He talked to the foreman to resolve problems. He filed grievances. Workers saw results and began to overcome their distrust. Sabino looked for opportunities to demonstrate how the contract helped. Before, there had been a caste system, with the foreman playing favorites. The others had drawn the worst jobs, the least overtime, the harshest conditions. Over time Sabino was able to level out assignments, workloads, and pay.

The next step in Sabino's education was bargaining. The Interharvest contract expired at the end of 1975, and Sabino was elected to the committee of workers who met with union negotiators and took part in deliberations with the company. Neither the union nor Interharvest paid workers for time spent on negotiations, so the Interharvest workers paid a special assessment to cover the salaries of their colleagues on the committee. The committee met often, because the Interharvest contract took on special importance. The union was about to embark on widespread negotiations, to turn the election victories into contracts. The leadership planned to use the Interharvest pact as a master contract. The Interharvest committee met at La Paz, and Sabino got to see Jerry in action. Sabino soaked it all up.

When the contract was nearly resolved, the company proposed to eliminate the nickel differential in the hourly rate for irrigators. Traditionally, the pairs who regulated the water flow were paid a few cents more than the field workers. Sabino steadfastly held out for his nickel. The issue was not just his own salary, Sabino argued, but a matter of principle: Never lose ground. Finally he got his nickel; the irrigators' salary went up to $3.15 an hour. Sabino took his place proudly at the table for the contract-signing ceremony. The union printed and distributed the Interharvest Master Contract, the model for future negotiations. The outside cover was an illustration of a worker in a field of lettuce, a giant eagle rising in the sky. On the inside the union reproduced photographs. There was Sabino, the irrigator who had held out for the extra nickel, signing his name to the contract he helped negotiate.

Sabino, front, holds papers during a meeting of the Interharvest negotiating committee at La Paz. Chavez sits with his dogs, Boycott and Huelga. (Walter P. Reuther Library, Wayne State University)

Jerry

Jerry had realized that the landmark law he had negotiated would end the guerrilla fights he so enjoyed. What he had not foreseen was how much the new law would alter his work and his relationship with the union leader.

Jerry received his first inkling when the Agricultural Labor Relations Board held its initial hearings. He had overlooked a small but significant detail in the final negotiations over the bill: symbols on the ballot, for workers who could not read. To his great annoyance, Jerry had mistakenly checked the item off his list. So when he and Chavez appeared before the

ALRB, Jerry was intent on making the strongest possible case to put the union's trademark eagle on the ballot.

The union prevailed, but Chavez was no help. At the start of the hearing in the state capitol, ALRB chairman Roger Mahony asked if anyone in the audience could not understand English. "Okay, there are three gentlemen at least, so if there is one, that's enough," Mahony said, directing his executive secretary to translate after each speaker.[12] Jerry watched Chavez tear up, overcome by the significance of the gesture and the union's progress in just a few short years. Jerry understood. But he wanted Chavez to engage in the nitty-gritty, to spar and scheme, the way they had done before. The union president could be both detail-oriented and strategically brilliant. But Chavez seemed not to focus on how to make maximum use of this new tool they had fought so hard to win.

Jerry, by contrast, was consumed by the details of the law. And that was the second realization that his life was going to change significantly. The law contained numerous deadlines for filing objections, appeals, and counter-appeals. Jerry had fought for strict time limits to protect migrant workers. He had not anticipated the magnitude of work those provisions would create. Almost every election generated appeals, which had to be filed within five days. The UFW automatically challenged any losses. Lawyers and paralegals gathered evidence, took sworn statements, and wrote arguments to convince the state agents that wrongdoing had marred the election campaign or the voting. In most cases the growers and the Teamsters also challenged UFW wins, if only to stall the certification. Separately, the union lawyers lodged complaints, called unfair labor practices. The law explicitly protected workers' rights to organize, but companies routinely threatened or fired union supporters. The remedies included large fines, reinstatement with back pay, and public apologies. Contract negotiations often triggered more charges, and sanctions if the union could prove the grower was bargaining in bad faith.

Jerry was skilled at delegating, but he found himself under pressure from the administrative demands. He had to lead his staff in a makeover from guerrilla warriors to labor lawyers; recruit more help; respond to nonstop inquires from union organizers around the state; and adjust to meeting the hundreds of deadlines for briefs, memos, declarations, and filings. The legal department jumped from a small office to eighteen lawyers and as many as a dozen paralegals. The young, close-knit group earned next to nothing but reveled in their status as nontraditional lawyers. Almost no one had actually practiced labor law before, and some were not even out of school. Kirsten

Chavez poses with the Salinas legal department, including (left to right) Tom Dalzell, just over Chavez's shoulder, Sandy, Jerry, and Glenn Rothner. (Walter P. Reuther Library, Wayne State University)

Zerger, a first-year law student in Berkeley, had signed up for a summer internship because working for the union fit with her ideals of social justice and her Mennonite upbringing. She ended up writing a manual that explained basic rules of labor law and cited relevant precedents established by the National Labor Relations Act.

The lawyers' work cycle mirrored the growing season. By late fall the harvest had largely ended. The frantic election activity segued into hearings to defend the victories, challenge the losses, and guard against attempts to weaken crucial state regulations, like those guaranteeing UFW organizers access to the fields. In San Diego alone, which was not one of the major agricultural areas, eighteen hearings on elections were scheduled for the last three weeks of November.[13]

By the time the state Senate and Assembly committees held a joint hearing on the implementation of the new law in late November, the state board was running out of money. Bishop Mahony testified that the pace and demand had been so much greater than anticipated that the board had rapidly gone through the initial appropriation of $1.3 million and was close to exhausting an additional $1.2 million emergency loan. The board had conducted 334 elections between September 5 and November 20, an average of more than six a day, and handed down fourteen decisions. Dozens more were pending. Asked what would happen if no further money was appropriated, Mahony said simply: "Well then we'll go out of business on January 31. Period."[14]

The legislature was not inclined to allocate more funds. The last election took place on February 6, 1976, seven days after the board technically shut down. Chavez blamed the growers and their influence in the state capital. He turned to Jerry to figure out ways to fight back. Chavez wanted to appeal to the public, relying on support the union traditionally enjoyed in urban areas. Chavez called executive board members the day the ALRB shut down. "We need to come back and stick growers with something. Wants authority to ask Jerry to prepare initiative," Eliseo wrote after the conference call.

Three days later Chavez told the board that Jerry was drafting a ballot initiative to make the ALRA part of the state constitution. The threat of a proposition would pressure lawmakers to reopen the state board.

By the end of February, Chavez relished an electoral fight, even if the legislature funded the ALRB. He got executive board members on the phone again and told them he wanted to put a measure on the November ballot whether or not the state board reopened. The climate would never be better, he said. He asked the executive board for permission to bring boycotters back to California to gather signatures to place the initiative on the ballot.[15]

Jerry had warned during an executive board meeting that a statewide campaign for a ballot initiative would be "a shitload of work." On the other hand, a victory would take the best labor law in the country and enshrine it in the California constitution. No future lawmakers would be able to touch it.

Eliseo

When the ALRB shut down, Eliseo took on another role for which he felt unprepared: department head in charge of contract administration. Now he had to figure out how to run an institution, not just a campaign.

He and Dorothy Johnson moved into a trailer at La Paz, a two-bedroom unit with some built-in shelves, luxurious compared to their past accommodations. The February 1976 move was their fourth in just over a year. Chavez had sent Eliseo from Cleveland to Chicago when the boycott there needed help, then to Oxnard in June to organize elections, then to Coachella in October to pick up the tail end of the growing season in the desert.

As head of contract administration, Eliseo took charge of two dozen field offices with about one hundred staffers. He assumed responsibility for making sure the handful of existing contracts worked and negotiating new ones as fast as possible. He had some familiarity with the issues from his one-year stint running the Calexico field office. But that had involved four contracts. Now there were almost two hundred election victories across the state. And not a single standard practice.

The union had no uniform rules for how to run the hiring hall—every field office did it differently. No standards for grievance procedures or what to do when a worker filed a complaint. No system to set priorities for the union's handful of negotiators. No plan for how to negotiate contracts at the dozens of ranches where the union was certified. In many places workers had had little or no contact with union staff since the election victory. Eliseo began to compile lists: companies with contracts, companies with certified election wins but no contracts, companies where negotiations were in progress. He sorted them by geographic area and by crop. He made notes to himself in the first weeks: "Recruit headquarters staff. Make sure every negotiating team has translator. Get copies of all contracts. Set up meetings with companies to bury hatchet."[16]

Before the law, the union had flourished with minimal structure. On paper Chavez had exercised central control; in practice his control had been somewhat illusory. Successful leaders like Eliseo navigated on their own, and as long as they produced results, their strategies went unchallenged. At the same time weak staff often escaped notice. Errors were overlooked as easily as the cash sitting in dozens of bank accounts opened in boycott cities, then abandoned. The union suffered no major consequences if a boycott leader inflated his numbers or failed to muster a picket line one weekend.

Eliseo realized that the stakes had become much higher, the results less subject to interpretation. Elections had winners and losers; contracts were signed or lost. A small mistake negotiating one clause could prove costly for years. The lack of standard practices became glaringly obvious—and legally problematic. Eliseo set out to build a structure that turned the momentum of the electoral victories into working contracts.

Chavez had been struggling to define his own role since the law went into effect. He was grappling with how to maintain control when he could no longer write the rules, when the need to delegate was obvious, and when the opportunities for subordinates to develop local power bases were just as clear. Chavez became intrigued by the science of "management" and saw salvation in a retired navy management guru named Crosby Milne. Like Chavez, Milne was a self-made man. He had spent his early childhood on a Canadian farm without indoor plumbing. He joined the navy as a mechanic and retired as a self-taught systems design expert. When his son dropped out of college to work for the union, Milne went to La Paz to see for himself what *la causa* was all about. Deeply religious and impressed with Chavez, Milne offered to help for a year in 1976. He considered the work his patriotic duty in the nation's bicentennial.

Chavez seized upon Milne's system, with its neat charts and boxes, clear lines of authority, and SAMs (Strategic Achievable Measurable objectives), as the solution for the unwieldy union. In the spring and summer Milne and Chavez held a dozen conferences, one for each department and entity in the farm worker movement. "In these conferences I am always saying that when the Union started, this was where we started—to organize workers," Chavez said as he opened the Organizing Department Reorganization Conference. "God, we never knew we would have to go into all these things: law, initiatives, politics, SAMs, goals, budgets, you name it; none of that. If I'd known that, I would have said, screw it. But it was essentially the organizing which I loved and I still like; but I can't do it these days. It's like candy behind the glass counter."[17]

When Chavez first introduced Milne to the board, Eliseo asked, politely, who Milne was and why the board should trust the retired military man in the union's inner circle.[18] Within a few months Eliseo had overcome his skepticism. "Before, we didn't have the rule of law," he explained to an interviewer from the union paper. "Everything we did had to be done through strikes and boycotts." Milne came along just as the union needed a structure in order to take advantage of the law and the new pathways to power. Eliseo called the transition the most significant change since the union was founded in 1962. The key, he said, was delegating power. When Milne had first asked Chavez to list the people who reported to him, they stopped counting at fifty-eight. Within a few months that had changed. "We're at the situation now where a lot more people have authority and power to make decisions," Eliseo said. "This has led to much, much, much better service for the membership. I think it's one of the best things that could have happened."[19]

Evidence of progress came in April. The union needed to conduct a petition drive to place on the November 1976 ballot the initiative that would make the ALRA part of the constitution. Volunteers easily gathered more than enough signatures—729,965—and for once the campaign did not bring everything else to a standstill. Chavez gathered the boycotters who had garnered signatures for a debriefing at La Paz, and Eliseo offered his congratulations. "It's really a sign of maturity for us, for this organization to do the kind of job that you did, while at the same time the rest of the work was being done," he said. "In the past there was a fire and all of us grabbed hoses and buckets and we ran and left everything hanging."

This time Eliseo's department was able to continue negotiating contracts. A year earlier the union had ten contracts covering 4,500 workers. As he addressed the boycotters on May 3, there were thirty contracts covered 15,000 workers. All together the union had won 225 elections covering approximately 39,000 farmworkers. Eliseo had six teams of negotiators working with seventy different growers. "If we do a good job of administering those contracts, then we're really going to have a strong Union," he told the boycotters.

Eliseo focused on defining structures and responsibilities for the ranch committees, the key group of farmworker leaders at each company. "We made a decision that for the union to really be strong, a lot of the power within the union needs to rest with the ranch committee," he told the boycotters. He explained his plan for subcommittees: one for health and safety, one for grievances, one for pensions. That way workers with questions would know who to contact in the fields, and those representatives could serve as liaisons with the union staff in the local office. Strong ranch committees, Eliseo said, made the union both more democratic and more efficient.[20]

But in private, at the next executive board meeting, Eliseo expressed frustration. The ranch committees always seemed to be a low priority. The workers had not received any training. Since the First Constitutional Convention in 1973, Chavez had talked about the importance of ranch committee bylaws and training local leadership. Three years later, nothing had happened. "We need to set up a program for the ranch committees and staff on how to have meetings, file grievances, generally how to administer the contracts," Eliseo argued. Fred Ross had been designated to set up training and education, but Ross, who did not speak Spanish, gravitated toward training the boycott volunteers and the English-speaking organizers. He kept not getting around to the ranch committees. Richard Chavez seconded Eliseo's concern; without sufficient training, the antiunion propaganda about bad contract administration would prove true. His brother acknowledged the need for worker involvement but made no specific plans. Chavez suggested the union encourage participation by commissioning an artist to design certificates for workers who attended house meetings.[21]

Eliseo was not at a conference three weeks later when Chavez expressed trepidation about empowering workers, particularly recent immigrants. "The newer they are in terms of immigrants the more money means to them," he said. Workers must be educated about the importance of sacrifice, Chavez said, praising the volunteers who led by example and shamed workers into understanding. He warned again about the likelihood that future leaders would abandon the union's commitment to pay its staff only a subsistence pay. "The moment this string of leadership goes, she's gonna go," he said. Huerta and Ganz were his chief backers in maintaining the volunteer system, he told the organizers. Farmworkers must understand the importance of sacrifice and the volunteer system before they assumed positions of leadership.

Those comments were edited out of the meeting transcript distributed to the board members. So was Chavez's conclusion: "You don't want farm workers managing the union right now. With the attitude they have on money, it would be a total god damn disaster, it would be chaotic. Unless they're taught the other life, it wouldn't work."[22]

CHAPTER 17

The Crusades

June 1976

Chris

The farm worker movement had taken Chris into worlds he'd never imagined during his sheltered upbringing in Upper Darby, Pennsylvania. Marches and fasts, mob lawyers' living rooms and jail cells. Chris still saw himself as passive in his private life, where he let Pudge make most of the decisions. But the union had enabled him to develop a forceful public persona that veered from righteously indignant to inspiringly charismatic. Now the Protestant minister embarked on another audacious venture: trying to establish a new religious order under the auspices of the Catholic Church.

Chris no longer fretted about being on the sidelines. He had found his new mission.

Chavez decided the time had come to pursue his dream of communal farms. He envisioned the farms as havens for poor people, a resource for the union, and a refuge for loyal supporters. He wanted a strong religious element and thought perhaps the collectives could be run by a new religious order. He had picked Oxnard for the first farm, with its fertile soil and year-round season. He had the perfect director for the endeavor, Chris. And a name for the new order: Los Menos. The Least. He took the name from the words of Jesus in the book of Matthew: "In as much as you have done it unto one of the least of these my brethren, you have done it unto me."[1]

Chavez had a long-standing interest in cooperatives for the poor. Real community would be vital, Chavez said, to keep people involved and avoid the fate of the faltering civil rights and labor movements. He read voraciously and studied the mistakes of the past. He had been exploring economic cooperatives since 1970, when he described his position as comparable to where he had been in terms of the union in 1965: "I was just talking about ideas and what could be done and a lot of people thought I was nuts."[2]

Six years later, with the state law imposing a welter of rules that held little interest for Chavez, he saw community as the future of his movement. He kept the plans from his own board, which would have been as skeptical as his friends in the labor movement. In the spring of 1976, while Crosby Milne worked on reorganization plans and Eliseo negotiated contracts and Jerry schemed about getting the Teamsters out of the fields and bringing the ALRB back to life, Chavez focused on building his community at La Paz and on more ambitious plans for communal farms.

Chris became Chavez's enthusiastic partner in the new endeavor. The two had long conversations, taped so that Chris could transcribe the notes and turn them into a proposal. They talked about selecting the first participants with care, not too "Anglo and educated," so that over time they could recruit farmworkers. Residents would live in separate homes but eat in a communal kitchen, combined perhaps with the church and classrooms. People would take vows of poverty and obedience and donate their money to the community when they moved in. They would commit to staying for at least one year, possibly four. The goal would be to have them stay for life.

The Order of Los Menos would serve the poor of the United States, starting with farmworkers. The first communal farm would serve as a "mother house" for the new religious order. The order would be unique, Chris wrote: "Protestant and Catholic, men and women, single and married, committed to justice, as political as necessary, organizing in the churches." Members would have to work for the UFW first—for as long as two years—before they could join the order. The communal Assembly would meet once every two years for five days, with three-day regional retreats every year. Its governing Policy Council would have five full-time members elected by the order's membership. There might be two religious orders—the first for people living permanently at the farm, the second for UFW staff who "want to join and accept disciplines," Chris wrote in a confidential memo to Chavez.

The union would provide money to buy the land. Chavez knew there was good farmland available in Oxnard. He had worked there in the 1950s, his first experience organizing farmworkers, for the Community Service Organization. The farm would grow and sell vegetables, row crops, cotton, wheat, and alfalfa, and raise cows for milk and chickens for eggs. The primary goal was to be self-supporting and over time to spin off more farms. The secondary goal of serving the world would be built in from the start. Tying the project closely to the union would meld the vision of an inward-looking, self-sustaining community with an expansive goal of changing the world.

"The community is an outgrowth of UFW struggle for justice," Chris wrote. The commune should be seen as part of the union, but separate. The union would give the commune assignments: to serve as a halfway house for prisoners, for example, or to visit old people in homes and hospitals. Residents of the commune would work on union campaigns. Leaders of the union could retire to the farm.[3]

Chavez directed Chris to research existing models, in particular the Hutterites, who had successfully developed multiple communities. Chris interviewed members of the Claretians to research the tax implications of land owned by religious groups. He explored the requirements and restrictions of canonical status. He talked with sympathetic Catholic priests for advice on how to approach the church. "Start in a friendly diocese. Lay and religious persons seek approval from that friendly diocese . . . with approval from that diocese, seek approval from Rome; at same time incorporate and go for IRS status with assistance from diocese," Chris summarized. He listed questions: Does approval from Rome carry restrictions? Could the new order get status from an existing order? And "what if the leader is a Protestant?"[4]

Worried that the spirit at La Paz was deteriorating, Chavez enlisted Chris to experiment at the union headquarters. Chavez focused particularly on the children of the movement leaders, a generation he saw as key to the future. "If we don't keep the kids, then we are in bad shape," Chris wrote. He arranged his schedule to split his time between La Paz and Los Angeles. He restructured the National Farm Worker Ministry to create a Department of Community Life. He sketched plans for regular liturgy, a celebration of special days, a communal kitchen and laundry, and a garden at La Paz. "Cesar wants to do the garden part of it," Chris wrote after a conversation with the union president. "Everyone has to work in the garden."[5]

Chavez also talked to Chris about Synanon, a drug rehabilitation program with several campuses, and its flamboyant leader, Charles Dederich. Like many in the union, Chris was familiar with Synanon's well-established center in Santa Monica, which often provided free medical and dental care for union families. Dederich had expanded and acquired a compound he called Home Place in the remote town of Badger, in the foothills of the Sierra Nevada Mountains. Home Place had morphed from a drug treatment center into an alternative lifestyle community. Chavez told Chris there were lessons in Synanon. The organization might even be a partner in developing the mother house, their first communal farm.

For both men, the plans were a welcome diversion from the mundane problems of building the union. They estimated the project would take one year to research and another year to locate land and identify the first residents. Chris needed to talk with experts about the IRS regulations for religious communities. Chavez sent Chris to see the papal delegate in Washington about the feasibility of establishing a new order. He needed to visit Hutterite communities, travel to Israel to see kibbutzim, and explore European communal models. But first, two battles at the polls intervened.

Gretchen

Gretchen Laue arrived in Providence, Rhode Island, at the start of Memorial Day weekend, a little more than a week before the 1976 Democratic presidential primary, seven months after she joined the union, and a lifetime removed from her Oregon home.

When Jerry Brown announced he would run for president that spring, the UFW embarked on another crusade. The union known for mobilizing foot power and mustering public support would do everything possible for the long-shot candidacy of the governor who had pushed through the best labor law in the country. The race was still open, although a Georgia peanut farmer named Jimmy Carter was taking the lead. Gretchen was a twenty-five-year-old boycotter in Boston with no experience on a political campaign. Her next-to-impossible assignment over the holiday weekend: Find a union printer willing to prepare hundreds of flyers, ready to distribute first thing Tuesday. Gretchen sat with the phone book and called every printer for miles. She finally found one who happened to be in the office despite the holiday, belonged to the printers' union, and wanted to help farmworkers. The flyers were ready on time.

Like many, Gretchen had ended up working for the UFW by accident. Her old Dodge panel truck, a secondhand U.S. Forest Service vehicle, had broken down in Boston, stranding Gretchen and Bobby the German shepherd. They had made it all the way from Oregon, driving on back roads to see the country. She slept in the bed she had built into the back of the truck and wrote on the fold-up desk she had constructed. She was particularly proud of her homemade washing machine, copied from John Steinbeck's *Travels with Charley*—a trash can strapped to the side of the truck with a bungee cord that agitated clothes in soapy water while she drove.

The Boston dealership that was supposed to fix the truck ripped her off instead. Gretchen was outraged, more because they took advantage of a single out-of-town woman than because of the money. She wanted to stay in Boston long enough to take the dealership to court, but she was broke. A friend had recently asked Gretchen her philosophy of life. Be a good person and smile a lot, she said. Her friend was appalled. So Gretchen was looking for meaning as much as a free place to live when she happened upon a sign soliciting UFW volunteers willing to work for room and board. She offered to stay six weeks and do office work. She said she would not be around long enough to be a crusader and was uncomfortable proselytizing for a movement about which she knew little. The boycott director wanted a three-month commitment. Gretchen agreed and moved into the attic of a crowded Dorchester house, a former rectory in a largely Haitian neighborhood.

Her first day on the boycott began with a four-hour staff meeting. Then, to her dismay, she was assigned to central Boston to do precisely that which she had said she could not do: leafleting, picketing, and as she wrote, "generally interrupting people in their comfortableness." But Gretchen had been reading the book of Matthew. She thought of Jesus as someone who made waves and confronted people even when the challenge made them uncomfortable. She decided she would try to picket for farmworkers, as much as the idea terrified her.

Her second day she went with three women to the UFW's Cambridge-Somerville support group. They set out to visit liquor stores and ask managers to remove Gallo wine from the shelves. When a store refused, they set up a picket line outside. "It wasn't hard because of the hours or the standing," Gretchen wrote in her journal that night. "It was hard because the owner had hired some picket breakers a few weeks before and a few of the volunteers and staff members had been beaten up." Then an older carpenter stopped his two young apprentices who were about to cross the picket line. He told the picketers he understood what it meant to fight to build a union. They're too young to understand, he said of his charges.

Each night for two weeks Gretchen collapsed late, every limb tired from walking, shouting, holding up signs. She felt exhausted, but alive. "The job was difficult, the time difficult but it also brings with it songs, interspersed with this driving need, short conversations with people who still have faith in building community and helping the oppressed. It's brought conflict with a few people and my intolerance for those who to me seem too weak, ironically, rather than the militant." She felt she knew her housemates well after only a couple of weeks as they talked about sacrifice, vision, and oppression.[6]

"And here I am," she wrote a friend, just after celebrating her twenty-fifth birthday, "six weeks later with picket lines every Thursday night and Saturday afternoon, calling people on the phone speaking to high schools, labor unions, and getting donations for the Union of everything from toilet paper to cash. And you know what John, I love it."[7]

Gretchen was the child of theater people, the oldest girl of seven siblings, just eighteen when her mother died. She had graduated from a Catholic girls' high school, where thinking about the future for her 35 classmates meant planning out lives as wives and mothers. Gretchen bucked that stereotype, although she was acutely aware of her desire to fit in and her reluctance to confront people or tackle missions that entailed risk. At various times she wanted to be a writer, a nun, a poet, a graduate student, and a teacher. She read avidly and possessed an extensive vocabulary, which until then had not included the word organizer. Now she became enthralled with the power of organizing. In an unconventional, irreverent family, she had rebelled by trying hard to be conventional. Now she discovered the thrill of challenging authority.

Her friends back home worried and sent her money and Cheerios. She munched the cereal on the picket line and mailed back the checks. "I'm not here because I have to be but because I want to be and really enjoy it," she explained.

She wrote newsletters, designed leaflets, and spoke to the press and church groups. She organized demonstrations outdoors and in corporate offices. She was naïve enough to be outraged when a secretary in an office they had barged into accused the boycotters of stealing her stapler—and then never apologized when she located the misplaced tool. At night Gretchen donned an oversize trench coat with pockets large enough to

hide buckets of paste and went out to plaster posters on any free sur-
faces she could. She lobbied stores to boycott Gallo. "Power," Gretchen
wrote. "It is a long time since I've contemplated it or been faced seriously with it."

By the time she went to Rhode Island for her first foray into electoral
politics, Gretchen was hooked. Her success in finding the union printer
over Memorial Day weekend drew attention; a week after the Rhode Island contest, she ended up Brown's campaign office manager for the New
Jersey primary.

Back in California, the threat of a ballot initiative was having impact.
The legislature agreed to increase funding for the ALRB in the fiscal year

Gretchen Laue, wearing multiple boycott buttons, proselytizes at a meeting.

that began July 1. The board would be open for business again by late November. But Proposition 14 was on the ballot and could not be removed. The union had to decide whether to wage an active campaign. At the executive board's June meeting, Chavez put the odds of winning at 40 percent and the cost at $1 million. He warned that the union was already in the red, spending $13,000 more per month than the money coming in. A campaign would mean sacrificing most other work. There would be no one left to organize, negotiate contracts, or work on the boycott. The board postponed the decision.[8]

A few weeks later Chavez nominated Brown for president at the Democratic convention in New York City. The Brown campaign had been quixotic and last-minute, but he did better than expected, and the UFW received credit. The union forces helped him carry Maryland as well as a slate of delegates in Rhode Island and New Jersey. The union was riding high, buoyed by an air of invincibility. Fred Ross was among the strongest voices urging Chavez to push for Prop 14. We will never be stronger, he said. To not campaign will look like a defeat.[9] After they returned home from the convention, Chavez endorsed a full-fledged campaign.

Gretchen and her boyfriend, whom she had met in the boycott house, drove to California in his yellow Volkswagen Bug. They took turns driving so they wouldn't have to stop to sleep. Her Forest Service truck had been wrecked by another boycott volunteer. Bobby the German shepherd was let out one day and never returned. Gretchen left her trunks in the Dorchester house, expecting to return in a few months. Virtually all the boycotters were summoned to California for the Prop 14 campaign. For all intents and purposes, the boycott was shut down.

Chris

Governor Jerry Brown was adamant that a campaign for Prop 14 would be a mistake, and he wanted one last chance to appeal to the union leadership. On the last Friday in July, Chris joined union leaders and workers for an evening mass in Delano in honor of Bishop Dom Helder Camara, the well-known Brazilian social activist. Chavez passed along word that Chris needed to attend an emergency meeting with Brown at La Paz the following afternoon. Chris had a conflict: He was scheduled to marry Eliseo and Dorothy Johnson in Delano.

They moved the wedding up three hours. Chris had watched Eliseo grow from a young rookie into an experienced organizer, completely loyal and yet with an independence that set him apart. Chris respected Eliseo and trusted his judgment. Like most people, the minister didn't feel he had broken through Eliseo's reserve. Chris performed a simple ceremony in the living room of Eliseo's mother's three-bedroom home on Albany Street. The couple took their wedding present of one hundred dollars from Eliseo's mother and spent half on a ring and half on a weekend honeymoon—a night in Visalia and a visit to Sequoia National Park.

Chris went straight from the wedding to La Paz for the Prop 14 discussion. Brown argued that the agricultural industry would spend heavily on a campaign and the initiative would polarize the state unnecessarily. He warned the union did not have sufficient experience with the big-budget mass media campaigns that were becoming common. "I don't see how the initiative can be justified in view of the fact that the money was appropriated and there is a Board," Brown said to Chavez in a phone call before the meeting.[10]

Chris had reservations, but kept them to himself. He anticipated difficulty generating moral outrage in the religious community when the union had already achieved its goal—the board was to reopen. Sandy understood that the union's political capital was at an all-time high, but he would have preferred they use the cachet to enforce the law and expand their base rather than engage in a fight that was more symbolic than substantive. He was unhappy about the initiative, but did not feel it his place to voice doubts. Eliseo focused on his job, which was vital enough to exempt him from most duty on the Prop 14 campaign. He issued the first uniform guidelines for operating hiring halls and for filing grievances. He was growing increasingly frustrated with the lack of enough good staff people. But he still voiced confidence that the union had matured sufficiently to do more than one thing at a time. "Because we're doing the proposition, it doesn't mean that contract administration comes to a halt," he said in September. Between June and September, the union had signed twenty new contracts, adding more than 2,100 members.[11]

By late summer, the campaign Eliseo dubbed "the crusades" eclipsed all other activity. Almost all the union staff were diverted out of the fields in the crucial months before the state board was scheduled to reopen. No one was preparing for the next round of elections. Marshall Ganz was in charge of the Prop 14 campaign, and—at Chavez's suggestion—Ganz asked Chris to be his number two. I want to see if you're as much of a son-of-a-bitch to work for as everyone says, Chris told Ganz. Chris opened the office at eight each morning. Ganz favored late-night debriefing sessions. After the first week Chris told Ganz to hold the meetings earlier or open the office himself. Other than that, they got along fine.

The campaign degenerated into the polarizing fight that Brown had predicted. Despite his warning, the governor did what he could to help the union. But the growers had used focus groups to identify an issue that resonated with voters: private property rights. Prop 14 would amend the constitution to include the access rule that had been upheld by the Supreme Court—the right of union organizers to enter the fields and talk to workers. That tiny piece of the broad farmworkers' rights initiative became the crux of the growers' campaign. In late summer the union devoted all its resources to registering new voters, in large part because the Democratic Party subsidized the effort. The growers were busy painting the proposition as legalized trespass. At a mid-September strategy meeting, Chris warned that the campaign could be lost by October if the union did not get its message out soon. The growers were successfully defining the proposition as the right to trespass on private property. The union needed to switch from registering voters to educating them, he urged. "We're getting burned already in the press," Chris said. Just get more people out on the streets campaigning, Chavez replied.[12]

Less than two weeks later the growers began a multimillion-dollar blitz of television ads. They never mentioned farmworkers or elections. They played off racist fears and featured small farmers who worried about their safety if strangers were allowed on their property: "I've raised my family and my daughters on this farm and we feel threatened . . ."[13] The union lacked the money to compete on the airwaves and the message to counteract the fear. Proposition 14 lost overwhelmingly, 62 to 38 percent. The union's invincibility was shattered.

Two weeks after the election Chris gathered the farm worker ministry board in Avon Park, Florida, for its semi-annual meeting. He reported on Prop 14 and the underhanded but effective campaign that had defeated the union. On the second night he was surprised to notice Chavez, though he often attended the meetings. Then Pudge walked into the room. She was supposed to be home in Los Angeles. The ministry was toasting Chris on his fifteenth anniversary and had flown the special guests to Florida as a surprise.

Pudge Hartmire had not expected to talk, but she found herself propelled to the podium. She talked about the Chris they didn't see, the Little League manager who studied new math to help his youngest son with seventh-grade algebra, the proud father who sneaked out the Friday before the election to the high school football field where his daughter was homecoming princess, and then raced back downtown to report for duty to Marshall Ganz. "I've never known anyone who has loved his work as much as he has. And I think I have all you people to thank for that," Pudge told the NFWM board and staff. "Because a person who feels happy, challenged and fulfilled is a secure and confident and content human being. Those are the only kind I think I am able to cope with some nights. Those are the only kind, I think, who make long lasting relationships in the long run, as far as marriage goes."

Cesar Chavez spoke at greater length, but no less intimately. He talked about the risk Chris had taken fifteen years earlier when he put the resources of the Migrant Ministry behind the farmworkers. "It's a type of help that probably can only be understood by either someone trying to organize a farmworkers union in 1962 in California or a person about to drown," Chavez said. "Never has there been a string. Never has there been a hesitation. Never has there been like, 'I've done so much for you now in a roundabout way you should do something for me.' And it is very seldom in our movement that this has happened." That quality made Chavez take advantage of Chris, a habit acquired in those early days. But beyond habit, Chavez said, he was comfortable asking Chris for favors, while he called on others reluctantly or because he had no choice. His comfort stemmed from Chris's tremendous respect "for the downtrodden and the exploited. I mean genuine and complete understanding about the value of human beings."

Chavez did not mention Prop 14. But he talked about how all your friends are with you in victory. "But when you have to deal with and grapple with a defeat, or maybe a sorrow, not all of them are there. And those that are there always stand up. They are always there and not only there but doing the right thing at the right time. There are not many in this world, not many that I know of. And Chris is there."[14]

CHAPTER 18

The Cultural Revolution

November 1976

Chris

Joe Smith walked his first picket line for the grape boycott while a high school student in west-central Illinois. He worked in the peace movement and took time out from school to campaign for Eugene McCarthy in Iowa and Wisconsin during the 1968 Democratic primaries. During college Smith lived in a Catholic Worker House, helping alcoholics and runaways, and organized a grape boycott in Davenport, Iowa. Eliseo knew the St. Ambrose College kid as a committed, salt-of-the-earth volunteer. After graduation, Smith taught ninth-grade English for a year, still searching for the place he could make a difference. In the summer of 1972, like many of his generation, he found his home in the UFW.[1]

Smith worked for two years on the Chicago boycott and then transferred to San Diego. When the UFW decided to revive *El Malcriado* in early 1976, Smith was tapped as editor of the union newspaper. He moved to La Paz. Chavez was clear about his past problems with editors who did not appreciate the nuances of the movement or had their own agenda. Smith had edited his college newspaper, but worried he was not qualified. He worked closely with Jacques Levy, a former reporter who had just completed a biography of Chavez. They cobbled together a small staff, hired a professional journalist as managing editor, and created work space in an unheated trailer with no electricity. Throughout the summer and early fall, they met regularly with Chavez.[2] In addition to overseeing the stories, Smith was in charge of recruitment, subscriptions, advertising sales, and obtaining a bulk mail permit to distribute the paper in a cheap and timely fashion.[3]

The first issue was published on September 17, 1976. Two days later Chavez led a scathing attack at an executive board meeting. He castigated Smith for failings that amounted to minor oversights and lapses of judgment: not running stories by department heads, antagonizing another union with a critical story. Smith apologized profusely and promised to take greater care. "It has become painfully clear to me that I do not have the experience, background, or sophistication to function as the newspaper's tactician or political watch dog," he wrote to Chavez and the board.[4]

Using Smith's mistakes as a springboard, Chavez then pivoted to a far more prominent target: Nick Jones, the national boycott director. Jones had been a loyal union worker for a decade. He had directed Smith in Chicago, then endorsed the younger man for the newspaper job. "I had a very shattering conversation with Cesar yesterday," Jones wrote to Chris on October 7.[5] Chavez accused Jones of disloyalty and deliberately undermining the Prop 14 campaign. At a secret board meeting, Chavez voiced his suspicions about Jones at length. After the election, Chavez was ready to act.

While Chris was in Florida preparing for the NFWM meeting, Joe Smith was fired. The charge was sabotage. Nick Jones was forced out by Chavez the next day amid similar accusations. The same week Marshall Ganz and Fred Ross brought all the Prop 14 volunteers to Hart Memorial Park, on the outskirts of Bakersfield. For three days they held court along the Kern River, interviewing volunteers, ostensibly to reassign them. The direct order was to root out the assholes—Chavez's term of choice for traitors, disloyalists, leftist agitators, and spies.

Smith appealed his dismissal to the union's executive board, and he appealed to Chris. "The danger here is obvious," he wrote. "I have been fired. My character has been defamed and slandered. I am accused of the most disgusting offense possible against this movement—of betraying the leadership, my friends, and the farm workers and being party to a conspiracy to destroy this union . . . If we are allowed to slander and slur one another in private without being held accountable for what we say, our potential for self-destruction is unlimited and uncontrollable." More than anything, though, what Smith wanted was a chance to keep working for the UFW, in any capacity. As he wrote simply: "The union has become the most important thing in my life."[6]

People habitually turned to Chris for advice and reassurance. He was a minister and a Chavez confidant, but above all an empathetic listener with a clear sense of right and wrong. Now he was buffeted with calls and letters. Jones and Smith asked Chris for help to clear their names, their baffled friends and colleagues demanded explanations, and outside supporters asked for reassurance.

Chris was upset. He thought Chavez had made a mistake. Chris spent hours talking to Smith and methodically followed a trail of clues, interviewing everyone who might help piece together the puzzle of why a midwestern kid who wanted nothing more than to work for the union the rest of his life had been cast out as a spy. A theory emerged. Smith had worked in Chicago with a volunteer who had accused a farmworker of trying to rape her during a driving lesson. She and Smith were friends. She ended up in California and had recently worked at the union clinic in Delano. On September 10, Chavez accused her of being a spy for either the CIA or the Communists and said her false accusation had ruined a farmworker's life. When she burst into tears, he viewed that as clear proof of her guilt.[7] Smith gave her a ride to the Bakersfield bus station. Then he went to see Chavez to plead her case. A few days later Chavez launched into his critical review of the newspaper and turned on Smith.[8]

Chris became convinced that Smith was guilty of nothing more than poor judgment on some of the newspaper stories and guilt by association. Jacques Levy vouched for Smith's good intentions: "From what I saw of Joe Smith, he was sincerely trying to do a good job to get out a good paper," Levy wrote Chavez.[9] Chris listed all the people he had talked to about the Jones-Smith affair, thirty-two union staff ranging from board members to Jerry to his secretary. He placed his notes in a file he labeled "The Cultural Revolution." Chris had begun comparing Chavez's house-cleaning to that done by Mao Tse-Tung, whose readings Chavez often used to open meetings. Chris put together his best argument for Smith as an innocent victim and went to see Chavez.

Chavez was courteous and patient in his explanations, confident that Chris would dutifully disseminate the rationales. But Chavez was unwavering. His first line of defense left little room to argue: You don't sit where I do. You don't know all the things I know. You are not in a position to judge. Chris knew, because he had seen it happen, that farmworkers around the state called Chavez with information. So Chris found the explanation plausible, though he still believed Smith was innocent.

Chris found the fallback defense even more unassailable. I could be wrong, Chavez said, I could be wrong. But for the sake of the movement, it's worth the risk of firing one person unjustly. Chris accepted the idea that the unity of the movement came first. Chavez's acknowledgment of his own fallibility helped Chris justify the actions. Mistakes happened; the fate of any one individual was secondary to the cause.

The fallout from the post–Prop 14 interviews led to more firings and transfers. Internal splits and rivalries widened. More volunteers were purged. Jones had a following on the boycott but was not popular among the union leadership in California. Chavez burnished Jones's credentials as a villain by spreading the word that he had plotted to challenge Marshall Ganz for a seat on the executive board. The *Los Angeles Times* published a story about the internal upheaval, based on Nick Jones's confidential resignation letter. The publicity exposed the divisions to a wider audience, but the story also handed union leaders a potent defense to use with insiders. To air complaints, no matter how serious, was to break a movement taboo. To go public was to sabotage the union. They dismissed Jones's protestations that he did not leak the letter.

As the news spread slowly around the country by mail and phone, more letters arrived at La Paz. Confused volunteers posed a basic question: Either a terrible mistake had been made in purging loyal staff members, or information needed to be shared to support the shocking charges. A typical letter, signed by all six members of the Seattle boycott office, called the Jones purge a case of red-baiting: "An atmosphere of suspicion has developed, in which preposterous accusations can be made and acted upon indiscriminately. People have been fired on the basis of flimsy charges against them."[10]

In early December Chris tried to catch Chavez after a meeting but had to settle for leaving a note instead. Good people in La Paz were concerned, Chris wrote. They believed someone had falsely accused Nick Jones, they saw echoes of McCarthyism, and they took away the message that this could happen to anyone. "Some very solid, serious people have had their sense of security shaken by the events *or* by the lack of explanation of the events. They want to stay for a long time (or for life) but they have a hard-to-define worry that maybe there will be more firings in the future," Chris wrote. He suggested a community meeting with Chavez.[11]

Chavez declined. Instead he dispatched Larry Tramutt, a Chavez loyalist who had taken over the national boycott operation, to New York to quell the rebellion. Chavez also sent Eliseo, the popular boycotter and board member whose presence would give the message credibility. The three met the day after Christmas so Chavez could run through the key points of the message they were to transmit: Joe Smith was fired for incompetence, nothing more. Nick Jones was not fired—he quit. He had resisted bringing boycotters to California to help with Prop 14. Charlie March, the New York boycott director and another Jones ally, had sent five kids to work on Prop 14 who were going on a trip to Communist China. March was on the hit list too, though he did not yet know.[12]

Eliseo was supposed to be visiting his in-laws in Seattle. Instead he left California before dawn, flew to New York, and met at six P.M. with the East Coast boycott staff. Eliseo knew all the boycott leaders well, and he knew March was one of the best. Just six months earlier Eliseo had given him a ten out of ten when the board ranked cities. Now March was deliberately not told about the meeting. Eliseo tried to find things he could say to the New York staff with conviction. Referring to dissident boycotters who argued their transfers were politically motivated, he listed union leaders who had moved from city to city. That kind of flexibility allowed the union to respond to crises. If you don't trust the leadership, he told them, you should leave. If you stay, you have to know you may be transferred wherever the movement needs you.[13] Ever since he had first read *El Malcriado* a decade earlier, Eliseo had watched the union be forced to defend itself against baseless charges that Chavez and his followers were a bunch of Communists. Now Chavez was doing the same thing to his own staff. Eliseo couldn't believe the accusations. Nor could he quite believe that Chavez could be so wrong.

Chris was still trying to help Smith. "Is there a place for Joe Smith" was number nine on his list of eleven things to talk to Chavez about at their last meeting in 1976. Number one was the reorganization of the National Farm Worker Ministry to create the community life department at La Paz.

Joe Smith wrote Chris once more a few days later. Smith thanked the minister and said their recent conversation was "a tremendous boost to my morale. I know that you cautioned me about raising my expectations but just to talk with you about everything meant a great deal to me. I am very glad to know that you remain concerned about what happened and committed to investigate it further. I have a lot of faith in your ability to handle this mess fairly and intelligently." He asked Chris to remember him in his prayers, and he ended with the traditional salutation of the farm workers movement. *Viva la causa!*[14]

John Moyer, the United Church of Christ minister who had been there for the union in Coachella in 1973 and many times before and since, had a talent for offering critical but nonjudgmental counsel. On the picket lines in Coachella, he had accepted without illusions the violence he witnessed perpetuated by the nonviolent union. Watching the purges unfold, Moyer did not condemn the turmoil, nor did he condone it.

Moyer worked in New York and knew Nick Jones and Charlie March well. Moyer rejected as absurd the idea they were disloyal or would subvert the union. As much as he felt for them, he urged Chris to focus broadly: "The real issues here deal with the future of the UFW and the NFWM . . . they have to do with trust, loyalty, delegation of authority, leadership, the movement from organizing in the fields to an established union, from powerlessness to power, from Fred Ross to Crosby Milne, from youth to maturity, from idealism to disillusionment." He reminded Chris of a speech Chavez gave to church people in 1966, when he presciently asked them to be there to help when the union ultimately gained power and the inevitable internal struggles would ensue. Now Chavez was struggling to reconcile his intellectual understanding of that turmoil with its emotional reality. "The delegation of authority, which Cesar so often talks about and which Crosby's reorganization demanded, involves the relinquishing of power and responsibility to others with whom the leader still has to relate. This is very, very difficult to achieve. It puts severe stress on the psyche of the leader. Things happen over which he no longer has direct control but for which he is still responsible," Moyer wrote to Chris.

Moyer concluded by placing the onus on Chris: "I think the National Farm Worker Ministry has an important ministry to the union leadership at this time, and your ministry to Cesar is crucial . . . What I am saying is: you are really the key guy, Chris. The time is now. It is a crucial task, and it will be a difficult one."[15]

Jerry

Jerry was not perturbed by the firings or the red-baiting. In Jerry's legal opinion, the union constitution clearly gave Chavez the power to hire and fire. As long as the moves didn't interfere with Jerry's operation, he really didn't care. Jerry was more annoyed by Chavez's penchant to microman-age and penny-pinch than by his personnel practices. Jerry had been try-ing for six months to get a few IBM Selectric typewriters for the legal department. Ellen had returned from Indiana after her first year of law school and spent the summer of 1976 working as Jerry's liaison in La Paz. One of her jobs was to handle budget requests. She asked for the typewriters, and Chavez turned her down flat. Are you sure? she asked him. He just looked at her over his half-glasses. Fucking A, I'm sure, he replied. Then Crosby Milne tried, and Chavez said he'd get the typewriters himself. Six months later the Salinas office had three legal secretaries and no Selectric typewriters.[16]

In terms of the big picture, however, Jerry felt upbeat as the new year began. He was on the verge of a major breakthrough: a deal to get the Teamsters out of the California fields. After several months of negotiations, Jerry had all but finalized an agreement whereby the Teamsters would neither organize farmworkers under the jurisdiction of the Agricultural Labor Relations Act nor negotiate new contracts where the Teamsters had won elections. In exchange, the UFW would drop its antitrust lawsuit against the Teamsters and agree not to pursue workers in related jobs, such as shed workers and truck drivers, which fell outside the purview of the state law. The ALRB was back in business, elections had resumed, and the union was piling up a string of victories in the vegetable fields of the Imperial Valley. With the Teamsters gone, the union would have a clear, unchallenged path to organizing in the fields. In high spirits, Jerry headed to a special executive board meeting that Chavez called in late February 1977 to discuss the union's future.

The location was Home Place, the Synanon drug rehabilitation community in Badger, fifty-five miles east of Fresno, just outside Sequoia National Park. Jerry drove up a winding, mountainous road and emerged into an eerie world. He found himself in a gleaming, clean compound, where all the residents had shaved heads and wore uniform overalls. An internal communications system called the Wire broadcast announcements, even in the bathroom. Today is the anniversary of the day I shaved my head, Jerry heard one resident proclaim. Smoking was prohibited. The before-dinner drink was a type of healthy gruel. Much of life at the cultlike community revolved around the Game, an encounter group exercise where players "indicted" one another for bad behavior and hurled obscenities in a therapeutic effort to enhance communication.

Chavez told the board he had brought them to Home Place to explain his ideas about community, to introduce the Game, and to solicit input on the future of the union. His unspoken agenda was to force a renewed commitment to the volunteer system and to a movement that offered community and shared sacrifice as psychic rewards for helping the poor.

Jerry walked into the meeting late, looked around in amazement, and assumed the role of the matador. The red flag he waved was a request from the paralegals to be paid $450 a month, instead of the standard five dollars a week plus room and board.

"I want to take a clear position," Jerry said. "And my clear position is that we're going to have to pay people." The high turnover they experienced under the current system was having a devastating impact on the union's work, Jerry argued, citing problems with a recent case. "We wasted a lot of time. We didn't value people's time. We didn't expect as much out of the people. I've gotten a proposal from the legal workers in the Salinas office. I think it's a well-thought-out, reasonable proposal. They want to get paid wages. My first reaction to the proposal was, 'Well, some of you aren't worth this, four hundred fifty bucks.' And it scared them. But as soon as I saw that, I think there's a way we don't value people's time because we don't put a price on it. And I think we're talking about competence and continuity."

Chavez insisted paying salaries was only one route to stability. "The crossroads right now is whether it's a movement or a union. We're at that stage where we have to make a decision," he said. The law had changed everything, he said over and over. The union now fought administrative battles in state hearing rooms, rather than confrontations on picket lines.

When Chavez said he would quit rather than be part of any union that paid salaries, Jerry took him on: "That's a big weapon: 'If you do it that way, you're not going to have me around.' So people don't consider that. We should consider that."

"We gotta have a philosophy," Chavez said.

"You know, I hated philosophy when I was in college because philosophy was always irrelevant to the facts."

"No, because you don't want to deal with it."

Chavez stressed that he had called the meeting to discuss *his* problems. And he laid them out: "This union, well, I organized it . . . The way we're going, we're not going to make it. We're not going to keep the ideals we talked about: being a different union, the brotherhood, kind of a community thing. Which is my bag. Which I need for whatever reasons. It's fast disappearing." At best, he said, the union would end up a small group of well-paid farmworkers.

Then he offered the solution. "I'm just convinced that the way for me, at least, for me personally, is to have a community like Synanon or close to that and start truly cooperative ventures." He outlined his ideas for communal living, weekly mass, union holidays, a farmworker prayer— concepts he had discussed at length with Chris but that were new to the rest of the union leadership. For two years, Chavez proposed, he would spend most of his time in La Paz, building the community. The first step would be to bring a dozen people to Synanon to learn to play the Game. Eventually the Game would be mandatory for all union staff.

The board members sat nearly speechless. Only Chris and Crosby Milne, familiar with Synanon and supportive of the larger mission of organizing the poor, were not surprised. Jerry offered to try the Game, but expressed reservations. He much preferred sending messages to people through others. "It's hard to be honest about certain things . . . you get things done more easily by sending certain signals indirectly," he said. "The Game may allow you to be honest, but there's a price that may be paid." He could not foresee how large that price would be.

The next evening Synanon founder Chuck Dederich addressed the board. Over two decades Dederich, a reformed alcoholic, had built Synanon from a tiny experimental program into a nationally renowned drug treatment program based on a "tough love" approach. He had parlayed the acclaim into financial success, cultivating a devoted following that donated generously and enabled him to amass a real estate empire. More recently he had shifted from treating addicts to building a community where people stayed for life. Chavez envied Synanon's efficient operation. The cars all ran, the campus was immaculate, the organization never struggled for money.

The Game was an integral part of the Synanon therapy, and Dederich arranged a demonstration for his UFW guests. He explained the triangle (work life, where the boss is the top point) and the circle (the Game, where everyone is equal). He brought them into the Game room. The observers sat on bleacher seats above a recessed pit in the middle of the room, where players sat in a circle. Richard Chavez walked out soon after the insults and obscenities began. Jerry got in the ring with the Synanon players, and so did Chris. They each got gamed on the same issue: Why aren't you in La Paz? The Synanon players called Chris a "professional humiliast." They gave Jerry an even harder time: You abandoned your friend Cesar and moved the legal department to Salinas. Jerry was taken aback. Until then he had thought Chavez was fine with the lawyers working in Salinas. Strangers attacking him for his refusal to live in La Paz sent a clear message.

Jerry could hold his own in any contest of verbal wits, and he gave as good as he got. He called Dederich a schmuck. Chuck the schmuck. The unfamiliar obscenity delighted the Synanon faithful. In the post-mortem

discussion, Chavez recounted Jerry's performance with relish. The matador lived to fight another day.[17]

Eliseo

Eliseo was appalled by the Game, but more alarmed by the way the conversation progressed over the three-day meeting. He had arrived at Home
Place expecting to prepare for a tough election campaign, discuss ranch
committee bylaws, and hash out strategic priorities. The Teamsters settlement provided an opportunity for the union to set its own agenda. At last,
they could play offense instead of defense. But that required formulating
strategy. Chavez had shuffled the board members around again and reas-
sumed most statewide responsibilities. Eliseo had gone from running
contract administration to Coachella field office director. Marshall Ganz,
no longer organizing director, was in Calexico. Both arrived at Home
Place prepared to debate key decisions: Where to focus finite resources.
Grapes versus vegetables. How to deal with the ALRB.

Chavez presented a concise litany of the union's problems: insufficient
resources, difficulty keeping good staff, too few contracts, staff isolated
from the members. All at the moment of great opportunity. "The road is
open, and we ran out of gas," Chavez said. "The Teamsters are gone . . .
here's this tremendously great opening to just charge through and get the
job done. Look, there's nothing between us and getting the workers organized right now . . . All the obstacles are removed. And we finally climbed
the hill and we're at flatland, and we can't go."

Eliseo agreed with that assessment, but he struggled to understand the
leader's proposed solution. There were only two options, Chavez kept saying. They could start paying people and be like a regular union. That was
fine, but he would leave. Or they could become a real community. Throughout the debate he skillfully kept the conversation on track and adamantly
insisted on those two options. No compromises. He batted down every attempt to analyze the very real problems the union faced.

As the meeting wore on, Eliseo listened in confusion as Chavez focused
almost entirely on the needs of people who worked for the union, not
farmworkers in the fields. At every chance Eliseo suggested they discuss
the ranch committees. He kept trying to focus the discussion on the need
to recruit more farmworkers, who were unwilling to give up their jobs to
work for the union. When Chavez talked about why volunteers were unhappy at La Paz, Eliseo tried again: "Cesar, the main reason for that is be-

cause you have a staff up in La Paz that is basically ninety-five percent nonfarmworkers . . . if you had fifty percent farmworkers at La Paz, I bet that that would take care of a lot of those problems. If you look, every staff we've got, in any field office, the majority are not farmworkers."

Eliseo was usually adept at proposing specific solutions. At most meetings his points were clear and focused. But now his comments reflected uncertainty as he strained to understand Chavez's arguments and to reconcile his own conflicts. Eliseo worried the union was in trouble. But he defended its success in personal terms when Milne raised a question: "Crosby, when I came to this country I started working at ninety cents an hour. Eight years later I was making a dollar five. In the last eleven years wages have tripled since the union got started." Eliseo argued they had to find a way to persuade more farmworkers to join the staff, but rejected the idea of salaries. He said people who worked for the union needed time off, but that work was what really recharged him. He believed most volunteers could take on more responsibility, but only if they were trained. And he kept circling back to the point that bothered him most. They had to have more farmworkers in leadership positions.

Eliseo tried out loud to formulate a solution to the dilemma he saw so clearly: "We're working against ourselves. The more we work to improve the wages and working conditions of the workers, the less incentive they have" to work for the union. Irrigators at one of the large Coachella companies were making $13,000 a year. "I'm going to go say to a worker, 'You're making $3.40 an hour, you're getting this and this and this . . . come and work for *cinco pesos por la causa*'?"

He tried to come to grips with the needs of the union versus the movement. "I think at least in my case the fact that there wasn't money involved in it made that commitment stronger to stay here," Eliseo told the others. "And I know that's true for a lot of the people I work with." But he warned that the farmworkers now under contract didn't share the movement philosophy. The union's public image was changing too. The UFW's shift from underdog to establishment made it harder to attract the kind of passionate talent that had built the union. "The fact that we don't pay is a strength but it's also a weakness. We attract every twinkylander around and then once we got them we don't know what to do with them."

Chavez pounced on that to reinforce his point: "It really means we go to the very poor. We go out and build our staff, at least, with the very poor. They're the ones who have needs."

Eliseo had been under the impression that everyone on staff was treated more or less the same. He knew some people had special arrangements for help with mortgages, loans, and other obligations. But subsistence pay was the policy; people lived on five dollars a week, plus handouts from family and friends. When the board bantered with Jerry during a break, someone joked about Jerry's salary and the lawyers' munificent $600 a month wages. Eliseo had been on the board three and a half years. The passing comments were as much a revelation as the Game.

"Can I ask a question?" Eliseo interrupted Chavez as he began the afternoon session. "Why do we pay lawyers six hundred bucks? As opposed to other people? Because it seems to me it's a radical departure from what we're doing."

"Because we couldn't get lawyers and we thought that we had to pay them six hundred dollars," Chavez answered. "Not now . . . but in those days. So the decision was to make an exception, with doctors and with lawyers."

"I thought lawyers were coming because of Jerry's magnetic personality," Eliseo said dryly.

"That and six hundred dollars," Chavez replied without missing a beat.

"You've got certain people who are getting a salary that's considerably above and beyond what most of the other people are getting . . . I never knew that such a policy was made and I wanted to raise it and find out why," Eliseo persisted.

He didn't get an answer. Chavez deflected the discussion. Ganz fell asleep and began to snore. Chavez declared the board was at impasse on the question he kept pressing: Pay salaries or form a community.

The realization that some staff already earned salaries changed the equation for Eliseo. Crosby Milne proposed a half-volunteer, half-paid system and pushed Chavez on why he rejected the idea.

"Why?" Chavez said. "Because I won't let that, I won't be here and be a part of that, that's number one. No way I would be a part of that. I wouldn't."

"Well, you're already doing that," Eliseo shot back.

"We get paid," Jerry said, backing him up.

Eliseo was so serious and studious that he was the least likely to play smart aleck, sufficiently in awe of Chavez that his arguments were always respectfully phrased. But now the thirty-year-old became close to defiant. He challenged Chavez directly on point after point. Baffled but still determined, Eliseo tried at every chance to steer the conversation back to the real problems the union faced in the field.

"Hey Jerry, you want to talk about something interesting for a change?" he said, as Chavez mused about creating community. "Let's talk about the ALRB!"

"I'd like the board to finish my problems before we get to your problem," Chavez said.

"The problem is that your problems aren't as interesting as our problems," Eliseo responded.

"I know. But just give me . . . I got a couple more," Chavez said.

"No, no, you got no problems—let's not pay anybody, let's do games, whatever you want, and let's go after the ALRB," Eliseo said, near desperation.

Next Chavez told the board he planned to send his own people into the regional offices to evaluate staff and weed out those who were performing badly. Eliseo jumped on that. Where was Chavez going to find people competent to evaluate the organizers on the ground? Eliseo asked. "If I hire them, I'm responsible for them. And if I'm hiring nothing but a bunch of assholes who aren't doing their job, then I shouldn't be director . . . you should fire me."

By the end of the three-day meeting, the board members were so confused, they sounded slap-happy. Chavez allotted the final ten minutes to discuss the urgent strategic questions facing the union: where to focus their organizers, and whether to fight in the grape vineyards or in the lettuce fields. Eliseo needed an answer on whether he was getting help for the campaign scheduled to launch in less than a month.

Chavez told Eliseo, Marshall Ganz, Richard Chavez, and Jim Drake to meet and work things out. You can meet in the car driving back to Delano, Chavez said. His brother was indignant: You're talking about a half-day strategy discussion, not a car ride. Like the others, Richard Chavez said he had thought such important discussions would be the focus of the meeting. The union president metaphorically shrugged, delegating the key decision of where to focus the union's organizing power and expressing no interest in taking part in the deliberation.[18]

Often events come into focus as watershed moments only long after the fact, a fading memory in the rearview mirror. Eliseo did not need to drive very far down the mountain from Home Place to realize that he would look back on that meeting as the time when everything changed.

PART V

A Movement or a Union?

April 1977–July 1978

CHAPTER 19

The Purges

April 1977

Chris

In early spring, Chris left for Europe. The month-long trip was his first real vacation in years, courtesy of a little money that had come along with the tributes from the farm worker ministry at his fifteenth anniversary party. He did some sightseeing with Pudge, but he justified the trip by researching collectives. He spent five days on an Israeli kibbutz, visited an ecumenical religious community in Taize, France, and then checked out the Community of the Ark in southern France.

When Chris walked back into his Los Angeles office on May 13, his assistant, Sue Miner, handed him a pile of letters and urgent messages. They chronicled in wrenching detail events that had unfolded in his absence. The word purge had entered the UFW vocabulary, soon to be as universally understood as "*viva la causa.*"

The first letter came from Richard Cook, Chris's good friend and de facto number two in the ministry. Shaken, Cook had sat down on April 6 to begin a long letter he knew Chris would not read for weeks. But Cook wanted to get everything down while his thoughts were fresh. He had just gotten off the phone with a friend, Judy Kahn, whom he had recruited for the union six years earlier. She had lived in La Paz and worked in the financial department. Until yesterday. At a community meeting at La Paz on April 4, Cook related, Kahn was one of a half dozen people fired in a kangaroo court. She was accused of being the "master counter-organizer," out to sabotage the union. The attacks were brutal, and they were carefully planned. Kahn pleaded guilty only to griping at the communal kitchen in the run-down rooms they still called the Hospital. "Judy said that the real reason for her firing is that the administration at La Paz is in chaos and scapegoats were needed," Cook wrote. "At one point in the 4/4 meeting, Cesar said, 'We knew about you a long time ago.'"

By the time Cook reached the last sheet of his ten-page letter, he told Chris he was writing through tears, tears that he could not share with anyone else. "I don't want to do anything that would weaken Cesar's leadership or weaken the movement," Cook wrote. "Yet where do I go now with my anger and hurt? And isn't this the same kind of question that Judy and others have, too? What do I do with my frustration without being disloyal?"[1]

Deirdre Godfrey had also worked in financial management and shared the same messy kitchen with Kahn. From Godfrey, Chris received Copy #15 of the epistle she mailed to union leaders on April 25. She numbered the letters carefully to keep the contents confidential. Godfrey had been a strong boycotter, and Chris knew her well. In La Paz she was frustrated by the isolation of her job and the living conditions in the Hospital. She had already resigned from the union and had planned to leave in June when she was expelled during the meeting that became known as the Monday Night Massacre. "I have never spent such a fearful night as the one following that meeting: with security people surrounding the pay telephone, threatening to throw me out the gate after I had gone to Tehachapi to make a call arranging for a place to go, and marching through the halls every two minutes all night," she wrote. ". . . I shall never forget the frenzied, hate-filled faces and voices of people who had been warm and friendly with me right through to the hour of the meeting."[2]

The purges widened, and the postmarks came from farther afield. On May 4 Sister Mary Catherine Rabbitt wrote Chris from Denver. She was on the NFWM board representing the Sisters of Loretto, the order that had sewn Huelga flags and marched on picket lines in the grape strike a decade earlier. Now she wanted answers. A popular Denver boycotter was among those purged. "We *all* are very concerned about this and are uncomfortable with the silence of the union in responding to these charges . . . we would be deeply saddened if such allegations of a 'witch-hunt' prove to be true," Rabbitt wrote. "We would hope that in some way you will be able to convey our concerns to Cesar and to the Union. We feel that the union *does* have to be accountable to people who are loyal supporters."[3]

Chris composed a response, so artful that his letter became the model. He ran the letter by Chavez before sending it off. Chris expressed appreciation for the opportunity to address vexing questions. He offered inside information: With the boycott shut down, the union needed to trim staff and shift volunteers to new jobs. Not everyone could make a successful transition. Then Chris articulated the kind of heartfelt and eloquent rationalization that kept so many in the fold:

"Not everything that happens within the movement is wise, right or just," he wrote to Rabbitt.

> Farm workers are human beings and so are their leaders. You and I are quite conscious of that reality from our own experience within the churches . . . I don't know about and/or understand everything that happens within the union and I am a lot closer than most supporters. I can't imagine myself making judgments about the heart and soul of the movement based on what happens to some volunteers, even to some of the best and most dedicated volunteers. The UFW is a farm workers' movement! The changes that are happening within the farm workers' community represent human liberation beyond anything that could have been dreamed of 15 years ago. The leadership is disciplined, determined, persistent, committed to non-violence and holding firm to a vision of a poor people's movement within the U.S.[4]

In the weeks after his return from abroad, Chris distributed talking points to help his staff respond to critics. He stressed that the same people who expressed qualms about Chavez's strong leadership and the cult of personality praised such attributes in Ho Chi Minh, John L. Lewis, and Mahatma Gandhi. Chris compared Chavez's housecleaning with Mao's Cultural Revolution—messy to look at up close but serving a larger goal: "Clearly, Cesar has embarked on a mini-cultural revolution within the UFW, using the Synanon game and other tools of leadership. He is determined to carry it through and he is certain that it will help the movement, while at the same time knowing that it may not always be right or accurate or wise in particular cases."[5]

Like Cook, many people were loath to talk about events for fear of hurting the cause they believed in. But they needed to talk to someone, so they turned to Chris. They worried about discouraging others from helping the UFW, but they knew nothing could disillusion Chris. He repeated what he viewed as a profound truth: Those who committed their entire lives, who never thought about going back to school or taking another job or going on vacation, those people had special privilege to make their own decisions. Unity is more important than always being right, he told the doubters. If we make a mistake, we can adjust. But if we're not together, we can't survive.

He believed that with all his heart. Even when the witch-hunt hit close to home.

For several years the National Farm Worker Ministry had run an after-school program in Delano. The Huelga School was Chris's pride and joy. When he was ready to expand the program into a licensed school, Chris recruited Shelly Spiegel. She was a teacher in a poor Mexican area of Los Angeles, who spent her weekends urging people to boycott Gallo wine. When Chris made the offer, Spiegel's mother was appalled, convinced that her thirty-year-old daughter would never find a Jewish husband in Delano. Spiegel went anyway. During the summer of 1976, while others celebrated the nation's bicentennial and cheered the Tall Ships, Spiegel raised money in Los Angeles so she could teach farmworker children in Delano. Then she went door to door on Delano's west side, persuading parents to entrust her with their kids.

She watched the school take shape as if by magic, that UFW way of creating something from nothing. A four-foot fence needed to obtain state certification suddenly appeared. Volunteers poured cement for a basketball court. The longshoremen's union donated a cargo net that became a climbing fence. In September twenty kindergarteners and first graders boarded a new minibus with eagles on the side. The Huelga School parents paid minimal fees but pledged to attend Friday night union meetings, help on the boycott in Los Angeles one weekend a month, and pitch in when the union needed them. The school educated kids who were outcasts in the Delano schools—and organized their parents, helping to overcome skepticism and hostility toward the union that went back to the botched contracts and the hiring halls of the early 1970s. The Huelga School became a powerful organizing tool, enticing workers to embrace a union that was changing their lives. When Chavez came to visit early in 1977, he was so impressed he asked Spiegel for a proposal to create ten schools. "He said children all over California could benefit from such a program," reported *Hijos del Sol* (Children of the Sun), the bilingual school paper. ". . . He wanted Shelly and Chris and some of the parents to come up with some ideas on how to make better programs and how to expand these programs."[6]

Two months later Chavez was still raving about the Huelga School, but increasingly eager to jettison other services that sapped the union's resources. Two weeks before his fiftieth birthday, Chavez told his board he felt trapped: tied down by the demands of administering contracts ("a string around your neck"); frustrated that he could not focus on helping the poor, the senior citizens, the alcoholics, and the prisoners; and frightened by the prospect of the UFW becoming the kind of traditional union he had always disdained. He felt stymied by the challenge of teaching farmworkers to value sacrifice and disgusted by those who expressed no gratitude for their contracts but instead made more demands. ("Every time we look at them, they want more money. Like *pigs*, you know. Here we're slaving, and we're starving and the goddamn workers don't give a shit about anything because we don't train them, you know, we don't teach them anything.")[7]

Chavez's tolerance for dissent diminished as his frustration increased. More purges ensued. Slough off the old, his mentors at Synanon urged. Complaints about the lack of democracy, Chavez declared, came not from farmworkers but from those who felt they took a "step down" when they joined the union staff. Like the teachers at the Delano day care center. Chavez had decided the preschool drained resources and did not help the movement. He ordered it shut down. The day care center teachers helped parents lobby to reverse the decision. Their "counter-organizing" enraged Chavez. He fired them.[8]

Shelly Spiegel had worked closely with the day care center director, and they were friends. By the time the union's executive board convened at La Paz on June 30 for its summer meeting, the charges of counterorganizing had mushroomed into accusations of sabotage. The dominant theme for the meeting was infiltration by agents intent on destroying the union. Chris knew Spiegel was under suspicion. He knew without question that Shelly Spiegel was not a spy. For once, he tried to take a public stand.

Sandy

Sandy arrived at the summer board meeting determined to turn defeat into victory, the UFW way.

He was incensed about how the state labor board had run elections in the recent Coachella campaign, where the union fared badly. Weak support among grape workers and a disorganized campaign had contributed to the UFW's poor showing. But the growers used flagrantly illegal scare tactics, and incompetent state board agents failed to intervene. The union had filed dozens of complaints with the ALRB, charging the growers with unfair labor practices. Sandy was eager to follow up. "We've got probably the best set of cases to try to get bargaining orders, which is the right to bargain without winning an election, than we've had yet," Sandy said near the start of the board meeting. "It was just, as far as I'm concerned it was just ridiculous, what the growers did. And I think they got away with it 'cause of the board. I never felt more frustrated!"

Maybe it was because Coachella had been the first place Sandy had worked in the fields and seen the union's power; maybe it was because he was invested in the law he had helped craft; maybe it was just because he liked to win. But Sandy really wanted to engage all the minds in that room to brainstorm about how to attack the growers in Coachella. Instead, he listened to discussions that seemed irrelevant at best, vicious at worst.

First, Chavez staged a demonstration Game, playing with the group from La Paz who had been trained at Synanon. For an hour they shrieked and cursed each other out. Then Chavez went around the room and asked what people thought.

"I think it's very good," Jerry said enthusiastically. ". . . The thing that's amazing is how tough we are. There are a lot of good lawyers."

"Oh, I thought it was true. I thought all the stuff was true," Sandy deadpanned when Chavez called on him. A few people laughed.

"Very interesting," Eliseo said, totally noncommittal. That elicited laughs too.

Next, Sandy listened again to Chavez obsess about the phone bill and berate those who failed to fill out telephone chits, sheets that indicated each call, its destination, and its duration. Unlike the expletive-laden rant during the Coachella strike four years earlier, this time Chavez praised the legal department for being under budget. Jerry proudly explained they had stopped accepting collect calls from the union's field offices. "Who would ever think this would come from Salinas legal," Chavez marveled. "If they can do that, everything is possible."

Soon the tone changed. The meeting degenerated into a no-holds-barred attack on the oldest member of the board, Philip Vera Cruz.

Good enemies had always been central to Chavez's strategy. His union did not depend on contracts or money to be strong, he often said. Like the "non-violent Vietcong," he needed only three things: a disciplined staff, the support of the people, and a good villain.[9] Villains helped Chavez generate excitement, bring people together, and direct their collective anger toward action that furthered his goals. "When we had a visible opponent," Chavez reminded the board members now, "we had unity, a real purpose. It was like a religious war."

The Teamsters and the growers had been wonderful villains. Now targets like Philip Vera Cruz would have to suffice. He was a leftist Filipino leader, strongly ideological and not inclined because of age, health, and temperament to do the strenuous work expected of everyone else. He was the only board member who had declined to go out on the boycott. The seventy-two-year-old hardly spoke during board meetings, but took many notes. Nobody was likely to spring to his defense.

Chavez accused Vera Cruz of planning to resign and write a book critical of the UFW. He had already handed over his notes to leftists intent on destroying the union, Chavez charged. Vera Cruz denied the accusations but doggedly refused to say much else. One after another the union leaders jumped in, verbally abusing the elderly man, who barely responded.

Sandy was silent. He didn't understand what was going on or the need to savagely humiliate Vera Cruz, who had already said he would resign. As Chavez hammered on the dangers the union faced, he revealed a personal twist: The assholes were out to sabotage his marriage. His wife had intercepted love letters. He was not sure he was still married. He had warned her this would happen. This is how they operate, he said. The women either seduce you to get information or else they frame you.

Gilbert Padilla said he planned to resign. He wasn't angry, just bewildered. He couldn't follow what Chavez was doing anymore. Jerry and Chris urged him to stay and play the Game. Jessica Govea was near tears. She talked about meeting Padilla as a child, when he worked for the Community Service Organization and came to her house with Chavez and Fred Ross, and they changed the direction of her life. "You were the sparks, you know, in my family's life, in my life," she said. Now she worried the cycle would be broken. "We've gone around and started sparking a hell of a lot of people's lives. The thing I'm worried about is that if we're so hurt . . . It's a really beautiful thing that's been built over the years . . ." She choked up.

A few minutes later Chavez suddenly turned to Sandy.

"Sandy, I haven't heard you say anything. In fact, your expressions are so, I've been looking, I can't even read. You're just very noncommittal. You haven't said anything, you haven't done anything, you haven't even shown any nervous signs. Nothing."

"Just like Mr. Spock over there," Jerry said.

Sandy felt like he had wandered into some dysfunctional family quarrel that he had no right to witness. Atypically incoherent, he stalled for time. "One of the reasons is, I'm not so sure that I have the right to be here, just sitting here. Because the other people here go back a lot longer than I do. But I am here, and obviously I'm thinking . . . I guess one of the ironic things to me is I'm supposed to be trained to use words and I don't find it that easy to use them." He verbally fumbled until he put together words that made sense to a lot of people: "The fear I have is that we're on the verge of something really, really big, and yet feeling like maybe we'll blow it, you know. I think everybody in this room must feel that at some point. It's so hard to do it all."[10]

Chris

Chris was not worried about the future of the union. Like his religious faith, his belief in Chavez never wavered. The minister's fears were much more personal. He was torn between defending an innocent friend and not jeopardizing the relationship central to his life.

"Dolores and I are coming apart at the seams over Shelly," Chris said, bringing up the Huelga School. Huerta lived in Delano, and her daughter was one of Shelly Spiegel's star first-graders. Huerta praised Spiegel as a teacher even as she enumerated her sins: She was a ringleader in a conspiracy among the Delano staff. She threw parties and excluded Huerta. Spiegel deliberately scheduled events to conflict with union needs. She befriended the disgraced day care teacher. She tried to undermine Huerta among the parents. "Shelly cannot damage me with the membership in Delano," Huerta said defiantly. "None of them can fuck me up with the members. I mean none of them. I don't care how hard they try . . . because my roots go back many years."

You don't get it, Chavez said to Chris. You are all blind to the conspiracy and danger. Chris acknowledged he was not in Chavez's seat. "But what I know is, when somebody gets focused on as being a problem, all kinds of unrelated facts, incidents, relationships begin to automatically fall into place," Chris said. ". . . Those pieces may or may not add up to anything. But they add up to something because somebody with power has indicted them. All I'm pleading for is that we also listen to another interpretation of those events. So we don't screw good people who shouldn't be screwed."

Jim Drake asked permission to tell the thirty-five people something that Chris had recently confided. He was afraid to raise these issues for fear he himself might become suspect. "My God, what are we? What have we become?" Drake said. "If Chris Hartmire is afraid to express things openly because he's afraid he's going to be accused of being part of a conspiracy, what more is there to say?"

Even then, Chris blamed himself. He was making Chavez's job harder: "We're afraid because we don't have the balls . . . Why are people afraid? They're afraid to wreck their friendship."

"Also, Chris, you're afraid because you may be wrong," Chavez interrupted.

"I'm willing to accept that as a possibility," Chris replied, "but I don't think that's the real root of it . . . I get a lot of shit from the outside world over all that's happened the last five months. I defend the union, and I think I interpret it better than anybody else probably does, so that people understand and stay with us." But, Chris added, emphatically, "the last five months have not been exactly normal."

There was another type in the union, equally as dangerous as the leftist infiltrators, Chris warned, his voice rising. "There are some people whose existence in life is made meaningful by kissing your ass," he told Chavez. "And they're dangerous people also. And they're going to go around hurting good people in the union just because they're kissing your ass. And I think you've got to watch for them too." He looked around the room, pleading for support. "Now, does no one agree with me?" As usual, no one was willing to publicly second an unpopular challenge. "Am I the only one who thinks that?" Chris appealed.

Chavez softened. He told Chris he could have input without fighting, that he had input all the time. Chavez talked about Winston Churchill, founders of movements and their fates. He could see the signs, that it was time for him to go before he was pushed. He talked about the impact of the landmark state law and reminded Jerry how he had called as soon as it passed and said, "Jerry, this changes the whole ballgame."

Jerry voiced sympathy. He urged the others to do as Chavez asked, to play the Game, to support his efforts to build community. "You trained us well, Cesar," Jerry said. "There's a lot of brain power around here. It's got to be hard for you to deal with the people in this room."

Chavez demurred. But at another point in the marathon meeting, he implicitly acknowledged the truth in Jerry's words. Chavez turned to the one person in whom he had confided his dream of a communal farm, and also his fears that one day the people he had trained would inevitably turn against him. "See Chris," Chavez said, "let me tell you what happens. And all of you should know this. When I came here, I had total, absolute power. That's how it got done. The whole cake was mine. Well, it was a little cake.

But it was mine. And then the cake keeps expanding. I try to keep being a proprietor. After a while, everybody built it. After a little while, if you have absolute total power, can you go to more total power? No. The only way to go is to go down. To go down, to have less power, is tough."

Then he addressed all of them, Chris and Jerry and Eliseo and the others who had been swept away by Chavez's brilliance more than a decade ago when they first met. "What you're saying, you've grown up," Chavez said. "You've grown up. And now it's very hard to face me on an equal basis. As it should be. And all of you are growing up . . . You're sure you now own the union."[11]

Eliseo

Eliseo did not consider himself anything near an equal. But he was confident he understood what the union needed to do. When they were not talking about conspiracies, at its heart the question the leaders debated at the meeting in the summer of 1977 was what it meant to organize workers.

Chavez made his current definition clear: Organizing was winning elections. He insisted that organizing, negotiating contracts, and administering those pacts were three separate functions. To succeed right now, the union must concentrate on only one. Eliseo did not accept that proposition. Organizing was developing leadership at each ranch, to involve the workers in everything from negotiations to grievances. "A contract is not just a piece of paper that you go and sign with an employer," he said. "It's an instrument of power." The union derived strength not from negotiating holidays and higher wages but from giving "workers the experience of having power themselves, so they can start taking the company on and they've got a way in which to do that."

For months Eliseo had been arguing that the union was overextended and understaffed, with dozens of election victories on the books and no follow-up. Workers had voted for the UFW because they believed the union would represent their interests and deliver. "And that's not going to happen if we just keep jumping around all over the goddamn place," Eliseo said. "And we're leaving nothing but a trail of broken promises."

Chavez began to summarize Eliseo's comments. "Eliseo said basically two things. One is that getting a contract is like the final act in institutionalizing the power, but also he's saying that—"

Eliseo interrupted. "But it's the power of the *workers*, Cesar, the power of the workers. Not *our* power. People make that mistake."

"Isn't that the same?" Chavez asked.

"Well, no," Eliseo said. "Because a lot of people seem to feel that it's us. And it isn't. It's the workers themselves."

Chavez soon returned to his theme of infiltration. He handed out a confidentiality pledge that he had asked Jerry to draft. The one-sentence document said no one would speak about what happened at the meeting.

It was a foregone conclusion that Vera Cruz would refuse to sign. "Philip, legally it doesn't make a goddamn bit of difference whether you sign or not," Jerry said. "I can get your ass under the federal law. I can get your ass under the oral agreement . . . But as a matter of friendship, as an agreement of what we did in this room, it really hurts me that someone won't sign it. It makes me feel sick to my stomach."

"It scares me, Jerry," Vera Cruz said.

"Why does it scare you more than it scares me?" Jerry said. "I live by shooting my mouth off. It doesn't scare me."

Eliseo believed in the sanctity of the union. It wasn't that hard to convince himself there were enemies out to destroy them. Police had investigated credible death threats against Chavez. From time to time, Chavez went into hiding. Plenty of people still wanted to see the union fail. The idea that Vera Cruz had taken notes to use for some other purpose did not seem that far-fetched.

Eliseo pulled out a copy of the oath of office that the board signed in 1973 and began to read it to Vera Cruz. "Do you still believe in that?" Eliseo demanded. Vera Cruz was speechless. Eliseo persisted: "Are you telling us that it's not true? . . . It says you have to hand over all the papers."

"I cannot think straight," Vera Cruz said.

"Philip made friends outside who are opposed to us, and now he's in a bind," Chavez said. Triumphantly, he pointed to Vera Cruz's refusal to sign as evidence of his complicity in a left-wing plot to subvert the union, just months before its biennial convention. The attack had served its purpose. "The biggest thing," Chavez said, "was to get you guys at least partway convinced."

The meeting morphed from encounter group to church revival. One person confessed he had been seduced by the girlfriend of a purported spy. Chavez asked them to point to suspicious actions and people. Eliseo named someone who should be watched in Coachella: Doug Adair, better known as Pato. Pato had never been shy in voicing opinions. He had written Chavez to protest the purges during the Monday Night Massacre. Three weeks later Pato had written Chavez again when the union leader fired Joe Smith and killed *El Malcriado*, the newspaper Pato had worked for in its first incarnation. The feisty paper had been replaced with the *President's Newsletter*, which reported Chavez's activities using the royal "we." The *President's Newsletter*, Pato wrote, was "a fawning, sycophantic, self-serving sheet of narrow views and sanitized news, printed at union expense. We can, and should, do better."[11]

As soon as Eliseo mentioned Doug, Chavez jumped in and quoted from Pato's most recent letter. "Doug is one of them," he said, offering no proof but relating with relish a recent conversation when he had tried to send a message. "I go to Coachella and he's there and I look at him and I say, 'Hi Doug,'" Chavez said sweetly. "And I didn't say, 'Hi you son of a bitch.' I said, 'Hi Doug.' He said, 'Cesar you look so well, how are you?' I said, 'I feel pretty well. I'll be around for a *long* time.'"

When the board finally returned to the substantive question Chavez had posed—how to focus the union—Eliseo essentially took over the meeting. He proposed they concentrate on negotiating contracts, consolidate their victories, and target ranches for elections in Salinas, "easy pickings" where the union was assured of wins. Chavez pronounced the meeting a great success and promised to draft a plan to turn the board's momentous decision into action.

Eliseo's uncertainty about how to respond to the Game, the assholes, and the management problems contrasted sharply with his clarity about where the union needed to go. He spoke in favor of his resolution with real urgency and at greater length than was his custom. "We have a responsibility to all those people where we went and had elections to go out and negotiate those contracts and deliver on what we said we'd do for them. We have not done so up to now," he said.

"Let's look at history. Whether we like to or not. Let's look at it. What happened in 1973? Whether we like to or not, there were an awful lot of farmworkers at those ranches that we lost to the Teamsters, that it was not just a product of a sweetheart deal between the Teamsters and the companies. Oh, there were never any elections, we were right about that. But I tell you, there were a shitload of workers who were sick and tired that we didn't deliver on what we said we'd do. That was a period of no growth because we were out boycotting lettuce. But goddamn it, we didn't take care of the store. Face it, there were a lot of people there that we did not do a job with. We have to not repeat that mistake again."[12]

CHAPTER 20

In the Trenches

July 1977

Gretchen

Gretchen was back on the boycott, in charge of her own operation for the first time.

She had left the union in the fall of 1976, a few weeks before the vote on Prop 14. Her brother was ill, and while she felt guilty about jumping ship, her family needed help in Oregon. She found a temporary job teaching English and history at Sprague High School in Salem, and in the spring the district offered Gretchen a permanent position. She was tempted. But she reasoned that teaching shaped the next generation; in the union she could affect change directly. She flew back to California, ready to go anywhere, as long as the 1965 Valiant held out. In La Paz, Larry Tramutt was trying to rebuild the national boycott. He had worked with Gretchen during Prop 14. He snagged her for his staff and placed her in charge of the Los Angeles boycott.

In the age of elections, the boycott had become a modest, back-burner operation. Gretchen settled into the Los Angeles office, across the hall from Chris and the farm worker ministry, and immersed herself in an ongoing campaign to force an intransigent Coachella citrus grower to sign a contract.

Much had changed at Coachella Growers since the UFW easily won an election in November 1975–75 votes for the eagle, 22 for no union. Groves of young lemon, orange, and grapefruit trees had matured, turning Coachella Growers into the largest citrus ranch in the valley, with as many as 450 employees. At the same time, the grower had been systematically forcing out UFW supporters. The company stopped providing bus rides, making it impossible for workers without cars to reach citrus groves one hundred miles away from the main ranch. Supervisors cut workers' schedules to three days a week. They decreased the amount paid per bin of lemons.[1]

The controlling partner in the citrus company was Connecticut Mutual Insurance, one of the largest insurance companies in the country. Gretchen organized her staff of five to collect dozens of letters to the chairman of Connecticut Mutual expressing concern over the poor treatment of farmworkers. She worked with Chris to coordinate hundreds of calls a week to the chairman's office and organized delegations of religious and labor leaders to visit the insurance company. Then the boycott volunteers located policyholders and asked them to cancel if Coachella Growers didn't negotiate in good faith. Within weeks the company fired the law firm that had been stonewalling and hired a local attorney who promised to work toward a contract.

Gretchen's next boycott target was hers alone, and the campaign posed particular challenges. But Gretchen was the person unfazed by finding a union printer on Memorial Day weekend in Providence, and after two years with the union, she was even more fearless. So she nonchalantly took on a family-owned nursery an hour east of Los Angeles—a defiant, anti-union employer and a local institution.

The third generation of Lindquists ran Hemet Wholesale, a world-famous nursery that bred hardy ornamentals and roses. The Lindquists ran much of the city of Hemet as well. The part-time mayor worked full time at the nursery and was a partner in the company. His father was another partner, and chairman of the board of the largest bank in Hemet. His uncle was the publisher of the local newspaper and president of the chamber of commerce, his two sons were the editors of the paper, and the local municipal court judge used to be a salesman at the nursery.[2]

Hostilities at Hemet Wholesale had started before the election in September 1975. Company supervisors illegally banned UFW organizers from the property. They threatened union supporters and said Hemet Wholesale would go out of business if the union won. The UFW won overwhelmingly. Within six weeks the strongest union supporters had been fired, transferred, or harassed. The union filed unfair labor charges with the state. More than a year later the board concluded that the company had waged a "strenuous and unlawful battle to defeat the UFW." Hemet Wholesale was ordered to stop breaking the law, to read a statement to all its workers in which the company acknowledged wrongdoing, and to reinstate six workers who had been illegally fired, paying them two years of lost wages.[3]

The sanctions had no impact on Hemet Wholesale's stance at the bargaining table. The company hired an outside negotiator who commented at meetings about kissing the union negotiator, refused to provide necessary documents, and canceled bargaining sessions, claiming a tornado stranded him in Kansas—on a day there was no storm.[4] A year after bargaining allegedly commenced, the union filed another complaint with the state, and Chavez declared a boycott on Hemet roses and plants, sold largely in southern California.

Gretchen organized "flying picket lines"—as many as one hundred people went out each Saturday and protested in front of seven different retail nurseries in rapid succession. She deployed summer volunteers who went door to door in Hemet and collected five hundred signatures asking the city council to censure the mayor. She planned her biggest protest for the Hemet tourist attraction of the year, the Ramona Pageant. The day of the big event, the rain poured. More than 120 boycotters gamely carried billboards along with umbrellas and handed out eighteen thousand leaflets. Robert Lindquist, the mayor and nursery owner, sent Gretchen a note rubbing in the adverse weather. "Having received so many flattering allusions as to my great power and influence," Lindquist wrote, "it was impossible in this case, for me to restrain myself from further extending my influence heavenward."[5]

By May, all chains in the Los Angeles area that had carried Hemet Wholesale roses were "clean," as the boycotters termed it. By July, the company had fired its negotiator and scheduled a bargaining session.

For the union, Hemet Wholesale was a case study in the difficulties of obtaining a contract when an entrenched local business fought every step of the way. For Gretchen, Hemet was an opportunity to learn to manage a staff, wage a campaign, raise money, and recruit volunteers. She worked twelve-hour days, six-day weeks, with a tight-knit group of volunteers—and then went home and lived with them as well in a boycott house so full that a large closet became a bedroom. Gretchen thrived on the communal life, taking pleasure in the garden they planted in their backyard, where they hosted Saturday-evening barbecues for supporters after the week's last picket line.

Gretchen focused intently on work and screened out almost everything else. She had been on leave in Oregon during the height of the Cultural Revolution and was so oblivious to the purges that she did not realize that one of her staff members had been fired by Chavez. She was unaware of the intrigue in La Paz, the preoccupation with infiltrators, and the intense maneuvering to make sure no one disrupted the union's biennial convention. Gretchen was so thrilled to be chosen as a delegate to the Third Constitutional Convention that she ignored the implications of sharp stomach pains the week before and convinced the staff at the union clinic to give her pain-killers. Assigned to the food committee, she organized deliveries to the Fresno convention center and slept outside along with the other volunteers.

Inside, Chavez spoke of the need for radical change. Even the imagery reflected the shift in message. Murals of workers battling Teamsters had been replaced by a gigantic painting of the union president. Chavez stood in front of the mural, the waist of the painted Chavez looming above the real one's head. "Yesterday's actions and decisions, no matter how wise they may have been, inevitably become today's problems," Chavez warned. ". . . It is not difficult to get rid of total failures. They liquidate themselves. Yesterday's successes, however, always linger on long beyond their productive life. We must seek out those sacred tasks of the past that drain needed resources and scarce time and prune them ruthlessly so we can focus on the future."

Chavez also sounded one familiar theme: "Since this union was founded, it has been the dream of the leadership to build an organization led by farm workers," he said. ". . . It is important that the process of assuring the complete rule of the union by the farm workers begins now." He promised to restructure and train the ranch committees. He spoke of the broader future and the mission of creating community. He proposed one resolution to designate official union holidays and another to establish Founder's Day on March 31, his birthday. That was the day, Chavez said, he had decided in 1962 to form a union for farmworkers.[6]

Like many in the union, Gretchen had driven herself to the point of physical collapse. When the convention was over, she went back to the clinic. The doctor rushed her to the hospital for an emergency appendectomy.

She returned to work as soon as she could and passed on the themes Chavez had sounded at the convention. "Our dream is to be a national organization, to move from the fields into the city and become the Poor Peoples Union," Gretchen told a group of college students. First, the union needed their help to nail down contracts in California. "We haven't won yet," she said. "The next two years we'll have to fight like hell. The union is on the line."[7]

Eliseo

Eliseo left the Third Constitutional Convention as second vice president, one notch up in the union hierarchy, and happily retreated to Coachella, a post viewed as the union's equivalent of Siberia. For Eliseo, the inhospitable desert had become a refuge from La Paz. No matter how tough the problems in the Coachella Valley, Eliseo was confident he could devise strategies to cope.

The spring campaign in the grape vineyards that had upset Sandy underscored the reasons Coachella was an assignment few requested. Some of the difficulties were structural. The grape harvest lasted only a short time, and many workers passed through quickly en route north to the San Joaquin Valley. Historic tensions among Mexicans, Filipinos, and workers who migrated north from Texas complicated the organizing challenge. But the biggest obstacle, as Eliseo had pointed out to the board, was lingering resentment in the vineyards from the 1970 contracts that the union had mishandled. Eliseo found the election results disappointing, but not a surprise. The union's typical flood-the-zone approach had limited impact when so much distrust permeated the fields. Eliseo rebounded with a plan to consolidate the union's considerable gains in the citrus industry and a determination to formulate a longer-term strategy to overcome anti-union sentiment in the vineyards.

Union supporters had gravitated to Lionel Steinberg's large ranch, the first UFW contract in Coachella. Eliseo was renegotiating the Steinberg contract, and he intended to make it the model for future pacts in grapes. He aimed to negotiate one strong contract in each crop, which would set standard for wages and working conditions. Then he could use the first contract to speed up negotiations with other growers in the industry and put competitors on an even footing. One of the growers' biggest complaints was that union contracts placed them at an economic disadvantage. Lionel Steinberg railed during negotiations about how the hiring hall impeded his ability to employ experienced workers. He was embarrassed to tell other grape growers that his crews pruned an average of only 2.5 vines per hour, making his costs as much as forty dollars per acre higher than those of his competitors.[8]

Eliseo had followed Chavez's dictum to focus on negotiations. Chavez wanted more income from dues, and he exhorted compromises to gain new members. "We really need to be flexible," he told the board. "People who are negotiating are going to have enough power to sign contracts."[9] Four months later he refused to sign off on a contract Eliseo had negotiated because of a minor clause. Eliseo pointed out the contradiction. "How will a negotiator effectively engage in collective bargaining if he/she knows that what agreements are reached are conditional on your later approval?" Eliseo protested in a letter to Chavez. "Most people would become afraid, and this is the case now, to move from what they know you'll approve. In effect you'll become the master negotiator for the state, present at every table. This is not healthy for the union." Chavez marked up and filed the letter, writing "not so—full authority" in the margin. But he approved the contract.[10]

More and more, Eliseo was questioning policies and challenging Chavez's judgment. Eliseo asked why Spanish translations of contracts were so poor, in some places different in meaning—leading to major difficulties. He questioned the wisdom of keeping the union's headquarters at La Paz, in the middle of nowhere. He denounced as child labor a motion to have the union dispense field jobs to underage workers, a request by parents who wanted families to work together. He rejected as unrealistic a new personnel policy that required a letter of recommendation from an employer.

"I think we're going to have a hard time getting some employers to give farm workers a recommendation to come work for the union," Eliseo argued. Chavez vehemently defended the policy as an integral part of his new management system: "There's nothing like a letter from an employer. Good or bad it tells you something . . . I have a need to know who the guy is."[11]

Chavez was still struggling to impose structure on the unwieldy union. His most trusted and capable partner was Sister Florence Zweber, a nun who had come to the union from the Mayo Clinic. She was an experienced accountant, and Chavez put her in charge of straightening out the union's chaotic finances. She had gradually made progress, though the jargon and structure of white-collar finance often clashed with the realities of the fields. Chavez enthusiastically embraced her new management system—the Planning Programming and Budgeting System (PPBS)—and in September 1977 he summoned the board to a restructuring conference.[12]

In the three months since the tumultuous meeting where the board had voted to concentrate on negotiations, nothing had changed. The union had about seventeen thousand members (the numbers were inexact and constantly fluctuated, depending on the amount of work available), covered by ninety-nine contracts. The numbers had been stagnant in the year since the ALRB reopened. Now Chavez outlined the structure he had developed with the help of Sister Florence. Their proposal organized the union by function, like a hospital flow chart. The board members were skeptical. "Unions aren't hospitals," Eliseo wrote.[13]

Out loud, Eliseo ran through a litany of the things he did each day and a list of his staff. "Now what is the problem—is it the system or is it the fact that there are not enough people to do the work? . . . I don't think it is the system breaking down. We just don't have the resources."

"I feel exactly the same way," said Richard Chavez.

"We are not trying to tear down the plan," Eliseo told the union president. "What we are trying to do is tell you, from our experience of dealing with day-to-day problems of administering and negotiating contracts, of our suggestions for making it more viable."

The problem, Chavez insisted, was not people but planning. Even when they adopted a plan, board members failed to follow through. He returned to his favorite example, berating the union leaders for not properly filling out telephone chits: "You are not using them because you don't have time to use them or for whatever reason, but you are fucking me over. And it is not being done."

Chavez argued that his plan aimed to decentralize authority; the board members told him the proposal would centralize more decision-making in La Paz. He countered that the plan would be so clear that no one would need to call for guidance. "What is happening today in the union, we have several unions going around and that is dangerous," Chavez said. "The situation is desperate. Something has to be done."[14]

Chavez had polled the staff on whether the UFW should be a business union or a movement, and now he polled the board. Even those most ideologically committed voted for business union. "Our business is take care of home base—our members—have to deliver on our obligations," Eliseo wrote. "B.U. means that we don't run off to do crusades, instead of service our membership."[15]

To Eliseo, the solutions proposed in La Paz seemed as intellectually disconnected from the work as the union's headquarters was from the fields. Back in Coachella, he tried to block out the confusion. He worked closely with Ruth Shy, his deputy in the field office, who had long ago dropped out of the Sisters of Loretto. They shared a commitment to the workers and an ability to filter out the troubling issues. Shy worked closely with the ranch committees, and she could see workers change, literally from week to week, as they began to understand their own power. Eliseo signed a landmark citrus contract that included a provision where workers could renegotiate rates as conditions changed and strike if no agreement were reached. Hemet Wholesale signed a contract on November 21, and Coachella Growers a few days later. Eliseo credited the boycott with forcing both companies to negotiate. The union pursued a bad-faith bargaining case against Hemet Wholesale and eventually obtained a $192,500 settlement.[16]

As long as he could see progress, Eliseo buried his questions and endured the wearying lifestyle. He had grown up in the union. The teenage picket captain from Delano was now a thirty-one-year-old father. Dorothy was on leave, taking care of their infant son. Eliseo had a family, no financial security, and no prospect of even a savings account. He asked Chavez about the possibility of setting up a trust fund for his son. Chavez promised to get back to him with some ideas, but he never did.[17] Eliseo hated to ask the union for money. So did Dorothy; she grimaced every time she remembered having to ask for ninety dollars to pay a dental bill in Calexico, when she bit down on Milk Duds and broke a filling. The communal lifestyle they had accepted without question was more problematic as a family. It bothered Eliseo that he could not buy his son new shoes. He had to rely on the union's community grab bag. In November, Eliseo had to write Chavez and ask for help. Despite saving all they could, they were $150 short for a planned trip to visit Dorothy's family in Seattle over the Christmas holidays.[18]

In early 1978 Chavez began another reorganization. He talked to Eliseo about the possibility of handling the vegetable industry, where all the contracts would be up for negotiation by year end. When Chavez sent out memos announcing new assignments for Marshall Ganz, Gilbert Padilla and Dolores Huerta, Eliseo figured he was next. He sat down and composed a detailed memo on what would be needed for an effective transition in the Coachella office, to preserve the momentum they had built.[19]

Chris

Chris was delivering the message of change to his board with far greater clarity than Chavez was to his. Chris opened a report to the NFWM board with a quote from Chavez in a recent interview: "The ALRA has changed everything. It has affected everything we do, even our way of thinking . . . We now are faced with trying to find out how to maintain the vitality we had, so that it goes beyond just shouting 'Viva la Huelga.' . . . We had a kind of community. We were united because the persecution made us united. We had an urgent cause. But in fact, we were not really united in terms of staff and in terms of community. We discovered that quickly."

The message, Chris reported succinctly, was profound: "What has worked for 12 years is no longer adequate. The old is being cast off in favor of new methods, new people and new priorities."[20] Chris's next report opened with an even more blunt quote from Chavez: "The same people who struggle and win and build an organization are often-times the ones who then destroy it by fighting each other."[21]

Chris saw the challenge that Chavez faced: How to manage the transition from cause to union without sacrificing the movement? Chris eagerly pitched in to help. They still talked about the Poor Peoples Union, but the day-to-day work of the UFW consumed Chavez. The dream of a communal farm in Oxnard run by a religious order had faded into less ambitious goals in La Paz: a community laundry room, weekly mass and liturgy. Chris formed an outstanding citizen committee, a pet committee, and a beautification committee. He chaired a meeting to pick the twelve most important dates in the union history, one to celebrate each month. He advised on how to furnish the Game room in the north unit. He drafted the UFW prayer.

Chris became the union's liaison with Synanon, sending groups up to the Home Place for training and coordinating the Games at La Paz. He began to see that Chavez was using the Game to put certain people together and engineer particular attacks. All but a few holdouts played the Game at La Paz every Wednesday. Then Chavez began requiring union staff from around the state to come to La Paz on Saturdays. Chris reported to Chavez regularly on who refused to play. Among the most adamant was his brother. Chris quoted Richard Chavez: "It is not helping people, in fact the people I relate to are being screwed up by the Game."[22]

In the fall of 1977 Chris found himself embroiled in a much more public confrontation. Chavez traveled to the Philippines, a misguided effort to reach out to Filipino workers who distrusted the union. Ferdinand Marcos hosted the UFW delegation. Chavez was quoted in the *Washington Post* praising the dictator's regime. Human rights advocates and religious leaders protested. They sent Chavez and Chris information that outlined well-documented human rights abuses, thinking Chavez had erred out of ignorance. Then they called on him to renounce the earlier statements. Chavez refused. Chris faced enormous pressure from all denominations. His own board wanted the National Farm Worker Ministry—in theory, an independent group—to make a public statement. Leader after leader urged Chris to distance himself from Chavez's defiant defense of the repressive regime. Chavez was stubborn. He was not going to abuse the hospitality of his hosts by criticizing their regime, he told Chris. In an attempt to quell the controversy, Chavez asked Chris to host a town hall meeting for religious leaders.

On a Saturday afternoon Chris sat on the Delano High School auditorium stage, uncomfortably aware that the meeting was only making matters worse. Officials who had flown in from the Philippines read prepared statements on behalf of the government. Chavez backed off from praising martial law but reiterated that he was impressed with the country and had not witnessed evidence of brutality or torture. One after another, Chris's staunchest allies criticized Chavez. They went to a nearby Mexican restaurant for dinner afterward, and Monsignor George Higgins turned down two requests that he sit at Chavez's table. Higgins ended up next to Chris, and the labor priest harangued Chris all night about his refusal to stand up for what was right.[23]

Chris focused on the critics' self-righteousness and their paternalistic attitudes. He half-convinced himself that Chavez might be right, clinging to that hope to get through the first real clash between his church family and his union family. Chris had not faced such pressure since he had first committed the Migrant Ministry to help the union in 1965 and jeopardized all his financial support. Then he had been absolutely sure he had chosen the morally courageous path. Now he struggled to justify his position. He argued that others who had not fully committed themselves to the cause, like Higgins, should not be casting stones. Chris chastised his own board. "The farm workers now have their own Union and their own leadership," he said. ". . . We, as supporters, may not always agree and we are free to say so—but we are not in a position to dictate what the UFW and its leaders do and I hope we will not use our support to try to blackmail them into doing things *our* way."[24]

John Moyer, the United Church of Christ leader, had actively supported efforts to expose the Marcos dictatorship and its policies of torture. He urged Chris not to dismiss or denigrate critics. "What the left has failed to do, Marcos has succeeded in doing by giving Cesar the royal treatment and, in a sense, putting him in debt to the Marcos government for the support of Filipino workers in the UFW," Moyer wrote to Chris. "Maybe this was necessary, but, my God, what a price to pay. I just hope *he* is aware of that."[25]

In reply, Chris acknowledged his own "captive conscience." He was honest about his priorities: "I am not proud of it but I have seen it for what it is . . . maybe because I am chicken or maybe because my conscience isn't as important as some other things I value."[26]

Chris never seriously considered taking a stand on the Philippines. He defended Chavez and rationalized the trip as part of the ongoing struggle to reshape the union. "I am clearly susceptible to Cesar's personality and power, but I am not blind," Chris wrote. "I will know it when he becomes someone entirely different."[27]

Sandy

Sandy had been clear, since the first phone-bill rant during the Coachella strike, that he had joined the union for the cause, not the man. So like Eliseo and many others, Sandy immersed himself in work. He oversaw a team of attorneys and paralegals who handled all work before the ALRB. They operated on adrenaline and intellect, without a complete set of labor law books and with minimal experience. Five years' practice, which would have put him at the bottom rung of a major law firm, made Sandy a senior counsel in the farm workers union. Sandy did not need Crosby Milne's boxes and charts to figure out his own goal: to mold the law to the best possible advantage of farmworkers.

What Chavez dismissed as mundane, nonmissionary work, Sandy saw as central to the cause. No other state in the country had anything like California's Agricultural Labor Relations Act. Each of the early cases Sandy tackled set a precedent that could affect workers' rights for generations. For the opportunity to witness the landmark law actually help farmworkers, Sandy could tolerate the diatribes about telephone chits. He could tune out the purges. He could give up his Memorial Day to watch one of the union vice presidents inspect the lawyers' cars, insisting that Sandy open the sealed radiator on his Datsun so the executive board member could measure the fluid level.

An early victory had given organizers the legal right to be in the fields for an hour before work, an hour while workers ate lunch, and an hour after work. Next, the state board ruled that if a grower did not provide an accurate list of employees before the election, the vote could be overturned. A challenge by the union to the vote at Hansen Farms, where Jerry had been beaten up during the 1970 strike, yielded a ruling that an employer could not promise workers better wages and conditions for voting "no union." A Teamster victory at Oshita became an often-cited case after the board threw the election out and ruled that the employer improperly gave health insurance to workers just before election day in an effort to win their votes. In the spring of 1977 there were 133 cases in various phases pending before the state board, and dozens more in court.[28]

Sandy's second priority was educating the union's motley crew of far-flung volunteers. First he wanted them to understand the gist of decisions. Elections often were won by a handful of votes, and victory could hinge on understanding minor technicalities in advance: whether the office secretary was eligible to vote or the difference between shed workers at a company that handled only its own produce or one that was a commercial operation. Second, the union needed to apply standards uniformly—not one of its strong suits. Lawyers could find themselves in trouble if they argued that a Salinas organizer had acted in accordance with union policy—only to discover the policy in Coachella was entirely different. "I can't emphasize enough that everybody in the Union who is connected in any way with organizing or negotiating and so on should read all the opinions," Sandy wrote in summarizing recent ALRB cases. "Each of the opinions contains the substance of what this law is really all about."[29]

Sandy also had a temper he was more than willing to use. The union had won an election at O.P. Murphy, a tomato grower south of Salinas, on September 30, 1975. For two years the company stalled, first fighting the certification, then refusing to bargain for a contract. In the fall of 1977 two members of the negotiating committee were fired, and their crews walked off the job in protest. Word spread, and soon all five crews stopped picking tomatoes. O.P. Murphy fired them all. When the workers found themselves replaced by a labor contractor's crews, the strikers went into the fields and talked the scabs into walking out too. The Monterey sheriff ordered the strikers out of the field. Five were arrested, cited, and released. The next day the same thing happened. This time the workers were charged with felony counts of conspiracy to commit trespass. Two days later a brawl with scabs in the field ended in more arrests. The strike leaders were charged with attempted murder. Sandy called around, and when he couldn't locate the workers by four twenty P.M., he went to the jail. He was denied permission to see the workers and ordered to leave. Sandy did not usually take no for an answer without a fight.[30]

Judge William F. Moreno was home watching a Saturday afternoon football game on television when a deputy sheriff called, requesting permission to lock up a foul-mouthed lawyer who was insisting on seeing his clients. The judge thought the workers had not yet been booked and the lawyer was a public defender not yet appointed to the case. He said yes. Sandy was exchanging angry words with the jail officials when several deputies suddenly jumped him from behind. They ripped his shirt, pulled off his belt, and injured his neck. Then they charged him with resisting arrest and threw him in jail. On the arrest form where it said "weapon," the police officer wrote "hands, feet and mouth." Under "motive," the officer wrote "personal satisfaction." The only part of the report Sandy acknowledged as accurate was his repeated use of the expression "Fuck you, man."[31]

First the sheriffs threw Sandy into the cell with the workers he had been asking to see. Then they put him in an isolation cell. A few minutes later, the sheriffs were surprised to see Judge Moreno. "This is one judge that believes in action," he later explained from the bench. "When I found out we had a lawyer in our jail that was arrested for disturbing the peace, I went down there to the jail." When Moreno understood that the strikers had been arrested and booked early in the day, and he saw Sandy in a torn-up shirt, sitting in an isolation cell, Moreno ordered the prisoner released. The judge arranged for Sandy to talk with his clients. When the case came before him a few weeks later, Moreno recommended the district attorney dismiss the charges. "You know, if I were a lawyer out there and I was thinking I was getting ripped off, I would probably get a little bit vocal too," Judge Moreno said in court, "and I suppose that there is no lawyer worth his salt that isn't going to get upset at one time or another when he thinks he's getting the runaround."[32]

Sandy wanted to sue for false arrest. Jerry convinced him to drop the threat as part of an overall settlement. Two years later the ALRB awarded O.P. Murphy workers back pay for having been wrongly fired by a company that had bargained in bad faith.[33]

CHAPTER 21

Visions Collide

February 1978

Jerry

Chris passed on the article with an enthusiastic endorsement: "Jerry, this is worth reading and then rereading with care." Jerry handed the story out to his staff with his own commentary: "For those who think this is only a reorganization."

In the interview published in *Sojourners,* a Christian social justice magazine, Chavez focused on the importance of community. He emphasized that the union faced a crossroads. Either we become a real community, he said, or it's just a regular nine-to-five job. "If we choose this community style we will have some kind of religion—either we invent one or we keep what we have, but we cannot be without one. It is very meaningful and important."[1]

In notes and conversations Jerry began to telegraph the shift. When Ellen Eggers was nearing graduation from law school in Indiana, she assumed she would go to work for the union. On February 8 she called Jerry. He told her they were not hiring. In fact, he confided, he expected the legal department to shrink. Ellen was disappointed and started looking elsewhere. Part of the appeal of the union had been the feeling that she was really needed; if there wasn't enough work, she saw no point going back.

Chavez had been needling Jerry about various things since the attack a year earlier at Synanon about abandoning La Paz. Too many lawyers. No Chicano attorneys. Resources devoted to unnecessary legal work. A year earlier Chavez had wanted the legal department to focus almost exclusively on election-related work and appeals to the state board.[2] Now he demanded a budget estimate before the union filed any unfair labor practice charge. Jerry told his staff they had to assess their work carefully.

Glenn Rothner, a young lawyer who had joined the union in 1975, responded with a five-page memo he entitled, "Up a stream of consciousness without a paddle." He didn't have the time, he told Jerry, to add up all the court cases, unfair labor practices, and administrative appeals he was supposed to be handling in Fresno, his area of responsibility. He wasn't pushing aggressively to resolve issues, even on elections dating back two years, because he didn't have time to prepare properly for hearings. He invested hours in winning new elections, only to discover there were no organizers to run campaigns. Rothner had stopped at a bookstore on his way to a hearing and bought a couple of Ross Macdonald mysteries and an eight-cent chocolate sucker, which he made sure to finish before arriving at the UFW office because he felt guilty about the indulgence. He saw his own harried work as a reflection of the union's problems: "We tailor our work to the latest fad or crisis. Since we don't have enough staff, time, or resources we end up being jugglers rather than lawyers . . . juggling is just not my idea of a way to help the union grow."[3]

Other lawyers expressed similar frustrations. Jerry had never enjoyed administration, and he grew tired of the complaints. He had tried to protect his staff from La Paz and Chavez's micromanaging, while also shielding Chavez from the growing discontent in Salinas. Chavez wanted the legal department to play the Game, and Jerry decided that might be a good idea. Take himself out of the middle, let the lawyers see what dealing with La Paz was really like, and let Chavez see what a bunch of quick-witted lawyers could do in a verbal sparring match.

By the spring of 1978 ninety-four people on the union staff were playing the Game, in offices around the state. Chris traveled to different sites and distributed an explanatory handout: "Most organizations destroy themselves unless they find a way to deal with each other . . . The game is a tool . . . lie, exaggerate, use humor, no violence . . . keep it a mystery for workers. Like any game, the more you play, the better you are and the more you like it."[4]

Once the legal department began playing the Game, the personal dynamics in the small department changed irrevocably. The lawyers were skilled debaters, trained to go after the jugular, and they knew each other well. Personal tensions that had not been impediments to collegial work suddenly became grist for sharp attacks. The alleged boundary between "in the Game" and "outside the Game" disappeared. The department split in two factions. People ended up in tears, which made Jerry uncomfortable. Still, he presented himself as an advocate in his mid-year report to the executive board: "We have spent a considerable amount of time and energy playing the Game. On the whole, I think the Game has had a positive impact on the Legal Department, though some have suffered some considerable pain as a result of it . . . I have found that bonds develop between the people that really play and that the people that don't play, tend to isolate themselves."[5]

The Game exacerbated another gulf—between Salinas and La Paz. The lawyers made clear their contempt. "Legal staff are organizing and pushing their feelings, e.g., waste of time to come to La Paz, game isn't working, the real work of the union is 'out there,' La Paz staff are brown-nosing 'moonies,'" Chris wrote. Jerry told Chris derisively that the La Paz people were not taking on the lawyers enough. "He wants us 'to take off the gloves—if we know how,'" Chris wrote.[6] The fourth Saturday that the lawyers made the four-hour trip to La Paz to play the Game, they arrived in matching shirts and ties, prominently carrying copies of *Time* magazine. The executive board, at Chavez's request, had declared a boycott on *Time* after the magazine published an article describing Synanon as a "kooky cult," where men were forced to undergo vasectomies, couples were ordered to wife-swap, and a grand jury was investigating allegations of child abuse.[7]

In and out of the Game, the lawyers began to ask about money. Most of them earned $600 a month. They depleted savings or relied on family outside the union to pay their bills. They were getting older and wanted some security. Some asked Jerry for increases. If they were going to have to put up with the Game and the ensuing problems, at least they should be able to pay for basic living expenses without relying on their parents.

Chavez's opposition to paying wages had been unwavering. When the paralegals had asked for salaries a year earlier, Chavez had presented the request to the executive board as Exhibit A in his argument for a community dedicated to subsistence living: "There is no movement," Chavez said, so the paralegals sought wages as a substitute for the security a movement would offer. "They work right alongside the attorneys . . . We have these gaps, these special kinds of treatment, based solely on the triangle," Chavez said, invoking the Synanon symbol for the work life.[8]

Nonetheless, Jerry thought a request to modestly increase the lawyers' salaries would receive a different reception. The lawyers were already paid; the question was how much. Chavez had always been a pragmatist, willing to pay for services he needed. Jerry viewed the issue as solely a financial question and was confident he could cut a deal. Tell them to put it in writing, Chavez responded when Jerry broached the subject.

Tom Dalzell was in Calexico when Jerry called and told him to write a letter asking for a raise. Immediately. The Dazzler wrote that he had postponed dental work, given up health insurance and liability car insurance, and spent $1,000 of his $1,400 in savings. Like the other lawyers who spent a lot of time on the road, he pointed out that the union's two-dollars-a-day food allowance did not cover meals. He earned $650 a month and asked for an additional $400.

Sandy's note was typically understated. "I have worked in the Union for five and one-half years, and, not surprisingly, I am now nearly five and one-half years older," he began. "I have reached, if not passed, a time in my life when I must do some planning for the future." At thirty-three, he did not want to continue to rely on his parents to supplement his $7,200 income. He and Kirsten Zerger were planning to get married. She had a young daughter. "This is not an easy subject to raise. I have stuck with this work for obvious reasons and I would like to see the creation of a National union. I know the road ahead is a long and difficult one. I would like to make my contribution to that fight, and I think I have something to add to it." He asked for a raise to $17,500.[9]

Most of Jerry's $29,000 salary had been paid for the past two years by the United Auto Workers union, which had been subsidizing the UFW for more than a decade. The UAW leaders had decided the farm workers union should by now be self-sufficient. They had initiated a phase-out that would reduce weekly checks to the union from $6,200 in early 1976 to zero by September 1978.[10] The UAW eliminated Jerry's salary grant as well. "So now I, too, need money," he wrote Chavez.[11]

Separately, Jerry forwarded the letters he had collected from his staff. "People have overcome their fear and guilt in relation to raising these issues and at the same time have recognized a need to confront the long-range future," he wrote Chavez. ". . . This is not easy for them as it was not for me."[12]

In the imagery of the movies Jerry loved, the lawyer handed the union president a loaded gun.

Eliseo

Eliseo finally received his new assignment in the spring of 1978, though it was not one he and Chavez had discussed. Just months after Chavez had pushed the board to do nothing but negotiate contracts, he placed Eliseo in charge of organizing. Chavez made the switch in response to concern from Governor Jerry Brown, who worried that the landmark labor law could become a liability in his reelection campaign if the union did not begin actively organizing again.[13] Eliseo took over a department that had all but disappeared.

Before he could begin to plan, he found himself back where he had started three years earlier—in Oxnard, meeting with workers at Egg City. The state had scheduled another election at the egg ranch, years after a box of challenged votes from the original election had been stolen. While Eliseo was meeting with the Egg City workers at night, he heard a rumor that seven crews of lemon pickers at Coastal Growers Association had walked off the job, angry with the rate they received per bin of fruit. The next morning some citrus workers showed up at the union office. Eliseo went with them back to Coastal Growers, the area's largest citrus harvesting company.

Workers milling outside the gates of the citrus company headquarters cheered the arrival of *la union* and lifted Eliseo on top of a car. He looked down on close to a thousand lemon pickers in their customary white hard hats, like a sea of mushrooms. The union is hard work, he told them. If you just want a raise, go talk to the boss. The more he told them how difficult a strike and election would be, the more the workers cheered. Eliseo directed them to line up by crew, pick a representative for each crew, and sign cards. They did, standing in lines one hundred deep to wait their turns.[14]

The ALRA had a provision for an election within forty-eight hours if the majority of workers at a company went on strike. The union had invoked the rule only twice before. Eliseo filed for an election at Coastal Growers on March 29. Two days later hundreds of workers waited in the early-morning rain until state agents opened the polls. Eliseo waited nervously next door. He did not really know these workers. He had not had time to do all the usual due diligence. When the polls closed, he joined several hundred lemon pickers to watch the vote count in the cafeteria of the labor camp at 5th and Rose, where most of the workers lived. Each time an agent held up a ballot marked with the eagle and called out

"Union de Campesinos," Eliseo made a mark on his yellow pad. He crossed off each set of five, then circled each set of 50. After about 90 minutes, the sheet was covered with 897 marks. Only 42 workers had voted against the union.

Even in elections with such lopsided tallies, growers often filed appeals that blocked state certification for months. Without certification, the union could not even commence bargaining. Such delays frustrated workers and created a quandary for the union. Years often went by between an election and a contract. Workers who originally campaigned for the union were long since fired or moved on in disgust. Eliseo had an idea for a way to break that cycle. After the Coastal Growers election, he kept the lemon pickers out on strike. The company was desperate to get the harvest going again. Eliseo explained what it would take to get workers back in the lemon groves. After four days Eliseo and the Coastal Growers vice president jointly signed a stipulation waiving all objections and asking the ALRB to certify results immediately so they could start bargaining. Work resumed.

When negotiations stalled, Eliseo responded with Plan Maraña, or Operation Tangle. Workers showed up in the morning, messed up the trees, dumped lemons on the ground, and then went home. After a few days the company locked them out. The strike was on again. Eliseo negotiated an arrangement with the labor camp where the workers lived, and the union paid $9,936 to cover food and lodging. The union used connections in the Brown administration to persuade the state unemployment office to put most of the strikers on unemployment. More than nine hundred workers stayed out on strike, with the help of $36,000 in food assistance from the union.[15] Eliseo put the pickets to work circling the Elks Lodge while he finalized a contract inside.

Within eight weeks, two thousand workers at six citrus ranches had voted to join the union, by overwhelming margins. The UFW won the Egg City revote as well. Eliseo began his new job as organizing director with a boost of energy.

The Oxnard activity sharpened the contrast with La Paz. While Eliseo had been setting up conferences to train ranch committee leaders, Chavez focused on classes for the children of the movement leaders. The children would stay, he believed, unlike newer recruits to the union staff who had not endured the "wounds and scars" that bound the older generation to the cause and to one another.[16] Chavez had abandoned his iron-clad resistance to accepting outside funds and obtained more than $600,000 in grants from the federal government for training programs. He set up a school for negotiators and enrolled the children of La Paz, including his son, his son-in-law, and Dolores Huerta's son. He designed a curriculum for the negotiating class that included labor history, contract language, UFW history, and Spanish. He also included a unit on mind control; Chavez had taken a course and believed the mind-control techniques would help negotiators to relax at key points during deliberations.[17]

When Chavez announced that his next school would be for organizers, Eliseo urged him to select only students with particular aptitude. Chavez disagreed. For years he had valued organizers above all other disciplines. He had viewed good organizers as a special breed, extremely difficult to find, and blessed with a single-minded commitment that verged on fanaticism.[18] But his perspective shifted sharply as he faced the exigencies of trying to hold his movement together. Loyalty and longevity trumped talent.

Anyone could be an organizer, Chavez now declared. "The life of the union depends on teaching people," he said. "Unless they're really, really very dumb, I think they can be taught. If they have the interest, they can be taught."[19]

Jerry

The lawyers' requests for raises were not on the agenda for the June 16 executive board meeting. Chavez brought the subject up. The proposed salaries had to be weighed in the context of the union's precarious finances, Chavez said, but more significantly as a philosophical choice. He warned of consequences. If the board did not approve the raises, the attorneys might quit. If the board did grant the requests, the decision would exacerbate tensions with volunteers. The legal department would have to shrink to stay within budget. And last but not least, Chavez wanted the legal department in La Paz.

Chavez rebuffed several suggestions to deal with the lawyers' requests as a budget issue, divorced from the larger question of paying salaries. He insisted they were linked. Jerry had provided the perfect opportunity to force a referendum on the volunteer system that Chavez believed so vital to the cause.

Chavez raised two questions: Was it too late for the lawyers to embrace the volunteer lifestyle? And why were they really working for the union? He saw only two options: Convince the lawyers of the value of subsistence lifestyle, or cut the legal department to a handful of people who would do only specialized work. Finally, Chavez said the issue was too important to resolve without further thought. He adjourned the meeting for one week.[20]

Jerry drove back to Salinas, distraught. He stopped along the way and called Sandy's house late at night, then arrived there close to four A.M., in despair. Jerry was in mourning before the votes were counted.

Chavez exploited the break between meetings to generate support for his vision of a volunteer movement. He circulated the salary requests and solicited input from the union staff. Many had not known the lawyers were paid. Chavez asked Gilbert Padilla to chair a community meeting at La Paz on June 19, at which he juxtaposed the union's shaky financial state with the lawyers' requests. Letters from staff members to Chavez overwhelmingly criticized the greedy attorneys. This was blackmail. Let them leave. Find people who truly cared about the union. One person did suggest reducing other costs, including the meals served every weekend during the Game—$300 to $400, or twice the average lawyer's salary.[21]

Jerry lobbied too. He worked hardest on Padilla, who had been openly questioning whether Chavez had gone a little crazy. But their discussions ended acrimoniously. Jerry was furious that Padilla of all people would not support the lawyers. As baffled as he was by Chavez, Padilla shared a commitment rooted in their common experience decades ago in the Community Service Organization: Money screws things up. The appeal of sacrifice was powerful, and Padilla believed Chavez's axiom that you can't organize poor people if you make too much money. Padilla rationalized the decision in financial terms—he was the secretary-treasurer, and the union could not afford to pay all its staff. But he shared Chavez's emotional commitment. Jerry saw the decision as strictly economic: Paying modest salaries would not in the end cost more than a crazy-quilt volunteer system that paid room and board, credit card bills for gas, and a dozen other special deals.

Chavez had asked all the lawyers to come to the board meeting. When they declined, he went to Salinas instead. The meeting began inauspiciously when Jerry and Chavez were inadvertently locked out and Jerry had to call upstairs to get the door opened. The discussion did not go much better. Positions only hardened. Chavez found the lawyers hostile and arrogant, and they found him inflexible and unappreciative. As important as the money, the lawyers did not want to live at La Paz, and they made that clear. They told Chavez the union should pay people and get rid of the incompetents, and that would solve a lot of problems.

Without Padilla's support, Jerry didn't have the votes. He called board member Pete Velasco the night before the meeting. Jerry knew Velasco would vote with Chavez. Jerry also knew Velasco could be relied on to deliver a message. "Won't attend meeting. Don't want to get angry. Upset. Got kids—want send college," Velasco wrote, taking notes of the conversation. The UAW had cut off his stipend, Jerry told Velasco, and he planned to leave August 1. "Sorry, Pete. Goodbye."[22]

When the board reconvened on June 25, Velasco delivered the message. Chavez reiterated that the debate was over philosophy more than money. He rejected suggestions to deal with the lawyers as a budget item and insisted on a referendum on the union policy of subsistence wages.

Like Chavez, Eliseo also argued philosophy, not economics. For him, the broader issue was about farmworkers, not lawyers. If we're serious about turning the union over to farmworkers, he said, we should pay salaries. He suggested a policy similar to other unions, which stipulated that no staff could earn more than the highest-paid union member. He rejected outright Chavez's contention that students in the negotiations and contract administration school were the future of the union. They are not farmworkers, Eliseo pointed out. He disputed Chavez's contention that voting to pay wages was tantamount to destroying the union. Finally, when the stalemate was clear, Eliseo gave up. Maybe we are all on different wavelengths, he said. We just don't understand where each other is coming from.

At Chavez's request, the minority faction, the four younger members on the board, drafted a proposal. The idea endorsed by Eliseo, Jessica Govea, Marshall Ganz, and Mack Lyons called for phasing in salaries over time, paying stipends in accordance with seniority, contributions, and responsibility. They explicitly defined the long-range goal as a union for farmworkers, not a poor people's union. Chavez offered a counterproposal: Continue the volunteer system, liberalize benefits slightly, and continue to pay for professional services only until the union could build up those departments and staff them with volunteers. He also told the board he had decided to resign, regardless of the outcome of the vote. He wanted to move on to his next endeavor, after an orderly transition.

For four years Richard Chavez had been the board member who spoke most openly and consistently in favor of paying salaries. But he could not in the end vote against his brother. Richard Chavez tried to combine the two plans, suggesting they delay the payment of wages for one year, until the union was in better financial shape. His brother ruled the amendment out of order.[23]

The union founder prevailed by the slimmest of margins. The volunteer system would continue. The legal department would move to La Paz and be replaced by volunteers who embraced the union's lifestyle. Chavez said he would pay Jerry his full salary during the transition and keep a number of other lawyers for two years. But like the title character in his favorite movie, *McCabe and Mrs. Miller*, Jerry had negotiated himself into the ground.

Chris

Marshall Ganz called Chris right after the vote. Ganz was freaked out and wanted to talk confidentially. They met for breakfast in Los Angeles. Until very recently, Ganz had been one of the most outspoken and ideologically committed supporters of the volunteer system. He had argued that paying salaries would destroy the movement. But Ganz had never questioned the need to pay for professional help. He put lawyers and doctors in a separate category, and their salaries posed no contradiction for him. When Chavez used the lawyers' request to reopen that exception, Ganz saw the move as an attempt to kill the legal department. During his work organizing the vegetable workers, Ganz had come to view the lawyers as essential. Dismantling the department would be disastrous.

Chris offered his usual reassurances. Chavez has not lost interest in the union, Chris told Ganz. "I am sure some of it bores him but that has always been true to one degree or another," Chris wrote in a follow-up note. "I think it is more true to say that some elements of the union's philosophy, life and work are crucial to him and it is hard for him to see himself leading a movement that is without these elements (e.g. subsistence life-style, non-violence, sacrifice, service)."[24]

Chris had several long conversations with Chavez in the days that followed. Chavez expressed outrage at the idea of paying staff. He felt betrayed by people he had thought shared his vision and the sacrifice it entailed. The contention that farmworkers had to be paid to work for the union incensed Chavez. This was a direct challenge to what he knew best. He would recruit farmworkers who wanted to sacrifice for the struggle. Chavez, Chris concluded, was preparing to move on to his next, grander phase and leave the running of the union to others. "I can't keep forcing my will on everybody else," Chavez told Chris. "I really thought they believed in the same ideal—we all started with it." Chavez would leave—but not until he could ensure an orderly transition, so that the union would survive. He would not continue to risk his life for an organization run by people who did not share his ideals.[25]

Chavez had often spoken bitterly about his experience with the Community Service Organization; members had adopted a middle-class agenda and stopped helping the poor, forcing him to leave. "He has told me several times that he is in exact spot he was in with CSO," Chris wrote in a confidential note to Jerry, instructing Jerry to tear up the note after he read it. "I don't want to talk with Marshall about this, right now, because it may feed into his convenient thoughts about Cesar as the possible betrayer of 'all we have worked for these many years.' I think Cesar honestly believes a good transition can be made, sometime in the next few years."[26]

Chavez's deliberations were fueling Chris's own identity crisis. The minister was forty-five, torn between home and work, uncertain if he should quit, but unable to leave. Chavez wanted Chris in La Paz. Pudge was unwilling to move from Los Angeles until their youngest was out of high school, in three years. Chris drafted letters he never sent, two to Chavez explaining why he could not move, one to Pudge wondering if he should do something else. "I am definitely going through some kind of identity crisis: am I Chris Hartmire, the old timer and UFW leader or am I Chris Hartmire, the church person, the supporter who organizes all the other supporters? I am most comfortable in the second role; unfortunately the union doesn't need supporters in the same way it used to. Sometimes I think I should just get out of it altogether and do something entirely different. But it would be a devastating time for someone like me to leave. Somehow the union has to make this transition from la causa to a bread-and-butter union."

John Moyer was a friend to Chris and one of the national ministry's most significant supporters. As secretary for special programs in the Board of Homeland Ministries, which chartered the Migrant Ministry, Moyer had gone to Delano in 1965 when the strike started. He had been at every important event since. Social causes were his passion, and helping farmworkers had become his primary mission. Blunt, with no tolerance for bombast or bureaucratic hierarchies, Moyer always sat in the back of the room at meetings so he could slip out. He was courageous in his stands and down to earth, a poor politician but a determined leader. And like Chris, John Moyer was an eloquent writer and insightful thinker. In 1978 they exchanged a series of letters that identified the profound issues hanging over the union and the minister, and the decisions that would shape the fates of both in the coming years.

Moyer: "When does a person (Chris) stand over-against a friend (Cesar)? What happens to the relationship when you do this? To what degree is your identity and integrity and *uniqueness* as a person submerged in your relationship to Cesar? Does loyalty mean the immersion of the life of one person in the life of another?"[27]

Chris: "You are right on in terms of an emerging identity crisis (mine)."[28]

Moyer: "The Philippines trip has raised the larger issue of *what constitutes ministry* to the union. What has happened on this particular issue is *symptomatic* of what I see to be a growing sign of unhealth: *namely the identification of loyalty with acquiescence.* There seems to be the growing assumption within the union that those who do not agree with Cesar on *every point* are, ipso facto, disloyal to him and to the union. If, in fact, this is a general assumption and a working one, the union is in *real* trouble."[29]

Chris: "Cesar is involved in a *major* internal struggle to pull the union out of the past and into the future. Coupled with that is the battle to avoid paying salaries by building community and keeping the spirit of service and sacrifice alive in the movement."[30]

Moyer went to see what was happening for himself. He spent a few days at La Paz and talked to a dozen people. He watched the Game. He spoke at length with Chavez. The observations all reinforced Moyer's concern. He found La Paz oppressive and stifling, the Game destructive, and good people demoralized. Chavez was micromanaging and growing more isolated. Moyer relayed his concerns to Chris:

> I sense that Cesar is having a real struggle with his leadership role. Like many other founders of movements, organizations, revolutions he is having trouble letting his child grow up. He speaks eloquently of enabling people to grow and make their own mistakes, and then he fails to do what he speaks of. He gives people responsibility, then does not give them the freedom to do their job, even becomes paranoid when he does not know everything that is going on. And, of course, the paranoia grows as the union grows because there is more and more that he *cannot* know. Delegating responsibility is the hardest task for any leader: to let go, to hold people accountable, but to *let go.*

Moyer considered the movement the most important thing that had happened in the country in a long time. He cared deeply that Chavez find his way and the union get back on course. A failure would hold ramifications not just for farmworkers but for social advocates and for the church. "My worry is what I perceive to be a widening gap between Cesar's idealism and his actual performance," Moyer concluded in his letter to Chris. "I think you can help him reverse that trend. I don't know anyone else who can."[31]

The cumulative stress became too much. The Huelga School, the purges, the Philippines, Chavez's pressure on Chris to be in La Paz, all took an emotional and physical toll. One of Chris's children became seriously ill. Chris himself was having digestive pains, which he ignored. Toward the end of the summer he was in La Paz and felt sick. He had a bloody stool. He looked pale and shaky but thought nothing of driving himself two hours back to Los Angeles to see his doctor. The doctor admitted him to the hospital immediately. Chris regurgitated blood and fainted in the wheelchair. He was in intensive care for several days, recovering from a bleeding ulcer.

Eliseo

After the adrenaline rush of the citrus strikes wore off, Eliseo tried to muster the spirit to begin his new job. He sketched out an organizing strategy for Fresno, Salinas, and Santa Maria, arranged a trip to Florida, and began to research Texas and Washington state.

He put together a plan and called his small staff to a conference. He explained his first rule of organizing, so important that he capitalized the sentence in the handout: WORKERS MUST DO THE WORK THEMSELVES. An organizer's role, Eliseo explained, is to coordinate action, strategize, plan, analyze and evaluate. "The organizer should work as a staff person to the workers at the ranch particularly the comité central. The organizer should plan time well so that he can plan and teach workers," he wrote. His experience in the citrus campaigns had only reinforced his determination to train ranch committees and involve them in running the union. "We have to change our ways; it is possible for workers to do anything if we are willing to take risks and let them.[32]

Eliseo gave Chavez a proposal for a campaign to tackle ranches in Salinas and Santa Maria, where the union had never made inroads against the Teamsters. Eliseo presented a detailed ranch-by-ranch analysis that explained the crop, the workforce composition, and timing and assessed their chances of winning elections. He included an itemized budget that

called for adding fifteen organizers to the department, which was bud-
geted for twenty-six people. The cost for the extra volunteers would be
$340 per person, or $5,100 each month during the ten-week campaign.[33]

At a lunch meeting in the communal dining room at La Paz, Chavez
unexpectedly attacked Eliseo. The ostensible justification was the organizing proposal. Chavez berated Eliseo for requesting additional staff and
making unreasonable demands. For Chavez to go after people like that in
public was not unusual. But he had never jumped Eliseo. Most of the executive board listened in stunned silence. Eliseo left the room and walked
outside. The attack only confirmed all the thoughts he had been pushing
away for months—his conviction that the union was moving in the
wrong direction and there was no place for the work he wanted to do.

On June 28, three days after the vote on the lawyers and subsistence
pay, Eliseo met privately with Chavez. Then he went home to Fresno and
told Dorothy they were leaving the union. He typed a letter requesting a
leave of absence. Chavez was not interested in building a union for farmworkers in a way that made sense to Eliseo. He had been struggling for
months to reconcile everything, to convince himself that somehow it all
made sense, that Chavez had a grand plan. The decision to get rid of the
legal department. The Game. The preoccupation with traitors. The lack of
focus on organizing. The inability to keep a stable staff. The crusades. The
reluctance to train ranch committees. Now he could no longer hold it all
together, just do his work and ignore the rest. He did not tell Dorothy any
of those things. He simply said it was time to do something else.

The pattern was clear. To question was to challenge; dissent was tantamount to disloyalty. That left Eliseo no option but to leave. He could no
longer stay and go along quietly with the program. He would never be
disloyal to the institution and the man who had shaped his life. Eliseo was
an optimist, like any good organizer who must believe that the impossible
can be done. But he was also a realist. To stay and try to fight Chavez was
not an option. He could not conceive of winning, even if he could have
brought himself to take the leader on. Besides, there lingered a scintilla of
doubt. Maybe he was wrong. Maybe Chavez did know best. It is so hard to
believe that heroes have feet of clay.

Eliseo went on leave, with the understanding that he would soon resign. Chavez made no effort to persuade him to stay. Chavez had asked
Eliseo to represent the union in July at a conference of agricultural organizations in Costa Rica. Eliseo offered to withdraw, but Chavez told him to
go anyway. As his last official act as second vice president of the United

Farm Workers, Eliseo took a bus from Fresno to Los Angeles and flew to Costa Rica on July 8.

He had never been to Costa Rica. He bought souvenir T-shirts for his son and noticed how much of the music came from Mexico, as he wandered around the capital city of San Jose the day before the meeting began. A taxi took him up into the mountains to the retreat where the conference was held. As an opening exercise, the delegates were instructed to write a short answer to the question, "*yo quien soy?*" Who am I. They pinned the answers to their shirts and walked around the room, getting to know one another as they read the responses. Eliseo didn't know what he was going to do when he returned to California. He didn't know where he was going to work or live. He had no savings. He did not own a car. He was walking away from the only job he had known since he stopped working in the fields at the age of nineteen.

Soy un trabajador tratando de crear una mejor vida para su familia, read the sign on Eliseo's shirt. I am a worker trying to make a better life for his family.[34]

PART VI

Up from the Fields

July 1978–January 1989

CHAPTER 22

Quiet Before the Storm

August 1978

Mario

Mario Bustamante always remembered the Salinas summer night in 1970 when he first heard the farmworker clap. A quiet, rhythmic sound, starting slow. Then faster and louder, faster and louder, faster and louder, until the Evangelical church on Market Street filled with a powerful roar. Mario was twenty-one, and the image stayed with him long after the sound had faded.

Mario had worked in the California fields for one third of his young life, ever since he left his Mexico City home and crossed the border to find his father. Salvador Bustamante was cutting lettuce, and his son soon ended up a lechugero too. The job suited Mario's personality. He was physically strong, mentally quick, and fiercely headstrong.

He first joined the union in Calexico in 1969, when the service center opened in a cramped, cricket-infested room in the Hotel El Rey. Dues were $3.50 a month, and the union filled out tax returns for members. Mario was always calculating the odds; three months' dues cost less than paying someone to do his taxes. He viewed the union solely as a business proposition. The next summer, Mario went with his father to hear Cesar Chavez speak at the Salinas church on the eve of the 1970 lettuce strike. A few weeks later he walked out on strike from Merrill Farms. He volunteered for marches and weekend boycott duty. He hung around the union

Mario Bustamante exhorts workers in Salinas during Chavez's thousand-mile march.

office as if it were his club. When Chavez came through the Salinas Valley on his thousand-mile march the summer before elections began, Mario corralled workers to join the morning masses and nightly rallies. When a group along the route badmouthed Chavez, Mario got into a brawl defending the union leader.

Mario first worked under a union contract in crew number seven at Interharvest. The lettuce cutters were grouped by speed—the trios that could finish their fields by one thirty, by three thirty, by five P.M. Crew number seven always was first out of the fields. Mario averaged fifteen dollars an hour and boasted he never worked more than a thirty-hour week. For Mario, the union was still about the fight in the streets, not his day-to-day life on the job—until he went to work for Green Valley Produce. The union had won an easy victory at Green Valley, a Salinas cooperative that harvested lettuce for a dozen growers, and soon signed a contract. Mario joined a new crew that Green Valley added in the spring of 1976. His larger-than-life persona made him well known, and the twenty-seven-year-old lechugero was elected union steward.

Mario didn't know exactly what the job entailed, but he knew what he did not want to do. He had watched the union use the *tortuga* to force Interharvest to meet demands. Mario did not approve of "liberating ranches" by ruining production. The tactic made no economic sense. Mario was a firebrand, but his imposing physical demeanor—at six feet, he towered over most workers, and the physical demands of cutting lettuce gave him an athlete's build—masked the fact that he was always thinking. The union had yet to write ranch committee bylaws, so Mario learned on his own. He read the contract. He explained the medical plan to workers. He learned grievance procedures. He watched Jerry negotiate, feet up on the desk with that "fuck you" swagger that radiated power. Before the union, if a foreman didn't respond to complaints, workers had no recourse. The contract gave the workers power, and Mario was eager to use it to address injustices. He also preached responsibility. The company pays us to pack twenty-four good heads of lettuce in a box, he told his crew. If we pack twenty good and four bad, it's like a mechanic who services your car and puts on one bad tire. One of the most potent arguments growers used against the union was that companies would go out of business. Mario told his crew they had to prove that wrong. The eagle must be a symbol of quality.

In 1977, Mario attended his first union convention. In 1978, the Green Valley workers elected him president of the ranch committee. The union had become more than a social club for Mario. As a child in Mexico City, he had attended school in the evening, the second shift for the kids who had to work. He had arrived at school so tired he often fell asleep. He dropped out after fifth grade. As an adult, he was frustrated and occasionally angry that his lack of education so curtailed his choices. He loved to talk, but spoke only Spanish, recoiling at the sense that people who heard his broken English thought he was stupid. By the time he became ranch committee president, Mario saw the union as a way to change his life. Before, the only options were to be a worker or a foreman; the exploited or the exploiter. The union offered a third way.

Mario's younger brother was becoming a leader in the fields too. Chava had finished high school in Mexico City in 1967 and gone to visit his brother in Calexico for a two-week vacation. He saw Mario driving a 1959 Cadillac Seville, and Chava decided to stay. Though he emulated his older brother in many ways, Chava Bustamante was not a classic lechugero. He could not keep up with Mario, a head taller and stronger by far. Usually Chava worked as the box closer, the least physically demanding job in the trio, stapling the cartons shut. More than once Chava sat down in frustration on a lettuce box in the middle of the field, protesting his brother's relentless pace. The long days that began before dawn with only headlights from trucks to illuminate the fields left Chava bent in pain. The first time he thinned tiny seedlings with the short-handled hoe, his hands were clenched for days, and he could not stand upright. Eventually, he learned to make the pain bearable the way many did—by using amphetamines. Drugs and alcohol were common, often supplied by the boss. Where Mario loved working in the fields and relished the physical labor as well as the fellowship, Chava enjoyed reading and writing poetry. For Chava, the union was a way to achieve dignity as well as control over his own body.

Mario and Chava's father was an ardent unionist, well known to the UFW staff. When elections began in 1975, the Salinas field office director needed help. He tapped Salvador Bustamante's younger son. Chava became the lead organizer working in the fields at California Coastal, a large lettuce and vegetable grower. After the union won the election, Chava was chosen ranch committee president at Cal Coastal and led negotiations on the first contract. One of Chava's key demands was an eight-hour day. When the company rejected the proposal, he organized a petition drive. When the company dismissed the petitions, Chava organized a work stoppage. After the second break at three P.M. in the Soledad fields, three crews refused to go back to work. The company president threatened to fire Chava if he ever did that again. But the workers got their eight-hour day.[1]

Later, Chava watched Jerry negotiate. Chava loved listening to the lawyer spar with growers at the bargaining table. The sharp attorney thought so fast on his feet, avenging all the wrongs that had been done to the workers in the fields. Shoes untied, hair uncombed, Jerry winked at the workers as he played with the men across the table, teaching the workers by his body language, as well as his words, not to be afraid. Chava dedicated a poem to Jerry, "La Poder vs. La Astucia"—The Power vs. the Astuteness. The last verse read:

> Poor fools! Those who think
> That power comes from money.

Without contemplating
That real power
That which is real and lasting
That is the one which is given through justice.

Each fall, when the lettuce harvest finished in Salinas, most of the lechugeros moved south to Calexico for the winter growing season. In the late summer of 1978 the talk was about the contracts that expired in a few months. The union hoped to negotiate a master agreement with the vegetable companies. Chava told his brother they needed help organizing workers at Cal Coastal, a primary target if the union called a strike. So Mario went to work there as well. They both looked forward to seeing Jerry in action again.

Sandy

Sandy also awaited Jerry's next move, to see how he would fight to preserve the legal department. Sandy and the Dazzler could not imagine walking away. Nor could they see Jerry abandoning the cause they had fought for together. So many battles remained. Important cases were on appeal, and most of the contracts were up for renegotiation. Sandy assumed the lawyers' expertise would prove too vital for Chavez to just throw away.

When the executive board rejected the lawyers' salary requests, board members stressed their desire to keep Jerry.[2] Shortly after the board vote, Sandy headed to La Paz in the passenger seat of the blue Dodge Colt that Jerry absent-mindedly drove in fifth gear, regardless of his speed. Sandy was just along for the four-hour ride; he waited while Jerry met with Chavez, then the two lawyers turned around and drove home. Jerry was initially pleased. He had bought a year or more for half the department, enough time to litigate some key cases. Always Eeyore to Jerry's Tigger, Sandy poured cold water all over that. Keeping half the people meant firing the other half. Jerry became sober. He pulled off at a rest stop on Highway 46 to call the legal department in Salinas from a pay phone. He told the staff to assemble in the office, though it was already late at night.

At the meeting that became known as the Night of the Long Knives, Jerry explained that the legal department would be phased out. Chavez wanted volunteer lawyers, living at La Paz. Jerry outlined a transition and said half the staff would have to leave right away. He named names. Sandy thought about quitting, but he would have felt like a deserter. Besides, there was still work to do.

Sandy also knew that despite the feud with the attorneys, Chavez had always appreciated the legal department's devil-may-care attitude. Most of all, he liked that they almost always won. The union had amassed an impressive record. Some of the work was defensive. Sandy had spent weeks handling a tricky arson case that had grown out of the 1973 strike; he kept the workers out of jail even after they were caught more or less red-handed. He had spent a month in Coachella fighting Keene Larson in court when the grower tried to bar the union from picketing. Despite dozens of lawsuits, documented violence, and questionable behavior, the legal department had saved the union from paying a major settlement in any venue. They plastered growers with so many interrogatories that even companies with strong claims backed down rather than turn over sensitive business data.

On the offensive side, the union's record was more significant, since many decisions would affect policy for generations. The victories set labor law precedents in administrative hearings and court cases. Sandy had won California Supreme Court cases that established the principle that growers had to deal with the ALRB rather than do an end-run around the state board by going straight to the court. The union lawyers pioneered novel attacks, like the antitrust suit. They presented cases to the state board that won hundreds of thousands of dollars in back pay for workers unjustly fired. The union had recently won the first "make whole order," directing a recalcitrant company to pay employees the difference between their actual wages and what they would have earned under a contract, back to the time the company stopped bargaining in good faith.

Sandy foresaw an urgent need for strong, creative legal work to cement the union's progress. Growers and labor contractors were finding loopholes or strategies to circumvent the law. Workers had filed the first petitions to decertify the union at several ranches. Companies where the union had won elections claimed to go out of business—only to reincorporate under a different name and claim the union had no right to represent the workers. In Oxnard, citrus ranches were pulling out of the giant harvesting co-op that Eliseo had organized. The manager was desperate; labor contractors lured away his business with promises of cheaper costs and no union interference.

Sandy assumed that Chavez, a pragmatist and master negotiator, would reach some accommodation with Jerry. The idea of a smaller legal department came as no surprise. For months, the message from La Paz had been to settle litigation, drop cases that would not lead to new contracts, and handle as little ALRB work as possible. Where the union once automatically challenged elections they lost, they now filed a challenge only if victory seemed assured.

Jerry had another motivation to shrink the department. The emotional fissures precipitated by the Game had not healed. Sandy figured Jerry might use the salary requests he had solicited as a way to negotiate for a smaller, stable, better-paid department. Sandy made schedules and helped parcel out the work of the lawyers who left. Jerry walked around singing "Did You Ever Have to Make Up Your Mind," one of the Lovin' Spoonful's greatest hits.

"Jerry responds to the pain and problems of the union with a bitter, almost hysterical laugh," Kirsten Zerger wrote in her diary. "Sandy responds by crawling inside and pondering the pain he feels for the union and himself."[3]

Summer turned to fall as Sandy waited for Jerry to act and struggled to make sense of his actions. One day Jerry urged his staff to negotiate with Chavez; the next day he told them to find new jobs. He refused to divulge his own plans and played one lawyer against another. Still, Sandy thought Jerry would keep fighting for a cause he believed in. That was what Jerry admired and emulated in Chavez, and what Jerry had taught his staff. He modeled the behavior that Sandy embraced, the behavior that freed him from the constraints of acting like a lawyer. Sandy refused to believe this would be the end of the legal department. He was baffled by Jerry's apparent refusal to do what he always did—find a way to change the outcome. But Sandy figured Jerry must have a plan. He just wasn't sharing it.

By November no plan had emerged, but plenty of blame had been thrown around. Former friends were not on speaking terms. Eight lawyers were gone, two more had given notice, and the six who were left felt overwhelmed by uncertainty and anger. They wrote to Jerry and Chavez, asking for clarification and presenting an ultimatum: Tell us our future by December 1 or we'll leave by March 1. The act of solidarity caught Jerry by surprise, and he belittled their negotiating technique. Sandy viewed the letter more as a farewell than a bargaining tactic.

The lawyers closed on an elegiac note: "We are bound because of a shared and rich past with the Union. We are nearly the last remnants of an effective Legal Department and are bound, ultimately, together and to the Union, by a mutual wish to maintain the exuberance, joy, and quiet satisfaction of contributing to this historic fight for human dignity, economic democracy, and political power."

Sandy provided the final line. He didn't need to look at the piece of paper he carried in his wallet with the Dostoyevsky quote. He knew the passage from the *The Brothers Karamazov* by heart: ". . . still let us remember how good it was once here, when we were all together, united by a good and kind feeling which made us . . . better perhaps than we are."[4]

Sabino

Sabino was starting to realize how much he didn't know. Workers were carefully shielded from internal machinations at La Paz. They did not know about the fight over the legal department. Chavez specified that workers not be told about the Game. But Sabino began to have more questions. People left without explanation. Eliseo, the charismatic Mexican leader whom Sabino had admired from a distance, had abruptly disappeared. There had been talk in the fields that the young farmworker was the future of the union. Sabino was disappointed that Eliseo had abandoned them without a word. Questions about departures elicited only gossip, and the gossip was always the same: They left because they wanted to make money, or they took money, or their wives wanted money. The official news of Eliseo's resignation reached Salinas in late summer, accompanied by official spin. "Story already is that he wasn't a good negotiator or organizer and all he wanted was money," Kirsten Zerger wrote in her diary. "How far from the truth. How sad we are at this state of revising history so soon. I wonder if people will buy it really."[5]

Sabino would not have begrudged money to the union staff members. He had always been appreciative of, but somewhat puzzled by, the volunteers who embraced poverty as a way of life. The workers themselves rejected that lifestyle—as Chavez noted with frustration. During the 1976 negotiations on the Interharvest contract, Sabino and his co-workers politely declined the skimpy vegetarian food that Chavez favored. They would rather buy their own food than eat subsistence fare. They were working hard in order to live well.

The internal strife was about to affect the vegetable workers directly. Contracts covering thousands of workers at thirty companies in the Salinas and Imperial Valleys expired at the end of 1978. Two thirds of the companies primarily grew or harvested lettuce.[6] The union was late getting ready for negotiations and woefully unprepared. Chavez stalled on decisions about his team. Jerry would have been a logical choice, until the collapse of the legal department. Eliseo was gone. Marshall Ganz had worked most closely with the vegetable workers but was so shaken by the vote on the volunteer system that he considered leaving the union. Ganz went to work on Governor Jerry Brown's re-election campaign. Jessica Govea went with him.

So the old team was largely absent on the last Saturday in August when Sabino traveled to La Paz, one of 140 leaders from the vegetable companies invited to a summit to prepare for negotiations. Chavez hosted the ranch committee members from twenty-seven vegetable companies. He gave tours of the union headquarters. They sang "Solidaridad Pa' Siempre" and "No Nos Moveran." A priest recited the Farm Worker Prayer.

Clearly and frankly, Chavez laid out problems with hiring halls, seniority lists, pesticides, and the union's medical plan. The innovative insurance plan was designed for workers who moved from ranch to ranch, so they would be covered no matter where they worked. The reality proved very difficult for the understaffed union to manage. Chavez promised improvements. "It's a tremendous problem," he said in Spanish. ". . . *brumoso, latoso, complicado y tardoso* [*sic*]" (foggy, annoying, complicated, and late). He explained the unique difficulties he faced administering not just the medical plan but the entire organization: Where other unions had ten thousand members all working permanently at one or two plants, he had ten thousand members spread among dozens of ranches, moving back and forth between jobs, working one month and off the next. He explained the solution: a full-time union representative at each ranch, paid by the company, similar to provisions in autoworkers' contracts. "If we don't get this, it's impossible to administer the contracts," he said.

He also warned about a more intangible threat. The union's success had made it a target, he said, for Marxist youth longing to undermine the organization. The workers must stay vigilant and root out infiltrators. "Where there is honey," Chavez said, "there are flies."[7]

Chavez split the meeting into five groups to develop specific contract proposals and report back to the whole conference. Sabino was in the Yellow Group. They produced a detailed list of demands: Grievance meetings conducted bilingually, so workers could understand them. Seniority clauses written in clear language instead of legalese. Strict language on pesticides, because supervisors gave no warnings or lied about how soon workers could safely return to the fields.[8]

At the end of the day Chavez proposed the union negotiate with all the

The newly elected negotiating committee for the vegetable industry, including Chava Bustamante (standing, third from left) and Sabino (back row, third from right), with Chavez and executive board members Gilbert Padilla (back row, middle) and Richard Chavez (back row, second from right).

vegetable growers together. Mario moved that the group adopt the idea of an industrywide committee: "We have to negotiate with this structure, because we do not have force if we do it one by one." The motion passed unanimously. The workers proceeded to elect ten members to the negotiating committee. Chava received the second-highest vote total. Sabino was right behind in third place. Both viewed their new post as another big step, a chance to influence life for workers not only at their own ranches but across the industry. "We leave this conference united, in solidarity and brotherhood," Chavez said, "dedicated to our mission, determined to achieve new objectives in the long road to make a better life."[9]

No workers were privy to the executive board deliberations just two weeks later, when Chavez struck a very different tone. He had sent his senior people to Salinas to prepare for negotiations, and they returned with grim reports. They found four-year-old checks worth hundreds of dollars in insurance payments to workers—in unopened envelopes gathering dust. Complaints about the medical plan were rampant. Grievances went unresolved. Employers were ready to capitalize on the workers' dissatisfaction by encouraging decertification votes.

Chavez reacted with anger. He sought scapegoats and returned to his theme of infiltration. He blamed the "RUs"—Revolutionary Union communists—and their allies, assholes who were deliberately screwing up the medical plan. The others told him just as angrily that the problems stemmed from the union's incompetence, not sabotage. Chavez turned on them. They failed to see the danger, didn't root out problems, and forced him to do the dirty work. They hurt the union by arguing with him and countermanding orders. "You've got to follow a leader," Chavez said. ". . . Leaders either fall or stand on what they do. They do something good or something bad, and you give them a chance. But while they're leaders, you follow. Not that you don't talk back, but there's a way of doing it. You support. Even if you criticize, you do it but you support the way it's being done. You begin to argue, it's destructive."

Finally the board agreed to stopgap measures. They dispatched a team to Salinas to meet with workers and stall until Chavez figured out his negotiating team. Chavez dubbed it *Plan A Flote*. The goal was simply to stay afloat.[10]

September and October passed with no union proposals and no chief negotiator in place. When Ganz returned from the Brown campaign after Election Day, he and Chavez had an acrimonious meeting. Ganz finally agreed to research the economics of the vegetable industry to help the union formulate demands.

The results were startling. Wages had fallen far behind during the double-digit inflation of the late 1970s. Corporate profits had soared: Salinas lettuce growers cleared $71 million in 1978—an increase of 975 percent in eight years. Wages for farmworkers during the same period went up only 85 percent, to $3.70 an hour. Farmworkers had received smaller increases than the companies' other employees. The biggest jump in farmworker wages had taken place before the contracts were signed—growers handed out raises just prior to elections in the hope of convincing workers to reject the union.[11]

Sabino traveled with the negotiating committee to visit workers at each company. With charts and graphs, Ganz laid out the case to workers for demanding significant increases. The bottom line was clear: The bosses were getting richer, the workers were losing ground. When Sabino addressed a group of workers in Salinas on January 17, some members hesitated about voting to authorize a strike. The union's strength during the winter was in the Imperial Valley, Sabino explained, but they would need support in Salinas too. He briefed workers on negotiations. The executive board had voted three days earlier to authorize a strike fund. "We have to be strong, united," Sabino told the crowd. Then he asked them what they thought. *"Sí se puede!"* the members shouted. The strike vote was unanimous.[12]

CHAPTER 23

The Dream Strike

January 1979

Mario

Winter lettuce in the Imperial Valley matured after about sixty days. Three or four more days, and the leaves began to bolt. By the end of January heads of worthless lettuce littered hundreds of acres in the Imperial Valley. Mario surveyed the damage, as he checked on picket lines and scabs in the fields where he had once picked lettuce. He was working as an organizer instead of a lechugero, and he loved it.

Mario had gone to work at Cal Coastal before the season began in the Imperial Valley. While his brother went from ranch to ranch with the negotiating committee and explained the economic imperative for the strike, Mario prepared workers for the day-to-day reality. Life will be tough on the picket lines, and scabs will not be tolerated, he warned. Anyone weak should leave now. By December, when the season started in Calexico, the Cal Coastal workers were primed.

The union finally presented its economic proposal to the vegetable growers a few days after the contracts had expired. Demands included an increase in the minimum wage from $3.75 to $5.25, a significant boost in employer contributions to the health and pension funds, a cost-of-living adjustment, and union representatives paid by the company. The growers rejected the proposal as absurd—their anger compounded when the union published its opening gambit in a Mexicali newspaper. The growers cited

President Carter's wage guidelines, designed to help the economy rebound from the long recession. The union retorted that the guidelines applied only to those earning more than four dollars an hour. Growers pointed out that lechugeros worked piece rate and earned far more. Only a few months of a year, the union responded. Growers counteroffered a 7 percent raise, in accordance with the Carter administration guidelines.

When a strike seemed inevitable, the negotiating committee gathered at La Paz with union leaders. Ganz presented a company-by-company analysis of the union's strength in a marathon meeting that lasted until dawn, figures scrawled on giant sheets of butcher paper taped up around the room. When he ranked companies according to how strongly the workers would support a strike, Cal Coastal topped the list. Each company elected a strike coordinator to lead the fight. The Cal Coastal workers chose Mario.

On the morning of January 19 the strike began at Cal Coastal. Almost all the 350 workers stayed out of the fields. The next day Vessey went out. Then Mario Saikhon. On the fourth day workers at Sun Harvest—the giant company formerly called Interharvest—joined the strike. More than two thousand workers at the four companies marched on picket lines instead of working in the fields.

Mario began each day driving house to house in Mexicali at three thirty A.M. to round up strikers and direct them where to report for picket duty. At eight A.M. the strike coordinators met with Ganz in the Calexico strike office. They counted strikers on picket lines and scabs in the fields and identified fields ready for picking—and picketing. Most days they targeted one company where workers were not on strike and pulled them out to disrupt production. Mario kept track of the Cal Coastal strikers— who had taken a job elsewhere, who was helping with the strike. The first goal was to keep workers out of the fields. The second was to persuade them to picket. Mario kept his strikers busy to distract them from the temptation to return to work. He organized card games and soccer games and found money to keep his strikers well fed.

The growers tried to salvage the crop by employing their families, students, winos, and anyone else they could find, an assemblage the strikers derisively called "the circus." Harvesting lettuce required skill and physical stamina. It was not a job for novices. What lettuce the circus managed to cut was badly done, the unappealing look likely to lower the price.

By the time Chavez came to Calexico two weeks into the strike, about three thousand workers had essentially shut down eight companies that normally supplied one third of the nation's winter lettuce. Chavez called

Mario talks to workers at El Hoyo during the strike.

the strike "a dream that at one time we thought impossible." The big drop in supply had driven up the price, and growers still in business were reaping large returns. But ranches idled by the strike were losing hundreds of thousands of dollars a day.[1]

"It is our sweat, our backs, our muscle that have made the farmers of the Imperial Valley the rich men they are today," Mario told a reporter two days after Chavez's visit. "For years they have been using and wasting our people's lives in the fields. All we want is a little security and the hope that our children won't have to work so much for so little pay."[2]

The union made noises about a boycott of Chiquita bananas, a lucrative and easily identifiable product of United Brands, owner of Sun Harvest. On Saturday, February 10, Chavez and the negotiating committee sat down for the first time with Sun Harvest. They had just begun to talk in the basement of a Los Angeles church when word came that a striker had been shot. Rufino Contreras, twenty-eight, had been among a group of strikers who tried to chase scabs out of a Mario Saikhon field. The trespassing technique was not officially sanctioned but widely used. A foreman and two other Saikhon employees opened fire. One bullet hit Contreras in the head. He collapsed face down in the lettuce field. His brother and father watched him die.

Thousands mourned for several days. Chavez held a mass on Saturday night in El Hoyo (The Hole), the large parking lot alongside the border where labor contractors picked up workers who crossed from Mexicali each morning. On Sunday night a candlelight march shut down the border crossing. On Valentine's Day Chavez led another mass in El Hoyo. Then more than seven thousand mourners walked in a funeral procession that stretched for miles along the rural roads of Calexico.

The strikers shut down the border again two weeks later. This time they stopped cars with workers trying to cross from Mexico and forced them back. The one-day work stoppage, designed to frighten away scabs, turned into a riot. Like the Pied Piper, Mario drove in a pickup with a loudspeaker on top, leading caravans to the fields. Strikers broke irrigation gates and flooded fields. They slashed tires and overturned tractors. More than one thousand strikers rushed into the Maggio fields and threw rocks, chunks of cement, and metal stakes, first at workers and then at police. Helicopters buzzed the fields during a two-hour confrontation. Police called Arizona and San Diego for backup when they ran out of tear gas.[3] Mario had been a ringleader, careful to not be a perpetrator, but he thought it prudent to leave town. Mario made his way to Salinas, to begin strike preparations up north.

Ganz had become protective of Mario. Before the strike the only Bustamante that Ganz knew well had been Mario's father. Salvador Bustamante had been the first farmworker Ganz met in the Salinas valley, and the older worker had guided the rabbi's son around the lettuce fields. When Salvador Bustamante died in 1977, Ganz attended the funeral, the coffin draped in a red and white flag emblazoned with the black eagle. Ganz liked good students, and he had not thought of the impulsive Mario in that role. Mario was a Chavista, faithful verging on fanatical, willing and able to punch someone out on a picket line for criticizing the leader. But as the strike progressed, Ganz saw Mario as a curious student with an innate grasp of power and leadership. Ganz was impressed with Mario's courage, but also with the shrewd mind behind the bravado.

The more Mario worked with Ganz, the more the lechugero liked the organizer's style. Ganz was neither afraid of the workers nor overly deferential, like many union volunteers. He demanded a lot, but he respected results. Mario also valued results, but the tools available to him had always been limited. Relying on street smarts, he tended to resolve problems by taking matters into his own hands. The idea of learning a more sophisticated approach intrigued Mario. One of his early, vivid memories of the union was the 1970 strike headquarters where Fred Ross had posted giant maps of each ranch, detailing the boundaries, the crops, and the crews. Now Mario had an opportunity to study firsthand that school of organizing.

Gretchen

Gretchen found herself fascinated by the same lessons. She had been sent to Calexico to help manage strike benefits, another posting for the Catholic schoolgirl who saw herself as a loyal servant to the movement. The office job turned into her first immersion in the world of Mexican farmworkers, the people behind the cause.

Gretchen had entered the union like so many others, an uninformed, enthusiastic, but naïve boycotter. She had gained greater sophistication about organizing as boycott director in Los Angeles and through political campaigns, but she knew little of the fields. Almost none of the union staff were farmworkers, so Gretchen had minimal contact with the people she was trying to help. Her assignments had shifted as frequently as the union's priorities; perpetually short-staffed, Chavez moved resources wherever he needed them most. He had assigned Gretchen briefly to the organizing department, despite her lack of Spanish. (It's like boxing with one hand, he told her; if you're good enough, you can win anyway.) Then she helped out on Governor Jerry Brown's re-election campaign. Then to La Paz for two months, to help computerize the troubled medical plan and study insurance alternatives in preparation for the vegetable negotiations. When the strike started, Gretchen was sent south to help.

She spent twelve-hour days inside a second-story room in a concrete bunker at the end of a Calexico cul-de-sac. Gretchen sat just to the right of the entrance, next to Jessica Govea, who became a role model and then a friend. Competent and self-assured, Jessica had been elected to the union's executive board. Now she was in charge of administering strike benefits. She and Gretchen kept lists of strikers, calculated who qualified for unemployment, and dispensed gas money and strikers' pay. Strikers were eligible for $25 to $50 a week—depending on the size of their families—if they presented a form signed by their coordinator certifying they had spent the requisite hours on picket lines. They collected groceries at a warehouse across town, stocked through a food drive that Chris coordinated from Los Angeles. Once a week volunteers loaded a half dozen trucks with beans, rice, flour, lard, cornflakes, soup, canned tomatoes, potatoes, milk, sugar, and oats. During the first three months of the strike, sixty-three trucks delivered 1.15 million tons of food.[4]

Gretchen's job was writing checks. Her passion was taking notes. Every day she crossed the outdoor landing to the large room on the other side of the stairs where Marshall Ganz met with the *concilio* of strike coordinators. Gretchen tried to attend every meeting, sometimes two a day, standing in the back and writing in her journal. She had seen Ganz organize political campaigns, but never workers. She listened as he taught them, with his disciplined approach, to be accountable for the strike. Soon she learned as much from the workers as she did from Ganz. She watched the strike coordinators diligently take their own notes, the drab room becoming the classroom the workers had never had an opportunity to attend. She witnessed the transformation, as they developed confidence in their own ideas and coalesced into a team.

In the relatively few hours she spent outside the office, Gretchen was also falling in love with the dusty border town of Calexico. No weather was too hot for the Oregon native. More important, she was fascinated by the culture and the community. The border defined the Imperial Valley, distinguishing it from other major agricultural regions. Most workers lived with their families in Mexicali rather than in the labor camps and run-down barracks prevalent in the other valleys. Many lechugeros ended up with one family in Mexicali and another in Salinas. Unlike farmworker towns where workers came and went with the seasons, life in the Imperial Valley had a certain permanence. Workers came home to Calexico, even on weekends when they labored more than five hundred miles away in Salinas.

Then Rufino Contreras was shot and killed, and life in the Calexico strike office changed overnight. Gretchen was alone when she heard the news, and then the whirring of helicopters overhead. Mostly she felt shock. Soon Chavez arrived, and everything went into high gear.

The whispering campaign began before the mourning ended: Marshall Ganz had sanctioned "rushing the fields," a potentially dangerous but common trespass. Chavez replaced Ganz with a loyal subordinate, Frank Ortiz, whose style was far less collegial. He clashed with the workers immediately. By mid-March, Chavez's dream strike was in disarray. Strikers stopped showing up on picket lines. Scabs filled the fields. Ortiz had misjudged when work would move north, letting the Imperial Valley strike operation break down weeks before the harvest ended. Jessica and Gretchen couldn't dispense benefits because they didn't know which companies Ortiz had called out on strike. The antagonism was so crippling that Chavez called a special board meeting at La Paz. He urged the board to play the Game: "There's no way of cleaning ourselves up short of playing the Game." The voices were harsh and tight among those who once had bantered easily. Ortiz complained that no one would cooperate: Gretchen stonewalled him, Jessica disappeared, Tom Dalzell did not return calls.

"The son of a bitch won't cooperate," Chavez said about Dalzell. ". . . He figures Frank is on the other side, he was on the other faction."

"Well, what faction am I, Cesar?" Jessica challenged him.

"Well Jessica, I think you're in Marshall's faction," Chavez said, speaking in an affectless tone to the woman he had known since she was seven. "I'm not sure. Let's face it, that's what's happening in this union. That's what's happening."[5]

Gretchen was clearly in Marshall's faction. Shortly after the confrontation among the board members, Chavez dispatched a handful of people to five cities to lay the groundwork for a new boycott against the lettuce growers. He sent Gretchen to Boston, the city where she had stumbled into the union. She hosted meetings for new recruits and told them the story of how her truck broke down and she ended up in the union by accident.[6] She was still fascinated by power, the draw that had kept her in the union long after her three-month commitment. But three and half years later she returned as an organizer, committed to fight for the rights of the farmworkers whose lives she had begun to understand.

Sandy

Sandy went down to Calexico to help after the killing in the fields. He was wrapping things up, still numb about the idea of leaving, trying to disconnect. Chavez had rejected the ultimatum from the lawyers in their impassioned letter that ended with Sandy's favorite quote from Dostoyevsky. Sandy and Jerry were on shaky terms, the kind of baffled fallout that can happen only among close friends.

In Calexico, Sandy and the Dazzler collected statements while the union lobbied for criminal charges. Jerry had sent Sandy to represent the union, but Chavez dispatched his own lawyer from La Paz who blocked Sandy from talking to the sheriff. That tension typified the confusion and mixed messages Sandy had encountered for months.

Helpless and angry, he watched things fall apart like in a slow motion

Jerry and Sandy in the office they shared until the final, tense months of the legal department. Sandy and Kirsten Zerger took a roll of pictures during one of the last staff meetings in Salinas. (Kirsten Zerger)

movie. After all those years of battling recalcitrant state officials, the current members and the general counsel of the ALRB were as favorable as possible to the union. But the union was too paralyzed to take advantage. In Oxnard the huge gains among citrus workers evaporated as growers pulled out of the harvesting association and went to labor contractors. Sandy convened a meeting to help the new legal staff and field office directors figure out strategies, but the union lacked the organizing strength to fight.

Sandy had become accustomed to Jerry's preference for indirect communication. Now Jerry tried in his oblique way to transmit the message that the legal department was history. He typed notes on small slips of white paper and mailed them in unsigned envelopes. Each lawyer received a quote from Jerry's favorite movie, *McCabe and Mrs. Miller*, which ends with the charming hero bleeding to death in the snow. A paid assassin hunts down McCabe after he turns down a mining company's offer to buy his whorehouse. Sandy's note was a line the hitman uses after McCabe blows his one chance to make a deal: "You weren't far apart, were you?"

Sandy decided he would take a long trip to Israel after he left the union, something he had wanted to do since growing up as one of the only Jews in a small town in western Pennsylvania. Then he would look for work. Kirsten Zerger had been applying for jobs, but Jerry was making her search difficult. Kirsten was only twenty-eight, one of the smartest, toughest lawyers in the department, more comfortable than most taking Jerry on. When they had played the Game and the women indicted Jerry for sexism, Kirsten had led the charge, sitting on his lap to make her point. But in the last fragile days of the legal department, Jerry gained the upper hand. He threw roadblocks in the way of her job search and told Kirsten she couldn't have time off for interviews. Finally, he reduced her to tears. Sandy's bafflement turned to anger. He had had it. Jerry made no effort to salvage the department, played one lawyer against another, and criticized their negotiating tactics—and now he was angry that they were leaving. Sandy stormed down the hall to have it out.

The second-floor offices in the ornate Glickbarg building had doors with glass windows in the middle and transoms overhead. Jerry and Sandy had shared an office until recently, and the door was almost always unlocked. Sandy grabbed the doorknob with his left hand and banged on the glass pane with his right to push open the door. The door was locked. In his fury, Sandy just pushed harder. He punched through the glass. Jerry was on the phone, and Sandy stood in the doorway, blood dripping on the floor, the two lawyers screaming at each other. Well, you don't have to kill yourself over this, Jerry said, as someone found towels for a tourniquet. Kirsten drove Sandy to the hospital, where they sewed up the partially severed tendon in his wrist with twenty-five stitches.

Two days later the union president came to see Sandy. Chavez asked Sandy to stay. The union needed him. Chavez talked politely and persuasively, in that way he had that made people want to do things for him. Chavez explained his vision of a volunteer legal department, how important that was, and how badly he needed Sandy during the transition. Chavez said he had always known the lawyers were good, but he hadn't realized how good until people pleaded with him to make them stay. Even the governor. Chavez apologized for not having paid more attention to their work or shown more appreciation. Sandy gestured toward the sling on his arm, and Chavez quickly assured Sandy he didn't need to explain. But Sandy wanted Chavez to understand that the fight with Jerry had been the culmination of months of misery, and it was time to go.

Sandy typed up an account of the meeting that night, while it was still fresh. Chavez "didn't need to come and lay himself open to me, and I wasn't going to extract anything from him," Sandy wrote.

I know it must have been hard for him, it must have been somewhat humiliating for him. I felt bad enough as it was. I felt this
pervasive sense of sadness in there with him, that it was too late,
where has he been, why didn't he come sooner . . . At one point I
got this feeling of a person being offered something and you
know you really can't accept it, you can't even talk about it in
good faith anymore. So I tried to tell Cesar about how terrible it
was in the office, and that I really needed a rest.[7]

A few weeks later, the turmoil in the legal department became public. In
late June 1979 the union submitted a new list of attorneys who would be
appearing before the state agricultural labor board. Jerry was not on the
list. Newspapers bannered headlines. The union downplayed the moves.
Jerry said he was staying with the union in a different role and denied reports of philosophical disputes. The union's legal expenses underscored
that the fight had been about control, not money. In the year since Chavez
had begun to dismantle the Salinas legal department, the number of union
attorneys had dropped from sixteen to eight. The exodus forced Chavez to
rely on outside lawyers, who charged retainers and billed by the hour. The
union had spent 50 percent more on legal personnel.[8]

Sandy packed up and scrubbed the house at 125 Key Street that he
shared with Kirsten and another lawyer. He was determined to collect his
full rental deposit from the Salinas Bean Company Retirement Plan.
When the Bean Company representatives came to inspect the house,
Sandy worried about a slight residue of mold. But the only thing that
interested the landlord's agents was the big story in the local paper—the
breakup of the UFW legal department.

Just as the strike around him reached its peak, Sandy left Salinas. He
packed up his Datsun and drove east to visit his future in-laws, a prominent
Mennonite family in Kansas. The Fourth of July was approaching. Sandy
did not feel much like celebrating. He had been grieving for a long time,
and it was past time to leave, though it still felt strange, almost scary. Ten
years ago he had headed west, driving until he could go no farther. West was
where you went to seek adventure, to explore new frontiers. West was where
he had discovered a way to be a lawyer that made him proud. He had found
friends and a role in the civil rights struggle of the West. Now he headed
east, unsure what lay ahead, neither captive nor liberated, mostly just
melancholy about what might have been.

CHAPTER 24

Victory in Salinas

June 1979

Sabino

When the lettuce season began in Salinas and the strike barreled into the lush green fields, Sabino went to work each morning—organizing picket lines. The strike became his job.

The union rented out a labor camp and transformed the barracks into strike headquarters for Sun Harvest. Hundreds of workers reported for picket line assignments in the morning, picked up food rations in the afternoon, and organized carpools to Calexico on weekends to collect their unemployment checks. Sabino's assignment was to organize the fifty *huelgistas* manning picket lines at a Chualar field, south of Salinas. He worked as carefully at his new job as he had when he regulated the flow of water in the fields.

The commitment of the Sun Harvest workers had become more apparent as the strike wore on. Imperial and Salinas, the two primary areas for lettuce, bookended the growing season. In between, lechugeros normally hopscotched to Arizona and the San Joaquin Valley. Sun Harvest assumed that striking workers would not relocate to fields where they would not work. But without pickets the strike would fizzle. So when the season began in Arizona, the union rented buses. Each morning strikers left Calexico before dawn for the hourlong ride to picket the Yuma fields. A few weeks later the union rented a school in Fresno and prepared for the same routine. The first day of work pickets outnumbered the thirty Sun Harvest workers by almost three to one. "We have a lot of strength in this company," Marshall Ganz boasted to the executive board as he briefed them on the strike. "It's something really, really special."[1]

Sun Harvest, the largest lettuce grower in the world, shipped ten million cartons of lettuce a year with a sales value of $50 million to $70 million.[2] If Sun Harvest cracked, other companies would follow. The company was also the UFW stronghold, the oldest vegetable contract with the most loyal union workers. And Chavez had already threatened a full-scale Chiquita banana boycott. So Sun Harvest became the union's primary target.

By the time the season began in Salinas, the pattern had been set. For Sun Harvest workers, strike duty was a job: Show up in the morning, picket all day, collect unemployment or strike benefits at the end of the week. Sabino attended the daily meetings for strike coordinators as well as the negotiating committee sessions. Most days he directed the picket line in Chualar. One committee of workers had responsibility for hustling donations of food. In the late morning they spread their bounty out in the shade of the parked cars that lined the field. Everyone shared. Sabino savored lunchtime, for the camaraderie as much as the food.

The strikers' disciplined routine flowed from the unity of their leaders. They stuck together even as the strike slogged on and spirits flagged. They vowed to reach a contract deal for all the companies, not just one or two at the expense of the others. They came to see how growers often played the lechugeros against the steadies. They determined to form their own alliance and end the era of divide and conquer. Ranch committee leaders had never worked together before, even within Sun Harvest. The large company had multiple committees—steadies in Salinas, lettuce workers in Imperial, Salinas, and Huron, celery cutters in Oxnard. As he got to know his colleagues, Sabino found one of the older lechugeros particularly impressive. Cleofas Guzman was short, strong, and animated, a gregarious leader who commanded respect and affection. He always had a smile and a friendly word, as well as wise ideas for strategic moves.

Sabino's quiet leadership, rooted in his ability to negotiate compromises and create consensus, was better suited for peace than war. The first time Sabino tried and failed to persuade scabs to leave the fields, he reported back to a meeting, dejected. Ganz maneuvered the irrigator to the side and taught him a basic lesson: Keep your own spirits up, and don't depress the others. Sabino quickly became another devoted student of

Ganz. Unlike some, Sabino never tired of Ganz's endless meetings, his omnipresent clipboard and lists and pedantic style. Sabino had always learned by watching others. Now he studied how to coordinate actions, exert pressure, and motivate people.

As the strike approached the six-month mark, picket lines dwindled. The union had struck only the eleven companies where the UFW support was strongest. That made it easier for growers to recruit scabs. At the other ranches workers adopted what they dubbed "pre-huelga" tactics—sporadic and unpredictable walkouts and slowdowns. Mario had returned to Green Valley, where he led the workers in Plan Canguro (Plan Kangaroo: skip every other row) and Plan Maraña (leave the fields a tangled mess). Some days the lechugeros showed up, worked for two hours, then left. The strategy effectively sabotaged the growers. But within weeks they fired the workers. Mario, Sabino, and the other leaders argued that the union needed to expand the strike to all vegetable growers with union contracts.

Chavez reviewed the strike from afar and reached a different conclusion. He decided the union could not win. In early summer he told the staff in La Paz to prepare to go to the cities again. "The strike has lost its punch," he said. Only a boycott would be effective.[3] On July 23, Chavez called union leaders to La Paz to plan a full-scale boycott. The union would target Chiquita bananas, immediately after the biennial convention in mid-August.[4] Chavez had moved the convention to Salinas to honor the strikers. Ganz proposed marches that would converge in a massive rally to kick off the convention. He hoped the show of force might impress both Chavez and the growers.

Sabino was focused on the strike, intent on winning, and in the dark about Chavez's lack of faith. The irrigator looked forward to the convention, confident that delegates would follow the strike coordinators' recommendation and endorse a general strike. Others might go off to cities to boycott, but Sabino knew his workers wanted to stay and fight. He helped organize the marchers, who converged in a rally of more than five thousand on a Saturday afternoon at a Salinas school yard.

Nine years earlier and just a few miles away, Sabino had walked out on strike from Merrill Farms, a young, anonymous irrigator marching in a sea of people, along with Mario and Cleofas Guzman and all the others he did not yet know. They had chafed in a world where their intelligence far outstripped their education. Sabino had always known he was not just short and hardworking, cute with big ears. He had not known whether the rest of the world would ever see him as anything else. When he told people about the UFW, Sabino said the union was about people at the bottom, moving up. He was living proof.

Mario

Mario arrived at the convention exhilarated by the marches and ready to lead workers at Green Valley on strike. He listened to the fiery speeches at the rally, then headed that evening to a special meeting of strike coordinators with Chavez and the executive board.

Chava, normally less ebullient than his brother, came to the meeting particularly subdued. He had been arrested twice, fired from his job, and faced a possible prison sentence. His problems had begun on the first day of work at Cal Coastal's Salinas ranch. About sixty-five strikers had been picketing at the entrance to the labor camp when the company buses drove out at six thirty A.M. to take scab workers to the fields. Chava and a dozen others ran alongside the buses. When they slowed to pass over railroad tracks, workers threw rocks. Chava was arrested, and the company used the charge to fire him.[5] The UFW filed a complaint with the state, arguing that Chava was unfairly singled out because of his union activities. Two months later Chava was stopped while cruising around Soledad with another ranch committee president at four A.M. Police found the makings of a simple gasoline-in-a-jug explosive in the car. Similar devices had been used to blow up packing sheds and cars. Chava faced six felony counts. The union had hired a skilled defense attorney, and Chava was following his advice to the letter. The prospect of several years in prison terrified him. He had stayed away from the strike, but he joined Mario and the others at the meeting with Chavez on the eve of the convention.

The four dozen workers waited while the executive board met, then filed into the room after ten P.M. and stood around the table where the board sat. They were leaders at companies on strike, as well as representatives of ranches that expected to be called out on strike in the next few days. They had learned to organize through the strike and to support one another. They felt they owned the strike.

They all knew Jerry was in serious talks with Meyer Tomatoes. Chavez began by briefing them on the negotiations. He was taken aback when Mario asked who would sign off on the Meyer contract if they were all busy at the convention. Ganz jumped in to explain that the industry-wide negotiating committee recognized that an early contract would set precedents. They had agreed to weigh such decisions jointly. Chavez made clear he viewed the decision as his prerogative, not theirs. "I think we have the right to have an opinion," Chava countered. "From the beginning, we formed an industry committee. We negotiated as an industry because it affects us all."

Chavez moved to his major point. "The union is broke. We have spent $2.8 million dollars on this strike," he said. They must shift to a boycott in order to win. "We've always gone to the boycott with the strikes we have lost. It takes more time but it is easier to win. It is a sure win."

Respectfully, the workers disagreed. Chava took the lead. He was always a good debater, well informed and willing to challenge. He also came prepared. He had gotten wind of Chavez's purpose in advance, and the workers had held their own pre-meeting. When Chavez said that boycotts never lasted more than three months, Chava shot back, "What about Gallo?" Gallo was an exception, Chavez acknowledged.

Chava insisted that a boycott alone was not acceptable. They must begin a general strike as well. "Because if we don't do it, the high morale and all the desire that they have had for so long to go on strike, and the morale especially of the strikers that believed they had the back-up of the general strike, that morale will fall to the floor," Chava said. "It will sink to the lowest depths. We have to make a decision that we will have to live with forever."

Chava pointed to Green Valley, where his brother worked, one of the many lettuce cooperatives. Without the pressure the union had built up through the strike, growers could pull out of the cooperative and use nonunion harvesters instead. "What will happen to the strength we all have right now?" Chava asked. "Where will that strength go?"

A strike is for everyone, not just you, Chavez replied. "We don't know if we will win . . . and if we do it will take a long, long time," he said. "And we will have to commit all the resources of the union . . . I can't do this in good conscience."

When Chavez argued a strike would commit workers not represented in the room, the workers all chimed in: Let's put it to a vote. Mario was confident the workers at Green Valley would voice support. If the union walked away from the strike now, Mario argued, "I know with this all their spirit and all the faith they've had in us will hit bottom."

When the meeting ran past midnight with no resolution, Ganz suggested they resume the discussion after the convention. He said the delegates would support a three-pronged attack—the strike, boycott, and a legal assault. As the meeting broke up, Mario made one last statement: "If tomorrow there is a resolution from the executive board that there is going to be just a boycott, I'm going to oppose it." Ganz and Chavez assured him that would not be the case.[6]

The next morning Mario went to the Resolutions Committee meeting. He arrived a few minutes late and asked Gilbert Padilla, the committee chair, to see the resolutions already approved. Mario looked at Resolution 10, and he exploded. Resolution 10 listed all the forces arrayed against the strikers, concluded no end to the strike was near, and resolved that the union would place its full force behind the boycott. This was not the deal last night, Mario yelled at Padilla. Fine, write what you want, Padilla said.

In Spanish, Mario sat down and wrote an amended Resolution 10:

Whereas, workers at different companies have now been on strike for seven months, and we know well they have sacrificed everything for the good of all, and

Whereas, strike votes have been taken at the other companies where contracts have expired . . .

Whereas, we must extend the strike because we feel that thus we will achieve the speediest victory . . .

Be it resolved, by the members of the United Farm Workers of America, AFL-CIO, to extend the strike, in order to do the right thing as men and women and to set an example for our children.[7]

Jerry

When the delegates convened for the Fourth Constitutional Convention, Jerry was not there to hear the testimonials for the legal department he had created. He was negotiating.

For once, the Teamsters had really helped. A wildcat Teamster strike at Bud Antle, one of the big three lettuce growers, had forced the company to increase wages to five dollars an hour. Suddenly the UFW's proposal did not seem so out of line. Jerry knew he was running against the clock and Chavez wanted to end the strike. But Meyer Tomatoes needed a break too. Tomatoes were rotting on the vine.

Jerry was closeted at the house of the attorney for Meyer when convention delegates took their seats on folding chairs in the Hartnell College gym. They paid tribute to the widow of Rufino Contreras. They cheered Jane Fonda when the actress promised to promote the Chiquita boycott on her upcoming movie tour. Ganz read a telegram Gretchen had sent on behalf of the Boston boycott: "We in Boston are thinking of you as you make very important decisions about the future of the union." Chavez called Chris up to the stage and introduced him the same way as usual: "He has always been at our side, never, I say this here and wherever I go, with all the help that he has given us . . . never has he asked for anything."

None of the Salinas legal department heard Rosario Pelayo read Resolution 2, thanking the lawyers for their years of outstanding service. Then a striker from Mario Saikhon read Resolution 3, thanking Jerry Cohen. The crowd gave the absent attorney the traditional farmworker applause.[8] The night before, Dolores Huerta had objected to honoring the lawyers who were selling out for money. Chavez had explained he couldn't welcome the new lawyers without thanking the old.[9] The union president took the microphone to speak on Resolution 4, applauding the new attorneys who were "dedicating themselves unselfishly to improving the lives of farm workers." Chavez introduced the team, six Chicano lawyers, two just admitted to the bar in June, two still studying.[10]

The convention worked through all the other resolutions, skipping number 10. Then Mario went to the microphone and read the resolution he had written. The delegates cheered, and the measure passed by acclamation.

Delegates and visitors were straggling out of the convention around seven P.M. when Chavez rose from the rocking chair he favored to ease his back pains. He had been fasting for eight days. "Fasten your seatbelts," he said. "There is an important announcement to come." Jerry made his grand entrance, conga-dancing down the middle aisle with the negotiating committee from Meyer Tomatoes, sporting bright yellow Meyer caps. Jerry announced they had a deal: A 43 percent raise over three years, retroactive to January 1, increased medical and pension contributions, and two unheard-of provisions: a cost-of-living increase and a full-time union representative, paid by the company. "I think this is proof, proof of the kind of force we have when we use it," Jerry told the cheering workers. He brought Tom Dalzell up on stage and thanked him for his help. "*Vivan los abogados!*" the delegates shouted.[11]

On Monday morning Mario waited for Ganz to resume the boycott-versus-strike discussion. Nothing happened. Chavez had left. Furious, Mario went and found Ganz. There is no money, Ganz told him. They've shut the bank accounts. No more strike benefits. Ganz was due in La Paz the next day for a three-day conference to plan the boycott. He did not go. He defied Chavez and stayed to help escalate the strike. When the vegetable ranches opened at the end of the week, workers at West Coast farms, a large lettuce grower, walked out on strike. The action was unauthorized but effective. Two weeks after Chavez had told the workers they could not win the strike, West Coast agreed to the best contract the union had ever signed.

Jerry used that pact as leverage to finalize a deal with Sun Harvest. They signed five days later. The base wage went from $3.70 to $5.00 immediately. Jerry celebrated with the workers and the staff. They began drinking in the afternoon and later competed in sprints in a vacant lot next to the union office. They ran elimination rounds until only Jerry and Cleofas Guzman were left. In the last race Jerry suddenly collapsed. He was so drunk and the pain so severe that he thought he had been shot. He had partially severed his Achilles tendon.

His leg in a cast, Jerry stayed at the negotiating table. Two days after Labor Day, the strike leaders planned work stoppages. There were no strike benefits, but workers walked out anyway. An early heat wave helped their cause. On September 12 the growers lined up to sign contracts: Arrow, Associated, Veg Pak, Veg-a-Mix, Harden, Sakata, and Valley Harvest. Jerry held court at the Towne House Hotel. He called Chavez and urged him to come. Chavez stayed in La Paz. On September 14 two more growers signed, including Green Valley Produce.

A few days later a different celebration took place at La Paz. Farmworkers graduated from an English class. The students and their guests gathered in the North Unit, the old hospital building that had become the social center. The proud graduates put on a slide show for their families, the La Paz community, and most of the union officers. The slides ended with a familiar refrain, the same message that Eliseo had delivered at a boycott conference in almost the same spot less than eight years earlier: The union is not Cesar Chavez. The union is not La Paz. The union is the workers.

Graduates and guests, board members and union leaders, trooped down to the communal kitchen for a celebratory lunch. They had barely sat down when Dolores Huerta rose and began to grill the teachers. She demanded to know who had suggested such subversive thoughts. Someone must have put the workers up to voicing such disloyalty, and she wanted a confession. The meal ended before it began. Two teachers were fired later that day.

The union is the workers had been their campaign slogan, the essence of the UFW's appeal as the union waged war against the Teamsters and piled up election victories. But that was four years earlier and another era. The union was Cesar Chavez, and to suggest otherwise was treason.

CHAPTER 25

A Different Union

January 1980

Ellen

Ellen had just graduated from law school in Indiana when the union called. The legal department had gone from an overstaffed operation in Salinas run by the legendary Jerry Cohen to a bare-bones operation in La Paz run by a young lawyer named Marco Lopez. He offered Ellen a job for the customary room and board and the upgraded salary of ten dollars a week. She had already committed to a law firm and felt obligated for at least a year. By the end of 1979, Ellen longed to return to the union. She regretted not being able to work for Jerry, but she had never cared about the money. She had not begrudged the lawyers' salaries, but assumed she would not take one herself. Her mother had sent Ellen a quote from Albert Einstein because the sentiment reminded her of Chavez. Ellen pinned the quote to her refrigerator wherever she lived: "I am absolutely convinced that no wealth in the world can help humanity forward, even in the hands of the most devoted worker in this cause. The example of great and pure individuals is the only thing that can lead us to noble thoughts and deeds. Money only appeals to selfishness and irresistibly invites abuse."

Ellen arrived at La Paz in mid-January, moved into a trailer, and was happily reunited with her first two friends in the union, Chris and Ruth Shy. Shy ran contract administration. She was busy implementing a victory in the new vegetable contracts—the position of paid union representative.

The paid reps, as they became known, would earn their normal salaries but work full time handling grievances and resolving problems. The union had to establish procedures to select the paid reps and spell out their responsibilities to both the union and the company. After a series of meetings with Chavez, Shy drew up a plan. The members would elect ranch committee presidents who would serve as the paid reps. Shy wrote an election manual and distributed detailed instructions on how to conduct secret-ballot elections. Finally, the ranch committees would have real power.

Ellen's mentor, Chris, had slowly recuperated from the bleeding ulcer. He split his week between Los Angeles and La Paz, where he focused on community life projects. The Game was more or less over. Chavez never explained why they had stopped, but Chris knew religious and labor allies had objected. Synanon's reputation had steadily deteriorated as state and federal investigations revealed violent, cultlike behavior. Chuck Dederich was forced to relinquish control of the organization he had founded after he pleaded guilty to conspiring to place a four-and-a-half-foot rattlesnake in the mailbox of an attorney who had successfully sued Synanon. Chavez continued to defend his friend and called on Synanon for help organizing the new legal department.[1]

Chris's other endeavors at La Paz flourished, and the activities and spirit appealed to Ellen. Weekends revolved around a communal project, often involving hard physical labor. Chavez kept coming up with new brainstorms. One month they dragged boulders from a creekbed to build a stone wall along the entrance road to La Paz; another month they cleared land to plant an orchard. On Saturdays everyone worked in the community garden. On Sundays Ellen went to mass, one of the few who attended regularly, a bond with Chavez.

Ellen found a very different union than the one she had left four years earlier, starting with her own department, now at La Paz. Jerry still worked in Salinas, negotiating with the holdout vegetable companies. Ellen still adored Jerry, despite undercurrents of hostility toward him at La Paz. Memos to Chavez complained that the ALRB and growers' attorneys did end runs around the new legal department and only wanted to deal with Jerry: "JC still trying to call the shots with the ALRB." "Need to define Jerry's role. Legal Dept. is paying a lot of money to have Jerry negotiate."[2] Chavez wanted to launch an apprentice program, to enable union faithful to become lawyers through a supervised program instead of law school. Chavez pointedly noted that the only apprentice Jerry had taken on was Tom Dalzell. Chavez warmly embraced Ellen and the other lawyers who had joined the La Paz staff, praising their commitment as he told them how the old department had been torn apart by the issue of volunteerism. "Don't live in past," Chavez wrote as he prepared notes for a planning conference with the new legal department. "Don't be afraid of change."[3]

Ellen liked being a pioneer in the new union. She spent two months studying for the bar, took the exam, then waited anxiously for the results. On the third Friday in May the pass list came out. Ellen's name was not there. On Saturday she moped. On Sunday she began to study again. Monday morning the fat envelope arrived, with the bad news and the reapplication packet. But as Ellen read the letter, she realized they had made a mistake: The score did not include points she had earned when she took the exam in the Midwest. She ran up to the North Unit, where Chavez had just opened a meeting with the newly elected paid reps from the vegetable companies. Ellen burst into the room and pulled Chavez aside, whispering excitedly. "This sister is a lawyer," Chavez said to the paid reps, explaining her roller-coaster emotions about the bar exam results. "Now she saw the paper, and she passed, and now we can welcome her as a lawyer. *Gracias a Dios.* Whew!" The workers saluted the new lawyer with the traditional farmworker clap.[4]

Sabino

Sabino was one of those applauding Ellen. He still could not quite believe he was there.

He had first watched the union leadership from afar, then edged closer and closer to the table, still not quite seeing himself take a seat. He had been drafted first as union steward, then ranch committee leader, convention delegate, and negotiating committee member. When the Sun Harvest contract called for two workers to be paid by the company and work full time on union business, Sabino decided to campaign for a leadership post. Cleofas Guzman had a lock on the first spot. Sabino was a long shot for the second. As an irrigator, he worked only in Salinas and was less well known than those who traveled around the state. Sabino ended up in a runoff against a lechugero and won. He attributed the victory to his fight several years earlier to keep the extra nickel for the irrigators. The workers had seen him fight for something. So Sabino proudly took his place among the first generation of farmworkers earning a salary to work for the union.

In late May he joined twenty other paid reps at the five-day training conference at La Paz. When Sabino found himself seated next to the union president at lunch one day, the irrigator picked up his name card and asked Chavez to autograph the slip of paper: *Para mi hermano Sabino, con admiración por tu valor y franceza* [sic]. *Viva la causa.* To my brother Sabino, with admiration for your courage and frankness. Sabino carefully saved the card.

Chavez threw out questions to the paid reps, just as he did at staff meetings, and recorded their answers on page after page of butcher paper. What is our mission? To organize and serve all the members. Who are our clients? The workers. The company. The consumer. What is the work of the representative? To administer the contract well. Chavez schooled them in the principles of "Management by Objective" and stressed his new buzzword: "quality." Sabino shared with the group a recent conversation with a foreman, who said the paid reps had already changed the image of the union. Before, union ranches had a reputation for inferior work. Now workers left their personal problems and quarrels with the company aside, and the quality of work had improved markedly, the supervisor said. "You have won the respect of the company and the workers," he told Sabino. Chavez applauded the change. "Between us chickens," he told the workers, the union had helped bankrupt companies in the past. They must not do that again. Mario, the newly elected paid rep from Green Valley, listened approvingly; he had been promoting the message of quality in his own crew for years. Chavez told them they must pass on the lessons from this conference. "Each of us must be a teacher," Mario said.

Several hours of spirited questions and answers ended with agreement on a five-word mission statement: *Calidad al pueblo nos conviene.* "Our mission is to give people quality" was the closest English translation, Chavez said. Then he posed the next challenge. How will you explain this to members? Doesn't better quality mean the boss gets richer? How does this help the workers? The paid reps turned to Guzman to answer. "Because with this we'll have more work, a better future for our families, better benefits," Guzman said. Better quality would protect against mechanization, he said, and a secure economic future for the company would help the workers too. They had come a long way from the tortuga.[5]

Back in Salinas, Sabino and Guzman divided up Sun Harvest's two thousand employees. Sabino represented the irrigators, tractor drivers, thinners, and broccoli and cauliflower workers. Guzman had the lettuce and celery. Sabino began his day at six A.M. at the union office. He sorted grievances and fielded questions from workers, complaints about bosses, and objections from the company. At night he often attended grievance hearings. The schedule kept Sabino busy, but he enjoyed the work. He also appreciated Guzman's companionship and counsel. Lechugeros tended not to treat steadies with much respect, but Guzman was different. When Sabino went home to Mexico to visit his family, Guzman covered for him. When workers grumbled because Sabino's brother got a dispatch, Guzman defended Sabino and put a stop to the sniping. Guzman led with a directness that inspired trust and attracted followers. Like Sabino, workers knew they could count on Guzman.

The leaders in the field had made a relatively smooth transition from wartime council to peacetime cabinet. Each Saturday morning the paid reps met with Marshall Ganz and Jose Renteria, the field office director, to review issues, discuss problems, and plan strategy. In addition to responsibilities at their own ranches, the paid reps helped the union organize at other companies. In the summer of 1980 wildcat strikes began in the garlic fields of Gilroy, a half hour north of Salinas. Workers picketed the Gilroy Garlic Festival and crowned a farmworker's daughter as their own Garlic Princess. Then they demanded elections. The union had no local staff, so the paid reps were dispatched to help in their off-hours. From La Paz, Chavez sent Larry Tramutt.

Tramutt's competence had made him a rising star, a loyalist whom Chavez had turned to for help in carrying out purges, handling the budget, and setting up schools to train negotiators and organizers. Tramutt liked La Paz, for the community and the proximity to Chavez. The young Stanford graduate found Chavez almost mesmerizing, in his power as well as his contradictions. He was intellectually demanding yet very human, taking time out to tell jokes or comfort a sick friend. He always pushed you to do more, yet didn't ask anyone to do things he himself would not do. He preached focus, but his insatiable curiosity ran in many directions at once. Even the pieces of Chavez that Tramutt had trouble accepting fascinated him—the leader's insistence that he could heal people with his hands, or his announcement one night that he had an aura. Sometimes late at night they drove with the guards thirty miles to Bakersfield to play handball. On the deserted courts, Tramutt saw Chavez's fierce competitive spirit unvarnished. He challenged every point and never gave up, no matter how far behind he fell. Sometimes Tramutt won anyway. He knew the handball court was the only place he could beat Chavez; in real life, his relentless drive meant he never backed down.

The paid reps had a reputation for independence, and Tramutt knew concern was building in La Paz about a Salinas power base. But he had no staff to run the Gilroy elections, so Tramutt warily welcomed the paid reps' help.

Then he saw them organize. They were confident and reliable, accustomed to teamwork, and able to speak to workers with unmatched credibility. Tramutt had sat through the fight over paying salaries to the lawyers and the debates over how to attract farmworkers to work for the union. Now he'd seen the answer. They held twenty-eight elections, winning all but two.[6] When Tramutt was summoned to meet with Chavez, he drove expectantly to La Paz, figuring Chavez wanted a briefing on the impressive string of victories.

Tramutt knew what the pursed lips meant as soon as he walked in. He had seen Chavez turn on other people enough times. Only I call elections, Chavez said. With all due respect, the workers do, Tramutt replied. Chavez asked Tramutt if he was taking his orders from Moscow. Tramutt knew it was time to leave. He told people he didn't want to get caught between Chavez and Ganz. He said he wanted to help the earthquake victims in Italy, the country of his ancestors. He asked for three weeks' vacation, pointing out he had taken only three days off in the past three months. Chavez wrote back that Tramutt's eight years with the union entitled him to only two.[7]

Sabino knew only that another one had disappeared. He focused on more pressing concerns. Serious problems with the medical plan persisted. The new labor-management relations committee at Sun Harvest had finally met. Chavez had said repeatedly that he wouldn't be happy until farmworkers were running the union. Sabino thought they were well on the way to making that dream come true.

Chris

In the beautiful rolling hills of the Napa Valley, Chris presided in the summer of 1980 at the wedding of Fred Ross Jr., the legendary organizer's son. The words that stuck in Chris's mind after the August 23 ceremony were not his own but those of Marshall Ganz. Why don't you come down to Salinas and see how a real union is run? Ganz had asked, something between a boast and a challenge. Chris took such implicit criticism as a Capital Crime. The loyal minister was on the verge of a move that would tie him even more closely to Chavez. Chris had decided to live at La Paz.

He had been restless on and off since the labor law passed five years earlier. His youngest was about to start his senior year in high school, and Pudge was willing to move to La Paz once their son graduated. Chris wrote Chavez to tell him the news. The next time the two men met, Chris happily recorded Chavez's response: "He is *very* happy about my letter, has been praying for it for 2–3 years."[8]

With renewed vigor, Chris resumed his role as cheerleader. He trumpeted the success of the negotiating school at La Paz. Subsistence living had not turned out to be the stumbling block it was thought to be in attracting farmworkers to the union staff, Chris said—an oblique slap at Eliseo's contention that the only way to involve farmworkers in running the union was to pay salaries.[9] Like Chavez, Chris overlooked that almost all the students were the children of movement families, not farmworkers.

Chris also boasted about the paid reps. "The most important feature of the new contracts is entirely new," he wrote in a Christian magazine. "Under the new contracts the elected President of the Ranch Committee (who stands for election every year) will be paid by the companies to do his/her job full-time. The new 'paid reps' have had two weeks of training at La Paz and are in the fields doing the work they did before—but now, full-time."[10]

As he worked out a transition, Chris broached to Chavez the idea of folding the National Farm Worker Ministry, which had less and less to do as the union focused inward. But Chavez said the ministry was politically useful. Chris, always careful to stay on message, wrote down his rationale as he prepared to make his decision public: "I am making this change because I know what has to be done in the union; it is something I can do and I feel called to do it. It isn't any kind of indictment on NFWM."[11] To his closest supporters, he was more forthright: "I have finally given in to the realization that I am doing no one any good by resisting a persistent internal call to go and do something new."[12]

Weary of educating successive waves of church people, Chris viewed the move as liberating. Finally he would shed his split identity. He brushed off friends' concerns. Jerry called Chris to say he should think twice about living in the closed world of La Paz and giving up his independent base. John Moyer, the United Church of Christ board member, had warned Chris strongly more than two years earlier, when Chris had been first tempted to move: "If you were in any way to relinquish your position as director of the NFWM and become part of Cesar's staff, there is no way you could perform that ministry to him. I have heard that struggle emerging in you often enough that I want to say that."[13]

By the end of 1980 Moyer was voicing his first serious differences with Chris in the fifteen years they had worked together. The board of the national ministry had always acted as a rubber stamp for Chris. Of all the board members, Moyer held the most sway, from financial and moral perspectives. Moyer had become convinced the UFW would never become a national union and expand outside California because Chavez could not delegate power. "The history is that the union has, since the signing of the first contracts, always operated on a crisis-reaction basis," Moyer wrote to Chris. "A brush fire erupts; all the fire trucks are rushed in to put out the fire, regardless of what they are doing. Crosby Milne tried to get the union to deal with this and, except for a short time, he failed."

Moyer reopened the decision that had been so controversial when the national ministry first convened in 1971. He argued that as a *national* ministry, they should work with other groups. He objected to Chris's assumption that if the UFW cut back on organizing, the ministry should scale back its horizons as well. "The UFW does not have a monopoly on service and sacrifice," Moyer wrote. He pointed to nascent efforts to organize farmworkers in Florida and Ohio.[14]

Chris fell back on the union's traditional defense. With enemies like the growers, with the full force of the agricultural industry arrayed against the union, Chris stressed indignantly, the UFW's survival was a miracle. The leadership had just spent one hundred hours developing a plan, he said confidently. They would move into other states within the decade. Moyer would see.

"We have been accused of being too close to the union, of lacking an independent, prophetic, Church perspective," Chris wrote as he prepared to leave his post at the National Farm Worker Ministry. "It is a troubling criticism because it is so close to the truth. We are one flesh with the people of the UFW. We, undoubtedly, *have* lost an independent perspective. In speaking to the public about the farm workers' struggle, we tell the truth, but not always the whole truth."[15]

Jerry

Jerry had a simple way of dealing with things that baffled him: He ignored them. While others deconstructed events and agonized over their meaning, Jerry moved on to the next fight. He liked to quote Jesus' exhortation to the apostles on how to behave when they were not welcomed in a town: Shake their dust off your feet and move on. As the lettuce strike waned, the dust began to pile up on Jerry's feet.

After the vote to dismantle the legal department, Jerry had felt liberated. He had thrown himself into preparing for his first argument before the U.S. Supreme Court. He felt he had turned defeat into victory, buying time to argue important cases and use the transition to shape their legacy—the implementation and interpretation of the ALRA.

Chavez repeatedly offered Jerry as much money as he wanted, to move to La Paz and train the new volunteer lawyers. But Jerry's life was in Monterey. He could not move to La Paz; nor did he have any interest in starting over with new recruits. Back in early 1979 Jerry had written his first resignation letter, saying he would leave in June: "You have always led by example," he wrote to Chavez, "so you know better than most that if the Legal Department is to be run on a volunteer basis it must be led by someone willing to set the example. I am not. I will always cherish the memories of the struggle and will miss all of you. Love, Jerry."[16]

When June came, the lettuce strike was in full swing. Jerry relinquished his title as chief counsel, but stayed. He plunged into negotiations, delighting in the drama, brinksmanship, and camaraderie of the workers who led the strike. He exulted in the final contracts. As the strike tapered off, Jerry kept negotiating with the companies that had refused to sign. After a while he began to wonder if Chavez really wanted more contracts.

Jerry urged Chavez to be more flexible. "I think it's time to change our bargaining posture in the vegetables. We should do whatever it takes to get contracts," he wrote Chavez in the spring of 1980. ". . . We are stagnating and on the defensive. Many resources are being used for few workers. We need to free these resources to consolidate and organize." He ended: "At some point, pure, pristine proposals need to be compromised into contracts." He underlined contracts twice.[17]

Jerry held on, even as he watched the union's position deteriorate around the state. Chavez had sent Gilbert Padilla to Coachella to negotiate a new contract with Lionel and Billy Steinberg. When Padilla arrived, workers were so angry that they threw rocks at him as he spoke from the back of a flatbed truck. They felt the union had abandoned them. A lawsuit to get retroactive pay from the last contract had never been resolved. Padilla, nicknamed the Silver Fox, soothed the workers. They negotiated a new contract. Padilla made the Steinbergs pay for the barbecue to celebrate. Billy Steinberg was still running the field operations, but he was also achieving success in his musical career. Linda Ronstadt had covered one of Steinberg's songs. "How Do I Make You" became a top-ten hit. When Billy Steinberg went out in the vineyards, the workers greeted him by bursting into song: *"How do I make you, how do I make you . . . think about me!"*

Padilla was having far less success. He grew increasingly baffled by Chavez. One morning Ellen, who was living temporarily in the Padillas' house in La Paz, awoke and heard Padilla on the phone, resigning from the union. Dolores Huerta had attacked him at a meeting of the credit union the day before and suggested he quit. Padilla got the message. Padilla had helped recruit Jerry to the union, more than a decade earlier. The Silver Fox's departure was not a shock, but more dust on Jerry's shoes.

Jerry became convinced that the way to preserve the union was to secure the base in Salinas. He put all his energy into settling vegetable contracts. The more vegetable workers, the greater their voting strength at the union's next convention, which would elect a new executive board. But Chavez could do the same math. Jerry decided Chavez did not want any more contracts because he felt threatened by the potential power of the Salinas workers. "Cesar has them at check mate," Kirsten Zerger wrote after talking to Jerry. There was no way to reach agreement on more contracts unless they made major concessions, Jerry told Kirsten. If they did that, Chavez loyalists would argue that Jerry and Marshall Ganz had sold out the workers. Jerry also voiced frustration that the strongest leaders in the fields, like Cleofas Guzman, would not take Chavez on directly or run for the executive board.[18]

Then Jerry thought he reached a deal with one of the holdout vegetable companies. He had agreed to give up the hiring hall for new workers, something the union had done numerous times. Chavez deemed the clause unacceptable. He claimed he had never agreed to relinquish the hiring hall, though two years earlier he had been the leading proponent.

Jerry decided there was not much point in sticking around. On November 24, 1980, he typed his second resignation letter. "I remain grateful for all I have learned in the union," he wrote to Chavez, "especially from you and Dolores about politics and negotiations, and intend to do something, I am not sure just what, to work for justice in some other sphere. Sometime, when you have the time, I'd like to get together and talk."

Jerry thought of Chavez as his teacher, and something more. They had started together when Jerry was twenty-six, in the kitchen of the Pink House on Albany Street, fighting a battle nobody outside really thought they could win. The Chavez kids babysat for Jerry's kids. Chavez had trusted Jerry with delicate internal problems. They were close. Jerry called and left messages. He tried to reach Chavez for three months.

Jerry sent one final note. "Well, Cesar, aren't you just a little ashamed of yourself?" he began. "Remember I am Jerry Cohen not Carl Sam Maggio," he wrote, referring to one of the owners of Sun Harvest. "Just because I disagree with you philosophically about paying staff and La Paz does not mean that when I leave I don't care about whether you and the union succeed. Now I repeat—aren't you just a *little* ashamed of yourself.

"Yours till Niagara Falls. Jerry."[19]

CHAPTER 26

You're With Us or Against Us

January 1981

Mario

Cleofas Guzman, the charismatic leader at Sun Harvest, was due to run a meeting in San Luis, a small border city at the triangular intersection of Arizona, California, and Mexico. On January 23 Guzman took the short-cut through Mexico en route to San Luis, where he planned to explain the union's medical benefits to Sun Harvest workers in Arizona.

The next morning Guzman's son-in-law called around because the lechugero had not come home. After a phone call and two trips to the union office, his son-in-law determined that Guzman had never shown up in San Luis. The family went to every jail and hospital in Mexicali, where Guzman lived. At the general hospital officials said there was no patient named Guzman, but on the way out his son-in-law saw a familiar pair of boots and pants. He made them check again and found his father-in-law.

Police said Guzman had been heading east on the San Luis–Mexicali Road when a cotton truck heading south on Ejido Benito Juarez ran a stop light as the lechugero approached the intersection. His car hit the truck about midway, the front end sliding underneath the box car. The brunt of the collision fell on Guzman's head.

Marshall Ganz and Jessica Govea were at a board meeting in La Paz when Chavez received a phone call, then delivered the bad news. They drove straight to Mexicali, arrived at the hospital around five thirty Sunday morning, and began making arrangements for a neurosurgeon to examine Guzman. He was paralyzed and semicomatose.[1]

Among those who had become known as Marshall's faction, nobody thought the collision was an accident. The truck driver never surfaced. The four-hour gap between when Guzman was hit and when he arrived at the nearby hospital went unexplained. None of the local union staff had thought to look for Guzman when he didn't show up, though he was extremely reliable.[2]

Mario based his suspicions on more than circumstantial evidence. Since the winter season began two months earlier, tensions in the union office had escalated sharply. Guzman, leader of the largest company, had had the first serious run-ins with the new director of the Calexico field office, Oscar Mondragon. Mario soon joined the fray. The paid reps had become accustomed to making decisions jointly and wielding authority. The new union staff were out to quash that power, not nurture it. Shortly after New Year's, Mario was looking over his seniority lists in a back room of the union office when he overheard his name mentioned upfront. Two well-known drug users were plotting with a union official to set up Mario by having him refuse to give them a dispatch to work. He walked into the room and challenged them to fight. They smashed a chair over his head, breaking Mario's nose. Then the field office gave them dispatches to work in the fields.[3]

Tom Dalzell, hanging out in Salinas trying to figure out what to do with his life, heard about the confrontation right away. He had spent a lot of time in Calexico and understood the politics. He assumed the attack was a message to Mario, sent by Manuel Chavez, Cesar's cousin. Manuel Chavez had worked on and off for the union since the beginning, sometimes as an effective organizer but often as a lone ranger who ran a group known for shadowy endeavors on both sides of the border. He had a lengthy police record.[4] Most people didn't want to know too much about what Manuel did. Cesar Chavez considered him like a brother.

Dalzell spread the word about Mario's broken nose among the ex-union crowd. "This is the only way that they can deal with Mario because on account of his big balls and mouth and courage and love of the fight normal political pressure will not work against him," Dalzell wrote. "And it isn't even clear that this abnormal Manuel pressure will work."[5]

A couple of weeks later Mario met with Guzman and a third paid rep for a drink at Hollie's Hotel on Imperial Avenue, Calexico's main street.

Guzman was known for his courage; now he was scared. He said police in Mexicali had warned him that his outspoken stance and arguments with union staff had made the lechugero a target. Guzman planned to move to the U.S. side of the border, where he would be safer. Before he could move, he was called to the meeting in San Luis and crumpled under the truck.

Mario was convinced the collision was a setup. He went to Salinas and met with the other paid reps to fill them in. Sabino was on vacation in Mexico, confident all was well back home because Guzman was covering for him on the job. When Sabino returned to Salinas and heard the news, he began to take a gun with him when he traveled out of town.

Chavez visited Calexico two weeks after Guzman was injured. The ranch committee presidents demanded a meeting. They complained about Mondragon, the new field office director. They asked for a clear delineation of their responsibilities compared to the union's office staff. Chavez promised to get back to them with answers. He told them Mondragon was in charge. Chavez also tried to shut down a prevalent rumor: Stop the gossip that his cousin Manuel had been involved in the crash that crippled Cleofas Guzman.[6]

Ganz and Govea were spooked. They had trouble believing the crash that had left the talented organizer brain-damaged was an accident, but they did not want to think about the alternative. They decided to resign. Chavez offered to send them on a trip to Israel to study agriculture and the kibbutz movement, as sort of a farewell present. They borrowed his cameras and made their travel plans.

They left behind the paid reps, struggling with a series of problems, with no support except one another. One by one, their allies in the leadership had walked away or been driven out, given up in frustration, anger, sadness, or fear. The medical plan was plagued by bureaucratic backlogs that delayed payments so long that workers suffered credit problems. The union was signing contracts in other industries with wages and conditions inferior to those of the vegetable workers. The paid reps knew that substandard contracts elsewhere could set a pattern that would be hard to overcome when the vegetable contracts expired in a year. They had learned the importance of looking at the big picture. And of sticking together. They began to talk about running their own candidates for the union board.

It had come to this: The farmworkers who had proudly gathered at La Paz less than a year earlier, hailed as the future of the union, now believed that Cesar Chavez's cousin had engineered an accident to knock off their most promising leader in the fields.

Gretchen

The whole Salinas gang showed up at the *carne asada* in mid-March to surprise Marshall Ganz on his thirty-eighth birthday and wish him well as he left the union. Most of the paid reps came to pay their respects and bid farewell. Jerry had just turned forty and was unemployed, rehearsing for a local play. Larry Tramutt had become Larry Tramutola, reverting to his original family name, and was raising money for earthquake victims in Italy. Gilbert Padilla was working two acres of onions and trying to get a state job. Gretchen found herself in a distinct minority—she still worked for the union.

Like Chris sticking his hand into the wringer on his mother's washing machine, Gretchen was getting pulled deeper and deeper into the workers' world.

After she left Calexico in the midst of the strike, Gretchen had bounced from the Boston boycott to the Brown for President campaign to the boycott in Rhode Island and back to California. She had picked up enough sophistication about union politics to realize that her ties to Ganz made her suspect. One of Chavez's sons-in-law had been sent to Boston to replace Gretchen as boycott director. When Chavez came through the East Coast on tour, he played a Game with the boycotters. Gretchen gamed him on having passed her over because she could not be trusted. She was pleased with herself for bringing the issue up and thought he took it well.

For Richard Chavez, Gretchen's enthusiasm and ability outweighed any suspicions about her allegiance. He had just taken over the negotiations department. The union had 130 contracts covering about thirty thousand members.[7] He was mapping out a plan to sign more and thought Gretchen could become a strong negotiator. She relocated to Salinas in the summer of 1980, moved into an apartment with Rosario Pelayo, and began to negotiate her first contract.

Her move coincided with the paid reps' efforts to help organize other companies. When the union tried to make a run at Merrill Farms, one of the largest nonunion lettuce growers, Gretchen went to the planning sessions. She had organized an election at Merrill two years earlier, losing by only five votes. Gretchen had met Mario briefly during the strike in the Imperial Valley. Their first contact in Salinas was not particularly auspicious.

Gretchen toasts Sue Miner, Chris's long-time assistant, at a surprise party to mark Miner's twenty-fifth anniversary with the farm worker ministry. Miner was a den mother to a generation of boycotters. (UCLA Charles E. Young Research Library Department of Special Collections, Los Angeles Times Photographic Archives, Copyright © Regents of the University of California, UCLA)

Mario bought her a hamburger, saying he knew the volunteers didn't get paid. She told him she was a vegetarian. He came back with Jell-O. She turned that down too. The Merrill campaign went nowhere because the union could not muster sufficient support. Mario proved more persistent in his courtship of Gretchen. When she disappeared from Salinas, Mario inquired where she had gone. When he learned she had moved to Napa to negotiate with several wineries, he offered to meet with the Napa ranch committees to explain how the paid reps system worked.

Gretchen's first negotiation, with Napa Valley Vineyards, took several months. She studied manuals and made late-night calls for advice to the other negotiators. She learned the minutiae of contract language and the art of bargaining. "Gretchen Laue is doing this—it is her first," Richard Chavez reported to the executive board, predicting a final agreement soon. "She has had ten meetings, most of the language is out of the way and [they] have had their first economic exchange. I knew it, I knew it!"[8]

By the time the Napa Valley contract was signed, Gretchen had become involved with Mario, largely against her better judgment. She told him

she did not cook, clean, sew, keep house, or do any of the things that traditional Mexican women did. Mario said he didn't care. He could buy all
those things. That statement stopped her cold, challenged all her precon-
ceptions. A farmworker buying services. Mario forced Gretchen to think
differently; that was a big part of his appeal. She kept finding herself surprised. Their differences seemed so vast that most friends thought the relationship was doomed. Chava warned his brother that he would get hurt.

The lettuce season had just begun in Salinas when Gretchen and Mario
went to the birthday party for Ganz. The paid reps were happy to be back
in Salinas, working with Jose Renteria, a field office director they knew
and liked. Gretchen spent her weeks in wine country, negotiating contracts, and her weekends in Salinas. Tom Dalzell, unemployed, cooked
Sunday brunches and played social coordinator for the loose-knit group
of current and former union staff who had stayed around the Monterey
Peninsula. Dalzell, Ganz, and Jerry engaged in another project, as they
tried to figure out their own futures as well as that of the union they were
leaving. In several long sessions they reconstructed in detail the events of
the past four years to analyze what might be salvaged going forward. They
studied the weighted votes from prior conventions to calculate what
might happen if workers really tried to take control of their own union.
They filled giant rectangles of butcher paper with columns labeled "La
Paz," "Strike," "Negotiations," "In the fields." They titled a column that detailed their own actions, "The Jedi." In the end they concluded the Jedi
warriors could not rescue the Republic after all.

Gretchen followed the frustrations of the paid reps and the growing
tensions from the sidelines. She tuned the problems out, in part because
she was oblivious to the depths of distrust between those who had long
fought on the same side. She saw herself as playing no role in the brewing
confrontation. Her workload increased as she gained experience and juggled multiple negotiations in the Napa and Salinas Valleys.

On Memorial Day weekend Sandy and the Dazzler threw a potluck
dinner and softball game in Berkeley, billed as the first annual reunion of
the old legal department. "Catch up on memories, pop-flys, and Life After
The Union," the invitation said. "Bring your softball equipment, but remember it's only a Game."9 Most of the old lawyers showed up, along
with many other union alumni. Gretchen was too busy with negotiations.

Chavez received a written report from an informant: The party became a sinister "counter-organizing" event that included a postgame
meeting to plot strategy. Chavez underlined certain names on the list of

attendees: Jerry, Sandy, Dalzell, Ganz. The union president wrote in the names of potential co-conspirators who were absent: Jessica Govea and Gretchen Laue.[10]

In Salinas another ominous gathering marred the holiday weekend. Oscar Mondragon arrived, telling workers he had been sent by La Paz to investigate complaints about the medical plan. In private conversations a different message from La Paz emerged. Mondragon accused Mario of exacerbating problems rather than solving them in order to create a political issue. He blamed Mario for instigating violence during the strike and intimated he was out to destroy the union. "He started accusing Mario Bustamante, saying he was a bad element," reported Hermilo Mojica, another leader among the paid reps.[11] The Chavez camp had hoped to enlist Mojica as an ally. They underestimated the workers' solidarity.

A week later the rhetoric escalated. Stephen Matchett, a close friend and former roommate of Gretchen, was among dozens of union volunteers summoned to a meeting at La Paz. Chavez delivered a blunt message: Malignant forces are out to destroy the union. You're with us or against us. There is no middle ground. Chavez spoke ominously about workers who had been tricked into selling out to the enemy, for money or for sex. He warned that a faction was trying to overthrow the president and the board. Everyone must choose sides. Stay and fight with us, or get out.[12] Jose Renteria, director of the Salinas field office, was forced to resign after he refused to help purge Mario and the other malignant forces.

Matchett came from a Quaker family. He had dropped out of Swarthmore, committed to finding a meaningful cause. Like Gretchen, he had started on the boycott and ended up in Salinas, where he worked as a paralegal. He had expected to work for the union for a long time. Meticulous, he never left work half-done. After he heard Chavez accuse workers of selling out, Matchett returned to Salinas, typed up a memo of his pending cases, disconnected the utilities at the union apartment where he lived, and left the keys on the table. He drove to Gretchen's apartment to fill her in and think about his next move.

Gretchen understood that she was being cast as a tool of Marshall Ganz, a Mata Hari who had seduced and corrupted a farmworker leader. But the idea seemed so preposterous she paid little heed. She focused on her work. She did not participate in the paid reps' discussions, or go along when Mario led the effort to find candidates for the executive board. The paid reps told Chavez they believed farmworkers should have a voice on the board. They notified him they intended to field a slate at the convention in late summer. He replied with the utmost courtesy, lauding their initiative. Mario and the others hoped to develop support around the state and field candidates from grapes, vegetables, and citrus. Concerns varied in different crops and regions. The workers had learned to organize. Chavez had said he wanted farmworkers to run the union, they repeated, though they no longer harbored any illusions.

Mario's brother had lost faith earlier than his friends. More than two years after the strike began, the union had finally signed a contract with Cal Coastal. The ALRB concluded that Chava had been fired for union activity, and the contract specified he was to be reinstated with full seniority.[13] But Chava had spent three months in jail, with a lot of time to think. His experience on the negotiating committee convinced Chava that the rhetoric about farmworkers running the union was only that. If he stayed, he would have to take on the institution and people who had gotten him where he was. He couldn't do it. He took a job as an outreach worker at California Rural Legal Assistance (CRLA). He traveled with Mario around the state to recruit candidates for the UFW board.

A few months before the convention, the administration in La Paz announced new assignments. Gretchen was to return to the boycott. She had no intention of going out on the boycott again. For one thing, she was committed to finishing her contract negotiations. For another, she was pregnant.

Chris

Chris arrived at La Paz just in time. Chavez took no chances as he faced the first open challenge, a challenge he had been expecting for years. With a convention fight looming and a steady trickle of prominent departures, Chris felt Chavez seemed particularly glad to welcome a close adviser who bucked the trend and embraced La Paz.

Chris had taken leave of the ministry shortly after Memorial Day. He was feted with gifts, tributes, and skits. While his title changed, his role did not seem all that different. The upcoming fight required a loyal administrator and skilled propagandist. Chris had plenty of experience.

The resignations of Ganz, Govea, and Padilla left three openings on the board. In July, Chavez appointed officers who would run for election at the fall convention. Chris wrote the press release, describing the three loyalists in glowing terms. There were "the two Arties"—Artie Rodriguez, a social work student from Texas and Chavez's son-in-law, and Artie

Mendoza, a likable organizer who had worked closely with the paid reps in Calexico. The third was Oscar Mondragon, the Calexico office director who had clashed with the workers and now ran the Salinas office as well. Mondragon had been convicted of arson for setting buses on fire during a 1974 strike in the Imperial Valley. Chavez asked his lawyers to research the legality of seating a convicted felon on the board. He anticipated the opposition might try to use the issue.

The paid reps ended up with two candidates: Jose Renteria, the former director of the Salinas field office, who had worked in the fields since coming to California as a teenager and worked for the union full time for five years, and Rosario Pelayo, a loyal Chavista for more than a decade. Her courage and fealty to the union were well known, not only in the Imperial and Salinas Valleys where she thinned plants and packed broccoli at Cal Coastal, but also in Coachella, where she worked in the Steinberg vineyard.

The campaign intensified as the showdown approached. Eight days before the convention Chavez asked Chris to witness calls that the union president placed to several paid reps, including Mario and Sabino. Chavez asked about problems with the medical plan. Chris took notes, though he did not speak Spanish. Once Chavez established that problems still existed, he directed Chris to draft a resolution for the board. The resolution authorized the president to send emissaries to Salinas to investigate the difficulties. That gave the board members an official pretext to be in Salinas.[14]

Chavez had another reason to send them to Salinas. He knew a sizable bloc of delegates from the vegetable companies would support Renteria and Pelayo. Chavez dictated an emergency measure that would circumvent the delegates and effectively take away their votes. The union board adopted an emergency rule: Fifteen percent of the workers at a ranch constituted a delegate body, and a majority of the delegate body could bind its convention delegates to vote for the Chavez slate. The board members descended on Salinas—ostensibly to resolve medical insurance claims. They circulated petitions to bind the delegates' votes. Mario and the paid reps were out to get Chavez, the board members told the workers. If you support Cesar, sign here.[15]

David Martinez, who had joined the board two years earlier, assumed a lead role. He spelled out strategy in an "Organizing Plan" that articulated the union's message: Marshall Ganz was "trying to screw C.C to take over the UFW," with the help of Jerry, Gretchen, and Larry Tramutola. Martinez instructed the campaigners to divide workers into three groups: for us, against us, in the middle. To those in the middle, the pitch was simple: There is no middle. You are with us or against us. To those supporting the Chavez slate, they would accuse Ganz of manipulating the paid reps ("how can they run the union") and allege that he resigned to escape charges, including his role in the death of Rufino Contreras.[16] Chris sat in on the board meetings where they discussed the need to recall and re-move the paid reps as soon as the convention was over. They talked about drafting an "anti-Marshall" resolution to present at the convention.[17]

Chavez appointed Chris as convention chairman. He spent frantic weeks organizing the logistics, housing, and meals, VIP-welcoming com-mittees, and simultaneous translation on the convention floor. He worked on the seating chart, careful to place the vegetable industry dele-gations in back, as far from microphones as possible. Chris compiled lists of companies, showing their weighted voting strength. He calculated how many delegate votes would be needed for a candidate to win.[18]

Chris was caught up in the fervor. Once again, Chavez had created an enemy, conjured up a good villain in order to rally everyone to do battle. Many found it easy to think the worst of Marshall Ganz. Chris had no personal animus against the former board member. But the minister was so far inside the union now, he saw the world in black and white again. There was an enemy, and the enemy had to be defeated. It was far easier—and more effective—to blame the rabbi's son instead of the workers actu-ally leading the revolt.

CHAPTER 27

Malignant Forces

September 1981

Mario

Mario arrived at the convention prepared to do battle, not optimistic about victory but not quite resigned to defeat. He thought his side might prevail on the merits. He knew the petition ploy all but ruled out a fair contest. Whatever the outcome, Mario would go down fighting. He took his seat in the back, with the troublemaker delegations.

Chavez set the tone in his opening speech:

> Now we come to this 1981 convention facing yet another assault on our beloved union. An assault even more menacing than the past conventions . . . More menacing because it is clandestinely organized by those forces whose every wish and desire is our destruction . . . Obstruction by those evil forces visible and invisible who work at every chance to destroy us—the growers, the teamsters, disaffected former staff, scoundrels, and god knows who, some unwittingly trying to reach the same goal—that is to bury our beloved union.[1]

The constitution required that the full convention ratify the emergency rule to bind the delegates' votes. Chavez brought the resolution up for a vote. Mario barreled up to the microphone. "To me, this resolution is unjust and undemocratic," he declared. Then he explained in simple math why the proposal was unfair. The convention delegates had been elected by all the members of each ranch. Under this change, if fifteen workers at a ranch of one hundred attended a meeting, and a majority of them signed the petition, they could bind the delegates to vote for the Chavez slate. That meant eight workers were speaking for one hundred—the vast majority of whom might not even be aware they had been deprived of their say. Mario finished up to applause: "This is a most shameful resolution for those of us who have believed in the democracy of this union."

Chavez called a vote. "The matter looks very split," he said, looking at the show of hands. A delegate quickly jumped to his aid, moving to reopen discussion because the members were confused. Chavez postponed the vote until the afternoon. During the lunch break the Chavez forces campaigned hard, using the most potent argument they had: The dissidents wanted to oust the beloved union leader. Flyers distributed during the break denounced the insurgents as puppets of "outside forces"—former union officials who had sabotaged the union's medical plan. Now they were intent on dethroning Chavez by controlling members of the board.[2]

After lunch, long lines formed at each microphone, but Mario managed to get the floor once more. "We were legally elected by all the membership in order to come and represent their interests as well as the interests of the union," he said. "Therefore this resolution seems to me completely absurd."

Chavez again called for a show of hands. The motion passed easily this time, amid shouts of *"Viva Chavez."* Mario and the others had decided that in essence, the rule deprived them of the ability to vote. They saw no point in staying. About fifty of the 350 convention delegates walked out of the hall to shouts of *"Abajo los traidores."* Down with the traitors.

Chava watched from the visitors' gallery, surrounded by people who had been his good friends and neighbors. Now they looked at him with undisguised hatred. On the floor below Mario broke the stick on his union flag in two and flung to the floor the red and black emblem he had often waved so proudly. The shouts followed him and Chava as the brothers walked out of the hall: *Muerte a los Bustamantes!* Death to the Bustamantes.

The next day, Doug Adair rose on the convention floor to nominate Rosario Pelayo. Pato knew Pelayo well; she was as loyal as they came and fiercely dedicated to the union. Pato thought she was exactly the sort of person who should be on the board to speak for farmworkers. The nomination was ruled out of order because Pelayo was not present. Instead the convention passed a resolution censuring the delegates who had walked out. For two hours speakers denounced the traitors, following the scripted lines that the board members had used in their campaign. Chavez lashed out at Mario for his parting shot at Oscar Mondragon as the lechugero walked out—"He yelled and said to Oscar: 'See how many contracts you get next year,'" Chavez told the convention—and at Sabino for being too close to the growers. "I would not take a cup of coffee from them," Chavez said, calling the growers scoundrels. He faulted himself for not making sure that Marshall Ganz had properly supervised the paid reps. Ganz had led them astray, Chavez said.[3]

Ganz had been living on the Monterey Peninsula, depressed. He had rebuffed requests from his former students to help them in their last campaign as union leaders. In the end, all the Jedi, those who had money, education, and alternatives, assessed the situation and declined to take the union on, concluding there was no way to succeed. Only the farmworkers, who had nothing to lose and everything to lose, tried to stand up to Cesar Chavez. They could not foresee how brutal the fight would be.

A week after the convention, Mario and Gretchen's son was born.

Sabino

Sabino did not attend the convention. He was not a delegate because he was a target.

David Martinez, the man Sabino had nominated to the executive board two years earlier, had come to see Sabino before the convention. Martinez gave Sabino the same choice the board member had outlined to others: You're with us or against us. There are people out to destroy the union. Tell me who they are, Sabino said. Mario Bustamante and Hermilo Mojica. It was not the irrigator's nature to idolize anyone, except perhaps his father. But Sabino had always spoken of Chavez with great reverence. He had believed Chavez when he said he would not die happy until farmworkers ran the union. But Sabino would never agree that Mario Bustamante and Hermilo Mojica were out to destroy the union. "I asked him how could I follow along with him and attack people who I knew were doing their jobs right," Sabino wrote shortly after the encounter with Martinez. "I told him that it was better to lose my job than to be forced to do his dirty work."[4]

Before the union, a farmworker could not challenge his boss without expecting repercussions. The union had taught Sabino a different way. He could stand up for what was right without fear. The strike had taught him the power of leaders working together.

Those were lessons he would need to draw on many times in the months to come. As soon as the convention ended, the executive board of the union descended on Salinas again. Huerta, Martinez, and Artie Rodriguez began visiting each vegetable company represented by the dissident reps. They urged the workers to oust their leaders, who were out to destroy Chavez. The elected ranch committee presidents served as the paid reps; if workers voted the ranch committee presidents out, they would lose the paid rep posts as well. Some workers were persuaded, but most backed up their ranch committee leaders. Chavez went to Plan B. At a meeting of the Green Valley workers on September 17, Huerta handed Mario a letter, firing him as the paid union representative. He was elected, not appointed, Mario told her. He took the letter from Chavez and ripped it up.[5]

A week later Hermilo Mojica was fired the same way. So was Juan Gutierrez, the paid rep at Cal Coastal. He was accused of having private meetings with Ganz and planning to form another union directed by Ganz.[6] Sabino knew it was only a matter of time. On September 29 David Martinez handed Sabino his letter. Like the others, the letter accused Sabino of failing to properly represent the workers.

Chris gave the union's public response. The convention had prompted Chavez to send a team to Salinas to investigate, Chris said. Based on their findings, Chavez had concluded that certain paid reps were not doing their jobs. The firings had nothing to do with the convention and did not constitute retribution.

Sabino went back to his job as an irrigator at Sun Harvest. But the Chavistas were not done punishing Sabino yet. On October 10 the union filed charges accusing Sabino of dereliction of duty as ranch committee vice president. He had failed, the indictment said, to inform members of a letter from the company ten months earlier explaining changes in the way celery was to be harvested. Sabino's trial took place five days later at Washington Middle School. He was convicted and stripped of his ranch committee post. Sabino appealed. He was not guilty, he said, and the judge and jury had violated his constitutional rights in a half dozen ways. They had failed to give adequate notice, the ranch committee had not voted, and the jurors had not been those specified in the constitution.[7]

After the strike Sabino had sat in judgment during numerous ranch committee trials to discipline strikebreakers. The union lawyers had carefully walked Sabino through the rules, warning that if they were not followed to the letter, the verdicts would be thrown out on appeal. Sabino had learned the rules. He knew his executioners had broken them.

The paid reps found an Oakland lawyer willing to take their case without charging for his time. He advised them to exhaust all internal remedies. They filed complaints appealing their removal. Sabino cited sections of the union constitution that guaranteed workers the right to support candidates of their choice. He said he had never been informed of any problems with his work. He pointed out that Chavez's letter offered no avenue of appeal and violated the constitution. Most important, he said: "I wish to make clear that I, Sabino Lopez, was never the personal representative of Cesar Chavez. I am the representative of the membership of workers at Sun Harvest, because I was elected by those members."[8]

Friends stopped talking to Sabino. You are out to destroy Cesar, they said. Sabino knew he had done nothing wrong. He wanted vindication. He wanted to clear his name. So with great emotional difficulty but no ambivalence, Sabino sued the leader he once revered and the institution that had taught him about power.

Chris

Chris once again assumed his role as defender in chief. The paid reps refused to go quietly. As the fights became more public, Chris found himself in the midst of a new religious firestorm. The charge was anti-Semitism.

The spark came from an unlikely source. Scott Washburn had joined the union a decade earlier, when he was just twenty-two. He had never held another job, except playing piano in a traveling carnival band. His whole family had ended up working for the union—his mother, sister, and two brothers. Washburn had grown up on union lore. He had spent hours driving around with Chavez, listening to the union leader's stories. Highly competitive, Washburn boasted one of the best win-loss records in union elections. In the summer of 1981 he was organizing farmworkers who lived in the canyons of northern San Diego County, burrowed into the hillsides under tarps and in makeshift shacks. The union set up a cooperative kitchen, trucked in potable water, and sent an armored car to cash the workers' checks. Washburn arranged basketball tournaments against the border patrol and hooked up a portable generator so workers could watch boxing matches on TV.

A few days before the union convention, some of Washburn's organizers were called to a meeting with Frank Ortiz; Washburn went along. Ortiz, a board member, was campaigning against the paid reps. He railed against Marshall Ganz and Jerry Cohen and told the group that the Jews were out to take over the union.

An anonymous memo in Spanish, handwritten in the distinctive lettering of one of the board members, laid out the same anti-Semitic arguments to use before and during the convention: The Jews want to take over the union. Ganz and Cohen, and the old legal department. The Jews used our people—Jessica, Eliseo, Gilbert—to control the legal department and the negotiators. They think they are superior to Mexicans.[9]

Washburn watched the vegetable workers walk out of the convention, and he felt sick. The place seemed toxic. He called Jerry and told him about the anti-Semitic comments. Jerry called La Paz. A few days later Ortiz wrote to Chavez: "This letter is to answer your question regarding the rumors alleging that I said some things about Jews at a meeting." Ortiz said he had explained that Ganz and Cohen were undermining the union, inciting the paid reps, and trashing Chavez. "I said, 'too bad these two guys had to be two Jews because our best support all across the country comes from the Jewish people . . . and now we had Marshal [sic] and Jerry working against us; that this was sad that they were Jews."[10]

The letter hardly put the matter to rest: The next complaint came from Monsignor George Higgins. The labor priest ticked off the recent departures of top union leaders, expressed alarm at the allegations of anti-Semitism, and demanded a prompt response. "In my opinion, Cesar, even the slightest compromise on the issue of anti-Semitism would seriously endanger the movement and could conceivably destroy it . . . As I see it, the truth is that the UFW is in serious trouble and that some of this trouble is strictly of its own making."[11]

Chavez passed the Higgins letter to Chris. Chris drafted five versions before Chavez signed off on a response, more than a month later. Chavez dismissed the criticism, declined Higgins's offer of help and chastised him for jumping to conclusions. Higgins immediately identified Chris as the likely ghostwriter.[12]

In October 1981, as the Dodgers met the Yankees in the World Series, Scott Washburn left the union where he had grown up. He had accepted everything else, even the way Chavez had demonized and purged Joe Smith, Washburn's best friend, back in 1976. Washburn had been able to justify a lot in the name of the cause—even lying and beating up scabs. But anti-Semitism crossed the line.

Chris worked to do damage control as the internal dissension became more public. Reporters called. "Anti-Semitism—Denied!" Chris wrote in his notes for a rebuttal to a *Los Angeles Times* reporter. Adopting Chavez's lingo, Chris wrote of the "malignant forces" out to destroy the union.[13] In a rare misstep, Chris told Washburn that the union leaders had been talking and agreed they could count on Washburn not to speak with the press. That infuriated him. Then he heard others insinuating that he had lied about the meeting with Ortiz. Washburn talked to the *New York Times*. He figured he could either be afraid the rest of his life, or take Chavez on.

The fault lines deepened. Several former union leaders had found work with California Rural Legal Assistance. Now Chavez made his displeasure with the agency clear. His son Paul led pickets at the CRLA office where Chava Bustamante worked. Jessica Govea discovered her contract was not renewed. Gilbert Padilla, also on contract, had thought he was in line for a promotion. Instead he was terminated. Padilla wrote to Chris, the man who had first found a way to pay Padilla to work for Chavez in 1963, two years before the Delano grape strike began:

> When I left, I left peacefully, however I have been bad mouthed and my name has been smeared . . . Executive board members, Dolores and Cesar have bad mouthed me, and now Cesar wants to decide whether I and my family should eat and decide where I should work. I ask you Chris, do you as a Christian man evaluate these actions on the part of the UFW leadership as an action that is truly non-violent? I want it understood that I am not asking you or Cesar or the UFW for a FUCKING thing. I am just saying to you, DON'T FUCK with me or my livelihood.[14]

Chris did not respond. There was really nothing to say, even for one so skilled in the art of salesmanship. The atmosphere at La Paz was the same us-versus-them, good-versus-evil culture that had characterized the union in its early glory days. Except the evil was not the growers, or the Teamsters. The enemies were former friends.

Ellen

The workers who had applauded Ellen when she passed the bar now faced her in federal court. On January 29, 1982, nine farmworkers sued Cesar Chavez, charging he had illegally removed them from leadership positions to which they were elected by their peers. The job of defending the union fell to Ellen.

In just two years Ellen had become the most experienced lawyer in La Paz. Of the six new attorneys Chavez had proudly introduced at the 1979 convention, only one remained. The union was trying with little success to recruit more lawyers. Solicitation letters touted the accomplishments of the legal department, pointing to landmark cases won by Jerry and the Salinas lawyers who were long gone. Three years after Chavez had threatened to resign over the issue and demanded lawyers embrace the volunteer lifestyle at La Paz, most of the attorneys earned more than twice what Sandy had made. The legal department was settled in new quarters in the refurbished North Unit. The rent was double what Jerry had paid in Salinas. But that was not a problem, the head of the department pointed out: The money went to one of the union's affiliated nonprofit corporations.[15]

Ellen felt uncomfortable taking on the paid reps, but the union was her client. The only alternative was to leave. She swallowed her qualms. Like Chris, she convinced herself that the workers had been manipulated by Marshall Ganz, the true villain. Just as the assumption had been at the graduation ceremony that someone had put the workers up to saying "the union is not Cesar Chavez," the union leaders now blamed Ganz for the actions of the workers. He had conspired with them to destroy the union. The workers could not possibly have accomplished this on their own.

"The UFW has reason to believe that former UFW staff persons were directing the actions of the plaintiffs while they were being paid representatives," Ellen wrote in an affidavit. "One of the reasons plaintiffs were removed is because the President of the union believed that the plaintiffs were unwilling to follow the policies of the union leadership and were instead taking directions from the non-UFW members, to the detriment of the union and the members. It is believed that these same persons have been behind the present lawsuit."[16]

Ellen had also learned from Jerry how to discourage hostile litigation through legal harassment: The union served the workers with 4,400 interrogatories and 163 requests to produce documents.[17]

Three thousand miles away, the woman who had established protocols for the election of the paid reps was working on an antinuclear campaign. Ruth Shy had stuck it out in La Paz long after many of her friends left. She was close to Jessica Govea and knew how painful her parting had been. Still, Shy had felt she could literally see the transformation in workers. To be part of that meant so much to her that she could overlook the purges and the pain. She had set up the system for electing the paid reps, written and distributed the rules manual, and stayed for the conference to work through union policies with the newly elected reps. Then she had written Chavez and asked for a six-month leave.[18] She had planned to return in the beginning of 1981. By then she had second thoughts. She stayed in New York and adopted a new cause.

A year later the paid reps filed suit, and Shy received calls from lawyers on both sides. She told Ellen and the paid reps' lawyer the same thing: She would testify if subpoenaed. She would not discuss her testimony in advance. When the trial began on October 25, 1982, Margaret Ruth Shy was the first witness. She sat in the waiting area, burying herself in a magazine to avoid glowering stares. Shy was cross-examined by the woman she had nurtured and convinced to stay with the union a decade earlier in Christine Jorgensen's house in Northridge. Ellen was so nervous that she later blocked out the interrogation entirely.

Chavez testified he had never agreed that the paid reps should be elected and did not even realize elections had taken place for some time. Shown a ballot, he said he had no idea where it came from. "I have never had any question whatsoever about whether the paid rep position is an appointed or an elected position," he said in his sworn affidavit. "After the contracts were signed, I began appointing people to fill the positions, pursuant to my authority under the union constitution."[19]

U.S. District Judge William Ingram's ruling on November 18, 1982, unequivocally rejected that version of events. "I conclude they were elected," he wrote about the paid reps. "There is no evidence, contemporary with the events, that supports the contention that they were appointed." The judge noted that Chavez was a busy man keeping track of many things, excusing him for testimony that could have constituted perjury.

The judge credited Shy. She testified that she had made election packets with Chavez's understanding and approval and kept him apprised of results after each election. Court exhibits included memos from Ganz announcing election results, copied to Chavez. The paid reps, the judge wrote, had "every reason to believe that they are elective officials; they were led to believe that by their union leadership and by the duly published processes of election."[20]

The judge ruled only on the first question: Were the paid reps elected? Now the case moved to the next phase: Did Chavez have a right to remove them? The union took a new line of attack. Ellen said she would prove that the nine workers were fired for "incompetence and insubordination" in their jobs as union representatives.[21]

"The union has really taken a beating . . . and we've lost a lot of supporters because people are believing things that aren't true," Ellen said in a newspaper interview. A month later, speaking with a *New York Times* reporter, Ellen called the paid reps " a threat to the survival of the union."[22]

Mario

The threat to the survival of the UFW lived in a trailer in Gilroy and made ends meet with odd jobs in factories and canneries, shut out of working in the fields he loved.

Mario had tried to keep working as a lechugero at Green Valley after he was fired as paid rep. When he walked onto the bus each morning to go to the fields, workers broke into rival chants and fought. After a few weeks, Mario gave up. He looked for work, but no one would hire the lechugero who had once worked in the fastest crews. Mario could not get a dispatch from the union, and growers were not about to hire a well-known union agitator. Mario took jobs where he could find them, in a cannery for a few months and then in a factory that made video toys. He badly missed the fields.

Mario, Gretchen, and their son Rafael had moved into a friend's trailer in Gilroy and then bought their own. Gretchen had worked for the union for another month after Rafa was born. She had a few contract negotiations she wanted to finish up. Then Paul Chavez showed up one day to pick up the ancient white Valiant, and Gretchen was done.

As he watched Gretchen and the other volunteers struggle to negotiate and administer contracts in the union's haphazard structure, Mario had come to believe the union needed paid, professional staff. The difficulties with the medical plan illustrated the problem of depending on an often-changing cast of volunteers. "We felt that the needs of the workers would be best met by an efficient and carefully run organization rather than by a family type structure," he said in a declaration. "It appears that another one of the drawbacks in the family structure is its intolerance of different opinions. The union has always been run according to the views of the President, Cesar Chavez. It became unable to deal with dissenting opinions. There can be no doubt that the other Plaintiffs and I were removed because Cesar perceived us to pose some kind of threat to his stronghold on the UFW, not because we failed to do our jobs."[23]

Mario kept fighting for *la causa* in every forum he could find. He urged workers to rescind the one day's pay that they contributed to the union's political fund. Dolores Huerta, the union's lobbyist, was fighting against the workers instead of for them, Mario said. He wanted his money back. He filed a complaint with the state labor board. He filed internal charges against the union officers, though he viewed the proceedings as no more than a joke. Mario accused the union leaders of spending members' money on the campaign against the paid reps. At first the union said board members "decided to use their own money for re-election campaign purposes. That money was pooled, and the Union was reimbursed for all expenses which were incurred in the campaign."[24] Then the story changed. The union produced statements showing a donor had deposited $10,000 in a campaign account and the union had been reimbursed for all costs from that fund. Mario demanded to see the canceled checks. The largest check repaid the fund for $1,698. It was dated September 3, 1981, but was not deposited until January 24, 1982—after Mario had filed a complaint.[25]

Shortly after they won the first round in federal court, the paid reps circulated a flyer telling farmworkers that Chavez had intended to use union money—their dues—in his campaign. "Here is the proof that through the court we forced Cesar to pay back the money he had misused," read the text above copies of the checks.[26] Chavez sued for libel and slander, seeking $25 million in damages from the nine farmworkers.

A few weeks before Christmas 1982 the paid reps began to fast outside the Salinas UFW office where they once worked, to protest the libel suit and draw attention to their cause. "We're only doing what Cesar taught us," Mario said during the eight-day fast. "To fight for justice."[27]

CHAPTER 28

A Dream Deferred

January 1983

Sabino

Sabino's faith had been destroyed, but the irrigator had yet to hit bottom.

Despite the initial vindication in court, the paid reps faced a lonely, up-hill fight. They held backyard barbecues and raffled off a television set to raise money for copying costs and depositions. Sabino knew the union's legal might and resources. They were farmworkers, taking on a world-famous icon.

Sabino took small victories where he could find them. He had known without question that the union violated its own rules when he was re-moved as vice president of the ranch committee. The mistakes were so egregious that he won reinstatement.[1] He continued working as an irriga-tor. When the Sun Harvest contract expired, Sabino sat on the negotiating committee, as he had each time before. None of the lawyers or negotiators who had bargained for the union in the past remained. Chavez led con-tract negotiations himself. Sabino attended meetings proudly. He ignored grumbling about the traitor. When people protested that a worker suing the union should not be at the bargaining table, Chavez shrugged. The paid reps will run out of money, he said.[2]

The company ran out of money first. At the end of 1983 Sun Harvest shut down. Company officials said the financial problems stemmed from $40 million in losses suffered during the strike.

Sabino looked for work, confident in his skill as an irrigator. He found a vegetable grower south of Salinas that needed irrigators and thought he was set. Then the manager recognized Sabino's name. One of the trouble-makers. No troublemakers hired here. Like Mario, Sabino discovered that he was cursed by both sides. At thirty-five, Sabino realized he could no longer work at the only job he knew. He had embraced the union as a way to get ahead, only to end up farther behind. Five children, no prospect of a job in the fields, and no other marketable skills.

He felt emotionally shattered, then physically ill. He went to a doctor and was taken aback by the diagnosis of depression. Finally, Sabino de-cided to learn English so he could find some other job. He remembered how Chavez had promised the paid reps English lessons, so they could ne-gotiate contracts themselves. Only a few years earlier, but another lifetime.

It turned out Sabino had skills he had not recognized. He had learned to organize. Lydia Villarreal had worked for the union in 1977 and then the following summer, while she was in law school. She ran the migrant outreach program at CRLA and had an opening for a community worker. Sabino aced the interview. The UFW complained when he was hired and threatened to picket his first day of work. Villarreal protected Sabino, eventually becoming a target of the union's ire herself.

Sabino was in court along with the other paid reps on November 30, 1984, to hear Judge William Ingram's ruling in the second phase of the suit. Once again Ingram was decisive:

> Although the court is hesitant to involve itself in intra-union dis-putes . . . the magnitude of the issues involved justifies such inter-vention. As to the facts, this court has ruled that plaintiffs were elected officials in its order dated November 16, 1982, and there is no dispute that plaintiffs were not granted a hearing nor subject to a recall election before they were terminated . . . The court finds that defendant Chavez's interpretation was not reasonable. Summary removal of elected union officials is not warranted un-der any reading of the constitution.[3]

Sabino felt triumphant. He knew the court case would drag on, its ulti-mate resolution and remedy becoming more moot every day. He had lost his job and his faith and hit the lowest point in his life. But he had stood up for what he believed in. The workers had proved to the world that they were right. Sabino had thought of the union as his second family—no matter how bad the discord, feuds, or fights, family is family. In the end, he discovered that was not true. Sabino was left wondering how all the grand hopes crumbled so fast.

Chris

Chris sank deep into the comfort of La Paz, satisfied with the routines, happy to be near Chavez, engrossed with the minutiae of his new administrative life. Like the rest of the union, Chris focused less and less on farmworkers, as he worked and lived in the bucolic retreat in the Tehachapi Mountains.

If he had had little independence from Chavez before, he now had almost none. That suited him fine; he did not have to struggle with conflicting loyalties. He worked on office projects and community-life tasks. Sometimes he chafed at the endless meetings, which functioned as an opportunity for Chavez to think out loud, rather than as a way to make decisions. Still, Chris felt liberated, no longer responsible for religious outreach or the public face of the union, except in crises. On a survey that asked the staff to list "What I do now" versus "What I would like to do," Chris wrote simply: "I like what I am doing now."[4]

He enjoyed the intellectual pursuits, though no enthusiasm lasted very long. Chris spent months reading Peter Drucker's theory of management and participating in mandatory group discussions; then Chavez dropped the study. He seemed to become bored with endeavors that did not yield quick results. Chris attended a brainstorming retreat that resulted in a one-word mission statement: "Our mission is food," Chavez wrote triumphantly.[5] Bemused, Chris wondered about the relevance but shrugged off any concern. Chavez knew best.

Chris's portfolio kept expanding. He took over the financial-management department. The union's finances became more complicated as Chavez spun off related nonprofit corporations that sought state and federal funds to build housing, run health clinics, start a radio station, and operate training programs. Next, Chavez assigned Chris to oversee acquisition of a new computer system. Chavez wanted to launch a direct mail boycott and fundraising campaign that would rely on computer-generated lists and letters. Chris obligingly dedicated himself to study the emergent industry of mainframe computers. Chris spent more than a year evaluating proposals and then overseeing installation of the new Sperry system.

The number of union contracts dwindled steadily, along with income.

Union dues had peaked in 1982 at $2.99 million.[6] Then the vegetable con-
tracts, the last union bastion, began to disappear. The complicated relationships between growers and shippers enabled companies still covered
by union contracts to shift more and more of their jobs out of the bargaining unit.

Lionel Steinberg, the first grape grower to sign a UFW contract, was the
last one left. He stayed with the union at the urging of his son, who put up
with the inept administration because he believed in the principle. In 1984,
Billy Steinberg had fallen in love and composed a song while driving his
red pickup truck around the vineyards. "Like a Virgin" was recorded by
Madonna at the end of the year and became one of the top hits of all time.
Billy Steinberg became a platinum-selling songwriter and finally left the
fields.

Around the same time, Chavez launched his new direct mail boycott. Instead of targeting a specific grower, he aimed at the state Agricultural Labor
Relations Board. Chavez cited poor enforcement and grower-biased rulings
and blamed Republican Governor George Deukmejian for the union's
losses in the fields. The law had proved a pyrrhic victory, Chavez argued,
because Republicans could gut enforcement. The union increasingly tried
to wield influence in Sacramento through the traditional route that Chavez
had once eschewed: money. In 1982 the union contributed more than

*Chris embraces Chavez as the two men leave a morning mass at La Paz in
August 1986.*

$780,000 to political committees, the biggest chunk to Assembly Speaker Willie Brown.[7]

From his home on the Monterey Peninsula, Jerry followed Chavez's attacks on the law. The attorney decided to speak up. He penned an op-ed piece in the *Los Angeles Times* challenging the union's defeatist line. "Junk mail doesn't organize people; people organize people," Jerry wrote, criticizing Chavez for using Republicans as scapegoats and relying on a direct mail boycott instead of old-fashioned organizing.[8]

Chris was assigned to respond. The minister had defended Jerry during the internal fights, when others condemned him as a co-conspirator in the Marshall Ganz cabal. Chris wrote Jerry a reproachful note:

> I have always assumed that you had more class than that, i.e. making "profound" judgments in public about the union (or any other organization) from a far-away place and a far-away perspective . . . Suppose you are dead right on everything you said, what is the point? What do you accomplish? Ego satisfaction? Visibility? Revenge? None of that makes any sense to me. It looks to me like the cynics here have been right and I have been wrong all along (another naïve minister bites the dust).

Jerry scrawled grades across the top of Chris's letter before mailing it back: C- for content, F for "Christian" charity.[9]

Chris wrote once more: "I guess I was not too clear. I have been in your corner in some nasty arguments over the last few years—I thought I was dealing with paranoia, nurtured by old personal hostilities. Needless to say, your article shook my foundations. Your non-response seems, in fact, to be a clear response—but not the one I was hoping for. Chris.

"PS Penmanship (yours)—F-"[10]

Ellen

Like Chris, Ellen embraced the camaraderie of La Paz, a community so close that when she traveled for work, a friend with babies the same age nursed Ellen's infant son. For a while Ellen also welcomed the frenetic pace and last-minute legal escapades. Gradually, the exhilaration faded into weariness.

Ellen lived with her son, the child of another union lawyer who had since moved to Sacramento. The day she gave birth, she had spent the morning on her hands and knees staining desks for the legal department office. She had moved from trailer-sitting to a room in the hospital to house-sitting for the Padillas to a trailer of her own to a tiny apartment in a triplex. Every place she went, Ellen pasted tiles on the floor and hung homemade curtains in the windows.

The priorities seemed to shift as often as she moved. One day she was helping on a libel suit in Marin County when she suddenly had to appeal a $100,000 judgment against the union from a car accident related to a picket line. Ellen typed furiously, then realized she could not possibly finish and drive to the courthouse ninety miles away in time to meet the deadline. A friend drove while Ellen finished typing on her lap. She signed the appeal on the hood of the car and rushed into the courthouse with five minutes to spare. That became the story of her life: celebrating the closest call yet each time she just squeaked by. After a few years the adrenaline rush from the shared sense of urgency wore thin. Ellen grew tired of the constant crisis mode and frustrated with Chavez's disinclination to see anything through, in play as well as work. The land she had helped clear for the orchard was still barren. The boulders she had enjoyed moving three years earlier still stood helter-skelter along the entrance road to La Paz, testament to another enthusiasm abandoned.

The stories she heard from friends about the direct mail boycott deepened Ellen's doubts. The volunteers still hung around supermarket parking lots, but now they clandestinely wrote down license plates of shoppers so the union could run the plates and send letters urging consumers to boycott that particular store. A far cry from the boycott that had drawn Ellen into the union. The new boycott slogan was *"Como siempre"* (As always). Ellen thought nothing could be further from the truth.

The litigation against the paid reps dragged on, increasingly pointless. In 1983 the union had amended its constitution to specify that paid reps were appointed. The contracts had expired at most of the vegetable companies; some were no longer in business. The paid reps had been driven out of the fields long ago. The union pursued its libel and slander suit, though there would be no money to collect if the UFW prevailed. Ellen happily handed off both cases to another lawyer.

Ellen stayed long past when she wanted to leave in order to finish a complex case that stemmed from the 1979 strike. All but one of the suits that growers brought against the union for strike-related damages had been dismissed or settled. Only the Maggio suit remained. The company's evidence of pervasive violence included videotapes, photographs, and numerous affidavits, some from former strikers. The facts were not really in dispute; the legal question revolved around the union's liability. The company argued that such widespread violence could not have taken place without being sanctioned, if not directed, by union leaders. Ellen knew it was a tough case. Chavez wanted to fight. The union rejected a settlement offer early on, which would have cost less in the end than the copying and filing costs for the multiyear litigation.

Ellen confided in Chris that she planned to leave as soon as the Maggio case was over. He sent her a note that told her to follow her heart. Ten years earlier he would have pulled out all the stops to convince her to stay. But the argument became harder and harder to make.

In early 1987 the judge found the union liable for $1.7 million in damages at the Maggio ranch. Ellen resigned a few weeks later. She parted on good terms, or as good terms as anyone could leave the union. She said her goodbyes at an outdoor potluck party at La Paz on a Saturday afternoon. Chris circulated a UFW flag that everyone signed. Ellen looked forward to relocating to Sacramento, where she could get radio reception in her car. She left La Paz with relief that she could finally move on, and deep fondness for the people she left behind.

Chris

The first small, nagging doubts that Chris allowed in began with the gala celebration for the twenty-fifth anniversary of the union, an elaborately choreographed tribute to the movement's founder, tightly controlled by the founder himself.

At the beginning of 1987 Chris did little else than prepare for Chavez's sixtieth birthday party. The union had adopted Founder's Day as an official holiday a decade earlier, but March 31 had never been the center of attention in this big a way. Chavez obsessed over every detail. He and Chris argued frequently. Recognition had never meant that much to Chavez during the years of the union's greatest fights and triumphs. Chris found Chavez's intensity about the event oddly self-important and a little unsettling. Chris had trouble summoning enthusiasm for the valedictory tribute.

There was little to celebrate. In the five years preceding the twenty-fifth-anniversary bash, the union had won elections or fought off decertification attempts at thirty-two ranches—and lost at thirty-nine.[11]

After Founder's Day, Chavez focused on pesticides. Posters featured a skull-like cluster of fruit with the slogan "The Wrath of Grapes." Chris was skeptical. He thought union supporters viewed contracts, not pesticide bans, as the real goal. The union produced a video about the dangers of pesticides. Chris met with Chavez in the fall of 1987, and the union president outlined the agenda: For three months Chris was to supervise distribution of thousands of videos, track the usage, and send follow-up letters. When the long-distance results were meager, Chavez dispatched Chris to various cities to hawk the movie and organize fund-raisers. Chris found the remnants of his old boycott network friendly, but puzzled.

In July 1988, Chavez began a fast to draw attention to the pesticide campaign. The Fast for Life turned out to be his longest—thirty-six days—and least successful. Chris helped stage-manage the event. He kept waiting for the response. The growers never called. They dismissed the fast as a publicity stunt undertaken because the boycott had failed. They said their grapes were safe. They seemed confident consumers thought so too. Chris wondered what Chavez would do next, after the drama of a thirty-six-day fast produced just deafening silence.

Shortly after the fast Dolores Huerta and Oscar Mondragon came to see Chris. They asked him to run for secretary-treasurer. Chris had always been reluctant to take a spot on the board, but the old reasons no longer seemed valid. He knew this was what Chavez wanted. At a one-day convention in Delano in October, Chris was elected to the second-highest-ranking position on the executive board. By prior arrangement with Chavez, Chris then took November and December off. He was weary and headed to Wrightwood, where the Hartmires had a small cabin in the San Gabriel Mountains, eighty miles northeast of Los Angeles.

While Chris was on vacation, an odd tale unfolded in the San Joaquin Valley. Bryce Basey, an independent accountant in Bakersfield who had worked for the union several years earlier, was going through a divorce. Prosecutors were tipped that Basey had stolen money from the farmworkers. Investigators determined that he had siphoned off eleven checks worth $417,163, most of which should have gone to one of union's housing projects in Fresno. Basey had used $130,000 to pay a delinquent tax bill for the union and transferred the rest into accounts for his personal use.[12] The thefts had occurred almost three years earlier.

Chris had been supervising financial management then, and he had hired Basey. As soon as Chris heard about the allegations, he called Chavez. Chris got through only to various aides. He returned to La Paz in January and immediately tried to talk with Chavez about Basey. The union president was friendly but busy, preparing for a week-long executive board meeting. He told Chris they would talk after the meeting.

Chavez devoted the first two days of the January board meeting to the dozen affiliated corporations that he had created in recent years—health and pension funds, a radio station, a lobbying foundation, a training institute, and the housing corporations. On Thursday, January 12, 1989, the executive board began discussing the Bryce Basey affair. An outside auditor summarized the facts. Suddenly, Chris found every eye in the room focused on him. Chavez led the charge. One by one, the union leaders turned on the man whose loyalty Chavez had so often extolled, the one person who had never asked for anything in return. The theft was a major public relations problem. Chavez had told Chris to fire Basey. Why had Chris defied Chavez? Did the minister not trust his leader? Did Chris have his own agenda? Bryce hadn't done this alone, Chavez said; he must have had help.

Chris had been the Game master. He knew how this was done. Each person had his part, the roles rehearsed in advance. Chris looked at Artie Rodriguez, cold as a block of ice. I preached at your wedding, Chris thought. He had to get out of that room. He went for a walk.[13]

Chavez appointed a committee to recommend what do about Chris. When Chris returned after lunch, the committee outlined options. Chris was the secretary-treasurer of the union. By force of habit, he kept taking notes:

> Question of my resignation as Sec-Treas
> Continue LOA—during it Cesar ask next constitutional officer to act as Sec-Treas
> If no wrongdoing—Chris resumes his duties
> If Bryce is guilty, Chris will tender his resignation (may not be accepted)
> If Bryce is guilty, then I take responsibility w/the public[14]

Then he stopped writing. Somehow, he got out of that room. Somehow, he stayed at La Paz for two more days, because he had promised to officiate at a retirement party. He wandered around the community he had once loved, waiting in vain for someone to say, "It's okay, we know you didn't steal any money. This is just a public relations problem." Somehow, Chris survived the party, and somehow he drove back to the cabin in Wrightwood. Chris soon realized he was on the outside, and he would never be back in. "It is kind of a Greek tragedy," he wrote in his diary. "Did I bring it on myself?"[15]

He called La Paz to set up an appointment with Chavez, and at seven thirty A.M. on February 15, 1989, Chris went to deliver his resignation letter. He expected a handshake and farewell. He was surprised to find Dolores Huerta at the meeting. She was there to bear witness. The abrupt departure of a union leader with a devoted following had to be justified as a betrayal. Chavez could not take a chance that Chris would speak ill of the union, though the union president should have known the minister better than that.

So as a parting gift, Chavez icily berated Chris. Chavez had seen this coming for a long time. Chris had been slowly but surely becoming disloyal. Chavez had been saying this to Huerta for months. Chris was becoming the most despicable noun in Huerta's vocabulary: Another Marshall. A traitor. Chris told Chavez he would never do anything to hurt the union. You've already done enough, Chavez replied.[16]

Chris didn't think till later about all the things he could have said, should have said. Why did you make me secretary-treasurer if you thought I had become disloyal? That's sort of a sensitive position for an asshole. At that moment all he wanted to do was escape the room, and the unreality.

He went back to La Paz once more with Pudge to clean out their trailer and pack up. Pudge needed to return a television stand to L.L. Bean and left the package with the guard at the gate for postal pickup. A staff member apologetically opened the box, following orders to make sure the Hartmires were not smuggling out files. When Chris went to Tehachapi to run errands, he kept noticing a farmworker he had met in Salinas. Chris realized he was being tailed.

Chris spent months in therapy, piecing back his identity. Once his counselor asked Chris to confront Chavez in an imaginary conversation, acting out both parts. You argue Chavez's position better than your own! the therapist exclaimed. Chris had an easy explanation. I've been doing that for twenty-five years, he said.[17]

Chris and Pudge sent out their annual Christmas letter a little early in 1989, closer to Thanksgiving. It seemed the easiest way to pass on the new address and reassure their friends. They had moved to Sacramento, where Chris worked at a homeless shelter run by his old friend LeRoy Chatfield.

"This has been a year of major change for us," Chris wrote. "After 27 years with the Migrant Ministry, The National Farm Worker Ministry and the UFW this was not an easy change and 1989 has not been a normal or a tranquil year. But here we are and here we plan to stay . . . and as we approach Advent we are tired but in good spirits and hopeful about the future."

Eliseo was running a union local in San Diego for the Service Employees International Union. He had called as soon as he heard that Chris had been cast out. Chris would always be grateful for that gesture. He had learned that when those you thought your closest friends turn against you, you find out who your friends really are, and you remember every one. On the bottom of the mimeographed Christmas letter to Eliseo, Chris added a short personal note.

"Thanks for your call, Eliseo, and your concern. It has not been an easy year but we are on our feet and doing well. We like Sacto! Do you ever get here? Please call if you do. Merry Christmas!"

Epilogue

They saw each other mostly at funerals.

When Fred Ross died in 1992, his son asked Chavez to deliver the eulogy and Jerry to officiate at the service in San Francisco. Chavez never responded. Jerry put him down on the program anyway. There was no way Cesar Chavez would not show up at the funeral of his mentor.

Chavez was hoarse and delivered a long, rambling speech. Gilbert Padilla walked out in the middle when Chavez credited the people who helped him start the union and omitted Padilla. Chris stayed in the back, careful to avoid any chance encounter with Chavez. Gretchen sat with Mario and their three children, the youngest almost five. Gretchen had worked for Ross in the mid-1980s, helping compile his papers, and Mario still remembered vividly how Ross had mapped out the 1970 vegetable strike.

After the service, Ellen approached Mario and pulled him aside. She had last faced him in a San Jose courtroom. She wanted to apologize. Ellen told Mario she had been wrong, and she asked his forgiveness. He was startled, and deeply appreciative that she had the wisdom to rethink her actions and the courage to apologize.

Chris was working on forgiveness too. In the spring of 1993 he went to a silent retreat at a Trappist monastery. "I started to pray for Cesar and the UFW," he wrote in a diary. "It is hard to be sincere but I am working at it. I know it is going to help." Chris read books that said you must confront the person you need to forgive. On March 14 Chris drafted but did not mail a letter to Chavez: "You decided to rip me away from a community I love and a cause to which I had given most of my adult life. It is still hard to believe that you did what you did—turning your back on 27 years of loyalty and collaboration to throw me out on the street . . . I have hated you for this, Cesar—both for what you did and for the way you did it. But time has past! [*sic*] I am older and am now a grandfather and have found a new life in Sacto."[1]

Forty days later, Cesar Chavez died in his sleep in Arizona, where he was testifying in a trial. His father had lived to be one hundred, and Chavez was only sixty-six. The grief was compounded by shock that he had died so young. Tens of thousands of people converged on Delano from around the world. Almost everyone came back, no matter the circumstances under which they had left. The funeral became a giant reunion, a celebration of all they had accomplished together, and a tribute to the charismatic leader who had changed their lives.

Eliseo walked through the streets of his hometown, where he had once picked grapes and where his sister still worked in the fields. The mourners marched across the west side of Delano out to Forty Acres. Eliseo asked everyone he knew to sign the flag that he carried. He wanted to save it for his daughter, who was twelve. Dorothy went to the funeral alone. She and Eliseo had separated. She was overwhelmed by the mass of people, the sheer humanity, the sadness.

Jerry's first impulse was to return to the Stardust Motel, to revisit the scene where twenty-three years earlier he and Chavez had negotiated the first grape contracts with John Giumarra. Jerry always carried the memory of that heady night, Chavez's remarkable triumph over an industry that had once seemed all-powerful. Sandy and the Dazzler drove together to Delano for the funeral, from the Bay Area, where they both worked as labor lawyers. They greeted friends they had not seen in years and shared only good memories. Along the march to Forty Acres, they passed children in a schoolyard, pressed against a fence where they had hung a sign that simply thanked Cesar.

Chris had returned a few days earlier to La Paz, amid many tears, invited by the family to help prepare for the funeral. He was happy to be involved, though it felt odd to be back. He sat next to Richard Chavez during the afternoon funeral mass, then talked till well past dark with dozens of old friends, watching as his children and grandchildren played, smiling as Ellen bounced happily from friend to friend. He kept a

Crowds line up for miles to follow Chavez's casket through the streets of Delano. (Scott Anger)

diary to chronicle the historic week: "It was a miraculous, peaceful closure for me."[2]

On the program for the funeral service was one of Chavez's most famous quotes, one that Chris had helped write during the 1968 fast: "The strongest act of manliness is to sacrifice ourselves for others in a totally non-violent struggle for justice. To be a man is to suffer for others. God help me to be a man." But the quote the mourners read substituted "humanity" for "manliness" and concluded: "To be human is to suffer for others. God help me to be human." Political correctness trumped truth. Those who inherited his union had learned from Chavez how to rewrite history to suit their needs.

Artie Rodriguez, Chavez's son-in-law, became the union's second president. He took over a family operation and a network of interlocking nonprofit organizations, most run by Chavez's son Paul.

When Jessica Govea died in 2005, the veterans and the ghosts gathered once more. The Salinas room filled with the legacy of the farm worker movement, a generation of activists who had come of age in the union. Most had trouble even imagining what their lives would have been like if not for the time they had spent together. They had long joked that the union was like the Hotel California in the Eagles song: You can check out any time you want, but you can never leave.

Their own transformation contrasted sharply with the lives of those working the fields that the organizers had once known so intimately. As they exchanged hugs at the National Steinbeck Center, the UFW had no contracts in the table grape vineyards or the lettuce fields. A handful of pacts in California covered barely five thousand workers. The landmark state labor law languished, almost unused. In the previous five years the union had won eight elections, lost three, and been decertified in three more.[3] A new generation of workers toiled in the fields, most without legal papers. Many were indigenous Mexicans who arrived not even speaking Spanish. They earned minimum wage, lacked health care, and desperately needed the kind of help the union once offered.

In lieu of organizing, the UFW of the twenty-first century had mastered the art of cashing in on Latino political power. The union leaders excelled at parlaying the memory of Cesar Chavez into millions of dollars in public and private donations. They redefined their mission as helping Latinos and signed up random workers who approached the UFW—a handful of taxicab drivers in Bakersfield, assemblers in San Jose who built prefab classrooms, parish workers in Texas. To include those workers and broaden the jurisdiction, the union excised the eloquent preamble to the constitution that Chavez had read aloud at the first convention in 1973: ". . . just as work on the land is arduous, so is the task of building a Union. We pledge to struggle as long as it takes to reach our goals."

The movement trademarked the slogan "Sí se puede," yes, it can be done, even as it adopted the posture that the state law did not work and organizing was all but impossible. They still had the eagle, as Rodriguez liked to point out, and they marketed that bird any way they could—on T-shirts, hats, and high-priced wine purchased by Latino professionals and Democratic politicians eager to express solidarity. Chavez's grave and former office at La Paz were transformed into a shrine and visitors center, financed with millions of dollars in state grants and built largely with nonunion labor.[4] In the fields, the only Cesar Chavez most farmworkers recognized was a famous Mexican boxer.

There was one final memorial for Jessica, in the Imperial Valley where she had done the work of which she was most proud. On Labor Day weekend in 2005 Gretchen and Mario hosted a commemoration in the border community that had once been Jessica's home. On Friday night Mario cooked *carne asada* outside their house. Filemon the donkey brayed. The smell of the marinated meat on the grill mingled with the fumes of spray paint as Rosario Pelayo and her old team from Calexico stenciled the UFW eagle on rectangular pieces of cloth. The next morning cars took off in a caravan, old UFW style, flags fluttering out the windows. As the caravan drove toward El Hoyo, the flags slowly unraveled in the wind.

There had been no contracts in the Imperial Valley for years. The building in the middle of El Hoyo that was once the vibrant union office sat shuttered, the colorful murals of heroic workers still clear on the inside walls. Three decades earlier a Mexican drum and bugle corps had played as the union flag rose over the office and the workers proudly took over El Hoyo. Now the lot alongside the border had reverted to its prior use: a shape-up center. In the predawn hours during the winter harvest, the lot filled each morning with hundreds of workers looking for jobs. The lucky ones boarded buses to the fields, powerless before the labor contractors whose existence was the reason the union formed. For now, the Third Way had disappeared. The options for a farmworker once more were stark and simple: to be the exploiter or the exploited.

Those who once dedicated their lives to Cesar Chavez's crusade now wince when they drive past farmworkers, hunched over rows of vegetables or trimming grapevines in the bitter cold. Once so certain they could change that world, the UFW alumni rue their failure. They applaud each other's individual accomplishments, but lament the lost opportunity to collectively achieve even more. The memories still cause pain.

But without hesitation, they would do it all over again.

As bleak as his legacy in the fields, Cesar Chavez left behind a generation imbued with the confidence they could make a difference and schooled in the ways to accomplish change. People touched by the farm workers movement during those exhilarating times, even briefly, found their lives irrevocably changed.

Shelly Spiegel, fired after one year as director of the Huelga School in Delano, married the union mechanic she had met that year (who became a lawyer) and dedicated her career to advancing bilingual education. Marion Moses became a doctor and established a pesticide education center. Kathy Fagan, who learned as a college freshman to set up picket lines for Eliseo in Chicago, specialized in occupational medicine and worked to combat environmental health problems in Ohio. Doug Adair became a date farmer in Thermal, near the old Steinberg vineyards where he once picked grapes. The organic dates from Pato's Dream Date Gardens proudly bear the union label.

The generation of activists who grew up in the UFW went their separate directions, but their paths often intersect as they build on lessons they learned together. Scott Washburn became Arizona state director for the Service Employees International Union, working for Eliseo. Washburn still organizes elections based on the four principles he learned in the UFW. In 2008 he led a successful drive to unionize Arizona state employees. Marshall Ganz returned to Harvard, wrote his Ph.D. dissertation about the early successes of the UFW, and became a lecturer at the Kennedy School. In 2008 he ran "Camp Obamas" around the country and helped build a grassroots organization during the presidential campaign. One of his students at Camp Obama was Shelly Spiegel's son.

Jessica Govea taught organizing at Rutgers and Cornell and spent the last part of her life passing the lessons of *la causa* on to a new generation of immigrants in garment factories and health care facilities. "I felt like I could do anything after being with her. And that is her legacy," Jessica's nephew, Juan Antonio Govea, said at her memorial. "Her legacy is that of empowerment."

UFW alumni found homes in the labor movement across the country. Chava Bustamante became a union leader after all. He spent nineteen years organizing low-wage workers in northern California, mostly janitors, and rose to deputy of an SEIU local. In 2007 he went to work for a labor-backed immigrants' rights organization, focusing on voter registration drives and political participation. Chava looks back on his years with the UFW as a voyage that gave him both a purpose in life and an opportunity to channel his passion for justice. Those twin forces have kept him going ever since.

Most of the attorneys who worked for Jerry in the Salinas office continued to practice labor law. Tom Dalzell went to work for the International Brotherhood of Electrical Workers Local 1245 soon after leaving the UFW. In 2007 he was elected to run the local in northern California as its business manager. He wrote a fictional account of his time in the UFW and researched slang in order to make his own character sound more clever than Jerry's alter ego. The novel remains a work in progress, but Dalzell became an expert on slang and published seven dictionaries.

Ellen Eggers worked as counsel to a public employees' union in Sacramento after she left the union. Shortly after Chris was purged, Ellen approached Chavez after he held a demonstration on the street near her office. He greeted her warmly until she asked about Chris. Then Chavez turned ugly and told her she was a terrible lawyer. She chased him down

K Street for several blocks, repeating her question. Her mother wrote the union out of her will because of the way Chris was treated. Ellen became a defense attorney in capital cases and worked for more than two decades defending death row inmates. She learned through that work about the importance of forgiveness.

Only a few stuck with the original cause. Dorothy Johnson became a lawyer and again took up the quest to improve conditions for farmworkers as director of the northern San Diego office of CRLA. She ventured into canyons where workers lived burrowed into hillsides under plastic tarps, taught them their rights, and battled some of the same growers the union had tackled decades earlier. In 2008 she helped the CRLA Foundation win a $675,000 settlement in a wage-and-hour suit against the company Scott Washburn had tried to organize twenty-five years earlier.

Sabino Lopez took a detour to San Diego, where he worked for Eliseo organizing janitors, than ended up helping farmworkers again in Salinas. He returned when Lydia Villarreal founded a nonprofit organization dedicated to improving farmworker housing. Sabino trains farmworkers, educates them about their rights, identifies leaders, organizes comités, and imparts the lessons he has learned over the past decades. Sometimes older farmworkers stop by, the ones who used to condemn him for trying to destroy Cesar, and they apologize and tell Sabino he was right. That means a lot to him.

Mario Bustamante bought a small taxi company in El Centro, began work most mornings before dawn, and passed on the lessons of organizing to his daughter. He and Gretchen chose to raise their children in the Imperial Valley, where they could become steeped in the worlds of both parents. Mario was denied a pension from the UFW because he fell short 175 hours in his seventh year, the year he was fired as paid rep and driven out of the fields. Mario never found a way to return to organizing farmworkers. But he never stopped helping others, whether they were passengers in his taxi, friends of friends, or members of his large extended family. His home, a sprawling former bracero camp, is almost always full of people and often functions much like the Service Center the union ran nearby, decades earlier.

Gretchen worked on political campaigns, taught farmworker children in the Imperial Valley, and then went to work for the University of California. She directed a statewide reading initiative and then found her home as director of an institute for professional development that trained teachers around the state. At the Salinas memorial service for Jessica,

Gilbert Padilla asked Gretchen to help him document the fading history of the Community Service Organization, where he and Chavez had first worked together. Gretchen raised money to conduct oral history interviews of the pioneer generation of CSO. She became convinced that CSO helped explain the trajectory of the UFW and decided to write a book about the organization. Gretchen and Mario visit Cleofas Guzman in Los Angeles, where he lives with his daughter and extended family. Once a champion runner, Guzman is confined to a wheelchair. He never recovered his mental acuity, though he usually recognizes old friends and reminisces about the UFW with both joy and pain.

Sandy Nathan worked as a labor lawyer in northern California, where he fought with the same compassion for the rights of seamen, transit, construction, utility, garment, hotel, restaurant, office, manufacturing, dock, and office workers—pretty much all workers except those in the fields. Kirsten Zerger became chief counsel for the California Teachers Association. She and Sandy married and in 1993 moved to rural Kansas. Kirsten helped found a community mediation center. Sandy commuted to California for his law practice, used his organizing skills to start a high school baseball program and pass a bond issue to construct ball fields, and served eight years on the Moundridge School Board. When his old wallet fell apart, he threw out the tattered quote from Dostoyevsky. He carries pictures of his grandchildren instead. In 2008, he returned to the San Joaquin Valley to help his son Jonathan on a college project, examining how Mennonite farmers responded to the UFW. The trip helped Jonathan understand more about his parents. The contrast between the valley today and three decades earlier was a bittersweet reminder for Sandy of all that was won and lost.

Jerry Cohen inherited real estate from his wife's family and applied his negotiating skills primarily to working out leases. The union had taught him to use his talent for raising hell to achieve practical goals. He taught a university course and was appointed to a judgeship by outgoing governor Jerry Brown. But pressure from growers scuttled the nomination. He helped old friends with causes when they needed legal aid. When CRLA tried to fire Lydia Villarreal, in large part because of pressure from the UFW, Jerry sued to help her keep her job. But he never found another cause that became his own. He read old English novels aloud and acted in amateur plays in Carmel, gloried in his Luddite refusal to carry a cell phone or use a computer, and became interested in groups working to save wildlife around the world.

Eliseo Medina organized janitors, college faculty, prison guards, and public employees in a dozen states around the country. No matter where or when, they voiced the same concerns he had first heard as a nineteen-year-old organizer in the Delano vineyards. Those desires for basic dignity and decent working conditions kept him committed to the ideal of unions as a way to empower people, in their lives as well as their work. He piled up one of the most successful organizing records in the country and was elected executive vice president of SEIU, the first Mexican American in the top leadership of the union. His crusade in the twenty-first century became the quest to provide legal status for the millions of immigrants in the United States without documents. He married Liza Hirsch, who also had worked for the union decades earlier and then became a labor lawyer. In 2007 Eliseo returned to Oxnard, happy to live in a farmworker community again. Sometimes he drives wistfully past the spots where he last organized farmworkers during the citrus strikes of 1978. On his wall is a framed copy of the oath of office, autographed by each board member at the first UFW convention in 1973.

Chris Hartmire worked for fourteen years at Loaves and Fishes in Sacramento and founded Clean & Sober, a residential recovery community for homeless men and women. In 2003, he and Pudge moved to Pilgrim Place, a church-affiliated retirement community thirty miles east of Los Angeles, where residents held a peace vigil every Friday before lunch during the Iraq War. Chris lost his boyish looks but none of his enthusiasm for helping others. He worked into his late seventies as a consultant to SEIU on a campaign to organize health care workers. In 2006 he flew to Miami when Eliseo fasted for eleven days to win a contract for immigrant janitors at the University of Miami. Late at night in the fasting tent, Chris told Eliseo the full story of how Chavez had turned on the minister who was once his trusted aide. Chris still believes he could not have played the same role in the farmworker struggle without turning his ministry into an arm of the union, though some days he wonders.

Acknowledgments

Many people made this book possible, above all those whose lives form the principal narrative. Mario Bustamante, Jerry Cohen, Ellen Eggers, Chris Hartmire, Gretchen Laue, Sabino Lopez, Eliseo Medina, and Sandy Nathan were true and steadfast collaborators, patiently tolerating my endless questions, from the most mundane to the extremely personal. They went along on a journey that I suspect proved at times more arduous than they had anticipated. They opened to me their homes, their minds, and their hearts.

Most of the other people who helped me understand and piece together the past are named in the book—though some to whom I am most indebted are mentioned only briefly. Those who generously shared their time and thoughts, dug through old files, schooled me about agriculture, labor organizing, and social movements, include: Doug Adair, Antonio Barbosa, Chava Bustamante, Bill Carder, Cois Byrd, Tom Dalzell, Marshall Ganz, Margaret Govea, Ellen Greenstone, Joe Herman, Dorothy Johnson, Howard Marguleas, Stephen Matchett, Liza Hirsch Medina, Roy Mendoza, Crosby Milne, Marion Moses, Consuelo and Esteban Nuño, Bruce Obbink, Gilbert and Esther Padilla, Jose Renteria, Jose Manuel Rodriguez, Lloyd Saatjian, Ruth Shy, Jennifer Sonen, Shelly Spiegel-Coleman, Billy Steinberg, Kenneth Thorbourne, Larry Tramutola, Lydia Villarreal, Scott Washburn, Joe Wender, Martin Zaninovich, and Kirsten Zerger.

Thanks for archival help to Isadora Mota at Amherst College, and to Kathy Schmeling and William Lefevre at the Walter P. Reuther Labor Library at Wayne State University, who graciously provided assistance time after time. I'm particularly grateful to Mary J. Wallace, audio-visual archivist at the Reuther Library, without whose help much of the research would have been impossible. Thanks also to Jim Stephens for his careful work rescuing ancient reel-to-reel tapes.

LeRoy Chatfield, the determined patriarch of the Farmworker Documentation Project, has assembled a very valuable resource (www.farm workermovement.org) for anyone interested in the history of the UFW. The thousands of photographs available on the site often inspired as well as educated me.

Peter Schrag, William Deverell, Nicholas Von Hoffman, and Jeff Rubin offered early encouragement and later advice. Thanks also to Simon Li, Dean Baquet, and John Carroll, for their support and help in shaping the stories I wrote for the *Los Angeles Times*, which led me to pursue this book.

The Alicia Patterson Foundation and the Berkeley Institute of Governmental Studies provided support that helped finance my research.

My agent, Gloria Loomis, believed in the book from the start. My editor at Bloomsbury Press, Peter Ginna, embraced the idea enthusiastically at the outset and offered astute suggestions and guidance throughout. Thanks also to Pete Beatty and Jenny Miyasaki at Bloomsbury Press for their careful editing and production work.

I was fortunate to have three readers whose insights and help throughout the writing were invaluable: Sam Enriquez, Geoff Mohan, and Michael Muskal. Michael, my husband, lived with this book almost as much as I did; his moral support, wise counsel, and abiding faith made this doable.

I end my thanks where I began: I am deeply indebted to the people who shared their lives with me and trusted me to tell their stories. One does not meet many truth-seekers; I feel privileged to have stumbled upon this particular group. I hope they believe this book was worth the sometimes painful effort to relive the past and that I have done justice to their remarkable history.

Notes

Abbreviations

The Walter P. Reuther Labor Library at Wayne State University in Detroit is the repository for the archives of the UFW and more than a dozen related collections. The UFW archives include extensive audiovisual materials, including hundreds of reel-to-reel tapes. The following are abbreviations for the collections I have cited most frequently:

ADMIN	UFW Administration
CENT	UFW Central Administration
INFO	UFW Information and Research
NFWM	National Farm Worker Ministry
NFWA	National Farm Workers Association
OOP1	Office of the President, Part I
OOP2	Office of the President, Part II
WORK	UFW Work Department
UFWOC	United Farm Workers Organizing Committee
UFW	United Farm Workers, 1986 accession

Jacques E. Levy, author of an early biography of Cesar Chavez, tape-recorded hundreds of conversations with Chavez and other top union officials and also recorded and took notes at key events during the union's early years. Levy transcribed almost all his tapes and eventually placed the entire collection at the Beinecke Library at Yale University. I have abbreviated references to these transcribed interviews as follows:

JEL	Jacques E. Levy Research Collection on Cesar Chavez

Other commonly used abbreviations which appear throughout the text and notes are:

NEB   National Executive Board of the United Farm Workers
ALRB   California Agricultural Labor Relations Board
ALRA   California Agricultural Labor Relations Act

1. *Huelga*

1 Cesar Chavez interview, May 23, 1970, JEL, Box 1, Folder 139, Yale.

2 Meeting agenda, Sept. 16, 1965, NFWA, Box 13, Folder 20, Wayne State.

3 Chris Hartmire notes, Jul. 1961, private collection.

4 Chris Hartmire, "The Church and the Emerging Farm Workers Movement, A Case Study," Jul. 22, 1967, private collection.

5 FBI memos, Oct. 11, 1965, at http://foia.fbi.gov/chavez/chavez1a.pdf.

6 Zaninovich, interviews by author, Oct. 2, 2006, Sept. 20, 2007.

7 Hartmire, "Some Comments on the Church's involvement in the Delano Grape Strike," Jan. 1966, private collection.

8 Hartmire, "The Church and the Delano Grape strike, A Partial Report," Feb. 1966, private collection.

9 Kern County Sheriff's Office, Oct. 19, 1965, JEL, Box 21, Folder 465, Yale; "9 Ministers Jailed in Grape Strike," *Los Angeles Times*, Oct. 20, 1965.

10 Memo, Oct. 17, 1965, NFWA, Box 6, Folder 15, Wayne State.

11 Hartmire, "Case Study."

12 Council of California Growers Newsletter, Oct. 4, 1965, San Joaquin Valley Farm Labor Collection, Cal State Fresno.

13 Tape of Hartmire speech, May 1979, UFW, Wayne State.

14 Hartmire, "Some Comments."

15 Zaninovich, report to Grape and Tree Fruit Council, Mar. 14, 1966, Farm Labor Collection, Cal State Fresno.

16 Hartmire to friends, Mar. 22, 1966, NFWM, Box 14, Folder 15, Wayne State.

17 Hartmire speech, Apr. 10, 1966, in author's possession.

2. Showdown at DiGiorgio

1 Judge Leonard M. Ginsberg, Order to Show Cause, *DiGiorgio Corporation vs. Cesar E. Chavez et al.*, No. 63606, Jun. 18, 1966, Ramona Pioneer Historical Society, Ramona, Calif.

2 Serda, interview by author, Jul. 11, 2006.

3 Hartmire to Forrest Weir et al., Jul. 5, 1966, private collection.

4 Ibid.

5 *The People of the State of California vs. Chavez et al.*, Case 3929, Ramona Pioneer Historical Society.

6 Hartmire to friends, Aug. 8, 1966, NFWM, Box 15, Folder 6, Wayne State.

7 Minutes, Aug. 19, 1966, OOP1, Box 44, Folder 11, Wayne State.

8 UFWOC flyer, n.d., private collection.

9 Chavez interview, June 11, 1973, JEL, Box 3, Folder 162, Yale.

3. Out of the Fields, Into the Streets

1 UFW Bulletin to members, Aug. 1, 1967, private collection.

2 Chavez interview, Jul. 1970, JEL, Box 2, Folder 148, Yale.

3 Kircher to Stanley A. Johnson, executive vice-president, Illinois State AFL-CIO, Sept. 13, 1967, William L. Kircher Papers, Box 21, Folder 11, Wayne State.

4 Medina, chronology of Chicago boycott and list of contacts from 1967 convention, private collection; "Farm Workers Union Passes the Hat to Fight Factories," Sept. 28, 1967, *Illinois State Register*.

5 Medina to Chavez, Sept. 1967, UFWOC, Box 3, Folder 12, Wayne State.

6 UFW newsletter, Jan. 3, 1968, private collection.

7 Hartmire, "The Church and the Emerging Farm Workers Movement, A Case Study," Jul. 22, 1967, private collection.

8 Hartmire to Migrant Ministry Action Mailing List, Jan. 25, 1966, private collection.

9 Chavez speech in New York, excerpted in *Catholic Worker*, Jun. 1968, private collection.

10 Kircher to Meany, Apr. 11, 1967, Kircher Papers, Box 7, Wayne State.

11 Minutes of meeting, May 12, 1967, OOP1, Box 44, Folder 17, Wayne State.

12 Cohen, Petition for Alternative and Peremptory Writ of Prohibition, *UFWOC vs. Superior Court of the State of California, County of Kern*, Aug. 28, 1967, private collection.

4. The Fast

1 Chavez interview, Jul. 8, 1973, JEL, Box 4, Folder 163, Yale.

2 Moses, Feb. 20, 1968, private collection.

3 Jerry Cohen Papers, Box 2, Folder 11, Amherst.

4 Cohen diary, Feb. 19, 1968, Jerry Cohen Papers, Series 2, Box 2, Folder 8, Amherst.

5 Hartmire to Action Mailing List, Feb. 26, 1968, private collection.

6 Chavez statement, Mar. 10, 1968, private collection.

5. Please Don't Eat Grapes

1 Tape of *The Bill Fields Show*, WGN, Jul. 28, 1968, private collection.

2 Medina to Chavez, Aug. 4, 1968, UFWOC, Box 2, Folder 1, Wayne State.

3 "Service for the Conversion of National Tea Company," circa 1968, private collection.

4 Balsamo, interview by author, Oct. 9, 2007.

5 Medina to Chavez, Apr. 12, 1968, Jim Drake Papers, Box 5, Wayne State.

6 Proceedings of International Association of Machinists and Aerospace Workers, Sept. 5, 1968, Chicago, in possession of author.

7 Chicago Typographical Union newsletter, *Reporter*, Apr. 1968, private collection.

8 *Chicago American*, Mar. 25, 1969.

9 Medina to Huerta, May 1, 1968, Jim Drake Papers, Box 5, Wayne State.

10 Chavez to Medina, May 10, 1969, private collection.

11 Tape of Delano meeting, Jan. 14, 1969, UFW, Wayne State.

12 Jewel press release, Dec. 5, 1968, private collection.

13 Chavez to Medina, Aug. 13, 1969, private collection.

14 "Chavez Optimistic about Grapes and Birchers," *Chicago Sun Times*, Nov. 13, 1969.

15 Medina to Chavez, Nov. 25, 1969, ADMIN, Box 24, Folder 11, Wayne State.

16 Hartmire, "The Challenge of the Farm Workers Struggle," Jun. 1970, private collection.

17 Hartmire to Chavez, Jun. 6, 1969, ADMIN, Box 10, Folder 14, Wayne State.

18 Tape of Jan. 1969 meeting.

19 Ganz interview, Apr. 8–9, 1994, JEL, Box 32, Folder 685, Yale; Giumarra testimony, *Congressional Record*, E8381, Oct. 9, 1969.

20 Hartmire to Medina, Dec. 4, 1969, private collection.

6. Making History

1 Harvard Business School Case Study 4-374-069, in author's possession.

2 Saatjian, interviews by author, Jul. 12, 2006, Nov. 14, 2006.

3 Hartmire to Medina, Dec. 4, 1969, private collection.

4 Harvard Business School Case Study 4-375-038, in author's possession.

5 Cohen memo, Feb. 26, 1970, ADMIN, Box 18, Folder 25, Wayne State.

6 Ibid.

7 Steinberg interview, Jun. 11, 1971, JEL, Box 6, Folder 198, Yale.

8 Levy notes, Jun. 26, 1970, JEL, Box 2 Folder 142, Yale.

9 Federal statistics cited in Jerald Barry Brown, "The United Farm Workers Grape Strike and Boycott," Ph.D. diss., Cornell University, 1972.

10 Tape of Dec. 1971 boycott conference at La Paz, UFW, Wayne State.

11 Chicago boycott newsletter, n.d., UFW, Chicago Boycott collection, Accession Apr. 4, 1974, Box 1, Wayne State.

12 Fagan to Chavez, Apr. 29, 1970, ADMIN, Box 24, Folder 12, Wayne State.

13 Jewel press release, May 4, 1970, private collection.

14 Tape of calls, Jul. 16, 1970, JEL, AV Box 58, Yale.

15 Levy notes, Jul. 17, 1970, JEL, Box 41, Folder 783, Yale.

16 Madeleine Cohen notes, Jul. 25, 1970, private collection.

17 Levy notes, Jul. 26, 1970, JEL, Box 41, Folder 783, Yale.

18 Levy notes, Jul. 27, 1970, JEL, Box 41, Folder 783, Yale.

19 Delano press conference, Jul. 29, 1970, JEL, Box 2, Folder 149, Yale.

7. Strike in the Salad Bowl of the World

1 Monterey County Agriculture Department, 1970 crop reports.

2 *Englund et al. vs. Chavez et al.* (1972), 8 Cal 3d 572.

3 "A Big Cut in Harvest and Shipment of Vegetables," *San Francisco Chronicle*, Aug. 26, 1970.

4 Levy notes, Jul. 29, 1970, JEL, Box 2, Folder 148, Yale.

5 Higgins press conference, Aug. 12, 1970, JEL, Box 2, Folder 149, Yale.

6 Venustiano Olguin affidavit, Aug. 31, 1970, ADMIN, Box 3, Folder 18, Wayne State.

7 Cohen interview, Dec. 18, 1973, JEL, Box 4, Folder 165, Yale.

8 Tape of boycott conference, Dec. 1971, UFW, Wayne State.

9 Higgins interview, Apr. 11, 1994, JEL, Box 37, Folder 743, Yale.

10 "Antle Lawsuit Continued," *Salinas Californian*, Sept. 3, 1970.

11 "Injunction Issue Simmers," *Salinas Californian*, Apr. 16, 1971.

12 Cohen journal, Sept. 19, 1970, Jerry Cohen Papers, Series 1, Box 1, Folder 5, Amherst.

13 Chavez, Sept. 15, 1970, JEL, Box 3, Folder 153, Yale.

14 Chavez, Sept. 17, 1970, JEL, Box 3, Folder 153, Yale.

15 Tape of NEB meeting, Jul. 1, 1977, UFW, Wayne State.

16 Chavez, Sept. 24, 1970, JEL, Box 3, Folder 154, Yale.

17 USDA statistics, 1970; Kirby Moulton, "California Fresh Market Grapes," Feb. 1975.

18 Medina to Moore, Jan. 2, 1971, UFW, Chicago Boycott collection, Box 1, Wayne State.

19 Tape of boycott conference in New York City, Dec. 1971, UFW, Wayne State.

20 Medina to Chavez, Mar. 17, 1971, OOP1, Box 11, Folder 2, Wayne State.

21 Chicago boycott newsletter, May 1971, private collection.

8. The Union Is Not La Paz

1 Chavez interview, May 23, 1970, JEL, Box 2, Folder 141, Yale.

2 Minutes of NFWM meeting, May 2–4, 1971, private collection.

3 Chavez to Ed Bradlee, Sept. 21, 1983, private collection.

4 Tape of conference at La Paz, Dec. 1971, UFW, Wayne State.

5 Chavez, Jun. 24, 1970, JEL, Box 2, Folder 144, Yale.

6 *California Migrant Ministry Newsletter* 3, no. 2 (Fall 1970), private collection.

7 Higgins to John Cosgrove, Jan. 15, 1971, Bishops' Committee on Farm Labor collection, Box 126, Folder: January 1971, quoted in Marco Glen Prouty, "Cesar Chavez and the Catholic Civil War 1965–1977," Ph.D. diss., Washington, 2004.

8 Minutes of NFWM meeting, May 2–4, 1971, private collection.

9 Tape of Dec. 1971 conference.

10 "UAW Helps Get Boycott Rolling," *El Malcriado*, Nov. 15, 1968.

11 Richard Chavez interview, Jun. 16, 1974, JEL, Box 4, Folder 173, Yale.

12 Tape of Dec. 1971 conference.

13 Ibid.

14 Calexico field office budget, 1971, ADMIN, Box 5, Folder 3, Wayne State.

15 Tape of Dec. 1971 conference.

16 Tape of conference in New York, Nov. 19, 1971, UFW, Wayne State.

17 Ibid.

18 Cohen journal, Sept. 19, 1970, Jerry Cohen Papers, Series 1, Box 1, Folder 5, Amherst.

19 Tape of Dec. 1971 conference.

20 Levy notes, Jun. 16, 1971, JEL, Box 41, Folder 784, Yale.

21 Tape of Dec. 1971 conference.

22 Harvard Business School Case Study 4-374-069, in author's possession.

23 Mahony to Chavez, Nov. 15, 1971, OOP2, Box 47, Folder 9, Wayne State.

24 Chavez to Mahony, Nov. 27, 1971, OOP2, Box 47, Folder 9, Wayne State.

25 Steinberg interview, Jun. 11, 1971, JEL Box 6, Folder 198, Yale.

26 Cohen, Jan. 29, 1971, JEL, Box 3, Folder 160, Yale.

27 Richard Chavez interview, Jun. 16, 1974, JEL.

9. Back to the Boycott

1 Conference transcript, Aug. 5–6, 1972, CENT, Box 4, Folder 51, Wayne State.

2 Chavez, "On Money and Organizing," transcribed from a talk on Oct. 4, 1971, in author's possession.

3 Tape of conference at La Paz, Dec. 1971, UFW, Wayne State.

4 Chavez, Feb. 13, 1970, JEL, Box 1, Folder 138, Yale.

5 Eggers affidavit, Sept. 11, 1972, California Secretary of State files, California State Archives, Sacramento.

6 Rosemary Cooperrider journal, n.d., private collection.

7 Notes from Feb. 1973 conference, ADMIN, Box 5, Folder 15, Wayne State; "Safeway Seeking to Curb Picketing by Chavez Union," *Los Angeles Times*, Feb. 10, 1973.

10. Holy Week

1 Dalzell journal, Apr. 1973, private collection.

2 Hartmire to friends, Apr. 17, 1973, private collection.

3 Riverside County Sheriff Department memos, Apr.–Jul. 1973, private collection.

4 "Struggle in the Fields," *Wall Street Journal*, Jun. 29, 1973.

5 Tape of rally, Apr. 19, 1973, UFW, Wayne State.

6 Sheriff reports, Apr. 1973; Dalzell journal, Apr. 1973.

7 Tape of rally, Apr. 19, 1973.

8 Ibid.

9 Dalzell journal, Apr. 1973.

10 Medina to Huerta, Jun. 1, 1973, UFW, Cleveland Boycott 1975 accession, Box 2, Wayne State.

11 Tape of Cleveland rally, Jun. 29, 1973, UFW, Wayne State.

12 Riverside County sheriff report, Jun. 29, 1973, private collection; Ochoa affidavit, Jun. 26, 1973, UFW, Cleveland Boycott 1975 accession, Box 2, Wayne State; Hansen interview by author, Apr. 13, 2008.

13 Tape of rally, Jun. 25, 1973, UFW, Wayne State.

14 Tape of rally, Jun. 25, 1973, JEL, Box 3, Folder 162, Yale.

15 Tape of rally, Jun. 22, 1973, UFW, Wayne State.

16 July 16, 1973, lawsuit, quoted in "Chavez Union Sues Teamsters, Growers for Strike Damages," *Los Angeles Times*, July 17, 1973.

17 Riverside Sheriff report, n.d., private collection.

11. Fill the Jails

1 Cohen, 1973 datebook, private collection; Dalzell journal, Apr. 1973, private collection.

2 *Fighting for Our Lives: The United Farm Workers' 1973 Grape Strike* (1975, Keene, California).

3 In re Berry, 68 Cal 2d. 137.

4 Transcript of conversation between Chavez and Giumarra, Mar. 1973, ADMIN, Box 11, Folder 18, Wayne State.

5 Cohen 1973 datebook.

6 Tape of rally, Jul. 24, 1973, UFW, Wayne State.

7 Levy notes, Jul. 28, 1973, JEL, Tape 120, AV Box 124, Yale.

8 Cooperrider journal, n.d., private collection.

9 Ibid.

10 Fr. Eugene J. Boyle et al. to Quentin Reynolds, Aug. 3, 1973, in Cooperrider journal.

11 Memo, Jul. 30, 1973, ADMIN, Box 5, Folder 46, Wayne State.

12 Hartmire to Those Persons Who Went to Jail, Aug. 21, 1973, private collection.

12. The New Union

1 Woodcock memo, Oct. 10, 1973, Leonard Woodcock UAW President Papers, Box 43, Folder 6, Wayne State.

2 Chavez, Aug. 21, 1973, JEL, Tape 121, AV Box 125, Yale.

3 Tape of Dec. 1973 NEB, UFW, Wayne State.

4 Transcript of proceedings of 1973 convention, in possession of author.

5 Ibid.

6 List of candidates, private collection.

7 Convention transcript.

8 Levy notes, Sept. 23, 1973, JEL, Box 6, Folder 205, Yale.

13. Dark Days

1 Dalzell journals, Nov. 1974, private collection.

2 Nathan to Chavez, Jan. 7, 1974, Marshall Ganz Papers, Box 8, Folder 5, Wayne State.

3 Corky Larson to Chavez, Feb. 5, 1974, in Harvard Business School Case Study 4-375-038.

4 Chavez interview, Mar. 19, 1974, JEL, Box 4, Folder 171, Yale.

5 Einar Mohn quoted in report by Jane Yett Kiely to Safeway, Mar. 21, 1973, in author's possession.

6 Harvard Business School Case Study 4-375-038.

7 "Grape Pact Signed Within Four Hours," *Los Angeles Times,* Apr. 18, 1974.

8 Medina, "Setting Up a Boycott," Apr. 16, 1974, UFW, Cleveland Boycott 1977 accession, Box 3, Wayne State.

9 Medina report to NEB, Jun. 6, 1974, private collection.

10 Ibid.; Medina to Ohio boycott coordinators, May 4, 1974, UFW, Cleveland Boycott 1977 accession, Box 3; notes, n.d., UFW, Cleveland Boycott 1975 accession, Box 3, AFL-CIO Convention Folder, Wayne State.

11 Medina to staff, Dec. 19, 1973, UFW, Cleveland Boycott 1975 accession, Box 1, Wayne State.

12 "A Fast of Hope," *Cleveland Plain Dealer*, Sept. 25, 1974.

13 "Farm Worker Boycotters Learn by Doing," *El Malcriado*, Nov. 2, 1973.

14 "Meany Sees More Farm Strife," *Los Angeles Times*, Feb. 23, 1974.

15 Cohen report, Oct. 7, 1974, Marshall Ganz Papers, Box 7, Folder 30, Wayne State.

16 President's report to NEB, Jun. 1974, Marshall Ganz Papers, Box 8, Folder 6, Wayne State.

17 Ibid.

18 Richard Chavez interview, Jun. 16, 1974, JEL Box 4, Folder 173, Yale.

19 Levy notes, Oct. 6, 1973, JEL, Tape 123, AV Box 127, Yale.

20 Tape of NEB meeting, Dec. 16–23, 1974, UFW, Wayne State.

21 Hartmire notes, Dec. 10, 1974, private collection.

22 Tape of Dec. 1974 NEB meeting.

23 Chavez speech, Mar. 17, 1974, JEL, Box 4, Folder 168, Yale.

24 Tape of Dec. 1974 NEB meeting.

25 Richard Chavez interview, Jun. 1974.

26 Medina report to NEB, Jan. 17, 1975, private collection.

27 Chavez to Medina, Dec. 7, 1973, ADMIN, Box 11, Folder 18, Wayne State.

28 Tape of NEB meeting, Oct. 12–15, 1974, UFW, Wayne State.

29 Tape of Dec. 1974 NEB meeting.

14. The Best Labor Law in the Country

1 Tape of NEB meeting, Dec. 17–23, 1973, UFW, Wayne State.

2 Tape of NEB meeting, Oct. 12–15, 1974, UFW, Wayne State.

3 Cohen and Nathan interview, Jun. 19, 1975, JEL, Box 29, Folder 571, Yale.

4 Tape of Oct. 1974 NEB meeting.

5 Medina report to NEB, Jun. 1975, INFO, Box 11, Folder 6, Wayne State.

6 Tape of NEB meeting, Dec. 16–23, 1973, UFW, Wayne State.

7 Brown inaugural address, Jan. 6, 1975, www.californiagovernors.ca.gov/h/documents/inaugural_34.html.

8 Cohen to Chavez, Jan. 29, 1974, Jerry Cohen Papers, Box 2, Folder 11, Amherst.

9 Cohen and Nathan interview, Jun. 19, 1975.

10 Tape of NEB meeting, Mar. 25–28, 1975, UFW, Wayne State.

11 Ibid.

12 Dalzell memo, Apr. 11, 1975, UFW, Box 41, Wayne State.

13 Chavez interview, May 17, 1975, JEL, Box 29, Folder 575, Yale.

14 Tape of Dec. 1974 NEB meeting.

15. Elections in the Fields

1 Tape of NEB meeting, Jun. 13–18, 1975, Wayne State.

2 Ibid.

3 Ibid.

4 Chavez interview, Aug. 1, 1975, JEL, Box 29, Folder 572, Yale.

5 Ibid.

6 Press release, Aug. 30, 1975, UFW, Cleveland Boycott 1977 accession, Box 3, Wayne State.

7 Medina memo, Sept. 20, 1975, private collection.

8 Nathan interview, Sept. 24, 1975, JEL, Box 29, Folder 577, Yale.

9 Ellen Greenstone affidavit, Sept. 11, 1975, private collection.

10 Nathan interview, Sept. 24, 1975.

11 Medina notes, n.d., private collection.

12 Medina to Chavez, Aug. 10, 1975; Medina notes, n.d., private collection.

13 Medina notes, Aug. 1975, private collection.

14 Medina notes, Sept. 4, 1975, private collection; "Border Patrol Hurt Effort at Farm, UFWA Charges," *Los Angeles Times*, Sept. 5, 1975.

15 Medina report, Sept. 20, 1975, private collection.

16. Transitions

1 Hartmire notes, May 6, 1975, private collection.

2 Hartmire to NFWM board, May 13, 1975, private collection.

3 Hartmire to Action Mailing List, May 30, 1975, private collection.

4 Tape of meeting, Sept. 22, 1975, UFW, Wayne State.

5 Senate-Assembly joint hearings on implementation of the ALRA, Dec. 19, 1975, California State Archives, Sacramento.

6 Hartmire speech, Nov. 11, 1975, private collection.

7 Hartmire to Chavez, Sept. 1975, private collection.

8 Govea memo to Toronto boycotters, Aug. 3, 1975, private collection.

9 Transcript of 1975 UFW convention, Aug. 15–17, 1975, WORK, Box 7, Folder 7, Wayne State.

10 Almaraz memo, "The New Mural," n.d., private collection.

11 Transcript of 1975 convention.

12 Transcript of ALRB hearing, Aug. 29, 1975, ALRB files, Sacramento.

13 *El Malcriadito*, Nov. 1975, Farm Worker Collection, Southern California Library for Social Studies, Los Angeles.

14 Senate-Assembly joint hearings on implementation of the ALRA, Nov. 25, 1975, California State Archives, Sacramento.

15 Medina notes, Feb. 6, Feb. 9, Feb. 24, 1976, private collection.

16 Medina notes, Feb. 20–28, 1976, private collection.

17 Transcript of conference, Jul. 4–6, 1976, OOP2, Box 1, Folder 18, Wayne State.

18 Minutes of NEB meeting, Feb. 16–21, 1976, UFW, Box 27, Wayne State.

19 Tape of Medina interview, Sept. 76, UFW, Wayne State.

20 Transcript of meeting, May 3–4, 1976, UFW, Box 55, Wayne State.

21 Minutes of NEB meeting, Jun. 13–15, 1976, OOP2, Box 1, Folder 18, Wayne State.

22 Two versions of transcript of organizing conference, Jul. 6–8, 1976, ADMIN, Box 29, Folder 21, Wayne State.

17. The Crusades

1 Hartmire notes, Jun. 1976, private collection.

2 Chavez interview, Feb. 1970, JEL, Box 1, Folder 138, Yale.

3 Hartmire notes, Jun. 25, 1976, private collection.

4 Hartmire notes, May–Jun. 1976, private collection.

5 Hartmire notes, Jul. 23, 1976, private collection.

6 Laue journals, Oct. 1975, private collection.

7 Laue, n.d., private collection.

8 Minutes of NEB meeting, Jun. 13–15, 1976, OOP2, Box 1, Folder 18, Wayne State.

9 Ibid.

10 Transcript of July 27, 1976, conversation, UFW, Box 54, Wayne State.

11 Medina report to NEB, Sept. 14, 1976, private collection.

12 Tape of NEB meeting, Sept. 15, 1976, UFW, Wayne State.

13 NFWM newsletter, Fall 1976, private collection.

14 Transcript of speeches at testimonial, Nov. 16, 1976, private collection.

18. The Cultural Revolution

1 Smith résumé, private collection.

2 Smith to NEB, Sept. 22, 1976, private collection.

3 Smith to Chavez, Sept. 22, 1976, private collection.

4 Ibid.

5 Jones to Hartmire, Oct. 7, 1976, private collection.

6 Smith to Padilla, Nov. 17, 1976, private collection.

7 Tape of NEB meeting, Jun. 30–Jul. 2, 1977, UFW, Wayne State; Hartmire notes, Dec. 15–16, 1976, private collection.

8 Hartmire notes, Dec. 10, Dec. 15, Dec. 16, 1976; Smith to Hartmire, Dec. 20, 1976, private collection.

9 Levy to Chavez, Nov. 17, 1976, UFW, Box 54, Wayne State.

10 Seattle staff to Chavez, Dec. 13, 1976, OOP2, Box 3, Folder 22, Wayne State.

11 Hartmire to Chavez, Dec. 1, 1976, private collection.

12 Medina notes, Dec. 26, 1976, private collection.

13 Medina notes, Dec. 27, 1976, private collection.

14 Smith to Hartmire, Dec. 20, 1976, private collection.

15 Moyer to Hartmire, Nov. 23, 1976, private collection.

16 Milne to Chavez, Mar. 13, 1977, OOP2, Box 47, Folder 18, Wayne State.

17 Tape of NEB meeting, Feb. 25–27, 1977, UFW, Wayne State.

18 Ibid.

19. The Purges

1 Cook to Hartmire, Apr. 6, 1977, private collection.

2 Godfrey to Hartmire, Apr. 18, 1977, private collection.

3 Rabbitt to Hartmire, May 4, 1977, private collection.

4 Hartmire to Rabbitt, May 25, 1977, private collection.

5 Hartmire to staff, May 31, 1977, private collection.

6 *Hijos del Sol*, Feb. 1977, Pete Velasco Papers, Box 7, Wayne State.

7 Tape of NEB meeting, Mar. 15, 1977, UFW, Wayne State.

8 Edy Scripps to Chavez, Mar. 30, 1977, OOP2, Box 3, Folder 22, Wayne State.

9 Chavez, Mar. 17, 1974, JEL, Box 4, Folder 169, Yale.

10 Tape of NEB meeting, Jun. 30–Jul. 2, 1977, UFW, Wayne State.

11 Ibid.

12 Adair to Chavez, May 1, 1977, OOP2, Box 3, Folder 23, Wayne State.

13 Tape of June–Jul. 1977 NEB meeting.

20. In the Trenches

1 Larry Tramutt memo, Mar. 10, 1977, ADMIN, Box 29, Folder 26, Wayne State.

2 Tramutt memo, May 11, 1977, UFW, Box 52, Wayne State.

3 ALRB decision, 3 ALRB No. 47, Jun. 17, 1977, www.alrb.ca.gov.

4 ALRB decision, 4 ALRB No. 75, Oct. 29, 1978, www.alrb.ca.gov.

5 Lindquist to Laue, May 9, 1977, UFW, Box 52, Wayne State.

6 Chavez report to convention, Aug. 26, 1977, and resolutions from convention, in possession of author.

7 "United Farm Workers Seek Support on Campus," *Daily Titan* 20, no. 29 (Oct. 26, 1977).

8 Medina notes, May 30, 1977, private collection.

9 Tape of NEB meeting, Nov. 24, 1976, UFW, Wayne State.

10 Medina to Chavez, Mar. 10, 1977, OOP2, Box 47, Folder 17, Wayne State.

11 Tape of NEB meeting, Jun. 30–Jul. 2, 1977, UFW, Wayne State.

12 "Comprehensive Planning and Management Project," Sept. 1977, private collection.

13 Medina notes, Sept. 28, 1977, private collection.

14 Transcript of planning conference, Sept. 28–Oct. 2, 1977, UFW, Box 31, Wayne State.

15 Medina notes, Sept. 28, 1977, private collection.

16 ALRB decision, 4 ALRB 75.

17 Chavez to Medina, Feb. 1978, private collection.

18 Medina to Chavez, Nov. 7, 1977, OOP2, Box 47, Folder 17, Wayne State.

19 Medina to Chavez, Feb. 21, 1978, UFW, Box 59, Wayne State.

20 Hartmire report to NFWM board, Nov. 14, 1977, private collection.

21 Hartmire report to NFWM board, May 10, 1978, private collection.

22 Hartmire to Chavez, Feb. 13, 1978, OOP2, Box 9, Folder 18, Wayne State.

23 Higgins interview, Apr. 11, 1994, JEL, Box 37, Folder 743, Yale.

24 Hartmire to NFWM board, Sept. 31, 1977, private collection.

25 Moyer to Hartmire, Dec. 15, 1977, private collection.

26 Hartmire to Moyer, Feb. 23, 1978, private collection.

27 Hartmire to Moyer, Mar. 14, 1978, private collection.

28 Nathan memo to NEB, Mar. 11, 1977, INFO, Box 19, Folder 4, Wayne State.

29 Ibid.

30 Memo, n.d., UFW, Box 52, Wayne State.

31 Crime report, Monterey County Sheriff's Department, Sept. 18, 1977, private collection.

32 Transcript, *The People vs. Sanford Norman Nathan No. 81371*, Nov. 8, 1977, private collection.

33 ALRB decision, 5 ALRB 63, Oct. 26, 1979, www.alrb.ca.gov.

21. Visions Collide

1 *Sojourners*, Oct. 1977.

2 Tape of NEB meeting, Nov. 24, 1976, UFW, Wayne State.

3 Rothner to Cohen, Sept. 15, 1977, private collection.

4 Hartmire memo, Apr. 29, 1978, OOP2, Box 9, Folder 18, Wayne State.

5 Cohen report, Mar. 20, 1978, private collection.

6 Hartmire to Esther Winterrowd, May 8, 1978, private collection.

7 "Life at Synanon Is Swinging," *Time*, Dec. 26, 1977.

8 Tape of NEB meeting, Mar. 14–16, 1977, UFW, Wayne State.

9 Dalzell and Nathan to Cohen, May 24, 1978, UFW, Box 54, Wayne State.

10 Leonard Woodcock to Emil Mazey, Feb. 14, 1976, OOP2, Box 26, Folder 4, Wayne State.

11 Cohen to Chavez, Jun. 8, 1978, and Jerry Whipple to Cohen, Jun. 6, 1978, UFW, Box 54, Wayne State.

12 Cohen to Chavez, May 26, 1978, UFW, Box 10, Wayne State.

13 Minutes of NEB meeting, Oct. 10, 1977, private collection.

14 Minutes of NEB meeting, Apr. 3, 1978, OOP2, Box 1, Folder 22, Wayne State.

15 Financial report, May 9, 1978, private collection.

16 Tape of NEB meeting, Mar. 16, 1977, UFW, Wayne State.

17 Tape of NEB meeting, Oct. 23, 1977, UFW, Wayne State.

18 Chavez, May 23, 1970, JEL, Box 2, Folder 141, Yale.

19 Tape of NEB meeting, Jun. 15, 1978, UFW, Wayne State.

20 Minutes of NEB meeting, Jun. 15, 1978, UFW Box 27, Wayne State.

21 Letters to Chavez, OOP2, Box 36, Folder 26, Wayne State.

22 Velasco notes, Jun. 24, 1978, Pete Velasco Papers, Box 6, Folder 62, Wayne State.

23 Minutes of NEB meeting, Jun. 25, 1978, UFW, Box 27, Wayne State.

24 Hartmire to Ganz, Jul. 10, 1978, Marshall Ganz Papers, Box 1, Folder 5, Wayne State.

25 Hartmire notes, Jul. 8–12, 1978, private collection.

26 Hartmire to Cohen, Jul. 17, 1978, private collection.

27 Moyer to Hartmire, Feb. 24, 1978, private collection.

28 Hartmire to Moyer, Feb. 27, 1978, private collection.

29 Moyer to Hartmire, Feb. 28, 1978, private collection.

30 Hartmire to Moyer, Mar. 14, 1978, private collection.

31 Moyer to Hartmire, Jul. 11, 1978, private collection.

32 Medina, "Department of Organization Conference," May 31, 1978, private collection.

33 Medina to Chavez, Jun. 7, 1978, private collection.

34 Medina notes, Jul. 1978, private collection.

22. Quiet Before the Storm

1 ALRB decision, 6 ALRB 25, May 29, 1980, www.alrb.ca.gov.

2 Minutes of NEB meeting, Jun. 25, 1978, UFW, Box 27, Wayne State.

3 Zerger diary, Oct. 14, 1978, private collection.

4 Nathan et al. to Cohen and Chavez, Nov. 14, 1978, OOP2, Box 39, Folder 12, Wayne State.

5 Zerger diary, Sept. 6, 1978, private collection.

6 Contract renegotiations report, Jul. 8, 1978, private collection.

7 Tape of conference, Aug. 26, 1978, UFW, Wayne State.

8 Transcript of conference, Aug. 26, 1978, private collection.

9 Tape of Aug. 26, 1978, conference.

10 Tape of meeting, Sept. 10, 1978, UFW, Wayne State.

11 Ganz report, Dec. 1979, private collection.

12 "Valley UFW Members Vote to Authorize Strike," *Salinas Californian*, Jan. 18, 1979.

23. The Dream Strike

1 "Chavez Taunts Growers," *Los Angeles Times* and *Imperial Valley Press*, Feb. 2, 1979.

2 "Lettuce Strike Growing Bitter," *Los Angeles Times*, Feb. 4, 1979.

3 "New Violence Erupts in UFW Lettuce Strike," *Los Angeles Times*, Feb. 22, 1979.

4 Hartmire report to NFWM, May 15, 1979, private collection.

5 Tape of NEB meeting, Mar. 11, 1979, UFW, Wayne State.

6 Memos in Boston Boycott files, UFW, Box 2, Wayne State.

7 Nathan memo, Jun. 4, 1979, private collection.

8 Legal department expenditures, UFW, Box 38, Wayne State.

24. Victory in Salinas

1 Tape of NEB meeting, Apr. 22, 1979, UFW, Wayne State.

2 Ganz analysis, quoted in NFWM newsletter, May 1979, private collection.

3 Tape of meeting at La Paz, Jun. 1979, UFW, Wayne State.

4 "Boycott Planning Conference," Jul. 23, 1979, private collection.

5 ALRB decision, 6 ALRB 25, May 29, 1980, www.alrb.ca.gov.

6 Tape of meeting, Aug. 11, 1979, UFW, Wayne State.

7 Amended Resolution 10, UFW, Box 32, Wayne State.

8 Transcript of Fourth Constitutional Convention, Aug. 12, 1979, UFW, Box 32, Wayne State.

9 Tape of NEB meeting, Aug. 11, 1979, UFW, Wayne State.

10 Transcript of Aug. 1979 convention.

11 Ibid.

25. A Different Union

1 Memo to Chavez, Jun. 18, 1979, OOP2, Box 3, Folder 25, Wayne State.

2 Barbara Macri to Chavez, Dec. 10, 1980, UFW, Box 24, Wayne State.

3 Chavez notes, Aug. 25, 1980, UFW, Box 24, Wayne State.

4 Tape of conference, May 19–23, 1980, UFW, Wayne State.

5 Ibid.

6 ALRB records, California Agricultural Labor Relations Board, Sacramento.

7 Chavez to Tramutt, Nov. 12, 1980, UFW, Box 12, Wayne State.

8 Hartmire notes, Aug. 29, 1980, private collection.

9 Hartmire report to NFWM, May 15, 1979, private collection.

10 Hartmire in *Fellowship Magazine*, Jul. 1980, private collection.

11 Hartmire notes, Aug. 29, 1980.

12 Hartmire to supporters, Jan. 1981, private collection.

13 Moyer to Hartmire, Mar. 17, 1978, private collection.

14 Moyer to Hartmire, Dec. 9, 1980, private collection.

15 Hartmire, "Reflections on a Church's Ministry," *Migration Today* (1981), private collection.

16 Cohen to Chavez, Jan. 4, 1979, Jerry Cohen Papers, Box 2, Folder 11, Amherst.

17 Cohen to Chavez, Apr. 7, 1980, private collection.

18 Zerger diary, Oct. 6, 1980, private collection.

19 Cohen to Chavez, Mar. 4, 1981, private collection.

26. You're With Us or Against Us

1 Ganz and Govea report to Chavez, Jan. 31, 1981, private collection.

2 Ibid.

3 David Martinez deposition, n.d., in *Hermilo Mojica et al. v. United Farm Workers*, C282-0512 WAI, JEL, Box 33, Folder 694–95, Yale.

4 *The People of California v. Manuel Gonzales Chavez*, No. 11151, June 1964, private collection.

5 Dalzell journal, Jan. 14, 1981, private collection.

6 Chavez meeting notes, Feb. 10, 1981, UFW, Box 54; Carta Administrativa, May 3, 1981, UFW, Box 16, Wayne State.

7 Ganz plan, 1980, private collection.

8 Richard Chavez negotiations report, Sept. 2 1980, private collection.

9 Nathan et al. to Old UFW Legal, Apr. 15, 1981, UFW, Box 54, Wayne State.

10 Memo to Chavez, May 24, 1981, UFW, Box 54, Wayne State.

11 Statement by Mojica, May 24, 1981, private collection; testimony at "Trial of Oscar Mondragon," Aug. 22, 1981, UFW, Box 54, Wayne State.

12 Agenda for meeting, May 30, 1981, JEL, Box 33 Folder 694–95, Yale; Frank Denison memo to Barbara Macri, Sept. 21, 1981, UFW, Box 45, Wayne State.

13 California Coastal contract, Apr. 1, 1981, in possession of author.

14 Hartmire notes, Aug. 24, 1981, and Chavez memos, Aug. 25, 1981, UFW, Box 54, Wayne State.

15 Chavez to field office directors, Sept. 1, 1981, UFW, Box 54, Wayne State.

16 Martinez memo, Aug. 24, 1981, JEL, Box 33, Folder 694, Yale.

17 Notes from NEB meeting, Aug. 31, 1981, UFW, Box 20; meeting agenda, n.d., UFW, Box 54, Wayne State.

18 Hartmire notes, n.d., UFW, Box 32, Wayne State.

27. Malignant Forces

1 Transcript of UFW convention, Sept. 5–6, 1981, UFW, Box 30, Wayne State.

2 Convention handout, Sept. 5, 1981, in *Hermilo Mojica et al. v. United Farm Workers*, C282-0512 WAI, and *United Farm Workers of America v. Mojica et al.*, C82-6644 WAI, Federal Records Center, San Bruno, Calif. (hereafter referred to as "court files").

3 Transcript of 1981 convention.

4 Lopez declaration, May 18, 1982, court files.

5 Chavez to Bustamante, Sept. 17, 1981, court files.

6 Letters from Chavez to Mojica and Gutierrez, UFW, Box 22, Wayne State.

7 Lopez appeal, Oct. 25, 1981, UFW, Box 24, Wayne State.

8 Lopez appeal, Nov. 16, 1981, UFW, Box 22, Wayne State.

9 Memo, n.d., UFW, Box 54, Wayne State.

10 Ortiz to Chavez, Sept. 11, 1981, UFW, Box 54, Wayne State.

11 Higgins to Chavez, Sept. 21, 1981, private collection.

12 Chavez to Higgins, Oct. 21, 1981, private collection; Higgins interview, April 11, 1994, JEL, Box 37, Folder 743, Yale.

13 Hartmire notes, Oct. 5, 1981, private collection.

14 Padilla to Hartmire, Nov. 5, 1981, UFW, Box 54, Wayne State.

15 Macri to Chavez, Legal Department Budget Request, Mar. 1, 1982, UFW, Box 38; Legal budget, UFW, Box 13, Wayne State.

16 Eggers affidavit, Jul. 6, 1982, court files.

17 Diane Dickstein affidavit, Jun. 23, 1982, court files.

18 Shy to Chavez, Jun. 6, 1980, UFW, Box 23, Wayne State.

19 Chavez declaration, May 1, 1982, court files.

20 Judge William A. Ingram, Nov. 16, 1982, court files.

21 *Fresno Bee*, Nov. 20, 1982.

22 "Dispute Intensifies Over Cesar Chavez's Leadership of Farm Workers," *New York Times*, Jan. 3, 1983.

23 Mario Bustamante declaration, May 18, 1982, court files.

24 NEB decision, Feb. 6, 1982, UFW, Box 54, Wayne State.

25 Hartmire declaration, in *Mojica v. UFW*, Jun. 24, 1982, Marshall Ganz Papers, Box 1, Folder 9, Wayne State.

26 Flyer, n.d., in court files.

27 *Salinas Californian*, Dec. 10, 1982.

28. A Dream Deferred

1 Velasco to Lopez, Dec. 18, 1981, in *Hermilo Mojica et al. v. United Farm Workers*, C282-0512 WAI, and *United Farm Workers of America v. Mojica et al.*, C82-6644 WAI, Federal Records Center, San Bruno, Calif. (hereafter referred to as "court files").

2 Lopez declaration, Nov. 17, 1982, court files.

3 Judge William A. Ingram order, Nov. 30, 1984, court files.

4 Hartmire, Feb. 20, 1982, UFW, Box 10, Wayne State.

5 Chavez notes, Jun. 18, 1983, UFW, Box 26, Wayne State.

6 UFW 1983 LM2 report to U.S. Department of Labor, Washington, D.C.

7 UFW Political Action Committee, campaign finance filings, California State Archives, Sacramento.

8 Cohen, "UFW Must Get Back to Organizing," *Los Angeles Times*, Jan. 15, 1986.

9 Hartmire to Cohen, Jan. 18, 1986, private collection.

10 Hartmire to Cohen, Jan. 27, 1986, private collection.

11 ALRB statistics, ALRB, Sacramento.

12 *United States of America v. Bryce Lyn Basey*, Case No. 91-2087.

13 Hartmire diary, Jan. 12, 1989, private collection.

14 Ibid.

15 Ibid.

16 Hartmire notes, Feb. 15, 1989, private collection.

17 Hartmire notes, Sept. 1989, private collection.

Epilogue

1 Hartmire notes, Mar. 14, 1993, private collection.

2 Hartmire notes, Apr. 23–29, 1993, private collection.

3 ALRB statistics, ALRB, Sacramento.

4 Pawel, "UFW: A Broken Contract," *Los Angeles Times*, Jan. 8–11, 2006.

Bibliography

Library Collections

Jerry Cohen Papers, Amherst College Archives and Special Collections, Amherst College Library

Marshall Ganz Papers, Walter P. Reuther Labor Library, Wayne State University, Detroit

Jacques E. Levy Research Collection on Cesar Chavez, Yale Collection of Western Americana, Beinecke Rare Book and Manuscript Library

Fred Ross Papers, Special Collections, Cecil Green Library, Stanford University

San Joaquin Valley Farm Labor Collection, California State University, Fresno

Table Grape Growers Negotiating Committee Collection, California State University, Fresno

United Farm Workers of America Collections, Walter P. Reuther Labor Library, Wayne State University, Detroit

Books and Articles

Dunne, John Gregory. *Delano: The Story of the California Grape Strike.* New York: Farrar, Straus and Giroux, 1967.

Gordon, Jennifer. "Law, Lawyers, and Labor: The United Farm Workers' Legal Strategy in the 1960s and 1970s and the Role of Law in Union Organizing Today." *University of Pennsylvania Journal of Labor and Employment Law* 8, no. 1 (Fall 2005).

Levy, Jacques. *Cesar Chavez: Autobiography of La Causa.* New York: W.W. Norton, 1975.

Matthiessen, Peter. *Sal Si Puedes (Escape If You Can): Cesar Chavez and the*

New American Revolution. Berkeley and Los Angeles: University of California Press, 1969.

Pawel, Miriam. "UFW: A Broken Contract," *Los Angeles Times*, January 8–11, 2006.

Ross, Fred. *Conquering Goliath: Cesar Chavez at the Beginning.* Keene, Calif.: El Taller Grafico Press, 1989.

Taylor, Ronald B. *Chavez and the Farm Workers.* Boston: Beacon Press, 1975.

Web Sites

California Agricultural Labor Relations Board http://alrb.ca.gov

Farmworker Documentation Project www.farmworkermovement.org

FBI files http://foia.fbi.gov/foiaindex/chavez.htm

Index